CHABOT COLLEGE-HAYWARD

2 555 000 009679 5

100926   E
                          176
Horan   H8

Desperate women

Date Due

OC 2 9 78			
MAY 2 79			
MAY 2 9 '81			
MAR 4 - 1992			
MAY 9 '95			

CHABOT
COLLEGE
LIBRARY

25555 Hesperian Boulevard
Hayward, CA 94545

Desperate Women

BOOKS BY JAMES D. HORAN

OUT IN THE BOONDOCKS

U.S.S. SEAWOLF
(with Gerold Frank and J. M. Eckberg)

ACTION TONIGHT

DESPERATE MEN

THE PINKERTON STORY
(with Howard Swiggett)

DESPERATE WOMEN

By JAMES D. HORAN

G. P. Putnam's Sons
New York

COPYRIGHT, 1952

BY JAMES D. HORAN

All rights reserved. This book, or parts thereof, must not be reproduced in any form without permission. Published on the same day in the Dominion of Canada by Thomas Allen, Ltd., Toronto.

Library of Congress Catalog
Card Number: 52-9838

Manufactured in the United States of America

For Gertrude, whom the author is sure
he has made quite desperate at times.

100926

Foreword

THE stories of the life and times of my baker's dozen of America's most desperate women, points up, I believe, Hilaire Belloc's opinion that "readable history is melodrama."

My ladies range in culture and character from the incomparable Miss Van Lew of Richmond to China Polly in the wilds of Idaho, who was won and wed by Johnny Bemis, the tinware peddler who had the skill of a Jessamy Law with cards.

The prevailing note in all their lives was one of tragedy, although, as we shall see, there is an abundance of comedy, high romance, and not a little farce. Surely it can be said in the words of Meredith that Pearl Hart, Arizona's stage-coach robber, was caught in the "incredible imbroglio of comedy."

They all possessed a cold courage whether they were using their sex to steal military secrets or holding up a stage coach. Their appetite for life, action, and excitement was insatiable. They committed espionage as coolly as they sipped their tea, seduced men in high places for their country and their causes; held their liquor, rode like Comanches, dealt stud poker, packed guns, rustled cattle, and played road agent with great efficiency and picturesqueness. One cannot help but compare them with our ladies of today.

Strangely enough, they have been overlooked by historians. Perhaps we have forgotten that flirting fans and laughing eyes are never far distant from the rumble of guns, or that sunbonnets as well as the six-shooter helped to tame the frontier.

Some readers may criticize me for not including the good, honest women who never threw a gun or stole a horse, but with indomitable courage raised families and made homes in the wilderness. I agree they are more deserving, but they belong in another book. And as someone once said, good girls don't make good reading.

Several extraordinary discoveries of unpublished material in London, the National Archives, Library of Congress, the New York Public

vii

Library, and in many private collections, made this book a joy to write.

Hundreds of letters were written to beg, plead, and cajole old letters, diaries, pictures, and crumbling newspaper clippings and copies of family records, from their owners. My requests were granted with only three exceptions. As a working newspaperman, I find it ironical that the three who failed to answer were Wyoming newspaper editors.

Now to the pleasant task of acknowledgements. Of course, I owe a debt to many more individuals, historical societies, and libraries than are here mentioned.

Heading the list must be Mr. Sylvester Vigilante, Mr. Ivor Avellino, and Miss Shirley Barker of the American History Room of the New York Public Library. One need not travel to the far corners of the West to learn its secrets. They are all in Mr. Vigilante's vest pocket. I will always be grateful for their service, kindnesses, and friendship. One of the thrilling discoveries in writing this book was the discovery of Miss Elizabeth Van Lew's diary and papers in the Manuscript Room of the New York Public Library. I am deeply indebted to Mr. Robert W. Hill, keeper of manuscripts, and his gracious assistant, Mr. Edward B. Morrison, who made that discovery possible, and who were so lenient when the clock struck six.

There are constant adventures in writing history. One unforgettable one took place in the National Archives on a warm October afternoon, when a series of clues led me to Mrs. Greenhow's letters, then to letters of Belle Boyd and Pauline Cushman. But it was Mr. Richard G. Wood, and Mr. R. P. Flynn of the War Records Branch, National Archives, who broke the trail for me to follow. And it was Oliver Wendell Holmes who uncomplainingly left his work to act as my guide in that wonderful institution.

I have only fond memories of how Bess Glenn, chief of the Justice and Executive Section, and Josephine Cobb, chief of the Still Pictures Section, National Archives, acted so promptly on my many requests. Mr. David C. Mearns, chief of the Manuscript Division and Virginia Daiker, acting reference librarian, Prints and Photographs Division, and Mr. Donald Holmes, chief of the Photoduplication Service of the Library of Congress never grew weary of my queries, which usually ended with "as I am under deadline pressure, I would appreciate it if you would send as soon as possible, etc., etc."

Mr. Van Dyk Mac Bride responded at once to my request for copies of Mrs. Greenhow's pictures and letters in his collection. I am deeply indebted to Mr. Foreman M. Lebold of Chicago who gave me permission to use Mrs. Greenhow's letters now in his possession. Mr. Ralph G.

Newman of the well-known Abraham Lincoln Shop of Chicago kindly photostated them and sent them on.

Harriet H. Shoen, Ph.D., former head of the History Department at Davis and Elkins College, now engaged in preparing a textbook of enormous importance, kindly left her own work to send me Pryce Lewis' unpublished memoirs, and to spend an evening advising me on the part he played.

The slightest clue many times leads a writer to invaluable material. So it was in my case, when Mr. Virginius Dabney, editor of the Richmond *Times-Dispatch,* promptly published my request for information on Mrs. Greenhow.

This in turn was read by Mr. Donald J. Rulfe, who is writing a history of the theater in Wilmington. Mr. Rulfe advised me to contact Mr. Louis T. Moore, chairman of the New Hanover Historical Commission of Wilmington, North Carolina. A letter to Mr. Moore produced some excellent material on Mrs. Greenhow's death, including that fine article by Mr. Harry Hayden.

Mr. Clayton Torrence, director and corresponding secretary of the Virginia Historical Society, went to great lengths to obtain permission for me to have Miss Van Lew's scrapbook photostated. I found it most helpful.

India W. Thomas, house regent of the Confederate Memorial Literary Society of Richmond; Milton C. Russell, head of the Reference and Circulation Section, General Library Division, Virginia State Library; and August Dietz, Jr., of the Dietz Press, Richmond, were most helpful.

I was received with great courtesy in England. At my request, the Earl of Buckinghamshire, Hampden House, Bucks County, England, has made a survey of his family's papers which is still continuing as this foreword is being written.

Colonel Louis Sigaud, biographer of Belle Boyd, gave me leads and corrections of great value. Mr. George Bolds, last of the great frontier marshals, gave me invaluable background on my frontier chapters, as did Ramon F. Adams, of Dallas, Texas and Mr. Wayne Gard, of the Dallas *Morning News* and author of that unforgettable *Frontier Justice.*

Without the help and intelligent criticism of Zoe Tilghman, widow of Bill Tilghman, perhaps the greatest of frontier peace officers, I would have been unable to write the chapter on Rose of the Cimarron.

I can only recall with a great deal of pleasure the aid that Mr. Fred M. Mazzulla, attorney and collector of Western Americana, gave me on the Cattle Kate and Poker Alice chapters.

Grant and Carolyn Thomas Foreman responded at once and most cordially to my questions about Belle Starr, her piano playing, and her life at Younger's Bend.

Cohn Rector, last of "Hanging Judge" Parker's rangers, at ninety-two, dictated his memoirs of Belle Starr to Mrs. Rector who kindly sent them on to me. I am grateful to Homer Croy, who allowed me to use his research notes on Belle and who gave me good suggestions.

H. W. Kramer, advertising and publicity manager of the Cunard Steamship Company Limited, consulted their head office in Liverpool to check Calamity Jane's story that a Captain James O'Neil adopted her "daughter."

It took only one letter to send Mr. and Mrs. George L. Scott hurrying to the Portland Library to answer my questions about Harry Tracy. Only a crack newspaperman's wife could have replied with such detail. And another of Washington's better newspapermen, Duncan Aikman, author of *Lady Wildcats* which should always be in print, dashed off a prompt reply to tell me what he remembered about Cattle Kate.

Vilma Morelan, C.N., General Hospital, Grangeville, Idaho, took time out in a busy day to correct me on China Polly. And it was Idaho's historian, Sister Mary Alfreda, St. Gertrude's Convent, Cottonwood, Idaho, who rushed, air mail, special delivery, to a total stranger, her precious collection of pictures of Polly and Johnny Bemis.

Mr. Burton Rascoe, whose biography of Belle Starr is the standard reference work, saved me from bad blunders and gave me much good advice. Mr. Glenn Shirley of Stillwater, Oklahoma, who has written much of his state's rousing history, did valiant work for me on the Doolin gang and Rose of the Cimarron. Mr. William F. Kelleher, not only sold me good books, but also gave me the names of several important people in the West. The late Ralph Dudley, vice-president of the Pinkerton's National Detective Agency, gave me an important lead on Belle Boyd and Miss Van Lew.

Historical societies and libraries contributed a great deal to this book. I can only marvel how they are able, with skeleton staffs many times underpaid, to maintain their sense of humor and intellectual balance under the deluge of letters from demanding authors. It is a pleasure and honor to list them.

Agnes Wright Spring, executive assistant to the president, Frances M. Shea, librarian of the State Historical Society of Colorado; Lola M. Homsher, state archivist and ex officio historian of the Wyoming State Historical Department, and Mary Elizabeth Cody, Wyoming's state historian; Margaret Burke, librarian, The Natrona County Public

Library, Casper, Wyoming; Regina Willman and Maurene Chenoweth, librarian, Carnegie Public Library, Albany County, Laramie, Wyoming; Mrs. Ralph Catterall, the Valentine Museum, Richmond; E. G. Swem, librarian emeritus, and Herbert L. Ganter, curator of rare books and manuscripts, College of William and Mary, Williamsburg, Virginia, and curators, Mrs. C. E. Cook, Mrs. O. J. Cook, and Mrs. Rella Looney of Oklahoma's Historical Society. Also Robert W. Bingham, secretary and director of the Buffalo, New York Historical Society; Mrs. Anne McDonnell and Marguerita McDonnell, assistant librarians of the Historical Society of Montana; Dolores C. Renze, state archivist, State Historical Society of Colorado. Mrs. Gertrude McDevitt, secretary of Idaho's Historical Society and Mulford Winsor, director, Library and Archives, Phoenix, Arizona.

I must make a special tribute to the dramatic values of Eleanor B. Sloan, historical secretary of the Arizona Pioneers' Historical Society. It was Mrs. Sloan who found and sent to me the memoirs of Mike Rice, who knew Pauline Cushman.

I find it hard to adequately express my appreciation of the help, hospitality, and advice given me by Mr. Howard Swiggett. His friendship cannot be measured.

There is little question that I owe a great debt to Anne O'Shea, who helped to type the manuscript under the stress of a broken ankle and during the excitement of learning her charming daughter had won two scholarships. I am indebted to Florence and Maureen for "the little things" as they are called but which are never "little" to an author finishing a book.

It is a pleasure to remember the visit of Bob Amussen and Johnny King to Hole In The Wall. I recommend such working conditions to all publishers, editors, and authors.

Finally, as always, to Gertrude, who made me watch a queen when I wanted to talk about a Wild Rose.

J.D.H.

Horan's Boondocks.

xi

Contents

Sixteen pages of illustrations will be found following page 162

Book One: 1861-1865

I can retake the Valley and rejoin General McDowell but you must send new men to keep it. The women will take it if we don't.

—Letter of General James Shields to Secretary of War Stanton, in the Official Records.

The Wild Rose

ON THE afternoon of July 15, 1861, Donellan, a former Department of Interior clerk, was secretly rowed north across the Potomac below Alexandria, under orders to enter Washington and to see Rose O'Neale Greenhow, the most dangerous woman in the Confederacy.

His credentials were a scrap of paper on which Colonel Thomas Jordan, aide to General Beauregard, had written in cipher, "Trust Bearer."

In the early hours of the sixteenth, Donellan entered the city, which was ringing with the advance on Richmond of General Irwin McDowell's army. We know a rainy dawn was breaking when his carriage splashed up Sixteenth Street, passed the White House and St. John's Church, and stopped at 398, a two-story house with green shutters.

He was admitted by a maid and a few moments later faced Mrs. Greenhow, the beautiful Wild Rose of the Confederacy.

"Who sent you?" she demanded.

"Rayford of Virginia," Donellan said.

She studied him for a moment. "Your credentials, please."

Donellan gave her the scrap of paper. She glanced at it quickly, then said, "Thank God, you have come! I have news of great importance. You must return at once."

While Donellan ate a "hasty breakfast," Rose sat at her cherry-wood desk and wrote rapidly.

The market carts were beginning to creak across the Long Bridge into Washington when Donellan's carriage tore down Pennsylvania Avenue, his whip cracking like pistol shots in the opaque air.

He raced down the northern shore of the Potomac into Charles County, Maryland, where he was rowed to the Virginia side. There a man waited with a horse. A few miles beyond the ferry landing, Donellan ran into a cavalry picket in a meadow. He pulled up at the side of a waiting gray trooper.

"For Beauregard," he cried, as the cavalryman grabbed the dispatch

3

and galloped across the meadow, soaring over the fence like a fox hunter, and disappearing down the road toward Manassas.

Relays of cavalry couriers raced the dispatch to Beauregard, who did not see the message until eight o'clock that night. In his tent at Manassas Junction, where the bivouac fires glittered like fireflies against the dark hills, Colonel Jordan spread the dispatch on a field desk and deciphered it for Beauregard. It read:

> McDowell with 55,000 men will advance this day from Arlington Heights and Alexandria on to Manassas via Fairfax Court House and on to Centreville. . . .

Beauregard acted quickly. He advised Jefferson Davis of the intelligence he had received and urgently asked that General Johnson at Harpers Ferry reinforce him at once. Then he ordered General Bonham to abandon Fairfax Court House, fall back across Bull Run and dig in at Mitchell's Ford.

As the telegraph to Richmond clicked out the news, Jordan, in his tent, was writing to Rose:

> Yours was received at eight o'clock at night. Let them come: we are ready. We rely on you for precise information. Be particular as to descriptions and destinations of forces, quality of artillery. . . .

We do not know what the Southern Rose thought when she received Jordan's message the following day. Certainly she had every right to be irked by his demand for "precise information."

Hadn't she copied the intelligence she had sent him by Donellan from General McDowell's own orders?

2

The experiences of this Wild Rose of the Confederacy are so fantastic they are at first hard to believe, the more so because so much seems to rest on her own story, written later in the security of London.

Was she a woman of irresistible seductive powers, loved by a president and a vice president of the United States? . . . Did congressmen, senators, politicians, high army and naval officers tell her their country's secrets out of pure devotion? . . . Was one of her dispatches delivered in the tresses of one of her beautiful spies? . . . Did she take some part in the planning of a historic Caribbean revolution? . . . As the

4

a heady experience to have the most beautiful woman in Washington prefer to sit with him in the gardens of L Street, listening to his history of Tripoli rather than dancing with the handsome bucks who wore her heart on their sleeves.

Greenhow and she were married in Washington, living in a "fine establishment" on F Street near the Ebbet House. Rose sparkled in the company of her husband's friends. There was John C. Calhoun, electrifying the Senate with his thundering speeches; Congressman James A. Seddon, later the Confederacy's secretary of war; Robert Barnwell Rhett, leader of the South Carolina Secessionists and later member of the Confederate Congress; R. M. T. Hunter, Virginia's great politician and Jefferson Davis' secretary of war; Virgil Maxey, president of Rhode Island's university and a strong Calhoun supporter; J. L. Sullivan, owner of the powerful *Democratic Review;* and Jefferson Davis, whom she was to serve so faithfully in the dark days ahead.

But Calhoun was Rose's idol. It was the South Carolina statesman who formed her political philosophy of States' rights.

There is little doubt that the ruthless beauty, consumed with a burning ambition for power and position, guided her scholarly husband's political career. There is no direct evidence that she influenced Calhoun's decisions, but curiously, beginning in 1843, shortly after her marriage, one finds her husband mentioned frequently in the Calhoun letters.

Writing to R. M. T. Hunter in March of 1843, Calhoun disclosed that he had sent Dr. Greenhow south to establish the *Petersburg Republican,* "a Calhoun newspaper." If the paper "was successful," he wrote, he planned to have Greenhow bring it to Richmond.

Greenhow's editorship was evidently satisfactory to the Calhoun supporters because late that same year, Robert S. Rhett urged Calhoun to send Rose and her husband to New York to establish "another Calhoun newspaper."

The years passed. The country girl became a handsome matron, and as General Doster remembered, "famous for her beauty, brilliance of conversation, aptitude for intrigue and regal bearing," and the mother of two children.

The society which had at first only "tolerated" her now fought for her invitations. Statesmen of both parties, high officers of the Army and Navy, and foreign diplomats graced her table.

One of her frequent guests was James Buchanan, the squint-eyed senator from Pennsylvania. "Old Buck," as his friends called him, soon lost his heart to Rose who gave him her smile and nothing more. A

7

letter in the State Department Records, National Archives, tells us when Doctor Greenhow was taken ill it was Buchanan who insisted that Rose and her husband spend a holiday at Wheatland, his country place in Pennsylvania.

In 1845 Buchanan was appointed minister to England. He never forgot to write to Rose. Most of his letters, addressed to her from "your ancient and devoted friend," were chatty and friendly and usually ended with the cautious wish he were "home again."

In 1848 Doctor Greenhow published his important *History and Present Conditions in Tripoli* from his beloved French and Spanish sources. The book was well received and he followed it with an equally important history of Oregon and California.

Rose was now perhaps the most influential woman in Washington. She was also a woman with a tantalizing reputation for allurement. It is fitting that she should now appear to have helped plan a revolution with a romantic and handsome Spanish officer who had burning black eyes and mustachios which would have been the envy of any brigand.

It was late in 1848 when General Narciso López, commander in chief of the National Guard of Spain, and general of the Cuban Army was exiled from Cuba for his revolutionary activities. After many exciting adventures he arrived in New York as a movement to "liberate" Cuba was sweeping across the country.

Southern politicians, among them Calhoun, unofficially urged support of a revolution to overthrow the Spanish government.

López was given a hero's welcome in New York. A torchlight parade passed for hours under his window and crowds cheered him wherever he went. In 1849 he made a triumphant tour to Washington where he conferred secretly with many Southern senators and congressmen, among them Calhoun, who was later quoted as telling López, "The men of the South ought to flock down there in open boats the moment they hear the toscin."

Rose, always alert for a social lion, snared López as her house guest and gave him a glittering reception. Between receptions and gay levees where he charmed the women of Washington, López planned his revolution. And Rose, with her "natural talent for intrigue," helped him.

The plan was to raise an army of American "volunteers," equipped with rifles and small cannon, and to sail in transports from a Southern port. López said he was sure his mercenaries would be augmented by "thousands" of farmers and peons.

8

In 1849 López posted $10,000 in gold in a New York bank and offered Jefferson Davis command of his army. Davis declined. López next offered the post to Robert E. Lee. The Virginian toyed with the idea for several weeks, then refused, because, as Davis wrote López, "Colonel Lee felt it wrong to accept a commission in the army of a foreign power while a commissioned officer in the United States Army."

Lee had suggested Colonel G. E. White, a veteran of the Mexican War. López followed his suggestion and White accepted.

Recruiting offices were opened from New York to New Orleans. López offered his mercenaries $1,000 in gold and fifty acres of land in Cuba. Later he raised the ante to $4,000 and a hundred acres—or so he claimed. Apparently no one questioned his ability to pay.

The rendezvous selected for the invading armada was Round Tree Island near New Orleans. The departure date was kept a closely guarded secret.

Spain, hearing rumors of the rendezvous, protested vigorously. Then President Zachary Taylor issued a face-saving proclamation on August 11, 1849, warning Americans not to join the "criminal enterprise."

The expedition was ready to leave for Cuba. We do not know where López spent the last week before he departed for his homeland but it could well have been at Doctor Greenhow's house on F Street.

In the annual Report of the American Historical Association of 1904, is Rose's letter to Calhoun on the twenty-ninth of August. Rose wrote to Calhoun that the "main spring or mover" in the Cuban uprising, "has just left me after a parting breakfast before starting on his perilous undertaking. . . ."

The letter also gives Calhoun the departure date of the armada, a secret which López himself said was to be known only to Colonel White and a few trusted aides, because of Spanish spies in New Orleans. Rose wrote:

> The expedition sails on Saturday, that is to say a steamer with 1,000 men, from New York with one part of the force, and a steamer of 1,000 ton will sail from New Orleans with 12 or 15 hundred more men from New Orleans simultaneously. All are well armed and equipped and composed of picked men and officers, ready for the perils, the profits and the glory of the venture. . . .
>
> The government is in the secret and have done no more in the matter of the Proclamation [Taylor's] than regards that appearances demanded. . . .

9

Despite whatever aid Rose gave him, López' revolution was abortive. After a two-day raid he returned to Key West, then New York and Washington, where strangely enough his standing as a hero was greater than before.

There is no evidence that he saw Rose but it is likely that he did. Again American adventurers flocked to his recruiting stations. In 1850, with a larger force, López invaded Cuba but was defeated when the peons failed to join his revolt. Fifty-one Americans were executed, including W. H. Crittenden, who made his famous speech before a mob of 20,000. Asked to kneel, he shouted, "An American kneels to no man . . . and we always face our enemy. . . ."

A few weeks later López was garroted, a prayer for Cuba on his lips as the iron band choked him to death.

Rose may have grieved when she heard of López' death but the news a servant brought her on a windy night in March drove from her mind all thoughts of the romantic liberator whom the papers were now calling the "Washington of Cuba."

John C. Calhoun was dying.

With her husband, himself ill, she raced in a carriage to the Old Capitol Boarding House. How the memories must have engulfed her as she walked up to the entrance, its great arched window aglow with the lamps of the servants hurrying to open the door. As the cedar boughs creaked in the wind she may well have remembered the laughter of the gay young men who once called for her here; the last swift kiss in the carriage before her aunt swung open the door; Cave Johnson and the nights they danced away, and how the sad, scholarly man beside her wooed and won her in this very house.

Then the door opened and they went inside and climbed the creaking stairs.

All night she stayed at the statesman's bedside. The contemporary accounts speak with unfailing insistence of her wetting his parched lips with a damp cloth and listening to his dying prophecies of disunion. There is a macabre note to the death scene. On the same floor a drunken party was in full swing. As every hour struck, someone would open the door and ask in a hoarse whisper, "Is he gone yet?"

Calhoun died at six. As the bells of the city's churches tolled Rose closed the old man's eyes and kissed the cold cheek of her idol for the last time.

A strange fate would bring her back to this same room twelve years later.

In 1857 Doctor Greenhow, traveling on State Department business,

10

took Rose and his two daughters, Rose and Gertrude, to California. A few weeks after his arrival he was severely injured "in a fall down a grating" and died.

Rose sued the city of San Francisco for damages and collected an unknown sum. Then, in the mourning which she wore for the rest of her life, she returned to Washington with her children and rented a house on Sixteenth Street. Tragedy visited her again when her daughter Gertrude died.

Her admirer, James Buchanan, was now president. He was soon a frequent visitor and the Wild Rose became, as the *New York Herald* put it, "The Queen of Buchanan's rose-water administration."

General Doster remembered there was "much gossip" about Rose and the President of the United States, and that her house was known to be "the headquarters for the Democrats."

The carriages again lined up outside her door, discharging the belles in their low cut dresses with their beaux. In her parlor the brilliant sashes of the army officers mixed with the gold lace of the Navy and the broadcloth swallowtails of the politicians and the statesmen.

4

In 1859 Allan Pinkerton bought the railroad tickets for John Brown and his party and the raid on the United States Arsenal at Harpers Ferry exploded like a bomb in Washington. There were rumors of a slave uprising and the militia was called out. For days the name of John Brown rang in the halls of the Senate in bitter debate. Ben Wade of Ohio, who had sipped champagne in Mrs. Greenhow's house, swaggered into his seat with a brace of horse pistols and a challenging stare at the hotheaded senators from the slave states.

There was no more rabid supporter of the South in Washington than Rose. But strangely enough she continued to invite the "Black Republicans," as she called them, to her dinner parties. Two weeks after John Brown had been hanged she invited Senator Seward of New York and Congressman and Mrs. Charles Francis Adams of Massachusetts to her home. The rest of the guests were Southerners. When Mrs. Adams defended John Brown and his raid, Mrs. Greenhow left her neutral ground as hostess and answered Mrs. Adams with a furious harangue on Black Republicanism. Congressman Adams and his lady soon left.

In 1860 Lieutenant Colonel E. D. Keyes, military secretary to General Scott, met Mrs. Greenhow at a "general reception" in the home of her niece Mrs. Stephen A. Douglas, wife of the Democratic leader of the free states. Mrs. Greenhow was a frequent visitor at the mansion on I Street, just west of New Jersey Avenue.

Although he described himself at the time as "a man well on in years" Keyes had an eye for the ladies. When he wrote his memoirs twenty years later he still had a vivid picture of the attractive Southern women in their fragile dresses of gauze and gold who surrounded him that evening.

Mrs. Bass, another society woman, was "a handsome widow from Mississippi" and Mrs. Greenhow "the most persuasive woman ever known in Washington." It was Rose, he confessed, who brought him almost to the brink of the precipice, as he called it.

Keyes was appalled by the treasonable remarks of the ladies. He recalled how Mrs. Greenhow tried to undermine his allegiance. Rose, who perhaps had decided it was a waste of time to try her charm on the old soldier, shrewdly pointed out with an eye to the General's age, that the Southern coasts were "sickly" for summer campaigning. But Keyes, a strong Union man, was not to be diverted in his loyalty.

A bitter year passed. On a windy March 4, 1861, Mrs. Greenhow's friend, James Buchanan, passed the presidency on to Abe Lincoln of Illinois and returned to the rural peace of his country home in Lancaster.

In the South the Confederacy was actively preparing for war. The handsome little Creole, Captain Pierre G. T. Beauregard, resigned as the superintendent of West Point to accept a brigadier's commission in the Confederate Army. A flood of army and navy resignations followed. Among them was a young lieutenant from Virginia named Thomas Jordan. Before he changed his blue coat for a gray one, Jordan met Mrs. Greenhow at some Washington social function. The dashing Virginian completely captivated the Wild Rose.

Jordan, aware of Mrs. Greenhow's connection in high places in Washington, proposed that she act as a spy for the South when the war came.

It must have been an exhilarating moment for Rose. She was no longer the young belle who shattered men's hearts with a smile. The glorious nights were all gone. Now here was this young Virginian asking her to serve her beloved South, asking her to be an inspiration for all the women of the Confederacy!

It is a matter of record that Mrs. Greenhow accepted. And Jordan himself tells us in one of his letters to Beauregard that he gave the widow a cipher before he left Washington and adopted the name of

Thomas Jordan Rayford, Esq. of Richmond, to whom she would address her dispatches.

One wonders under what circumstances Mrs. Greenhow agreed to be a spy. Surely a man does not ask a woman at a dinner party to be a spy, at least not in 1861. Was it then in the intimacy of her parlor, the lamps turned low and the windows rattling in the night wind, that this woman possessed of "irresistible seductive powers" whispered to the dashing officer she would serve?

It is interesting to discover that for all her "great talent for intrigue" Mrs. Greenhow never learned that Jordan, who may have done all his recruiting of spies with the lights turned low and the champagne bubbling in the slender glasses, was regularly seeing another attractive widow, Mrs. Augusta Heath Morris "who lived in a fine style at Brown's Hotel."

Before he left for Richmond to become adjutant general to Beauregard, Jordan had "accredited" Mrs. Morris to act as a courier for Mrs. Greenhow!

5

On Saturday April 13, Sumter surrendered to Beauregard. Civil war was upon the land. Lincoln asked for 75,000 volunteers and sixteen states answered the call with the promises of money, arms, and guns. Church bells pealed and mobs cheered. And in Washington behind the blinds of the house on Sixteenth Street, Mrs. Greenhow planned her first move.

The uneasy day passed. Lee rode out of Washington to Virginia for the last time. Rumors that the Virginians were moving in swept the city. Panic spread. Shops closed and barricades were erected. Wagons loaded with rusty rifles and grapeshot creaked down the streets. Then the panic passed as the troops of the Seventh New York with the brave banners flying marched into the defenseless city.

On Independence Day there was a grand review of the New York regiments. Lincoln, General Scott, cabinet members, and staff officers returned the salutes of the troops. Before the parade was over there was a thick-scented carpet before the reviewing stand where the Garibaldi Guards had flung their blossoms.

As the warm dusk descended over the city, Chinese lanterns strung between poles and lampposts were lighted and the city glowed with a romantic blue light. In Willard's and Harvey's the Monongahela whisky and champagne flowed freely, and up the river at the Great

Falls the more expensive brothels patronized by the politicians blazed with lights.

Impatience swept the city like a fever after the grand review. The cry "On to Richmond" echoed everywhere. But in his tent General McDowell pleaded for more time to weld his army of new recruits into a disciplined fighting force. But the clamor rose. Discouraged and heartsick, McDowell at last spread out his maps and announced he was ready to advance on the heart of the Confederacy.

On July 9, Mrs. Greenhow sent this intelligence to Beauregard by Betty Duval, a beautiful young girl of eighteen. Rose sewed the cipher in a square of black silk and hid it in Betty's tresses. Betty left Washington on the afternoon of the ninth, dressed in calico and riding in a market cart. Somewhere along the Potomac, "at the home of a friend," she changed to a gray riding habit and was given a horse.

She pulled up at Fairfax Court House, the first outpost. A soldier told her it was commanded by General Bonham.

"Where is he?" she asked.

The soldier pointed to a tent in a pasture. A few minutes later she slid out of the saddle and entered the tent.

"General Bonham?" she asked breathlessly.

General Bonham, ruddy and silvery haired, rose. "I am General Bonham," he said.

Betty searched Bonham's face anxiously. "You *are* General Bonham?"

The General smiled. "I can assure you, Ma'am, I *am* General Bonham."

Betty entered the tent and plucked out her "tucking comb." From the tumbling masses of her hair fell the square of black silk. Ripping open the stitches, she handed the scrap of paper to Bonham.

He called for his aide as he read the message. Within a few minutes a courier was galloping down the road to Manassas with the scrap of paper inside his tunic. At Manassas, Beauregard "joyfully" read the message with its momentous news, from the woman, whom he later recalled, "lived in a house within rifle range of the White House."

Unfortunately, Miss Duval, that beautiful courier, will never appear again. What happened to her after that hot July day has been lost. All that we know about her is that she may have been the daughter of Margaret Duval who maintained a well-known boardinghouse on Pennsylvania Avenue and Seventh Street, not far from the home of Mrs. Greenhow. Her star boarder was General Winfield Scott.

McDowell had told his commanders he would advance on the ninth. But it wasn't until the sixteenth that his army moved.

14

As the first army wagons rumbled across Long Chain Bridge, Donellan, the clerk sent by Jordan, was knocking at Mrs. Greenhow's door. Within an hour he was racing to Manassas with her copy of McDowell's own order. About the time Jordan was decoding the cipher for his general, McDowell was sadly telling W. H. Russell, the *London Times* correspondent, he was having "great trouble" in obtaining information about the enemy's intentions or their numerical strength.

How did Mrs. Greenhow get a copy of McDowell's orders? The story is she got it from Senator Henry Wilson of Massachusetts, chairman of the powerful Senate Committee on Military Affairs, who was a frequent guest at her dinners. There is no conclusive evidence of this, although, when McClellan was marching to defeat at Antietam, Mrs. Greenhow states she sent Jordan a copy of the map used by the Senate Committee on Military Affairs with red dots to denote the army's route!

That she did send on to the Rebel high command military information is confirmed by the *New York Herald*, which stated after her arrest:

> We have in this matter [her arrest] a clue to the mystery of those important documents, maps and plans which the Rebels left behind in their hasty flight from Fairfax Court House.

On Wednesday the seventeenth of July, McDowell's advance straggled into the abandoned Fairfax Court House. The following day the army advanced on to Centreville and Bull Run, that "petty stream," the huzzas of the Northern press loud and shrill. There were tales of "great victory" and Seward, now secretary of state, told his friends the Union troops would be in Richmond by Saturday night.

When she heard the stories of the great "victories" Mrs. Greenhow smiled, but said little. So confident was she of the outcome of the battle she left on Friday for New York "to see a relative off for California."

Meanwhile the roads leading to Centreville presented an incredible sight. Mobs supplied with bottles of champagne and liquor streamed out of the capitol toward the battlefields. Matthew Brady, the photographer, with his black boxlike wagon, bounced along the ruts determined to capture a battlefield in his lens. Mrs. Greenhow's friend, Senator Wilson, armed with a shotgun, shared a carriage with his friends, Ben Wade, who carried his brace of pistols, and Zach Chandler, the target-shooting senator from Michigan. Congressman Ely of New York jounced along in a carriage he had rented for the enormous sum of twenty-five dollars. He complained of the choking dust and buttoned his long linen duster tight about his throat.

The "rude Colony" as Henry Adams called Washington, waited Sunday morning for news. The bars were crowded and trade was brisk in the three hundred or more brothels along Pennsylvania Avenue.

On a hill above Centreville sutlers hawked spy glasses to the crowds who peered down at the cloud of smoke from which emerged the crackle of musketry and the heavier crash of cannons. It was all very gay and everyone laughed when a drunken "gay lady" fell from a carriage in a froth of lace and petticoats.

And down in the smoke and flame of the guns General Jackson was winning his nickname in front of bloody Henry House.

A cool breeze gently played with the banners on the Washington roof tops as the sun went down. Then, at six, the bottom fell out of the gay world. A gray-faced Lincoln listened to the news, surrounded by his stricken generals and unbelieving politicians.

The battle had been lost. McDowell was falling back—back to Centreville, back to Fairfax Court House, back . . . back . . . to the Potomac.

The army had broken and fled. It was now a wild mob streaming back into Washington, the Confederate guns loud and ominous in its ears.

In New York at the Hotel Astor, Mrs. Greenhow heard the news and left by train for Washington. Aboard was a brother-in-law of Edward Everett, who tried to persuade her to leave at Philadelphia because the "mobs will surely rise in Baltimore." But Rose snapped back that her only fear was that she wouldn't be in time to greet Davis and "our glorious Beauregard" marching in triumph into Washington.

Another politician left the train at Philadelphia with the Wild Rose taunting him, "Ah, discretion is the better part of valor."

She arrived at six and went immediately to her house. Soon her parlor was filled. Who was present we do not know but from Pinkerton's later reports and her own captured correspondence we are tempted to wonder if among those who welcomed her home that night were Dr. Van Camp, the fashionable Washington dentist, who sent his son to the Confederacy; William Walker, a handsome young Post Office Department clerk who was one of her couriers; a F. Rennehan, who visited Mrs. Greenhow "at a late hour"; Miss Lily Mackall, her frail and faithful friend; her courier, Mrs. Augusta Heath Morris, who for all the sweet innocent role she liked to play, was a clever and dangerous spy; and Mrs. Baxley, a plain, dumpy woman whom General Doster was to remember so many years later as the most troublesome of the women prisoners in the Old Capitol Prison. And we would like to think that William Smithson, Washington's most powerful banker, leaned arrogantly against the piano as he listened to Mrs. Greenhow dramatically describe her trip to Washington and what she said to Everett's brother-in-law.

Then, as the July twilight fell over the city, Lizzy, her Irish servant, answered a knock at the door. She came into the room and handed Mrs. Greenhow a folded piece of paper. It was from Jordan. She proudly read it aloud.

> Our President and our General direct me to thank you. We rely on you for further information. The Confederacy owes you a great deal. . . .

It was one of her two greatest moments. The other was yet to come.

While Mrs. Greenhow and her ladies joyfully discussed the news of the battle, McDowell's shattered army poured across Long Bridge, Chain Bridge, and the Aqueduct, into the shocked and incredulous city. Pennsylvania Avenue was a bedlam of sutler's wagons, overturned carriages, army vehicles, ambulances, and thousands of weary frightened men. They sat on the sidewalks, lay in alleys, and pushed their way into saloons and brothels where they told and retold horrible tales of the gray lines which threw them back and the terrible Rebel cavalrymen whose flashing sabers loped a man's head from his shoulders like pumpkins from the vine.

Behind them in the darkness the wounded and the dead lay strewn for miles along the road which led to Fairfax Court House.

In Richmond there was great rejoicing. Bull Run had established, as an accomplished fact of military victory, the government of the Confederacy which before had been only a political assertion.

Years later when he wrote his own account of the battle, Beauregard did not forget the part played in that victory by the widow of Sixteenth Street. It was Mrs. Greenhow, he wrote, who had sent him the first dispatches with the news of McDowell's advance and an estimate of the Federal's military strength.

On the morning following the battle there were rumors of a Rebel advance upon the helpless capitol. Rose led her ladies out to the east portico of the Library of Congress to welcome "her glorious Beauregard." But she was disappointed. The fires everyone thought were from cannons were only cook fires.

Later the group rode back to the Senate and their bonnets were bright spots of color in the gallery. As she herself says, several of the senators, even some Black Republicans, crowded around her, some begging her to leave the city before the Rebels stormed across the Potomac.

There is little doubt that they *did* swarm around her as she claims. She was *the* woman to see in Washington of '61. As her captured correspondence shows, politicians were always calling upon her to get her to open closed doors or make some difficult appointment.

On the way out of the Senate Building she met Seward who told her nonchalantly that "nothing serious" was the matter and all would be over in sixty days with the Federals in Richmond. Rose thanked him for the "precious" information and said good-by. He never saw the cold contempt in her eyes.

On July 24, a small batch of prisoners was brought into Washington and an unruly mob stoned them. A company of militia delivered the men in dirty gray to the Old Capitol Prison. Rose soon heard the news. With her friend, Miss Mackall, she hurried to the prison in her carriage with what foodstuffs and fruit she had. Either there was no guard at the gate or the guard decided not to question the haughty women in black with baskets on their arms who swept past him.

The two women entered the prison yard and found the prisoners sprawled on the ground being harangued by William P. Wood, the ex-model maker, who had been appointed civilian superintendent of the prison. When he had finished Rose calmly addressed the prisoners advising them that the South "has prisoners 100 to 1 if the North wants to retaliate."

The weary men gave her three times three and a tiger. After emptying their baskets, the Wild Rose and the gentle Lily flounced out of the prison with Wood wondering how to deal with them.

Superintendent Wood would soon see her again.

That night Mrs. Greenhow and Miss Mackall sent the names of the prisoners south by courier. She also started a fund for Southern prisoners which was to provide many a captured gray trooper with a few simple luxuries.

The next morning she appeared at the prison gate. But this time the guard barred her way. Of course she wasn't stopped. "Channels" were soon opened by which she "communicated" with the prisoners and the

18

names of the captured Confederates to be dispatched to Richmond flowed without interruption into the house with the green shutters across from St. John's Church.

Several pathetic little letters in the State Department Records, National Archives, all written on scraps of blue wrapping paper, evidently with the same pencil stub, dramatically testify to the devotion the captured Confederate prisoners had for her.

Corporal Jeff Bates of the Alabama Rifles wrote, "We have received the articles you sent us. God Bless you. . . ."

A captain of a Georgia regiment swore he would "never forget your kindness"; a sergeant of the same regiment swore "everlasting gratitude" and predicted the South would never forget her. And so on.

There is a wonderful note from Private William Humphreys of the Eighth Georgia regiment, Company H. He first thanked Mrs. Greenhow profusely for the shoes and the shirt she had sent to him, then went on to say that "spirits of any kind except for medicinal purposes" were forbidden by prison rules.

With a chin-up attitude he agreed righteously, "and rightly so." The rules about spirits, he added, didn't apply to him because he didn't "care much about such things." However, he wrote:

I didn't need the ardent spirits but there are a number among us who occasionally like to share a glass with their friends. There are a great number of friends here.

There is little doubt that the Wild Rose made sure the "great number of friends" behind the gloomy walls of the Old Capitol Prison soon shared a glass.

For the next few weeks after the disaster at Bull Run, Washington worked feverishly to guard against attack. The saber-swinging Rebel cavalrymen were expected at any time. It was announced that the signal for the attack would be three guns fired by the Provost Marshal's Office, to be followed by the tolling of all the church bells in the city.

When she heard that the gas lamps burned most of the night in the War Department where the military was planning what to do should the Confederate Army cross the Potomac, Mrs. Greenhow immediately made it her business to meet the officer commanding the city's defenses. As she relates, she soon had the plan, plus blueprints of Fort Corcoran and Fort Ellsworth!

To familiarize herself and the other ladies with the Federal plans, she took them on a grand tour of the fortifications one warm Sunday afternoon. When they retired to her house for tea a plan was forming in her pretty head. It was one of the most fantastic of the war.

At the signal of attack the gentle ladies, aided by the few males in their group, would cut the telegraph wires to the War Department, kidnap the commanding general, and spike the guns of Corcoran and Ellsworth! With the city in a state of incredible chaos and with high army officers and War Department officials still bewitched by this strange woman, who can say the plan might not have been successful, at least in part—had Beauregard and Johnson been able to muster their own disorganized forces across the river for an all out effort to conquer the heart of America?

As Rose nonchalantly relates in her book, she sent the blueprints and the report of the military strength of Washington's defenses on to Jordan in Richmond.

This is not, as one might suppose, the exaggeration of a romantic woman. It is an incredible fact. That report is among the Captured Confederate Correspondence, State Department Records, National Archives in Washington.

This is what one enemy woman was able to send from a beleagued wartime capitol. Several pages long, dated August 11, 1861, it begins:

> The principal fortifications for the defense of Washington are in Arlington Heights and are of such nature that military men believe that 5,000 men could hold them against ten times that number. . . .

Each fort is examined minutely. Secret weaknesses in the earthworks are described; the number, caliber, and range of all fieldpieces are given. "The number of these guns may be doubled or tripled within the coming week so great is the supply constantly arriving." Regiments inside the forts are identified along with a military estimate of their fitness, condition of their morale, estimate of their officers' military experience, the percentage politically lukewarm; the number of muskets, shot, and grape issued them. Description of the fitness of horses and mules, conditions of wagons, ambulances, and stores were also included.

Allan Pinkerton labeled it: "Important military information for the Rebels. . . ."

Rose and her spies were hard at work when McClellan rode out of the West like a Lochinvar to supersede McDowell. He was dramatic and colorful. Reporters followed him everywhere as he inspected the city's fortifications. Soon he was their "young Napoleon."

Military discipline tightened. Tin Cup Alley, in the red-light district, was no longer strewn with drunken, half-clad soldiers. Provost Marshal Andrew Porter's men were everywhere, examining passes and uniforms and smashing the supply of wine and Monongahela whisky of any saloon owner who sold a soldier a drink.

McClellan soon discovered military information was being sent out of the city and brought in Allan Pinkerton who had protected his railroad from thieves, and appointed him head of the army of the Potomac's secret service. It was agreed that Pinkerton, the well-known head of the Pinkerton's Western Detective Agency, should go under the names of "Major A. E. Allan" and "R. Hutchinson."

The trail of treason was plainly marked and led to the house on Sixteenth Street. Soon "detective shadows" followed Mrs. Greenhow and Miss Mackall wherever they went.

When Mrs. Greenhow became aware that she was being trailed, she and her ladies made a game of it, losing their shadows by going into homes of friends and stealing out the back doors suddenly to come upon the unsuspecting operatives and demand haughtily, "Are you following *me, sir?*"

It was quite startling to the shadows who found themselves shadowed by the persons they were shadowing.

But for all of Mrs. Greenhow's games Pinkerton soon had enough evidence to warrant a raid.

On the night of August 21, 1861, Pinkerton took three of his best operatives, Sam Bridgman, William Ascot, and Pryce Lewis, to watch the house on Sixteenth Street. It was a stormy night and the rain came down in sheets. The three men took shelter under the dripping trees in front of St. John's Church across the street. When a lamp was lit in a front room they moved across the street and Pinkerton took off his boots and climbed on the "husky shoulders" of Lewis and Bridgman to peek through the blinds. In an "elegant" room lined with "valuable pictures and statuary" he saw Mrs. Greenhow reading.

They heard footsteps approaching and the bootless Pinkerton and his men hid in the bushes. A young officer entered the house. Again Pinkerton climbed upon the shoulders of his men and looked through the blinds. His "blood boiled with indignation" when he saw the officer hand the Confederacy's Wild Rose a military map and heard him, above the hiss of the rain, carefully describe for her the strength of each fortification on the map.

Mrs. Greenhow and the officer then left the room, returning within an hour "arm in arm." She escorted the officer to the doorway and the

21

crouching detectives heard what Pinkerton said, "sounded like a kiss."

Still bootless, Pinkerton ordered Bridgman and Lewis to watch the house and with Ascot hurried off into the rainy darkness after the young officer. But the officer discovered he was being followed and took to his heels. So did the detectives with Pinkerton slipping and splashing in the muddy road.

They chased the officer to his quarters, where a guard promptly arrested Pinkerton and his operative Ascot. They stayed all night in a verminous jail. In the morning Pinkerton, who was unwilling to disclose his identity, managed to smuggle a note to Assistant Secretary of War Thomas Scott, who came to the jail to "personally" release them.

The name of the officer who visited Mrs. Greenhow has been variously spelled Elison and Ellison. But in the recently discovered memoirs of Pryce Lewis, the Pinkerton detective who was sentenced to death in Richmond with Timothy Webster eight months later, Lewis identifies the officer as a Captain Elwood;* whom Pinkerton later had arrested.

General Doster reveals that in December 1862, while provost marshal of Washington, he was summoned to the cell of a Captain Elwood who had committed suicide by slashing his throat.

Elwood was locked in a small cell and seen only by a silent guard who brought him his meals. He was the prison's most mysterious inmate, for no one actually knew what crime he had committed.

It was said he had committed a number of offenses. Doster thought he had been jailed for misappropriating government funds and felt sorry for him. The case of the dead officer was so vivid in his memory twenty years later when he wrote his memoirs that he wondered why the Captain had not been given a court-martial, or if he had been found guilty of his crime why he had not been sentenced.

It was obvious that Doster never knew that Elwood had been in communication with the dangerous Rose. Had he been aware of this he surely would have remembered that in those long dead July days with Beauregard's aides peering through their glasses at the capitol's unfinished dome, such an act was high treason.

On the afternoon of August 23, Pinkerton—with boots on—surrounded Mrs. Greenhow's house with detectives. At about four o'clock Rose went out on her last promenade. She was not surprised to dis-

* According to Heitman's *Historical Register and Dictionary of the U.S. Army,* the only regular army officer of that name was Captain John Elwood of the Fifth Infantry, who died December 3, 1862.

cover she was being followed. On the twenty-first she had been informed she was "high on the prescribed list" and was to be arrested momentarily. Probably one of her "unconscious ducts" as Beauregard called them, had warned her.

However, instead of trying to get to Richmond she informed William Preston, American Minister to Spain, who was in Washington, and also "high" on the prescribed list, that he was about to be arrested. Preston fled to Richmond.

As she walked down the street in the August heat, she met a "distinguished member of the diplomatic corps" and allowed him to take her arm and escort her to the home of a friend "whose child was ill."

When she returned, she met one of her agents who told her between smiles and complaints of the muggy weather, that her house had been surrounded and two detectives were waiting at the door to arrest her.

"Wait on Corcoran's Corner," she told the agent. "When you see me raise my handkerchief it will be a signal that I have been arrested. Inform the others."

The agent bowed and walked away.

Rose raised her hand to her lips as if politely cutting off a cough, then turned and walked slowly down the street. She had swallowed the scrap of paper with the cipher before she reached her house.

As she walked up the steps, Pinkerton, in uniform, barred her way.

"Are you Mrs. Greenhow?" he asked.

"Yes," she replied, "and who are you?"

"I have come to arrest you, ma'am," Pinkerton explained.

Mrs. Greenhow, in her most regal manner, demanded, "And by whose authority, sir?"

"We have sufficient authority, ma'am," Pinkerton replied quietly.

She demanded a warrant but Pinkerton was now weary of her high-flung dramatics and told her that his warrant was the Secretary of State and the War Department. At this point Mrs. Greenhow raised her handkerchief to her lips and opened the door. The agent standing at "Corcoran's Corner" disappeared.

Pinkerton gave a signal and detectives from all sides "swarmed into the house like bees in a hive." The detectives commenced to go through the rooms. Once, as Rose said, she had to snatch something lacy and frilly from a detective's hand.

Pinkerton's men found themselves occupied with another member of the Greenhow household. Little Rose, then eight, ran out of the house screaming at the top of her lungs, "Mama has been arrested. Mama has been arrested." One wonders why Mrs. Greenhow went to the trouble of signaling her agent, when her child's powerful voice could have done just as well. Rose, surely her mother's daughter, climbed a tree, informing passers-by of her mother's arrest. Two detectives had to be dispatched to get her down from the tree and to carry her screaming and kicking into the house.

Within an hour all Washington buzzed with Mrs. Greenhow's arrest. More than one warrior in the War Department or statesman in broadcloth who had visited her "at a late hour" trembled when he heard the news.

The faithful Miss Mackall was the first visitor and was promptly arrested. She was searched by a female operative, then allowed to see Mrs. Greenhow who now had managed to get another of Jordan's ciphers from her desk and was wondering what to do with it.

Miss Mackall's appearance was most timely. She slipped the cipher into her friend's stocking. A few minutes later Pinkerton informed the widow she was to be searched. She protested violently at the "indignity" but was ushered firmly into a room where a woman detective, whose face reminded Mrs. Greenhow of an Indian-rubber doll, ordered her to strip to her "linen."

Each garment was carefully searched, then returned to her. She dressed in a cold rage and joined Miss Mackall in the library—where she had hidden a "batch" of Jordan's letters and intelligence ready for Richmond.

In the best tradition of all women spies, Rose, as she related, broke out her finest brandy, usually reserved for her distinguished guests, and invited the detectives to have a drink. They accepted.

Mrs. Greenhow claims she was in this way able to reach the hidden papers and stuff them down her bosom. Later they were transferred to Miss Mackall's stocking. She neglects to explain how she was able to persuade the detectives to get drunk under the eyes of their employer, nor does she explain how men as keen and observing as Pryce Lewis, did not detect the extraordinary fullness of her bosom which held the "batch" of secret papers.

But not all her papers escaped Pinkerton's detectives. Letters, dispatches and espionage reports, many torn into tiny pieces or burned, were discovered in the kitchen stove. In other hiding places throughout the house an "enormous file" of what Pinkerton, in his official report to Provost Marshal Porter and Secretary of State Seward, described as "treasonable correspondence" was found.

6

In the State Department Records, National Archives, there is a gray steel box marked "Civil War Papers, 1861-65; Greenhow, Captured Correspondence." To examine its contents is a fascinating experience. From the yellowing, charred and torn papers, emerges a strange woman of unbelievable power. These papers show her to have been the confidante of a president, senators, congressmen, secret agents, blockade-runners, spies, adventurers, and madmen.

They show that senators sought her approval of applicants who wished to enter West Point and Annapolis.

They showed she controlled more than fifty spies, forty-eight of them women, in five states, as far as Texas.

They show that her house on Sixteenth Street was used as a central clearing house for incredible military information sent on to Richmond from all parts of the country.

Among them is a letter of October, 1861, from William Durkin in New York, that he was sending on "for your approval" a list of officers under orders by the War Department to proceed with recruits to California and Oregon.

They show that in May, 1861, she managed to obtain a copy—by what means God knows—of secret order Number 16 which gave in detail the reorganization of the United States Army, bringing it to the strength of 18,954 men and officers.

A small, red leather covered diary, with Jordan's pseudonym and Rennehan's name scrawled across one of its pages, produced a second list of agents and several damaging notes on military fortifications and movements of army regiments.

It is plain the Confederacy's Rose had agents in the Navy Department. One wrote to her shortly before her arrest, enclosing a description and the dimensions of the new navy gunboats, still on the planning board.

The last paragraph of the charred note, taken as it were, from ten thousand later spy stories of both fact and fiction, reads:

I am afraid, dear lady, it will require three days to copy the plans. They are now in constant use. Still they shall be copied. . . .

There is also an outline of a plan to raise $10,000 to equip, by popular subscription, a small army for sixty days. The itemized list includes

100926

uniforms, muskets, shot and shell, medicine chests, boats, and fifty tons of coal.

There is no evidence that the entire sum was raised but there are initialed notes indicating that sums up to five hundred dollars had been contributed.

Across the bottom of the plan, Rose, probably in despair when she was unable to raise all the money had written, "Great God, on what a slender thread eternal matters hang. . . ."

It is evident that word had spread rapidly through the army that Rose was the one to see to get a promotion. After Sumter she received a flood of mail from captains, lieutenants, and privates seeking her aid!

Like Lieutenant Hamilton of the third Artillery, San Francisco, who wanted to be a captain, they all "had great faith" that she would help them.

The Catholic Bishop of California, and well-known historian, W. Ingraham Nix, pleaded with her to help him "out of a quandary" by obtaining one of General Washington's letters for "a young girl in Europe." Rose sent him the letter.

A small package, actually tied as it should be, with a faded ribbon, was the most fascinating find. These are her love letters from Senator Joseph Lane of Oregon, the half-mad blockade-runner; Parker H. French, and a mysterious "H——."

Lane was a handsome man and one of the most powerful politicians in the Northwest. Southern delegates who withdrew from the 1860 Democratic Convention at Baltimore, had nominated him as vice-president and Breckenridge's running mate.

It is evident that Lane was deeply in love with Rose but despised the aristocrats who flocked about her every night.

Once in a huff he wrote that his morning had been occupied by a hearing of the Senate Military Affairs Committee and explained why he hesitated to drop by in the evening.

> . . . and of the evenings you are surrounded by your admirers . . . I do not care for them . . . I do not care to meet them. . . .

But the Southern Rose had completely captivated Lane and even the "admirers" he detested failed to keep him away from the parlor on Sixteenth Street.

He wrote of a visit he had made when she was not at home:

26

It was only a quarter after ten when I left . . . I could not sit long. I was naturally impatient, restless and almost reckless . . . How could I stay long . . . ?

The love notes from Parker H. French are weird. Just before he was arrested by a Senate order after detectives had discovered he was organizing secret branches of the Knights of the Golden Circle in Boston and throughout New England, French, also known as Charles Maxy and Cornelius Murray, wrote Rose:

. . . I am now in the hands of doctors. The room is crowded with the souls of those who have lived in other days. . . . I have had a long pleasant chat with them. . . .

In another rambling, four-page letter he complained of being "chained to the skeleton of despair . . . badgered by fate . . . I stand at bay with Despair at my side. . . ."

Then later in March, 1861, when he was evidently recovering from his delirium, he wrote:

I have been very ill . . . soon I will be able to attend to business. The first will be that of which we spoke at our last meeting. I am not angry . . . but do not write me any more . . . tell no one where I am. . . .

There are eleven "H Letters"; one written on congressional stationery. With one exception all are signed with the initial "H." They had been marked by Rose: "Letters from H not to be opened—but burned in case of death or accident."

One bears a date, that of January 1861. It would appear they were written in a short period of time by a distracted man, desperately in love and unable for some reason to act freely in relation to the woman he was in love with.

One note runs through the eleven: "I love you. . . . I could not come last night. . . . I will come tonight. . . ."

There is some indication that he thinks his love is returned and yet there is an implication that Rose doubts the reality of the love of which he assures her.

It is said that these letters were from Henry Wilson, senator from Massachusetts and later vice-president. Yet manuscript experts declare

27

the handwriting is not Wilson's. If they are his letters, the question arises as to why Wilson, who served four years as the able chairman of the important Senate Military Affairs Committee, was not implicated by Pinkerton.

The answer may be that there was no evidence of treasonable communication in the letters which could well be explained as being the result of frustrated passion.

What the letters do unquestionably establish is that the desire for the Wild Rose drove someone who wrote on the stationery of the thirty-sixth Congress close to the breaking point with passion and frustration.

But if these letters are not Wilson's whose are they? This appears to be their sequence.

In the first "H" passionately begged forgiveness for failing to appear "at the appointed time." He explained that he was unable to get away because of important Senate business. He ended:

> You know I love you—and I will sacrifice everything on my own account. I have feared bringing you into trouble for I repeat to you that spies are put upon me but I will try to elude them tonight and once more have a happy hour in spite of fate. . . .

Apparently he never found his "happy hour" because the second note again begs forgiveness for not appearing. Now, although he is "exhausted" and "unless providence may put her foot against me," he vows he will see Rose that night. The letter ends: "That I love you, God to whom I appeal, knows."

The next three are hastily scrawled in pencil as if written on the arm of a chair. They are filled with a pathetic, unsatisfied passion, great anguish and suffering.

> I do love you . . . I must see you tonight . . . I am sick mentally and physically . . . nothing would soothe me as one hour with you . . . at whatever cost I will see you tonight. I will come tonight but at what hour I cannot say. . . .

There is evidence that Rose herself suffered in this unhappy affair. From the next letter it is plain she waited for hours for her lover and when he did not appear, sent him a bitter note of reproach.

"H" immediately replied, swearing eternal love and pleading with

28

her "never to doubt me." Then, in a businesslike way, he promised, "At ten o'clock tonight *precisely,* expect me."

Evidently they had their "happy hour" for on the next day Rose received a jubilant note. It read: "I am happy to say that I feel <u>particularly</u> [his underline] well this morning and can well account for the favorable change. . . ."

Then Pinkerton appeared on the scene and his detectives began shadowing Rose. She complained of this to "H" but he replied on congressional stationery, that he too was watched with "hawkeyed vigilance."

In the rest of the letters, some written in haste and in pencil "H" swears again and again "my love is all yours and yours alone."

On the last one he signed his full name. Rose carefully cut it out.

For what it is worth, the bundle is marked: "Love letters from Henry Wilson, U.S. Senator from Massachusetts." The words "supposed to be" are inserted by caret, between "letters" and "from."

Along with the love letters found by Pinkerton was a damaging dispatch from Donellan, introducing her to the bearer, Michael Thompson, "a true Carolina gentleman" who had volunteered to act as her courier to Richmond. The letter also pleaded with Rose to try to find out the movements of the Union Army "during the next two or three days."

Pinkerton immediately put his detectives on Thompson's trail.

The afternoon of the raid on Mrs. Greenhow's house, Pinkerton ordered Lewis and Bridgman to stand guard at the door and arrest all callers.

At nine, Walker, the Post Office Department clerk and Rennehan called. Lewis opened the door and the detectives pulled them into the house. Both men were indignant and told Pinkerton, summoned by Lewis, that they were merely "paying a social call."

But by this time the torn letters from the stove had been pasted together and there were the names of Walker and Rennehan. They were arrested and taken that night to Old Capitol Prison.

Meanwhile the Pinkerton men had learned that Thompson frequently visited a pretty young Southern widow, Mrs. H. Phelps.

Posing as a "true Georgia Secessionist," an operative—and it would be delightful to know how—got Mrs. Phelps to give him letters "to some friends who are right." The woman agreed. One of the letters she gave him was to Colonel Michael Thompson, a lawyer about fifty.

"Speak plain," Mrs. Phelps wrote the operative, "for he [Thompson] can be trusted."

Thompson, however, was not so gullible as his lady spies. He warned Mrs. Phelps that "the government detectives are trying all their games." Mrs. Phelps waved away his suspicions. Her friend from Georgia, she said, was a "Southern gentleman."

The net closed slowly about Thompson. The detective found he was in close contact with Mrs. Greenhow and the banker, W. T. Smithson, who was known in Richmond as "Charles R. Cables"; Van Camp, the fashionable dentist, and others. But Pinkerton wanted more evidence and the shadows kept at Thompson's heels.

Miss Mackall was released the night of the raid but after a change of clothing returned to join Mrs. Greenhow.

The morning of the twenty-fifth the search was intensified. Beds were taken apart, books examined leaf by leaf, and legs of tables unscrewed as Mrs. Greenhow, to Pryce Lewis, proudly compared herself to Mary, Queen of Scots.

There was humor too off stage. One of the detectives, a dashing Irishman tried to make love to Lizzy Fitzgerald, Mrs. Greenhow's servant, while another, a dour Scot, wept and begged the widow's forgiveness "for there's no telling what may happen."

Lizzy rebuffed the romantic Irishman and Rose told the weeping Scot to dry his tears and be off.

One of the papers Pinkerton's men did find that day, according to Mrs. Greenhow, was a "full and detached account of the administration and attempt on the life of President Buchanan at the National Hotel." She was undoubtedly referring to the night when she was present at Buchanan's inaugural party four years before, when many of them were stricken by a strange intestinal illness. The new President became violently ill and his young nephew died that night. Extremists in the Democratic Party raised the cry it was all a Republican plot but weeks later nearly all agreed with the official verdict that the illness had been caused by a leakage of sewer gas.

Mrs. Greenhow predicted the paper would never see the light of day. Curiously, it didn't. There is no mention of it among the Official Records, nor among the Captured Confederate Papers in the National Archives.

On the evening of the second day, while seated at the desk in the library, Miss Mackall silently motioned to Mrs. Greenhow, who walked across the room and joined her. Miss Mackall pointed at the desk. Mrs. Greenhow, as she relates, "almost swooned." She had used the blotter pad to dry the ink of the last dispatch she had sent to Jordan. Now it told the whole story. Before they retired for the evening the blotter had been tucked into the stocking of the faithful Miss Mackall.

A week passed. Mrs. Greenhow now decided to turn for help to the men in high places who once courted her favors. She wrote to former Attorney General Jeremiah S. Black and Senator R. J. Walker to visit her. But they never came. She had her revenge later, when she wrote her book. She was discreet about many names but quite careful to include Black and Walker as among men who knew her.

On the thirtieth the government served formal notice on Mrs. Greenhow that her house had been taken over for a female prison.

General Ben Butler—"Butler the Beast," as the New Orleans ladies called him months later—protested. He told the senators he hoped the government would consign Rose to his care at Fortress Monroe, where he would "put her through such an ordeal, she would never again endanger the loyalty of Union officers."

Butler was boasting. Superintendent Wood said later he would gladly handle a cage of hungry lions rather than Mrs. Greenhow, and Provost Marshal Porter cried he'd be damned if he wouldn't resign rather than take on Mrs. Greenhow "for one more day."

This handsome woman with a queen's bearing could put any man in his place, in boudoir or prison.

The War Department now took over control of the female prisoners. The detectives were replaced by thirty men from the Sturgis Rifles—McClellan's own bodyguard—under a lieutenant.

Accompanied by the officer, Mrs. Greenhow made a tour of her house denouncing "those unwashed, unkempt wretches [detectives]" for leaving their footprints on her rugs and handmarks on her linen.

Mrs. Greenhow and her daughter were assigned to one room in the house. The other rooms were stripped of their furniture and equipped with a bed, chair, and a washstand. The government's new "Greenhow's Prison," as the country's press called it, was ready for its occupants.

It took only a few days for the young lieutenant commanding the Sturgis Rifles to fall under Mrs. Greenhow's spell. He was soon buying fruit for her.

Mrs. Morris, who had been accredited to Mrs. Greenhow by Jordan as a courier, was the next prisoner. She was placed in a room next to Mrs. Greenhow but the connecting door was bolted and a wooden slat nailed across it. She wept all that first night and Mrs. Greenhow tried to comfort her in whispers under the door.

Mrs. Philip Phillips, wife of former Congressman Phillips of Alabama, her two daughters and her sister Miss A. Levy, were taken into custody the next day and brought to the Greenhow Prison.

31

While the ladies were assigned their rooms by the lieutenant of the Sturgis Rifles, Mrs. Greenhow had two distinguished visitors. One was Edwin M. Stanton, soon to be Lincoln's secretary of war. His companion was Colonel Thomas Marshal Key, an aide of General McClellan. Key seems to have been fond of roses—preferably wild. Stanton knew Mrs. Greenhow quite well and apparently asked her what he could do. He was nonplused when she promptly asked him to represent her in a habeas corpus action. Mrs. Greenhow still had her ear to the ground. Stanton, she knew, was now one of the most influential men in Washington.

The embarrassed Stanton refused and the men left. Pryce Lewis, in his memoirs, tells of another visit by Stanton. When he started to berate Lewis for some minor discourtesy to the women prisoners Lewis promptly ordered him out of the house with, "Now, sir, you march right out of this house."

The deflated Secretary of War quickly apologized and Lewis magnanimously accepted it.

Ironically, it was Stanton who approved Pinkerton's plan to send Lewis behind the Rebel lines. But the night they met, Stanton "gave no recognition" that he knew the embarrassed detective who had threatened to march him out of the Greenhow Prison.

Although she was confined to her room with a soldier at her door, Mrs. Greenhow continued to send her secret dispatches south to Richmond. But one of these fell into Pinkerton's hands and the amateurish cipher was broken.

Apparently Pinkerton rewrote, as bait, Mrs. Greenhow's dispatch substituting useless or minor information and sent it on to Jordan.

The dispatch found its way to Jefferson Davis. Acting Secretary of War Benjamin forwarded it to General Joseph W. Johnson, who in turn sent it to Beauregard and Jordan.

Jordan was not fooled. He wrote Beauregard:

The note in cipher is addressed to me, that is Thomas Jordan Rayford, a name I adopted before leaving Washington. This was for the purpose of cipher correspondence with Mrs. Rose Greenhow. It is quite possible that Mrs. Greenhow did not write this dispatch and it is simply a shallow device of the enemy to entice us into correspondence which shall fall into their hands. The cipher is now useless but it served our purpose when it saved General Bonham from disaster on July 17 [First Bull Run]. . . .

Jordan then went on to tell Davis he had heard that a large reward had been posted in Washington for anyone who could break Mrs. Greenhow's cipher.

"I am inclined," this practical man wrote, "to furnish the key to a friend of mine in Washington and let him have the consideration. . . ."

Jordan also assured Davis that Mrs. Greenhow was still operating despite her arrest. Her last intelligence, he said, informed them that Smithville was a new point of attack.

Back in Washington, the government gently juggled the explosive problem of how to deal with Mrs. Greenhow. There were numerous conferences between Pinkerton, Provost Marshal Porter, Secretary of War Stanton, and Secretary of State Seward as to what to do with this dangerous woman. Men in high offices, who feared they might be implicated in her affairs, were plotting to have her released. One must also consider her other powerful connections.

Her brother-in-law was James Madison Cutts, second comptroller of the Treasury. He and his wife—Mrs. Greenhow's sister, Ellen— were the parents of Rose Adele Cutts Douglas, the widow of Senator Stephen A. Douglas. Mrs. Douglas had now taken her aunt's place as the most beautiful matron of Washington society.

The brother-in-law of Mrs. Greenhow's sister, Ellen, was also a powerful ally. A nephew of Dolly Madison, he was an aide to General H. W. Halleck and later made a brevet brigadier.

Mrs. Greenhow's nephew, James Madison Cutts, Jr., was a powerful Washington attorney, an aide and later judge advocate on Burnside's staff.

Mrs. Greenhow was by now an international celebrity. W. L. Yancey, the Confederate diplomatic agent in London knew her and spread her fame about Victoria's court. In the United States the press was describing her as a beautiful romantic but dangerous spy. In Richmond people spoke of her in reverent tones.

The Wild Rose was fast succeeding in winning the role she loved so well.

In October, Walker and Rennehan, who had been arrested the night of the raid, pleaded to be released from their cells in the Thirteenth Street Prison. Provost Marshal Porter asked Pinkerton's opinion. He replied that the two agents should be detained until they had signed an oath of allegiance. A few weeks later they signed the oath and were paroled under close surveillance.

In mid-October a mysterious Mrs. Mary Onderdonk was brought

into the Greenhow Prison. She tried to become friendly with Mrs. Greenhow, but was ignored as "a woman of low type."

Mrs. Greenhow may also have deduced that Mrs. Onderdonk was a detective. She may have been right. In the comparatively short time of two weeks the lady was released on Pinkerton's orders.

In mid-November the pressure to release Mrs. Greenhow intensified. Stanton and Seward may have been weakening because they asked Provost Marshal Porter for a résumé of the Greenhow case. Porter turned to Pinkerton who wrote a vigorous report on the activities of the Wild Rose, denouncing the strange appeasement policy of the North.

After reviewing the raid, the arrest of Walker and Rennehan, and the finding of a "large amount of treasonable correspondence," he wrote:

It is a fact, too notorious to need reciting, that she [Mrs. Greenhow] was using her house as a focal center where treason found a resting place. Traitors were supplied with every need and care and supplied with every possible information obtained by the untiring intrigue of this remarkable woman.

Mrs. Greenhow has been the intimate of the very men who now lead the Rebel Councils and lead their armies. Since the commencement of this Rebellion, this woman, from her long residence at the Capitol, her superior education, her social powers, her very extensive acquaintances and her active association with leading politicians of this nation, has possessed an almost super human power, all of which she had wickedly used to try and destroy her government.

With her as with many traitors she has been most unscrupulous in the use of means. Nothing has been sacred for her appropriation, as by its use she might hope to accomplish her treasonable means.

She has made use of whomever and whatever she could as medium to carrying into effect her unholy purposes. She has used her almost irresistible seductive powers to win to her aid persons who are holding responsible places of honor. She has not used her power in vain among officers of the Army, but a few of whom she has robbed of patriotic hearts.

She has secret and insidious agents in all parts of the city and scattered over a large extent of the country. She had a long list of names in alphabetical order, a number of ciphers.

In her circle of influence were many women of various ages as

34

well as men. These women paid visits to the camps of Rebel generals and gave them the hand of friendship. They carried letters from Mrs. Greenhow's house with the most valuable of information statistical and otherwise which she received from the agents and employees of government departments and sent on the Rebel forces.

Pinkerton then went into the arrest of Captain Elwood who had come out of Mrs. Greenhow's house "at a late hour" and how he himself had been arrested and released by Assistant Secretary of War Scott. Pinkerton ended his report:

> It seems to me that this is a time when if ever the lines of demarcation between loyalty and disloyalty should be clearly marked as to admit very little doubt.
> I sympathize with any and with every person who is deprived of his liberty but it is far better that a few suffer than the lives of our best and brave soldiers should be sacrificed. . . .

In November one of Mrs. Greenhow's dispatches was confiscated. In it she confided to Jordan that Dr. Van Camp, for an unexplained reason, had destroyed a Confederate dispatch en route to her. Pinkerton's best shadows began investigating the dentist.

On November 26, two of his agents arrested Dr. T. Herndon, an army doctor deserting to Richmond. The physician confessed that Van Camp had supplied the carriage he used to flee Washington. He also revealed that a son of Van Camp had been wounded at Bull Run and was now on Beauregard's staff.

Pinkerton arrested Van Camp and the dentist was placed in the Old Capitol Prison. Several members of Congress interceded with Seward to permit Van Camp to take the oath and be freed on bond. But on the advice of Porter and Pinkerton, the Secretary of State refused.

In early December, Mrs. Greenhow suffered a hard blow. Miss Mackall had been ordered out of the Greenhow Prison in late November and had made a weary round of the offices of senators and congressmen appealing to them to force Mrs. Greenhow's release.

The strain of wading through the slushy and snowy streets in the bitter temperatures was too much for the frail woman. She caught a heavy cold and died of "a fever," probably pneumonia.

In a letter to Seward, Rose asked to be permitted to attend the funeral. It would seem incredible that a secretary of state would admit to a prisoner the effectiveness with which that prisoner, from her jail, was still communicating with the Confederacy. Nonetheless, Seward's letter of December 12 to Porter in the Official Records reads:

> . . . her [Mrs. Greenhow's] correspondence with the commanding general of the army besieging the capitol renders improper all interference in her behalf with the regulations established by the military authorities for the safety of the prisoners. . . .

What bitter rage must have welled up in her proud heart as she read Seward's refusal in the sickly winter light streaming through the wooden bars of her cell.

In late December, Mrs. James Madison Cutts, Mrs. Stephen A. Douglas, and a Colonel Ingalls were allowed to visit her for fifteen minutes "in the presence of a proper person." Ingalls tried in this short time to get her to "gracefully submit" to the government but she coldly rebuffed him.

The morning after their visit she wrote to Seward demanding to know the exact charges lodged against her. There was no answer. Rose fumed for a week—meanwhile smuggling out a dispatch to Jordan. It contained the minutes of McClellan's secret council and a copy of the map the army was to use. The map was the one used by the Senate Military Affairs Committee!

With the dispatch safely off to Richmond, the lady returned to the wars. She wrote a second scorching letter to Seward about the charges, smuggling out a copy to one of her agents who delivered it to Richmond.

It was published on page one of the *Richmond Whig*. The *New York Herald* reprinted it, describing her as "the most dangerous agent of a hostile army now besieging our capitol."

Repercussions shook Washington and reprisals followed. Mrs. Greenhow was deprived of writing paper and pen and informed that if she wanted candles she had to buy them out of her own purse.

Another of the blazing letters to Seward led the Secretary of State to declare he believed she was losing her mind. He sent a surgeon general of the Pennsylvania Volunteers to the Greenhow Prison to prove it.

The irresistible woman worked her magic. In the dreary room with the guards outside her door Rose and the surgeon general discussed life and the arts for most of the afternoon. The surgeon later informed Secretary of State Seward that there wasn't anything wrong with Mrs.

Greenhow's mind. Perhaps he wondered if there wasn't something wrong with Seward's.

Colonel Key, who had visited Mrs. Greenhow with Stanton, was next admitted. His visit would make a delightful scene in any play. Then about fifty, he apparently had more on his mind than questioning Mrs. Greenhow about her spy activities. As she relates, Key "pretended" to be deaf so she had to lean close to him. Once stirred by her nearness he tried to stroke her hand "to find out whether I had ever done any hard work."

Rose, the veteran of many such campaigns, said coolly it was her head that had labored more than her hands. This brought Key up short and he asked her gruffly under what conditions she thought she should be released. Rose replied, "Unconditionally," also indemnity for her losses and restoration of all lost property. Then, weary of leaning close and having her hands stroked, she sent the dashing Colonel away with the plea of a headache.

Meanwhile a patrol boat had captured the blockade-running schooner, *Lucretia,* and the agents who boarded her confiscated a package of letters from Jordan's spies.

The letters helped Pinkerton fit in some of the missing pieces in his spy puzzle. The "Colonel Empty" who had been sending valuable information through the lines to Jordan turned out to be the Washington attorney, Michael Thompson. His office was searched. A rebel flag, many letters, and a new cipher sent by Jordan were found in a desk of Lewis L. McArthur, Thompson's confidential secretary. Pinkerton hired a handwriting expert who compared the handwriting of the letters found on board the blockade-runner with letters written by McArthur. They were found to have been written by the same person.

The cipher was a good one and contained some of the symbols used by Mrs. Greenhow. Included among the letters found on Thompson's desk was one from Jordan praising Mrs. Greenhow and Thompson for the work they had done for the Confederacy.

"It will be understood and appreciated in the right places," Jordan wrote.

A dismal Christmas passed. Pinkerton sent in a detective named Applegate who charmed Mrs. Roberta Hasler, another attractive spy, into giving him three of Mrs. Greenhow's dispatches. But Rose soon found out who he was and notified Jordan.

Meanwhile, McClellan, now recovered from a severe attack of typhoid, was ready to advance on Richmond. Colonel Key and Assistant

Secretary of the Navy Gustavus V. Fox dropped in on Mrs. Greenhow in her prison to inform her she would soon be sent back to Richmond if she signed the allegiance oath.

Mrs. Greenhow probably used her superhuman powers, as Pinkerton called them, because by the time the two officers had left the Greenhow Prison they had given away their General's secrets!

That night the highly important intelligence was on its way to Richmond by way of Smithson, the treasonable banker.

It was the Wild Rose at her best. Her dispatch in the Official Records to Jordan reads:

> . . . and now today I have in my power to say that Kelley is to advance on Winchester, Stone and Banks are to cross and go on to Leesburg, Burnside's fleet is to engage the batteries on the Potomac. McClellan & Co. move up to Centreville, then on to Manassas.
>
> This information comes from one of McClellan's aides and Fox of the Navy Department.
>
> As I remarked to be prepared for them on every hand, and at every moment. Look out for a smash up. I send you papers containing Seward's letter.
>
> Now, my dear General, look out for a large army. Tell your men (God bless them) to cut and slay until every last man is destroyed. Do not let one come back to tell the sad tale.
>
> By God, General, give them the worst licking that any army has ever received!
>
> A confidential member of McClellan's staff came to see me and to tell me my case should form an exception and I only wish to gain time.
>
> All my plans are nearly completed.

How Mrs. Greenhow got out the information she does not say nor did Pinkerton know. But she writes vaguely of "engaging" herself at the time in "tapestry," using balls of colored wool which were delivered to her by the Provost Marshal's office. Her finished product was sent as gifts to friends. The messages could have been hidden in the balls of wool or the tapestry.

She also related coyly how a "little bird" perched on her shoulder, whispered in her ear, and winged to Richmond with her dispatches. Was this "little bird" a high army officer who was ready to risk career and country to serve her? . . . a helpless statesman torn between love and treason? . . . a scheming politician? . . .

Mrs. Greenhow now had become the tourist attraction in Washington. Crowds gathered daily on the sidewalk to stare up at the closed windows. The *National Republican* wrote an article about her, calling her "the beautiful Rebel of Sixteenth Street . . . the fascinating female spy. . . ."

Just before the year ran out, the informality of the prison routine vanished. A guard "—an unwashed ruffian—" was posted at her door day and night. Her intelligence system soon told her why.

An "escape plot" had been uncovered. She was said to have been its "ring leader." The plans for the "plot" were uncovered by a Captain Averil who had charge of the soldiers guarding the prison, when he broke open a cake delivered to the house. The New York and Washington newspapers made the most of the details of the "plot."

The year turned and there was another sensation. A portion of Lincoln's address to Congress had been printed in the *New York Herald* before he delivered it, and a congressional committee began an investigation. Chevalier Wikoff was subpoenaed and admitted he bribed the White House gardener to steal the President's speech.

The press soon forgot about it when the guns rumbled again to the south. But Wikoff sent Mrs. Greenhow a note asking her to help him slip through the Rebel lines and to give him a note of introduction to President Davis. He had a wild plan—which he said had been endorsed by Seward—of sending back "a compromise peace proposal." Mrs. Greenhow ignored his note.

Prison discipline continued to tighten. Little Rose, who formerly had been allowed to play in the front yard was now confined to the house. All laundry was searched carefully, and even a sprig of the lady's favorite jasmine which had reached her "without examination," brought the wrath of the Provost Marshal's office down on the head of Captain Averil.

In January, with dramatic suddenness, the War Department announced publicly that Mrs. Greenhow was to be removed from the Greenhow Prison to the more formidable Old Capitol Prison.

On a Saturday afternoon, escorted by "that German-Jew detective" as she called Pinkerton, she left her home for the last time.

The streets were packed and the windows of the neighboring houses filled with curious spectators eager to catch a glimpse of the dangerous woman. Men and boys clung to tree limbs or lamp poles. Even to a less theatrical woman than Mrs. Greenhow it was a dramatic opportunity. It was her second greatest moment. She saw her path to greatness clear before her. With little Rose clinging to her hand and Pinkerton at her side, she stood on the porch, calmly looking over the sea of faces. Her dark eyes were cool and contemptuous. She was Marie Antoinette persecuted by the dirty rabble.

The crowd waited breathlessly. They were not disappointed. Turning to the company of Sturgis riflemen she said in a loud, clear voice, "I hope in the future you men will have a nobler employment."

7

The Old Capitol Prison was an ugly, red-brick building on the corner of First Street and A Street. Its walls were rotten and vermin infested. Dust lay thick on the creaky stairs and rats scampered across its broad beams. The windows were cracked or without panes and wooden slates were nailed across them. Spaces between the main building and the extensions which sprawled into A Street were cut off by high wooden fences.

Fatty pork, moldy beans, or half-cooked rice, all swimming in grease, composed the menu for the prison's population of spies, blockade-runners, crooked contractors, deserters, Confederate prisoners, and contrabands.

Prisoners who had friends in the city were allowed food packages. The committee formed by Mrs. Greenhow managed to send in small items to the Confederate prisoners of war. It was not too difficult to bribe the guards. One of them, "a dastardly fellow," for a price allowed a Confederate officer to "escape" but shot him down as he was scaling a wall. The guard was "reprimanded" and sent back to duty.

In spite of the dreary cells and poor food, the prison had a lively social life. A bottle of Monongahela whisky could always be bought, and poker games—chips one cent—went on from dawn until the nine o'clock curfew. There was always a blue haze of tobacco smoke seeping out of the rooms and a great deal of singing, laughter, and horseplay.

The top floor of the two-story structure had five large rooms. Federal officers and men occupied three of the rooms. The central room, Number 16, was for the political prisoners. Bunks lined the walls. There was a cast-iron belly stove in the center, several plain wooden stools, and a pine table. The bunks were seldom used except by the bedbugs and lice. Officers and men slept on the floor or on the tables, a piece of cordwood for a pillow. Rebel officers and men were quartered in the north side of the building. They also slept on the floor and tables.

But despite the levity, an air of uncertainty and helplessness hung over the dreary building. Few knew the charges against them; no one the hour, or the day, month or year when they might receive a hearing. The sacred writ of habeas corpus had been suspended by presidential order.

As Seward wrote Lord Lyons, the British minister, a few days after Mrs. Greenhow had been arrested:

> My Lord, I can touch a bell on my right hand and order the arrest of a citizen in Ohio. I can touch the bell again and order the arrest of a citizen in New York. Can the Queen of England in her dominions do as much . . . ?

Superintendent Wood, "deeper in the War Department than any man in Washington," was a rough, good-natured man and a fierce abolitionist. His favorite subject was religion and he liked to shock Rose by scorning the Bible and confessing he was a pagan. Mrs. Greenhow relates that he always had a pamphlet of Tom Paine's writings stuffed in his pocket or a handful of antireligious newspaper articles. "His desire to make proselytes to his want of faith was the ruling passion of his soul," she recalled.

Mrs. Greenhow and little Rose were welcomed by Superintendent Wood who "seemed sensible of the honor" of having been appointed as her jailer. But he may have been nonplused when little Rose, after staring at him boldly for a moment, piped up, "You have got one of the darndest little Rebels here that you ever saw."

Mrs. Greenhow and her daughter were assigned a small room on the second floor of the prison's A Street wing. A solitary window looked into a dismal rear yard. A high board fence cut off all view of the street or the Capitol, where workers scrambled about finishing the huge dome. Apparently Pinkerton informed Wood he wanted to make sure Rose couldn't signal to any of her agents in the streets.

The room was quite different from the once cozy room on Sixteenth Street. It was plainly furnished with a bed, chair, looking glass, and sewing machine. Oddly enough, Wood permitted her to have her pistol—though without ammunition.

The room was bitterly familiar to Mrs. Greenhow. It was the same room in which she had administered to the dying John C. Calhoun. It was to be her home for five dreary months.

Once in the Old Capitol Prison, Mrs. Greenhow carried on a blazing feud with Brigadier General Stewart, the prison's physician. The buff, portly man, whom the widow described as "a vulgar, uneducated man, bedizened with enough gold lace for three field marshals," did not endear himself to the Wild Rose by his avowed love for the North and hate for the Confederacy.

The feud exploded on a bitterly cold day in January, 1862. Little Rose had come down with camp measles which swept through the prison. Mrs. Greenhow wrote a bitter letter to Provost Marshal Porter demanding the services of a physician.

Porter summoned Stewart and reprimanded him for neglecting his duty. The outraged physician hurried to the prison in his carriage and stormed up the stairs to Mrs. Greenhow's room, only to prick himself on the Wild Rose's thorns. She stood on the threshold refusing to allow him to enter. Her dark eyes flashing with anger and hate, she drove the physician into an apoplectic rage by her taunts and insults.

"I demand to be allowed to enter to examine your child," Stewart shouted.

"At your peril you will touch my child," Rose cried. "You, sir, are a coward and no gentleman thus to insult a woman."

Then she slammed the door in his face.

Stewart pounded the door, roaring that he must be admitted. Mrs. Greenhow pounded back shouting he would never be allowed to touch her child. The shouting and the pounding brought the officer of the guard on the double. He sided with Mrs. Greenhow and the Brigadier retreated—"slunk out," as Rose said.

Another physician was called and Mrs. Greenhow opened the door.

In late January, Mrs. Morris was transferred to Old Capitol Prison and a few days later was followed by Mrs. Baxley.

By February the lady spies apparently were getting on each others nerves. Mrs. Morris, whom General Doster found so attractive, smuggled out a letter to Jordan explaining that a "cabal" had been formed against her. Mrs. Greenhow, she added, was "drowned by mean ambition of being known (as the only one) in the good work and she is jealous of everything that surpasses her in loyalty and courage. . . ."

The Wild Rose could never stand an attractive rival.

Mrs. Greenhow, probably through bribed guards, continued to send on to Jordan in Richmond what military information she could pick up. But it wasn't like the summer days of '61 when all she had to do was lean close to a high-ranking officer or statesman and let the secrets pour into her ear.

As the weeks rolled by she flew into rages, insulted Wood and his guards, made impossible demands, and broke all the prison rules. She wrote letters to congressmen and senators, denouncing them and their prison, and more than once had Wood on the verge of tears.

"I'd rather resign than have Greenhow one more day," Provost Marshal Porter cried in exasperation.

Mrs. Morris summed it all up with a woman's eye. "Greenhow enjoys herself amazingly," she wrote Jordan.

In March, Stanton asked Pinkerton for a list of prisoners. In the list sent to the Secretary of War the indomitable widow was listed and described as "a dangerous and skillful spy who has been forwarding information to the Rebels."

On a blustery day in March, Mrs. Greenhow was brought before Stanton's two commissioners, General John A. Dix and Judge Edward Pierrepont, both prominent New Yorkers who had been appointed by Secretary of War Stanton to examine the numerous cases of men and women who had been unjustly imprisoned on charges of disloyalty.

Dix, secretary of the Treasury under Buchanan, knew Mrs. Greenhow. More than once he and his wife had dined at her table.

The hearing took place in one of the rooms of former Senator Gwin's house at Nineteenth and L Street which had been taken over by the government for use by the Provost Marshal's office. The hour's wait in a small, stoveless room did not sweeten Mrs. Greenhow's disposition.

The interrogation was "informal and marked with the most high bred courtesy," but if the commissioners thought they were in for an easy time with the Confederate Rose they were mistaken. She openly sneered at their "mimic court," heatedly denounced the Federal government, Black Republican dogs, President Lincoln—"that beast of Satan"—congressmen, the North, and the weather.

Rose's own speeches indicate to the reader she did not speak with the painful rodomantade she remembered in the safety of London. However, she believed—allowing for the times—she talked this way to Dix and Pierrepont.

"Charges? How many have you, sirs?" Then in a voice filled with contempt she answered her own question. "Now, isn't this a farce . . . isn't it so solemn . . . why, it's a perfect farce. . . ."

Once Pierrepont broke in to say that he supposed it was hardly worth while asking her to take the oath of allegiance or to give her parole.

Rose stared at him. "You would blush to do that, sir," she said. Pierrepont cleared his throat and said that's what he thought. He asked a lame question about the cipher she had used to communicate with

43

Jordan. She answered brightly that it wasn't anything important; it had been something she had used to while away her time "while ill."

It would have been interesting to have the opinion of that now lost leader, General McDowell, as to the importance of that cipher.

After several more pointless questions, which Mrs. Greenhow deliberately ignored or replied with ridiculously evasive answers, the two commissioners surrendered.

It is a wonderful scene to imagine. The regal Rose, her dark eyes flashing; and the two middle-aged men sitting behind the big desk, wishing to God they were at Willard's or Harvey's for a drink and spread of oysters—anywhere but in the presence of this woman who made them feel they were insulting a queen.

Finally the "examination" was over. The guards were summoned and both men stood up and bowed. As always Mrs. Greenhow left the field with honors.

"In these times," she said bitingly, "you should be in some more important business than holding an inquisition for the examination of women."

About the time she was flouncing out of Gwin's house to be returned to Old Capitol, her "glorious" General Beauregard in his tent at Manassas, was writing to a Miss Augusta Evans at Charleston, describing how Mrs. Greenhow had first sent him news of McDowell's advance and helped to win that first great battle for the Confederacy. "I was almost as well advised of the strength of the hostile army in my front as its commander," he wrote.

That same day young Walker, Rose's agent, petitioned Stanton to "modify" his parole. He was refused.

Rose returned to the prison in a cold fury. She drove Wood to distraction by sewing Confederate flags on her machine and frightening the guards half to death by suddenly producing her empty pistol and pointing it at their heads. Once she stole Wood's market cart, and while she sang "I'm off to Dixie," was pulled around and around the prison yard by the other prisoners to the cheers of the Confederate prisoners in the upper floor.

On April 22 word was slipped to her that the commissioners had agreed she should be released, but McClellan informed Stanton she had to be detained until the end of hostilities.

Unbelievable as it may be, the most powerful man in Washington ruefully admitted in a letter to the head of his secret service that Rose was too much for him.

"She knows my plans better than Lincoln," McClellan wrote Pinkerton.

Before April was out and the trees were budding along the avenue, Rose had established a system of obtaining news from Confederate prisoners and smuggling out the news to Richmond.

Then, on the last day of May, without any advance notice, she was informed by Wood she was to be sent to Fortress Monroe, then on to Richmond. There was barely time to dress little Rose, now a wan and listless child from the long confinement, and to collect her own meager belongings. With the good-bys of the Rebel officers ringing in her ears, she and her daughter were escorted from the prison. On the steps she was joined by Mrs. Morris, "that woman Baxley," a guard of six soldiers, and a lieutenant "dressed in full uniform with sword and carbine."

Conscious of the attention she was receiving, Mrs. Greenhow grudgingly admitted it was quite a military display, even for Black Republican dogs.

Word of her release had spread throughout the city and the Washington depot was jammed with a cheering crowd held back by a ring of soldiers' bayonets. Rose was again herself. She walked through the crowd, head held high, and spoke to the guards "in a theatrical manner."

At Baltimore more of her admirers gathered and cheered as she left the cars. With Mrs. Morris and Mrs. Baxley she was escorted to the Gilmore House where they received their friends. A *New York Herald* correspondent who was following the prisoners smelled a scandal brewing and the next day wrote there was a "wild levee" at the hotel that night. But General Dix, the commissioner, who, strangely enough, was present, denied the story with great heat.

There was a huge crowd at the wharf the next morning when Mrs. Greenhow, her daughter, and the other Southern ladies boarded the boat for Old Point Comfort. When Mrs. Greenhow stepped from the carriage, holding little Rose's hand, there was a loud cheer along with the chorus of "Maryland, My Maryland" and shouts of "God bless you, madam. . . ."

On deck she waved to the crowd. Men took off their hats solemnly and women wept when she lifted her daughter for all to see. Mrs. Morris looked miffed and Mrs. Baxley sniffed. Both women undoubtedly wondered what their sister spy had that they didn't have.

The journey was made that night under a clear and starry sky. The captain of the boat was a gracious fellow who thoughtfully provided sandwiches and iced champagne. The glasses were filled and Rose dramatically toasted Jefferson Davis and the glorious Confederacy. The toast was drunk while the captain, broad-minded as well as a fine host, turned his back.

One of the sights the ladies saw on their trip was the *Monitor,* with its low-armored deck and revolving turret. Six weeks before she had fought the Rebel *Merrimack* to a standstill.

On June 4, 1862, Mrs. Greenhow, a Confederate flag concealed in her shawl, and with her daughter clinging to her hand, touched the sacred soil of Richmond. General Winder received her and Jefferson Davis told her that night, "But for you, there would have been no Battle of Bull Run."

In Richmond she was given a heroine's reception. Beauregard visited her at the Mills House and gave her an escort to inspect Fort Sumter. We also know that Jordan left his camp at Manassas to see his Wild Rose.

On July 11 she sent a note to her old friend, Confederate Secretary of War Seddon, asking that she be made "a bearer of dispatches" so she could get transportation to Charleston. But the note never reached Seddon. It was intercepted by Federal cavalrymen.

Apparently that summer she had a housing problem. From Brown's Hotel where she was stopping with her daughter, Rose wrote to Jefferson Davis, asking his help in securing a small house.

After apologizing for bothering him with such a trivial request, she wrote: "I know you have so many people around you who must know of such things, thus I have ventured to ask this favor. . . ." *

Along with searching for suitable living quarters, Mrs. Greenhow invested heavily in cotton that summer.

In a letter to Smithson, the banker now on parole in Washington, she gave him power of attorney to sell all her stocks, securities, and dividends. The letter, in the Official Records, was confiscated by the Provost Marshal's office and led to the revoking of Smithson's parole. He was sent to Fort Lafayette as "a dangerous agent for Mrs. Greenhow," where he was detained until the war was over.

Judge Advocate Holt, in writing Stanton about Smithson's case in 1863, disclosed that Mrs. Greenhow's vault had been found through the confiscated letter. In it were 150 shares of railroad stock which Holt called "very valuable."

* Her underlines.

46

In July Rose left for London with letters of introduction from Jefferson Davis to Mason and Slidell.

We know from her letters that she said farewell to Beauregard on the twentieth. Writing from the Mills House, she thanked him for escorting her on a tour of Fort Sumter, the scene of his first great victory, and added she was leaving Richmond. On August 1, she wrote to him again, disclosing she was on her way to England. Always the espionage agent, she devoted most of her letter to an excellent review of the military situation in northern Virginia.

One of her letters to Jefferson Davis puts her in Wilmington, North Carolina, on the night of August 4. She was writing "a few hours" before she sailed aboard the blockade-runner, *Phantom,* and shortly after she had met with General Whiting, commandant of the port Lee called the life line of his army.

There are two cautiously worded sentences in the letter. One says the Federal Navy was "unusually vigilant" and had placed "a double line of blockers" before the mouth of the Cape Fear River. The Union Secret Service may have heard that an important agent would run the blockade that night.

The other discloses that Captain Porter, master of the *Phantom,* had refused to take Rose aboard unless she traveled "as a passenger," indicating Porter had refused to place her aboard secretly or to list her as a Confederate emissary.

She found Wilmington "the hottest and most disagreeable place in the world, and the very atmosphere seems laden with disease. The better class of the inhabitants have left the city. A great many people are here for the purpose of running the blockade—and I am surprised to see so many men who should be in the army."

Mrs. Greenhow also disclosed in her letter that she had conferred with General Whiting, commandant of the city, "who told me he was sure he could raise a brigade of cavalry among persons around here whom he knew if he were able to promise that those officers selected would be commissioned."

She wrote she had a letter from "an intelligent gentleman, Colonel Jones," who told her that the Union forces "were in complete possession of Louisiana and Mississippi."

Rose took her daughter along, possibly as a cover up, or because she had no one with whom to leave her. To the child, who had told Superintendent Wood she was the "darndest little Rebel you ever saw," running the blockade would be just another incident in her weird

47

upbringing. Already she had witnessed her mother's arrest by detectives and soldiers, saw her home turned into a prison, and had played ball along the dusty corridors of Old Capitol with the Yankee guards who used their rifles for bats.

The *Phantom* sailed in the early hours of the fifth. She quickly outdistanced the Union gunboats and disappeared in the mist.

Rose next wrote Davis on the nineteenth, from St. George, Bermuda, to relay information she had received "from a person whose position enables him to know most thoroughly of a decision that had been given by Crown attorneys, that all vessels on high seas were lawfully liable to capture even though the vessel and cargo were owned by British subjects."

She also described for Davis the arrival of the *Lee,* a blockade-runner which had been forced to jettison 150 bales of cotton to escape the Union gunboats.

She went on to praise the Confederacy's agent in Bermuda, a Mr. Walker, "who has a difficult and delicate port here." One of his greatest difficulties, she wrote, "is his processing of funds into gold and silver, there being no bank on the Island."

It is believed she sailed two days later on an English vessel.

Rose first stopped off in Paris. After putting little Rose in the Sacred Heart Convent she met in secret with Maury, the Confederate agent, and Napoleon III in the gaslit Tuileries. Then she went on to London. She was received by Queen Victoria at St. James's and was made much of by the Confederate commissioners.

She also wrote a book, *My First Year in Prison, and the Abolition Rule at Washington.* Besides being a best seller it was a powerful piece of Confederate propaganda. It is a book filled with fury and bombast but reticent when it comes to naming names—except when it came to naming Senators Wilson and Walker and former Attorney General Black.

Rose found her place in Mayfair and soon had a nobleman madly in love with her. His name has been lost but the *Wilmington Journal* and *Richmond Whig* later stated she was to have married him "that summer."

In September, 1864, Rose sailed for Richmond with several Confederate and British agents aboard the steamer *Condor.*

The *London Evening Mail* described the *Condor* as "a staunch three-funneled vessel, superbly adapted for her trade, with a great carrying capacity, drawing only seven feet of water and is as swift as a sea swallow."

Why Mrs. Greenhow left London may never be known but there are three possible explanations.

One is that she was the bearer of important diplomatic dispatches, possibly in connection with the alliance between England and the Confederacy which Henry Adams had written his brother, "had been negotiated behind our backs."

The second is that she was motivated by avarice and was hurrying to Richmond to use her influence with Jefferson Davis on behalf of a powerful English shipbuilder whose principal agent had been ordered to leave the Confederate states.

The third is that she was going to Richmond to help the shipbuilder only for patriotic reasons, after the builder had promised $10,000 to help her countrymen.

The first theory is supported by the fact the master of the *Condor* was one of England's most distinguished naval heroes and the favorite of Queen Victoria.

He was Admiral Hobart Hampden, hero of the war of 1854. Son of the eighth Earl of Buckinghamshire,* Hampden was an incredible figure, more out of G. A. Henty than out of life. He is described as a powerful man, well over six feet tall, with a handsome, weather-beaten face and pale blue eyes.

After winning the Victoria Cross in the Crimea, he was knighted by Victoria for his service to the Crown as special envoy to King John of Abyssinia. He was second in command of H. M. S. *Driver* in the Battle of Kronstadt. When Admiral Napier gave his famous command, "Lads, sharpen your cutlasses," it was Hampden who led his seamen aboard the Russian men of war. The next day he commanded the raiding parties which stormed the seven forts guarding Kronstadt.

He was always a favorite at court and upon his return from the wars he was appointed master of Queen Victoria's private yacht, *Victoria and Albert*.

The second and third explanations are partially supported by a letter the author discovered in the Library of Congress, published here for the first time.

The letter was from Alexander Collie, the English shipbuilder and owner of the *Condor,* the *Falcon,* and several other fast blockade-runners. From his office at 17 Leadenhall Street, London, Collie wrote

---

* In a letter to the author the present Earl of Buckinghamshire writes "it is perfectly true" that his dashing ancestor took the title of Hobart Pasha and died an admiral of the Turkish Navy. He adds: "I also believe it to be correct that he was a blockade runner."

to Mrs. Greenhow on August 9, 1864, that his principal agent in Wilmington, North Carolina, a Mr. Andrew, had been ordered to leave for England at once, "after he had brought that state in violent collision with the General Government."

Collie said he didn't know the details of the case but then went on to praise the integrity and intelligence of his agent, "who by his ability and success had caused the jealousy of some ill-conditioned rivals."

Collie added that before Andrew had sailed on the *Falcon,* "I had instructed him privately about many little things I wished him to do for various friends in the Confederacy, and I am sorry to think that those little things will now not reach the parties for whom they were intended."

Collie said he hesitated to ask the Confederate Government to rescind the order expelling Andrew, but again pointed out that his agent was "worth two" of any of his other agents, and with him in his employ, he could do "a great deal more for the Confederacy than with any other employees."

Collie said he was "very anxious" that Andrew again be reinstated in the good graces of the Confederacy, but shrewdly pointed out that he would not ask Davis to "grant me this favor, less what I do in other ways might be misconstrued."

He again used the phrase, "our business," and ended by saying:

> I may mention that I arranged with him [Mr. Andrew] to contribute $10,000 mostly to various charities through Mr. Seddon for six months. Good men were to be sent into the Confederate States for this purpose but my efforts in this way will now be necessarily limited for want of intelligence to carry them out.
>
> If you can aid in this matter privately* at Richmond, you will oblige me and I know that thereby you will benefit many of your countrymen, who need benefitting. . . .

In his letter, Collie uses more than once the phrase, "our business." Whether he meant that Mrs. Greenhow was financially interested in his blockade-runners, or whether he was using the phrase loosely, to include her as a patriot who was interested in any activity which helped her cause, we have no way of knowing.

However, there is no doubt that Collie was well aware of her influence at Richmond. His frank admission that he had "arranged" to pay $10,000 to Seddon's favorite charities, but must first have "intelli-

* Underlined by Collie.

50

gence" to distribute the money, is as bold-faced a bribe as any of Washington's mink coats or deep freezes of today. As we shall see, Rose carried $2,000 in gold aboard the *Condor*. Was it a bribe, or was it the proceeds of her book?

On the other hand, Mrs. Greenhow, who knew only too well how much $10,000 in gold would mean to the shoeless and hungry troops of Lee's army, may have been hurrying to Richmond to "privately" use her influence, not because of avarice, but because of that intense loyalty to the South which had caused her to serve as an espionage agent and to lose her fortune and her home.

Each theory, of course, is only supported by circumstantial evidence. The reader can select the one he likes best. As for the author, he prefers the more romantic one of the Wild Rose delivering secret dispatches to Richmond in connection with the alliance. It is hard not to believe that the future Earl of Buckinghamshire, hero of England's Navy, favorite of Queen Victoria, had been ordered to sail the *Condor* to America to make sure Mrs. Greenhow, and some highly diplomatic secrets were delivered safely to Wilmington, the port Lee said must be kept open if his army was to survive.

The *Condor* sailed for Wilmington from Greenock, a suburb of Glasgow, in mid-September. Fellow passengers noticed Rose carried a mysterious brown leather "reticule" dangling from her shoulder at all times. Some of them wondered if perhaps it contained secret dispatches to Jefferson Davis.

At Halifax the *Condor* took aboard another celebrated passenger, Professor James P. Holcombe of Richmond. Holcombe was one of the three Confederate agents who had met Horace Greeley at Niagara Falls in an abortive peace conference.

On the night of September 30, off the Carolina capes in a raging storm, the *Condor* ran the blockade. About midnight a Federal gunboat caught sight of her and gave chase. The wind shrilling in the rigging, the *Condor* took the bone in her teeth, knifing her way through the heavy sea. Decks cleared for action, the Federal gunboat raced in pursuit. As the hours passed the distance between the two ships closed.

At three o'clock in the morning, the *Condor* reached the mouth of Cape Fear River. As she flew up the river the pilot spotted a large white object bearing down on them. Thinking it was a Federal gunboat he shouted to the helmsman to swing her hard to port. The *Condor* answered her rudder. A moment later there was a sickening jar which shook her from bow to stern. The *Condor* had grounded on

New Inlet Bar, ironically only two hundred yards from the Confederate guns of Fort Fisher.

The white object had been the wreck of the famous blockade-runner, *Nighthawk,* which had been burned and wrecked in a fierce fight with the Federals before the *Condor* had made her appearance.

Now from his bridge Admiral Hampden could see the approaching Federal gunboats coming up to the stern, veiled in spray.

Mountainous waves began pounding the imprisoned ship. Soon she was shuddering and creeking in every joint. Below decks Rose and the other passengers huddled in their staterooms as the vessel rolled and pitched like a frenzied horse.

As the *Condor* wallowed helplessly, rockets zoomed upward through the windy blackness. There were now two Federal gunboats moving in for the kill. Someone shouted the news to the frightened passengers below decks. Evidently willing to risk a hazardous trip through the breakers in a small boat rather than again be imprisoned in Mr. Wood's verminous jail, Rose, a shawl about her head, ran up on deck. Drenched by the rain, she made her way up the slippery deck to the bridge. Admiral Hampden immediately ordered her below.

Above the howl of the wind, she cried, "I demand that you lower a boat."

Hampden refused. Rose then "ordered" him to give her a pilot and a boat. Again the *Condor's* master refused. As the spume hissed across the deck, the embittered master of the floundering ship and the determined woman with the rain-soaked black dress molded to her body by the wind, engaged in a bitter argument.

Rockets crisscrossed the sky. The boat began to list to one side. We know from the *Mail's* Richmond correspondent that the Admiral finally surrendered to Rose. He agreed to lower a boat, "although it was against his better advice."

The boat was made ready. Rose, who evidently knew what secrets the mail bags contained, carried them into the boat. Then she took her place midships, next to Professor Holcombe and a Lieutenant Wilson. The British and Confederate agents followed. Just before the boat was lowered over the side Hampden ordered his pilot to guide the whaleboat through the surf.

The men bent to the oars. As they neared the beach the howling of the wind and rain was lost in the booming thunder of the breakers. Without end the mountainous rollers lifted the tiny boat upward with a rush, only to let it drop sickeningly to the bottom of the trough.

It was "very near the beach" when a gigantic wave fell savagely on the boat, overturning it. Rose and the other passengers were caught in the terrifying undertow and sucked under.

Professor Holcombe, more dead than alive, fought his way to the surface and to the side of the almost submerged boat. The other men soon joined him. Battered almost into unconsciousness, but desperately clinging to the keel of the boat they were finally washed ashore.

Oblivious of the wind and the bone-chilling rain they lay on the beach like dead men. One by one, as their strength returned, they gathered in a wet, bedraggled circle.

Someone asked, "Where is Mrs. Greenhow? . . ."

There was no answer. The circle broke. Somehow they managed to start a fire of driftwood. Then the weary, shivering men began stumbling up and down the beach, crying her name.

"Mrs. Greenhow . . . Mrs. Greenhow . . ."

There was only the howling wind which tore the words from their lips and the thunderous crashing of the surf.

At dawn the wind dropped. The *Condor's* passengers and soldiers from Fort Fisher searched up and down the debris-littered beach. Across the gray sea in the day's first light they could see the battered *Condor*, decks awash. Beyond her prowled the watchful gunboats.

At eight the next morning a soldier found her body on the Fort Fisher Beach. She was lying on her side, her head pillowed on one arm. A few inches away was the mysterious brown "reticule." The soldier opened it. Two thousand dollars in gold flowed out on the wet sand. He put the bag inside his shirt and pushed the body back into the sea.

At ten-thirty the body was again found by Thomas E. Taylor, later the author of *Blockade Running* who was leading a volunteer searching party. He notified Colonel William Lamb, commandant of Fort Fisher who sent a wagon to take the body to Wilmington.

Rose was laid out in state in the Seamen's Bethel. The body was dressed by the ladies of the Soldier's Aid Society. As news of her death spread hundreds came by wagons and on horse. All day and night they shuffled past her bier.

As late as 1937, there were a few old people in Wilmington who still remembered that "in death the beauty of her womanhood was restored."

That night the soldier who had stolen the money appeared before Colonel Lamb, trembling and weeping. Confederate gunner Joseph

Blake of Wilmington recalled that the soldier told Lamb, "Colonel, there is one of two things I must do. I stole the money from Mrs. Greenhow's body. I must either give it up or go crazy."

Even in death few men could resist the Wild Rose.

While she lay peacefully in death in the Seamen's Bethel with the lamplight silhouetting her honor guard on the wall, a party of Federal raiders crept up the river in a small boat. Before they could climb up the sides of the *Condor* and burn her, Lieutenant Joseph Sowles, of Company A, Thirty-Sixth North Carolina Infantry, fired a warning shot and aroused the officer and men who had been sent aboard earlier by Colonel Lamb to guard the *Condor* from raiders.

It was hand-to-hand in the blackness. The Confederates swarmed on deck to meet the Federals climbing aboard with knives in their teeth. After a brief struggle the Federals withdrew. The alarm had now been sounded ashore and a courier sped to rouse Colonel Lamb.

A few minutes later the fort's big guns opened, smashing the Federal whaleboat to bits. But the Federal gunboats moved up and the night was soon bright with exploding shells, rockets, and musket fire.

One Federal gunboat was hit midships. As the "rip" in the river swung her in to shore, her magazine caught and she split the night with a tremendous roar. The survivors reached the beach and a bloody battle was fought on the sand until near dawn.

In the gray light the Federal gunboat smoldered on the beach. Dead men lay about her.

At four-thirty on Saturday, October 1, 1864, Rose's funeral procession wound its way slowly through the streets of Wilmington to Oakdale Cemetery. Shops were closed and hundreds followed the wagon, bearing the casket draped with the Confederate flag. A guard of honor of soldiers and sailors marched on each side. Among her mourners was Admiral Hampden.

At five o'clock under a dripping gray sky, Rose was laid to rest with Confederate muskets crashing above her and the guns of Fort Fisher defiantly booming their tribute as the Federal gunboats outside the harbor sullenly rode the swells in the dying light.

The stirring violence and grand pageantry for which she had such a passion in life, were an appropriate farewell for this indomitable woman who had always loved a good show and done her best to give one; who, as legend tells us, had sworn that should she die and be buried in Northern earth, she would rise from her grave and on ghostly knees crawl back to rest in the South's sacred soil.

In Oakdale Cemetery, a monument erected by the Ladies Memorial

54

Association of Wilmington now marks her grave. The inscription reads:

> *This monument commemorates the deeds of Mrs. Rose Greenhow, a bearer of dispatches to the Confederate government. She was drowned off Fort Fisher from the blockade runner, "Condor" while attempting to run the blockade on September 30, 1864. Her body was washed ashore on Fort Fisher Beach and brought to Wilmington.*

Not only a woman but an era that has gone with the wind, rests under the great white stone.

The Siren of the Shenandoah

WHAT is more satisfying to the romantic soul than to find that legend is reality?

Here is Belle Boyd, tall and graceful, a horsewoman at twelve; Stonewall Jackson's courier at seventeen; at eighteen, a dangerous spy known as the "Siren of the Shenandoah"; at nineteen, an inmate of Old Capitol with all the Rebel officers pursuing her. . . .

Robert W. Chambers and Joseph Hergesheimer, those great romanticists of yesterday, made her the heroine of their tales. But the moons which waxed and waned as she galloped across their pages were not all imaginary.

Of her service as a courier and dispatch rider, T. C. DeLong, high in the Confederate Army and Navy Departments, wrote in his *Four Years in the Rebel Capitol,* "Belle Boyd's name became as historic as Molly Pitcher's."

Douglas Southall Freeman, in his *Lee's Lieutenants,* describes Belle as "the most active and reliable of the many secret agents of the Confederacy."

More than one Union regimental history credits her with aiding in their defeat.

To a seaman on a Federal gunboat Belle was "a second Joan of Arc"; to the *New York Herald,* "a dangerous Rebel woman." The provost marshal of Washington remembered her "fine figure." To Superintendent Wood she was "the most persistent Rebel" the Old Capitol ever had—yet he helped to send her wedding trousseau to Richmond under a flag.

Like all good stories Belle's has a beginning, a middle, and an end. The beginning scenes are in the beautiful Shenandoah Valley from Martinsburg south to Front Royal. The time lapse is July, 1861 to the summer of '63. The middle is Old Capitol Prison and Belle's triumphal tour of the South. Destiny had no trouble with the end; there is moonlight, the deck of a captured blockade-runner, a man singing a love

56

song and a handsome Yankee prizemaster who woos and wins her. The end was in a moment of exquisite aptness, when, according to John Buchan's definition of romance, life turns artist.

2

Belle was born in Martinsburg, West Virginia, on May 9, 1844, in the home of her grandmother, Mrs. Samuel Boyd. She was christened Isabelle in honor of a great aunt. But she was always Belle to her family and friends.

A few months after her birth, the Boyds moved to Bunker Hill, a small village some ten miles away. Belle spent most of her younger years in their comfortable two-story house. In England many years later she would remember the scent of honeysuckle and the whispering of Mill Creek as it flowed over the rocks not far from her bedroom window.

When she was about eight, her father, Benjamin, moved his store to Queen Street, Martinsburg, and bought a house on 126 East Burke Street. Besides running his store, Boyd also managed a tobacco plantation.

Belle grew up in a house ringing with the cries and laughter of several brothers and sisters and, in addition, there were a large number of cousins scattered about the Shenandoah Valley who were frequent visitors.

Before she was ten she acquired her love for fine horses. By twelve she was a superb horsewoman.

Belle's favorite pastime was exploring the Valley, hunting out the old Indian trails and wagon roads.

Like the Cherokees who named the rolling river, she loved the Shenandoah; the crystal-clear water that by day mirrored the rolling white clouds and blue skies, and by night the soft moonlight and glittering stars. She knew almost every bend, inlet and ford. When there were gay picnics, it was Belle who led the way along an old trail or abandoned road to find some secluded spot.

She would travel these roads six years later, on a great black horse, guided only by the moonlight, with a dispatch bag instead of a picnic basket tied to her saddle.

At twelve Belle was sent to Mount Washington College for Women at Baltimore, where she finished a four-year course in French literature, music, and singing. While she was away, her family moved to 501 South Queen Street.

In the fall of 1860, Belle entered Washington society. While at the capitol she stayed at the home of Secretary of War Flood, soon to become a Confederate general. She was then sixteen.

After the fall of Sumter she returned home to discover that her father, at forty-four, had enlisted as a private in Company D, Second Virginia Infantry. But Belle was not surprised. She knew it was commonplace for the Boyds and her mother's people, the Glenns, to fight for their standards at any age. At sixty-four her great-great-grandfather enlisted in the Philadelphia Militia during the American Revolution. On her mother's side was grandfather James Glenn, a scout for General Greene, and in his late sixties, re-enlisting to fight under St. Clair against the Miami and Wyandots on the banks of the Wabash.

In June, Belle and her mother led a group of ladies to Harpers Ferry to visit their husbands and sweethearts. Discipline was lax and there were gay parties. The war, as Belle recalled, was "treated as a joke by all of us."

In July the laughter and the singing died away. The Confederate Army left Harpers Ferry to meet the advancing Federals under General Patterson. After a brief but bloody battle at Falling Waters the Confederates retreated.

On the afternoon of July 3, 1861, Belle and her mother stood on the steps of the store on South Queen Street watching the gray columns pass through Martinsburg. The two women found it hard to hold back the tears when Ben Boyd passed, his face gray with fatigue and his uniform covered with dust. But they smiled and returned his wave.

The last troops out of Martinsburg were Turner Ashby's riders. As he passed the Boyd house, the fierce, Arab-looking cavalry leader, whom Jackson was to call the greatest partisan fighter he had ever known, swept off his plumed hat. Belle waved and blew him a kiss. Soon they would meet again.

Two hours later the first Federal scouts entered the town. They were followed by a noisy band and the Second Pennsylvania Volunteers.

That afternoon Belle had her first experience with the Yankees. She was helping to care for two delirious Confederate soldiers in a temporary hospital, when a Federal officer, holding a Union flag, entered the room and called the two sick men "damned Rebels."

Belle gave him a tongue-lashing for his ungentlemanly behavior. The officer demanded to know who she was.

"A Rebel lady," Belle snapped.

58

"And a damned independent one at that," the Federal murmured as he went out.

The next day she met the enemy on much grimmer terms.

Independence Day dawned hot and sticky. Cannons greeted the sun. Before noon 150 barrels of liquor were "stove in." Soon the provost marshal's men were having a difficult time keeping the troops under control.

Groups of drunken soldiers prowled about the streets, shooting at windows, doors, and store signs. Someone repeated a story he had heard that Belle Boyd, a Rebel girl who lived on South Queen Street, had one wall of her bedroom covered with Confederate flags. Five drunken soldiers started out for South Queen Street with a Union flag, swearing to raise it above the Boyd house.

When Belle heard the pounding at the front door she ordered her servant, Eliza, to hide the flags. Then from a desk she took a pistol and joined her mother at the foot of the stairs.

The door went in with a crash. A spokesman for the soldiers held up the Union flag and shouted that they intended to raise it "above a damned Rebel's house."

Mrs. Boyd walked across the room to the soldier. She said quietly, "Men, the people in this house will die before they allow you to raise that flag above their heads."

She was pushed aside with a curse. Then Belle, "my blood boiling with rage at such indignity," raised the pistol. The soldier with the flag walked toward her. Belle aimed for his heart. When he was a few feet away she pulled the trigger. He fell like a butchered ox.

News of the shooting raced through the village. Another group of soldiers tried to set the Boyd house afire. Shots were fired and rocks shattered the windows. A crowd of ugly men were gathering in the shadows across the street when a provost patrol came up on the double.

On the day following the shooting the provost marshal sent for Belle. A hearing was held and she was exonerated of any blame. To prevent any further incidents, sentries were posted about the Boyd house.

Several of the officers who questioned Belle found her very attractive. Soon they were dropping by the Boyd house "to check on any complaints." Sometimes Belle invited them to tea. The town gossips reported she had been seen talking to Federal officers on the street instead of drawing aside as they passed.

Some of the townspeople began to avoid her. One was Miss Lucy Buck, who lived in the beautiful Bel Air, the Buck's mansion. She was to write much of Belle in her diary. She was in the garden one evening when Belle arrived. That night she wrote, "Nellie and I rose simultaneously and glided upstairs, telling R—— that should we be inquired for, we were not at home. . . ."

What Lucy and her friends did not know was that Belle was picking up bits of military information from the admiring Federal officers and sending it to Jackson's outposts in the Valley. Her courier was her servant, Eliza.

However, she was only an amateur at espionage. The inevitable happened. One of her messages was intercepted by Federal pickets. As her biographer, Lieutenant Colonel Louis A. Sigaud, who was decorated by Pershing for his own counterespionage service in World War I, says professionally:

> . . . she wrote her messages in "clear" [not enciphered] and in her own hand. This violated the important rule that the nature of the data transmitted and the identity of the sender must be concealed from the enemy in case of interception. When one of her messages fell into the hands of the Federals, her handwriting betrayed her.

The provost marshal sent for Belle. Captain James Gwyn of the Twenty-Third Pennsylvania Infantry took her to his colonel.

After a severe tongue-lashing, the Colonel read her the articles of war and dismissed her with a warning.

As she passed Captain Gwyn she looked up and whispered slyly, "Thank you gentlemen of the jury."

Soon Gwyn was dropping by again to see if Belle had any "complaints" to make.

In mid-July Belle visited her aunt, Mrs. James Erskine Stewart, at Front Royal, forty miles south of Martinsburg. She was there a few days when a dust-covered rider galloped into the village. He stopped only for a moment to dance his horse and shout the news.

Beauregard had smashed McDowell's army . . . the Federals were retreating back to Centreville . . . back to Fairfax Court House . . . back to the Potomac . . . some said Beauregard was going to march into Washington. . . .

Then with a whoop he was off. There was wild rejoicing—until the first wagons creaked into Front Royal with the wounded. Houses were turned into hospitals and the women of Front Royal became nurses.

Some of the wounded told the story of a beautiful girl who had warned Beauregard of McDowell's advance. They told how she had passed through the Union lines riding a market cart; how a planter had given her a horse to ride to Beauregard's headquarters where she delivered the vital dispatch hidden in her hair.

Belle thrilled to the story. She resolved to leave the caring of the men to less daring women. At the first opportunity she told her mother she would volunteer as a dispatch rider. She was then seventeen.

The summer passed. In the fall Belle and her mother traveled to the Confederate camp at Manassas to see her father. For several weeks they lived in a large farmhouse which had been set aside as quarters for wives and daughters of the troops.

There was a happy family reunion when Turner Ashby's troops galloped into camp. Among them was Mrs. Boyd's brother, James W. Glenn, one of Ashby's ablest captains. Captain Glenn was Belle's favorite uncle. He was a large and handsome man, full of fire and daring. Ashby thought much of him and mentioned him frequently in his dispatches.

Similar legends are told about Belle and Captain Glenn. One evening when Belle was about ten, the Boyds had some distinguished guests for dinner. Belle was instructed to keep out of sight because she was "too young." She flounced from the house and sulked all morning. But in the afternoon she returned, smiling slyly, a gleam in her gray eyes.

The party was successful. The wraps had been gotten and the good nights were being said, when there was a crash outside. The door swung open and Belle pranced in on her horse.

As her father reached out for her she said innocently, pointing to her horse, "Well, isn't he old enough? . . ."

It was told of Captain Glenn that once on a dare he rode his horse through the front door of "Mount Zion" his father-in-law's beautiful home at Milldale, Warren County, Virginia, and paraded up and down the fifty-foot long assembly hall.

We know that Belle rode as a courier between the camps of Beauregard and Jackson, soon after her visit to Manassas. How she was appointed is not known. Perhaps Captain Glenn saw in his niece his own recklessness and daring and recommended her to Ashby. There was also her expert knowledge of the terrain and her horse "Fleeter" which she had trained from a colt.

61

At the touch of her crop Fleeter would remain motionless. At another touch he would kneel; at another he would roll over and play dead.

Belle rode mostly at night. Until 1930 there were old men and women in Martinsburg who could still remember how they looked out their windows at the first sounds of the hoofbeats and saw in the moonlight the tawny-haired girl riding the big black horse down the main street.

There was little campaigning during the winter. Belle's duties slackened off and Fleeter remained in his stable growing sleek and fat. Ashby's Seventh Virginia Cavalry made Martinsburg their headquarters and there were rounds of dinners and levees.

In April, Jackson ordered Ashby to intensify the assembling of intelligence regarding the "position of the enemy's forces, their numbers and movements; what generals are in command, their headquarters and especially the headquarters of the commanding general."

During the winter Ashby had established an excellent espionage system. Reports from his spies behind the Union lines soon began to come in.

At his request Belle again took up her duties as courier.

Before he left to rejoin his regiment, Ben Boyd insisted that Belle leave Martinsburg, always in constant danger of occupation by the Federals, and stay with her grandmother at Front Royal. Belle agreed.

Miss Lucy Buck noted Belle's arrival in her diary. She wrote that Belle "seemed all surface, vain and hollow." Later, in reviewing the events of the day on which she met Belle, the mistress of Bel Air said that she had been "conscious of having compromised my dignity in mingling upon terms of equality and friendship with persons whom in my heart I despise. . . ."

In March, Mr. and Mrs. Stewart and one of their daughters, Fannie, left for Richmond. Their other daughter, Alice, remained behind with Belle, to take care of their grandmother, Mrs. Ruth Burns Glenn.

On the twenty-third of March Jackson was defeated by Shields' Regiment at Kernstown and retreated far up the Valley. Front Royal was occupied on the twenty-fourth. Mrs. Boyd was still at Martinsburg and when Belle heard reports of heavy fighting there she obtained a pass from the provost marshal to join her.

At Winchester, where she stopped overnight, an informer denounced her as a Confederate courier. She was arrested and taken to Baltimore. There was no evidence against Belle and General John A. Dix, who had felt the wrath of Rose O'Neale Greenhow, the South's Wild Rose, released her and gave her a pass to Martinsburg.

A few hours after her arrival she was ordered confined to the limits of the town. Mrs. Boyd appealed to the provost marshal and received a pass for both of them to return to Front Royal.

Meanwhile the Union Army was on the move. McClellan was moving up the Peninsula, supported by McDowell northwest of Richmond. When McDowell wired Washington he urgently needed reinforcements, the War Department detached Generals Shields and Geary from Banks' command and ordered them to join McDowell. Banks was instructed to defend Washington and confine his operations to defense. He retreated to Strasburg, stripped of most of his troops and guns.

Geary moved at once. Shields followed, slowly, almost reluctantly. Supporting McClellan's drive was not to his liking. His consuming ambition was to trap and destroy Jackson.

Shields marched eastward to join McDowell, via Front Royal, Chester Gap, and Warrenton, constantly seeking to have his route changed in an attempt to catch Jackson, who, McDowell wired him, was marching east to Hanover Junction on the line to Richmond, "so in coming east you will be following him." Jackson, however, was actually far southwest at Lebanon, White Sulphur Springs.

When Belle and her mother finally reached Front Royal, the Strickler House was ablaze with lights. A sentry told them that the hotel was now the headquarters of General Shields and his staff. Mrs. Boyd found her mother and niece in a small cottage in the rear of the hotel. The cottage, since torn down, was later known as "The Belle Boyd Cottage."

That evening Belle appeared before General Shields to request a pass to Richmond for herself and her mother. When he saw Belle, Shields had just finished an excellent dinner and was aglow from his after-dinner brandy. He teased her for a few moments, then let slip that in a few days she wouldn't need a pass; Jackson would be "annihilated" and she could travel wherever she wanted.

Then Shields introduced Belle to his aide-de-camp, Captain Daniel J. Kiely, a good-looking Irishman. While his general continued his bantering, Kiely had eyes only for Belle.

The next morning a bouquet and a tender love poem were delivered to the cottage. Both were from Captain Kiely. Belle did not discourage the Irishman. In the soft spring twilight they sat on the porch of the cottage while Captain Dan wooed her with all the eloquence of his race. Belle listened. Three years later she wrote she was indebted to Kiely—whom she discreetly calls "Captain D——" for "some withered flowers, remarkable effusions, and last but not least, for a great deal of important information which was carefully transmitted to my countrymen."

On the night of May 14, Belle was not surprised to see General Shields and his aides enter the Strickler House. From Kiely she knew that a council of war was to be held in the dining room.

Belle also knew that there was a hole in the closet floor of the bedroom above.

She tiptoed up the stairs to the bedroom. In the dark closet the hole in the floor glowed like a silver dollar. She could see Shields' florid face, a servant passing with a tray of glasses and a box of cigars.

When Shields began to talk she lay on the floor and glued her ear to the hole. She remained there for hours, listening and remembering.

When the clock in the dining room below her struck midnight she took one last look. The room was blue with cigar smoke. She could see snatches of blue uniforms, a table and maps. Her head was buzzing with a thousand details as she tiptoed down the stairs.

What Belle had overheard at the council was the possible route Shields proposed to take to trap Jackson; that Shields and General Geary were ordered to join McDowell to support McClellan; that Banks' force at Strasburg had been greatly reduced and above all, that a small detachment was to be left at Front Royal after Shields moved out in the morning.

Outside the house, Belle paused in the shadows. To rouse the servants—even her own—and get them to saddle a horse was to risk a commotion. It took her only a few moments to make up her mind. At Manassas Captain Glenn had told her of a "Mr. K——," a Confederate agent who always knew where Turner Ashby could be found. She must see "Mr. K——" at once!

Back in the cottage she enciphered hurriedly in a brief dispatch all she could remember. She took several passes released Confederate prisoners had given her to pass the Federal pickets on the road, then hurried to the stables to saddle Fleeter. Belle rode out of Front Royal under a beautiful moon. Twice she was stopped by the pickets but each time was waved on when she showed a pass.

When the last picket was behind her she drummed her heels on Fleeter's sides. The black horse flew down the road.

She rode about fifteen miles then swung off Gooney Manor Road to a side road which led through the woods to the farmhouse of "Mr. K——." In a few minutes she clattered up the steps to the porch and banged on the door.

A window was raised. A man's angry voice cried, "Who are you? . . . What do you want? . . ."

"It is I," she cried.

"You—? Who are you? . . ."

"Belle Boyd. I have important intelligence to communicate to Colonel Ashby. Is he here?" Belle shouted.

In the silence the sawing of the crickets and night insects seemed loud in the night.

"Wait a moment—I will come down," the man said at last. The window slammed.

A lock slid back and the front door opened. "Mr. K" raised his lamp. When the light fell on Belle's anxious face he drew her inside the house.

"My God," he said, "where did you come from, my dear? . . . How did you get here? . . ."

"I have no time to tell you the why or wherefore," she said rapidly. "Where is Colonel Ashby's camp? I must know at once."

She knew in a moment. Ashby, pistol in hand, swung open a door which led to a hall. His dark face lighted up when he saw her.

"Miss Belle!" he said as he slid the pistol back into its holster. "Is this you? Have you dropped from the clouds?"

Belle told him her story and gave him the ciphered dispatch. With Ashby's fervent thanks ringing in her ears she set out for Front Royal, skillfully guiding Fleeter down the back lanes and narrow trails she knew so well, whispering encouragement as he rose to soar over a pasture fence or across a creek; then down the Gooney Manor Road, her tawny hair streaming behind her in the wind and the light of the full moon lighting her way.

The first cock was crowing and the eastern sky was blushing a rose-pink when Belle unsaddled Fleeter, patted his head and tumbled into bed.

She was asleep when Shields marched his troops out of Front Royal. At noon the First Maryland Infantry along with several companies of the Fifth New York Cavalry, a battery of field pieces, some wagons and drivers—about a thousand men in all—occupied the town.

For a week a strange and ominous silence hung over the Valley. On the twenty-first, Belle and her cousin, Alice Stewart, obtained a pass to Winchester. Before they set out Belle charmed a young lieutenant

—whom she discreetly calls "Lt. H——"—into helping them pass the Federal pickets.

While Belle packed a bag the lieutenant drove her carriage to the Strickler House. Lucy Buck strolled by and noted that "a Yankee held the reins." As she explained in her diary that night, she was on her way to see Belle to ask her to carry a letter through the lines. She changed her mind, however, when she saw the Yankee officer. As she wrote:

> I concluded not to entrust my letter with one who appeared to be on such familiar terms with those whom we most dread, so crossing the street we went on up to see Cousin Mary. . . .

Evidently it never appeared strange to the mistress of Bel Air that she had planned to ask a woman whom she despised and considered socially inferior, to risk her life to deliver one of her illegal letters!

The Federal lieutenant escorted Belle and Alice to Winchester where they remained overnight. The next morning a Confederate agent secretly visited Belle and asked her to deliver two packages "to the Confederate Army."

One package is described as "important"; the other, "trifling."

Then handing her a scrap of paper he added, "This is a very important letter. Try to send it carefully and safely to Jackson or some other responsible officer."

Belle agreed to do what she could.

Belle gave the "important" package to Eliza who hid it in her clothes. The other she placed in a lunch basket and wrote across it, "Kindness of Lt. H——," believing in this way it would easily pass inspection.

She carried the small note in her hand—to be quickly swallowed.

At noon the merry party set out for Front Royal. As they reached the Winchester outskirts two detectives in civilian clothes rode across their path.

"What the devil does this mean?" the lieutenant asked.

"It means you are all under arrest," one of the detectives replied.

Belle tried to hide her trembling hands. "Why, sir?" she asked.

"For carrying letters," was the answer.

The detectives escorted the carriage to the headquarters of Colonel George L. Beal, commander of the Tenth Maine Infantry. When Beal asked Belle if she was "carrying any letters" she hesitated. Realizing that the basket would inevitably be searched she handed Beal the package "of trifling importance."

It contained a copy of the rebellious *Maryland News-Sheet.*

Beal slowly read the inscription "Kindness of Lt. H——." He glared at the helpless officer, now white to his lips. "What is the meaning of this, lieutenant?"

The officer swallowed but couldn't speak. Belle frantically came to his defense. As she raised her hand, Beal saw the small scrap of paper.

As Belle relates, he shouted, "And that—what is that?"

She shrugged her shoulders. "Oh, this is nothing, sir," she said. "You may have it if you wish."

As she tells it, she meant to swallow the note had Beal reached out to take it. But Beal swung back to the sweating lieutenant. As Belle remembered, "His wrath was now diverted from the guilty to the guiltless."

Beal cut off a blistering lecture to order Belle and Alice to proceed to Front Royal. As the two girls drove down the road they could still hear the bellowing of the outraged Colonel.

That Belle outwitted Colonel Beal and kept the "important letter" is partially confirmed by an Associated Press report published ten days later in the *Washington Star.* The accounts quote a Federal officer, saying that Belle made a trip to Winchester "in the company of a cavalry officer." She was arrested in the company of the officer, "but with her usual adroitness and assumed innocence she got clear of the charges of treachery and returned to Front Royal."

It is obvious that there is much more than these casual episodes. Many questions arise as to why the Federal commanders allowed Belle to return again and again. Evidently the Union officers were not sure and had they the evidence it would have mattered less. It is very hard to bring yourself to believe a pretty girl is a mortal enemy.

Although Belle considerately withholds the name of "Lieutenant H——" a search of the records of the cavalry units stationed at the time in Front Royal, strongly suggests he was Lieutenant Abram H. Hasbrouck of the Fifth New York Cavalry and adjutant of its Third Battalion. In all three regiments stationed there his is the only name which begins with *H* and he is the only one court-martialed.

Belle relates that her Lieutenant H. was dismissed from the service for aiding her. We know now that she was mistaken. Lieutenant H., or Hasbrouck, was dismissed on Dec. 20, 1863 on the more prosaic charge of "selling government horses."

Back in Front Royal she learned why she had been arrested. A Union spy, playing the part of a servant in the hotel, had seen the Confederate agent give her the packages. The information was telegraphed to Major James Tyndale, provost marshal at Front Royal. Tyndale wired Beal, who ordered her arrest.

While Belle rested and tried her best to ignore Clarke, the *New York Herald's* war correspondent who had been billeted in the cottage during her absence, Jackson moved out of Lebanon, White Sulphur Springs. His object was Front Royal where he hoped to capture the Federal garrison, get in the rear of Banks' reduced command, and force him to evacuate Strasburg.

A message brought Ewell west into the Valley. The brigade under Taylor, son of "Old Rough and Ready," left Ewell and marched west along the southern end of the Massanutten Mountain Range to join Stonewall near Harrisonburg. The rest of Ewell's command turned north to go east of the Massanutten with a rendezvous on May 21, with Jackson and Taylor near Luray.

Turner Ashby's cavalry continued due north toward Banks to maneuver before Strasburg and let Banks confirm his suspicions that Jackson planned a frontal attack on his lines. He was under orders to join Jackson at Front Royal.

Jackson and Taylor joined with Ewell at Luray and the entire command moved north. It rained all that day. As a dismal twilight fell over the countryside, the advance elements of the column camped in a dripping grove ten miles from Front Royal.

As Jackson wrote in his report, he moved at dawn up Gooney Manor Road. It was Friday, May 23. One of the weary privates in that long gray column was middle-aged Ben Boyd. Although the rain had stopped it was a tedious march. Gluelike mud clung to men's boots making them feel like lead, and the heavy guns sunk to the hubs of their wheels. At noon the advance scouts could see the steeple of the Front Royal church glistening in the brilliant sunshine.

At about that moment Belle was reading below stairs in the cottage. Suddenly Eliza burst in the door.

"Miss Belle," she cried, "I tinks the Rebels am acomin'!"

Belle rushed to the street. Federal troops were pouring out of houses; saddles were being thrown on horses, guns were bouncing down the street. A Union officer whom she knew slightly, ran by.

"What is wrong?" she cried.

He stopped and told her, "Jackson is coming up."

"Where are all your troops going?" Belle asked.

"We are trying to get the ordnance together. . . ." He started to go on. Belle grabbed his arm.

"What do you intend to do?" she asked.

68

"Burn it," the officer laughed as he pulled free. He called back, "as we'll burn the bridges to Winchester—when we're across."

He waved and disappeared in the swarm of blue-coated men. Belle walked back to the cottage. As she entered, Clarke, the war correspondent, ran down the stairs.

"Good God!" he cried, "what's wrong?"

Belle gave him a grim smile. "Oh nothing, Mr. Clarke," she said, "only the Rebels are coming and you had better get ready for a visit in Libby Prison."

Clarke ran upstairs to his room. Belle followed. She found a glass and went to the balcony. Her heart leaped as the gray column less than a quarter of a mile away, came into focus. She slowly lowered the glass and looked thoughtfully across the trees and roof tops.

The military situation, as she knew it from overhearing Shields' war council in the Strickler House, together with the information she had just received from the Union officer, slowly formed in her mind. Banks had four thousand men at Strasburg . . . Shields and Geary were southeast of Front Royal . . . west of the Valley was Fremont . . . there were less than a thousand men at Front Royal . . . the Federals planned to burn the bridges at Winchester . . . burn the material. . . .

As Colonel Sigaud points out:

> What the complete picture undoubtedly meant to her was that the Confederates could strike a smashing blow at Front Royal and perhaps against isolated Federal units, provided they knew where all the Union forces were and could avoid being trapped if they converged. . . .

As Belle realized, the information she possessed had to be delivered to Jackson. But how?

She went downstairs, pausing at Clarke's room. Through the half-opened door she could see the war correspondent throwing socks and shirts into a carpet bag. As the idea came, her eyes sparkled with delight. Softly she closed the door. Clarke was so engrossed in his packing he never heard the key click in the lock.

Belle offers a purely human motive for her act. "I just couldn't resist the temptation," she relates.

In the street she found several men excitedly discussing the Yankee's withdrawal. She told them of the information she had, then proposed that one of them take it to Jackson before he reached Front Royal.

They stared at each other. "You go," one said. Another added, "Yes, you go, Belle."

The minutes were slipping away fast. Belle realized that if Jackson was to get the intelligence she possessed, she had to deliver it herself. She ran inside the cottage, grabbed a white sunbonnet and hurried down the street, dodging the heavy guns, the companies of cavalry and marching troops.

Taking back streets and lanes she soon reached the limits of the town. Years later she would marvel at the ease with which she soared over fences and flower gardens. Then through an orchard and a pasture to Gooney Manor Road. Picking up her skirts she ran like a deer, leaping over mud puddles and wagon ruts. The road rose and fell. Her shoes were soon shapeless globs of mud. A sharp pain twisted like a knife blade in her side. She fought for breath but kept on. Federal pickets, driven in by Jackson's swift advance, spotted her. Rifles cracked. Minnie balls screamed through the air. Fear gave her wings. She flew down the road, leaving the pickets behind.

At the bottom of a rise in the road, she fell and lay in the mud for a moment to catch her breath. Pipes shrilled and there was a flurry of drumbeats. Belle looked up. The top of the rise filled with men in gray. The stars of the Confederacy hung limp in the still air. She rose and continued struggling up the road—only to find herself under a cross-artillery fire.

A Federal piece slammed. She threw herself to the ground as the ball burst less than twenty yards away, the fragments whistling through the air. Uninjured, but terrified, she rose and went on.

Two men watched her through their glasses. One was General Taylor who ordered his aide to intercept her. He did and Belle gasped out her intelligence. Taylor, as he relates in his memoirs, "believing in the correctness of the woman's statements, I hurried forward on the double, hoping to surprise the enemy's idlers in the town, or to swarm over the wagon bridge and secure it. . . ."

His buglers sounded the charge. With a roar Hay's Louisiana Brigade swept down the road. Another and another wave followed, the wild Rebel yell filling the air.

The second man who had caught Belle in his glass was Henry Kyde Douglas, one of Jackson's staff officers, and Belle's childhood friend. Douglas put his spurs to his horse and galloped down the hill as the Louisiana regiment began to move.

When Douglas reached her, Belle was sitting in the mud trying to catch her breath.

"Good God, Belle," Douglas said as he slid out of the saddle and knelt beside her. "What is it?"

"Oh," she whispered. "Give me time to catch my breath."

In a moment Belle outlined the information she had and added what the Federal officer had told her about burning the wagon bridge.

Douglas galloped back as Jackson came up from the rear "surprised," as he reported, to find the attack already had begun. He returned with Douglas and was introduced to Belle. When he asked if she wished an escort back into town, she refused his offer with thanks and then walked back to Front Royal.

Douglas never forgot that romantic touch to the day's battle. In his memoirs, *I Rode with Jackson,* published in 1940, he writes:

> Nearly exhausted and with her hand pressed against her heart, she said in gasps, "I knew it was Stonewall, when I heard the first gun. Go back and tell him that the Yankee force is very small— one regiment of Maryland Infantry, several pieces of artillery and several companies of cavalry. Tell him I know, for I went through their camps and got it out of an officer.
>
> "Tell him to charge right down and he will catch them all. I must hurry back. Good bye. My love to all the dear boys—and remember if you see me in town you haven't seen me today. . . ."

Jackson's troops needed no urging. They swept through the town, capturing the garrison and $300,000 worth of stores which the Union officers didn't have time to burn.

Then on to the wagon bridge. Flames were beginning to appear between the planks as Taylor led his men across. On the other side he turned to see who had been pounding behind him, urging him to ride faster. It was a grim-faced Stonewall Jackson.

Jackson's swift "foot cavalry" pressed on. Banks evacuated Strasburg but Jackson caught him at Middletown and broke his column in two. One part he chased through Winchester and Martinsburg up to the banks of the Potomac. The Federals had crossed but briefly before him and were streaming through Williamsport, Maryland.

Jeb Stuart and Turner Ashby were late in coming up or there might have been a roundup of Banks' entire command.

There is a wonderful last touch to that thrilling afternoon. Bone-weary and covered with grime and dust, Henry Kyde Douglas rode back to Front Royal late that afternoon. As he passed the Strickler

House he saw Belle surrounded by several admiring Confederate officers. Belle waved for him to join them.

As he leaned over to kiss her hand, Belle pinned a rose on his tunic.

"Remember," she whispered, "the rose is blood red, and those are my colors."

As they stood there, a line of captured Federals marched down the street. One was Clarke, the war correspondent, who had been caught going out his window. As he saw Belle he shook his fist.

"You'll rue this," he cried.

Belle winked and blew him a kiss.

Belle was heroine of the hour. On the porches and in the barracks her story was told and retold. Before the moon was up, she was an American legend.

However, there was one in Front Royal who was not impressed by Belle's exploit. In Bel Air that evening Miss Lucy Buck wrote in her diary:

> 'Tis said that she [Belle] wished some information conveyed to the army about the time of the keenest firing, and not being able to have anyone to go for her, she went herself to an exposed point, where the bullets fell like hailstones about her, riddling her dress.

She could not resist adding, "I know not what truth there is to the rumor."

It is unfortunate that Lucy could not have been in a quiet room of the Richards house, about a quarter of a mile from Bel Air, where a weary man in gray put aside his Bible to write a brief note. It read:

May 23, 1862.

Miss Belle Boyd,

 I thank you, for myself and the Army, for the immense service that you have rendered to your country today.

Hastily, I am your friend,
T. J. Jackson, C.S.A.

3

The Battle of Front Royal and Jackson's victory over Banks stunned Washington. As in '61 after the First Bull Run—ironically another battle in which a charming desperate woman, Rose O'Neale Greenhow played an important role—it was believed that at any hour Jackson would burst out of the Valley and take the capitol by storm.

The War Department was quite aware that with only 20,000 men Jackson had managed by his incredible swift marches and lightning blows to prevent 40,000 Federal troops from joining forces before Richmond—besides keeping Washington in a feverish state of anxiety.

On the twenty-fourth a jittery General John W. Geary, the former mayor of San Francisco, telegraphed Washington that Jackson with 20,000 men was marching eastward from Ashby's Gap toward Centreville, only twenty miles from Washington.

Lincoln wryly replied, "What became of the force which pursued Banks yesterday?"

The same day Lincoln ordered McDowell to abandon his support of McClellan and to take 20,000 men and head for the Valley at once. He was to trap Jackson and Ewell. Admitting the defeat of Banks was a "crushing blow," McDowell ordered Shields and Geary to return to the Valley at once and catch Jackson. Fremont, that same day, was ordered eastward to relieve the pressure on Banks by joining in the attack on Jackson. But Fremont, unlike the pugnacious Shields, had no desire to match arms and military sagacity with Stonewall. He took his time in reaching the Valley.

With Shields and Geary on the move, Jackson outnumbered as always, and with his men exhausted, moved down the Valley, leaving a small garrison of Georgia infantry behind at Front Royal. Eager as always to catch Jackson, Shields reached Front Royal after a forced march. So rapid had been his advance that the commander of the Georgia troops was caught by surprise. He abandoned the town in a hurry leaving most of his supplies and guns.

The swift attack caught Belle unaware. Shots were still being fired and Northern prisoners released, when an informer walked into Federal headquarters and denounced her as a spy. The informer's name was Annie Jones. Belle would meet her again under different circumstances.

The official reports of the Federal officers commanding the attack state that "one hundred and sixty Confederate prisoners, including Belle Boyd, a famous spy in the service of the Confederacy," were taken.

Belle was placed under house arrest. Sentries were posted at her door. But when her old friend General Shields arrived at Front Royal, he ordered her released. However she was kept under close vigilance by detectives.

On June 9, Shields, following Jackson, was defeated with heavy losses at Port Republic. Ambulances rolled back into Front Royal and private homes were turned into hospitals.

One of the seriously wounded was handsome Captain Kiely who had wooed Belle with his flowers and poems.

"Ask Belle to come," he whispered to one of his fellow officers. They sent for her at once. That afternoon Belle was seen galloping down the main street accompanied by a Federal officer.

"Where is the wounded Yankee?" she demanded of a servant.

The servant told her and Belle raced up the stairs, "entering the room without ceremony."

A small boy who watched Belle softly close the door of Kiely's room wrote about it many years later. He was "young Tom" Ashby. A half century later, as Dr. Thomas Ashby, he would remember the incident in his history, *The Valley Campaigns*.

The hot days dragged on. In the North the newspapers made Belle the heroine of many strange roles; a beautiful girl who rode a great white steed, waving a sword and leading howling Rebels into battle; a woman of great military sagacity who sat in the councils of Jackson and Ewell and told them what to do; a Molly Pitcher who loaded the cannons and directed their fire.

She was now and for always, "Belle Boyd, the notorious Confederate spy."

Belle dismissed the exaggerated reports as so much nonsense.

"As I believe the veracity of the Yankee press is well known and appreciated," she relates, "I shall give no more extracts from their eloquent pages. . . ."

Soon Captain Dan left for a Northern hospital. We don't know if Belle said good-by but we would like to think she slipped into his room at the Ashby house for the last time to give him the kiss he was so eager for.

There were rumors that Jackson was again moving north up the Valley against Front Royal. With Shields defeated in June and with a clear road ahead for Stonewall, the War Department ordered nearly all the troops out of the town, leaving behind only the Third Delaware Infantry.

Belle had continued her spy activities during the summer and was anxious to get off some of her information to Jackson. She was under daily surveillance and the strain must have been terrific.

One day in July she made a grave mistake. She was walking down the street when she saw two officers in ragged gray jackets, standing outside a tent where passes to Richmond were issued.

From the provost marshal she learned they were Confederate officers about to be paroled south. A plan formed in her mind. She asked the provost if she could invite them to dinner. Had Belle been less anxious to get off her dispatches she might have considered the readiness with which her request was granted and the fact that only one of the prisoners appeared for dinner. He was tall and handsome, with quizzical blue eyes and a face burned by the weather to the color of old leather.

An alert servant warned Belle, "Dat man ain't no Rebel. I seen him among the Yankees in de street. If he has got sech clothes on, he ain't no sech . . . dat man's a spy! Please God, Miss Belle, he am!"

Belle waved away the servant's warning. It was a wonderful dinner. The handsome blue-eyed man was a charming conversationalist, a perfect gentleman—and he had a pleasant singing voice.

It was a perfect evening. When he returned to his lodging in the home of a friend of Belle's, the "Confederate officer" wrote out his first report and signed it C. D. Smitley, Chief of Scouts, Fifth West Virginia Cavalry. His assignment was to investigate reports that Belle Boyd was sending treasonable dispatches through the lines to Jackson.

Other gay evenings followed. Smitley found Belle to be "a lady of culture, a brilliant conversationalist, expert with the piano and rather pretty."

One evening Belle and Smitley joined a group of Federal officers and their town belles. The handsome Smitley stayed at Belle's side. When she sat at the piano and sang "The Bonnie Blue Flag"—"in a sweet and sad voice"—he sat down and joined her. One of the Federal officers, long an admirer of Belle, glared at Smitley in a jealous rage for the rest of the evening.

A few nights later Smitley was with Belle at another gathering. One of the guests was the jealous Union officer. The hours flew. There was much singing, laughing, and piano playing. During the evening Belle impulsively asked Smitley if he would deliver some dispatches for her to Jackson when he left Front Royal. He said he would, and she gave them to him. When she was alone for a moment, the jealous Federal officer came over to whisper that she was a fool; the man she was laughing and dancing with was in reality a Federal scout. Belle gave him a scornful look and flounced off.

The party ended about midnight. Belle and the scout walked home arm in arm, down the wide, tree-shaded street, past the rows of tiny

75

Queen Anne houses with their walled gardens. They stood together at the cottage door, the air heavy with the intoxicating perfume of honeysuckle, and the moonlight streaming through the morning glory vines.

Belle got little sleep that night. Doubts lurked in the darkness. Was the Confederate officer really one of Jackson's troopers, or was he a spy as the Union officer had blurted out? . . . Had she played the fool? . . .

Weary and heartsick she rang the bell of the house where Smitley boarded. Her friends roused the scout who hurried downstairs. The parlor door was closed and they faced each other. For a long moment the only sound was the creaking of an army wagon moving down the street.

Then, as Smitley remembered it in his regimental history, "she wept like a child and demanded to know if I was a Union spy. . . ."

Unfortunately the romantic episode ends on this abrupt note. Smitley never told what happened next. However, we do know that Belle's dispatch containing military information was later delivered to Stanton. We must assume that Smitley, putting patriotism before love, denied with such emphasis that he was a spy, that Belle believed him.

Secretary of War Stanton acted quickly. On Tuesday, July 29, a carriage drove up to the cottage door. A Federal officer was admitted. A few moments later Eliza, weeping bitterly, told Belle that the provost marshal was waiting to see her.

She found the provost and a major of the Twelfth Illinois Cavalry. The third man was a short, bearded civilian with cold eyes. He was one of Baker's detectives with the horrible name of Cridge.

"Miss Boyd," Major McEnnis said, "we have come to arrest you."

"For what?" she demanded.

McEnnis handed her a note. It read:

> War Department
>
> Sir:
> You will proceed immediately to Front Royal, Virginia, and arrest, if found there, Miss Belle Boyd, and bring her to Washington at once.
>
> I am respectfully,
> E. M. Stanton.

She handed back the order to McEnnis. With a grunt the detective began to search the cottage room by room. Eliza, however, had slipped away to destroy as many ciphered letters and notes as she could find.

Cridge was very thorough. Within an hour he had a file of "treasonable letters."

At two o'clock she said good-by to her weeping grandmother and cousin Alice. Eliza begged on her knees to accompany her mistress but Cridge pushed her aside.

The whole village turned out to see her go. Major Sherman took elaborate precautions to see that Turner Ashby's cavaliers didn't rescue her. Belle's escort was nearly a hundred cavalrymen with fifty more spread out in skirmishing order.

From behind her curtains Miss Lucy Buck watched Belle's departure. She wrote:

> Belle Boyd was taken prisoner and sent off in a carriage with an escort of fifty cavalrymen today. I hope she has succeeded in making herself proficiently (sic) notorious now. They say they are going to put her within our lines and keep her there.

At twilight the party reached a Federal camp less than a mile from Winchester. The Official Records tell us that shortly before she had arrived the camp's commander, General Julius White, had wired Washington: "Cridge is here with Belle Boyd as prisoner. What shall be done with her?"

Assistant Secretary of War Walcott replied within the hour:

> Direct Cridge to come immediately to Washington and bring with him Miss Belle Boyd in close custody, committing her on arrival to Old Capitol Prison. Furnish him with as much aid as he may need to get her safely here.

White gallantly insisted that Belle have his tent. He told her she was to be sent on to Martinsburg in the morning.

During the early hours of the morning a cow blundered into the camp. A nervous sentry fired and called for the corporal of the guard. In a few moments the whole camp was aroused when someone shouted that Turner Ashby's riders were tearing into the camp to rescue Belle.

White, in his nightshirt, stumbled out of a tent, pistol in hand and restored order. The only casualty was the cow. During the shooting Belle had sat on the edge of her cot almost hysterical with joy at what she thought was a rescue attempt. When a sentry told her what had happened she buried her face in the pillow and wept.

77

At dawn the carriage and its escort set out for Martinsburg, reaching the town at two o'clock. The Union commander there informed her she was to leave for Washington at two o'clock in the morning. Belle pleaded with the commander to allow her to stay with friends but Cridge told the commander that was impossible. Instead she was brought to Raemer's Hotel where she held a brief reunion with her mother.

The train from Martinsburg reached Washington depot at nine the next morning. Cridge and his detectives had a difficult time making a passage through the large crowd to the carriage. When Cridge refused to answer one of her questions, Belle wondered if she was in "Russian Poland."

It was a short ride to Old Capitol. As he had done with Rose O'Neale Greenhow, Superintendent Wood personally welcomed Belle to his prison.

He opened the door, smiling broadly. "Well, well," he boomed, "so this is the celebrated Confederate spy! I am very happy to see you, Miss Boyd. Of course we will endeavor to make you as comfortable as possible. . . ."

Biting her lips to hold back the tears Belle followed Wood up the creaking stairs of the old prison to Room Number 16.

The doorway of every room they passed was filled with captured Confederate officers. The dirty, bearded men who had not seen a woman for months drank in every detail of what Wood described as her "fine figure." Not one made a sound. They only stared.

Her room was equipped with a looking glass, iron bed, table and chair and a sewing machine. The one window in the room looked out on the square and she could see the tiny figures of the workmen clinging like flies to the unfinished dome of the Capitol.

The menu of Old Capitol had not improved since that other tempestuous Rebel spy, Rose O'Neale Greenhow, had been there, and the food was abominable.

It is highly significant that Wood, one of the most influential men in Washington and Baker, head of the secret police, should have been selected by Stanton to question the eighteen-year-old girl.

Baker demanded to know if she would sign an oath of allegiance to the Union.

"Tell Stanton that if I ever do such a thing I hope my tongue cleaves to the roof of my mouth," Belle snapped.

Men crowded about the doorways of the rooms along the corridor. Baker stood up. "You will not sign the oath?"

"No!" Belle said.

"Then you'll rot here," Baker snapped.

"If it's a crime to love the South, its cause, and its president, then I shall rot here," Belle cried.

Cheers and cries of "bravo" echoed along the corridors. Without another word, Wood and Baker left the room.

The guard looked in a moment later then paced down the long hall. Something rolled across the corridor and into her room. Belle picked it up, then walked to the window. She opened her hand. It was a small walnut. On it a Confederate had painstakingly painted a tiny Confederate flag.

She pressed her face against the window and wept.

She stayed at the window all day. Her dinner grew cold. At nine the curfew was sounded. A guard came into Belle's room and turned down the gas. The prison was quiet. The only sounds were the pacing of the guard.

In Room Number 10 directly above Belle, Dennis A. Mahoney, editor of the *Dubuque Herald,* tossed restlessly on the table he was using for a bed. He had been jailed by Stanton for his fiery editorials denouncing certain Federal policies. Shortly after his arrest he was notified he had been nominated for Congress in Iowa's Third Congressional District.

Suddenly he slid off the table and went to the door of his room. He thought he had heard a woman's sad voice singing "Maryland, My Maryland." Then as he listened, the stirring words rose in the quiet of the prison:

> "The despot's heel is on the shore,
>   My Maryland,
> His torch is at the temple's door,
>   My Maryland,
> Avenge the patriotic gore
> Had wept o'er gallant Baltimore,
> And be the battleground of yore,
>   My Maryland!"

Men gathered at the doors of their cells. As Mahoney says in his *The Prisoner of State,* suppressed in 1863 by Stanton, "We wondered who was singing. When we were informed it was Belle Boyd, we all inquired about her."

Below in her room Belle sang with all her heart. Then, one by one, deep male voices joined her. Old Capitol rang with the voices of a hundred men and a girl. This was the South, the Cause; this was Jackson and his gray lines which stood like a stone wall; this was Beauregard, Barrow, and Bee; this was Turner Ashby and his cavaliers; this was the South that would soon be gone.

In the doorways of their cells, men sang at the top of their voices, tears streaming down their faces. They ignored the guards who shouted at them and waved their muskets.

As Mahoney said, "It was difficult to listen unmoved to this lady throwing her whole soul as it were, into the expression of the sentiments of the South, defiance of the North and her affectionately confident appeals to Maryland. . . ."

Months later, James J. Williamson, son of the designer and builder of the *Ann McKim,* America's first clipper ship, heard a fellow prisoner, Gus Williams, a Virginia planter, describe that night.

"When Belle sang," Gus said, "it made you feel like jumping out of the window and swimming the Potomac. Men walked off to one side and pulled out their handkerchiefs, wiping their eyes for fear someone would see them doing the baby act. . . ."

Finally the clear notes died away. There was silence again in Old Capitol. In Room Number 16, Belle lay on the cot and stared up in the darkness.

As she says, she was no longer afraid.

4

The day after her arrival Wood received orders from Stanton that Belle was to be kept in solitary. The order was issued after the *Washington Star* disclosed that a leading secessionist of Washington had paid her a visit while several other gentlemen "waited upon her."

War Department investigators were sent to question the *Star's* editors. They were told, "The editor is absent from the city."

The Official Records tell us that Assistant Secretary of War Watson then ordered Military Commandant General James Wadsworth of Washington to find out who violated the order to keep Belle in close custody and under whose authority this order was violated.

Wadsworth replied that same afternoon. He wrote Watson that Wood had allowed Dr. Hale, a Washington secessionist, to see her.

Belle never relates the incident. It may have been to protect Wood, who had taken a liking to the girl from Front Royal. Later he would defy authorities to send her a wedding trousseau under a flag.

General Doster, then Washington's provost marshal also visited Belle. As he recalled in his memoirs he found her reading *Harpers* and eating peaches. Doster found Belle to be a "lively spirited young Rebel." He agreed with Wood's approval of her "fine figure."

The second night of her imprisonment Belle was reading a Bible in the lamplight when she heard a soft tapping. She put the Bible aside and put out the lamp. As she relates the story—confirmed by Mahoney—she made a small hole in the ancient plaster with a table knife about where she could hear the tapping.

A note was slipped through the half-inch hole. In the moonlight which poured through the bars she read the brief cheery message from Fitzhugh, a Rebel officer.

The next night there was a tapping on the opposite side of the room. As before, she turned down the light and bored a hole in the plaster with the same table knife. A note from another Confederate officer was passed through.

As the days passed other prisoners bored holes in the plaster walls of their cells and, as Mahoney said, "there was a steady line of communication about the prison."

On the morning of her fourth day in Old Capitol a Frenchman passing her room managed to give Belle a small portrait of Jeff Davis. She hung it above her mantelpiece with the words scrawled above it on the wall, "Three cheers for Jeff Davis and the Southern Confederacy."

A guard informed Lieutenant Holmes, known to the prisoners as "Bullhead," that Belle had the picture in her room. Holmes rushed in and tore it from the wall. As punishment he ordered her door locked at all times.

The punishment was enforced for seven of Washington's hottest weeks. It was only after she had fallen sick that Wood learned of the Lieutenant's order. He immediately revoked it.

For the rest of her stay Belle carried on a blazing feud with her guards. As Gus Williams, the Virginia planter said, Belle infuriated the soldiers by singing "Maryland, My Maryland" at the top of her voice, emphasizing the words, "Huzzah! She spurns the Northern scum!"

When the guard stormed in to shout her down, she would meekly agree to stop. When they left she would pick up a broom and dust away their footsteps.

Sunday chapel in the prison yard was a big occasion. Belle, the only woman in Old Capitol at the time, was the star attraction. Mahoney

81

paints a wonderful scene of how she walked across the yard—a Confederate flag pinned on her bosom—with the fifty or more Confederate officers rising as one man to doff their caps.

"If she gave them one smile," Mahoney wrote, "it did more than preaching. You wouldn't hear a curse word all week."

On one occasion an infuriated guard lost his head and jabbed at Belle with a bayonet. The blade missed her by a fraction of an inch and pinned her dress to the wall.

There were angry shouts from the Confederate prisoners who witnessed the incident. For a moment it looked as if they would rush into the room. But Belle pushed the guard away and brushed him out of the room with her broom.

As Mahoney said, "He would have been torn to pieces by those angry men before it could have been known to the prison authorities."

Unlike Mrs. Greenhow, Belle's window looked out on the square. Officers leading troops down the street were often targets for her jibes. "How long did it take you to get back from Bull Run?" she would cry, or, "Where did Pope leave his coat?"

Her favorite was: "Are you coming or going to Richmond, sir?"

Once a soldier fired at her window. There was a tinkling of glass, then silence. A moment later a small Confederate flag was poked through the wooden slats to wave defiantly in the breeze. Even the Federals had to laugh.

Superintendent Wood may have remembered this incident when he wrote, "She certainly was the most persistent Rebel I ever had."

For some reason Belle discreetly avoids telling anything of her romance in prison. But Mahoney remembered it in wonderful detail.

One of the Confederate prisoners, lodged in a room across from Belle, was Lieutenant McVay, a cavalryman. McVay had been left for dead on a battlefield but revived as the embalmers were putting him in a dead basket.

After he had recovered from his wounds he was sent to Old Capitol.

McVay could only look and smile at Belle. However, love found a way. He wrapped his love notes around a marble and rolled them into Belle's room. Belle used the marble to respond. "The guard would spin about when he heard the noise of the marble rolling across the floor," Mahoney relates, "but it was always safe with Belle by that time."

But the romance ended abruptly on the evening of August 28. Old Capitol buzzed with the news. Belle was going home.

The Official Records tells us that General Wadsworth wrote to General Dix:

> I forward likewise Miss Belle Boyd, a young lady arrested on suspicion of having communicated with the enemy. I have agreed that she shall be placed over the lines by the first flag of truce which is in accordance with her wishes. No specific charge or information have been lodged against her.

The Rebel officer, Fitzhugh, accompanied Belle and together they rode in a carriage to the Washington depot. We know from the *Washington Star* that Southern sympathizers cheered them along the route.

No explanation can be found for Belle's release. As Carl Sandburg points out, "On the evidence she could have been legally convicted as a spy, shot at sunrise, and heard of no more."

The possible explanation of this apparent policy of appeasement, is that the North was afraid of retaliation. They had no desire to hang a lady spy. In Richmond, Miss Van Lew, that incredibly courageous woman was sending out dispatches containing highly important military information to Federal commanders, and in Tennessee Pauline Cushman was still riding for the Union.

Belle went to Richmond to be welcomed at the pier by Colonel Robert Ould, the Confederate exchange agent. On the road to Richmond, the Richmond Light Infantry Blues was drawn up in review in her honor. After a glorious week she left the Ballard House to board in a private home on Grace Street.

Old friends dropped in on her nightly. Once a Confederate officer called and left a small box. It contained a small watch and chatelaine. On the back was engraved, "In token of the affection and esteem of your fellow prisoners of Old Capitol."

Belle soon returned to Martinsburg, now occupied by the Confederates. Her father was home and there was a family reunion. In September she met Jackson and was made an honorary aide-de-camp. According to Belle, Jackson warned her to leave Martinsburg at once should he be forced to retreat.

In November, McClellan was replaced by Burnside. Martinsburg changed hands and Belle left for Winchester. En route she stopped overnight at Culpepper Court House where she stayed at the home of Mrs. Rixey, a favorite jumping off point for land blockade-runners.

Belle shared a room with a young lady who would write her reminiscences, *A Virginia Lady in the Civil War,* under the *nom de plume* of "Nellie Gray."

Nellie was planning to run the blockade the next day to see her husband in Baltimore. Just before going to bed she joined a group who were listening to a young girl describe the days and nights she had spent in Old Capitol Prison. Later she let them all admire a watch she said had been given to her by her fellow prisoners.

Nellie left the group and went upstairs. In the morning she found her bedfellow was the young lady who owned the watch. She asked her name.

"Belle Boyd," was the answer.

Nellie writes: "For the first time I knew that my bedfellow was the South's famous spy."

Nellie also tells of a visit by her brother-in-law, Dick. He was shoeless and shirtless, and his coat was a threadbare rag. Dick refused to enter the dining room. He insisted on talking to Nellie while hidden by a hat rack.

Suddenly the door swung open. Belle "took in the situation," and summoned the other ladies. Shirt, shoes, and stockings were begged or borrowed. As Nellie wrote, Dick was put in "Miss Boyd's hands and had a good dinner."

But Nellie never forgot the last scene: It was a bitter night. The windows were rattling in the wind when Dick said good night. Before he could open the door Belle placed her shawl about his shoulders, saying, "I can't let you go back to camp wearing a thin jacket, lieutenant, while I have this shawl."

She refused to take it back, telling Dick she could "get others where this came from."

In December, 1862, Belle visited her relatives in Tennessee. After a public reception in Knoxville in February of the next year, she was persuaded by the widow of her kinsman, Samuel B. Boyd, former mayor of Knoxville, to spend a long visit at the old Blount Mansion, one of the show places of the South and formerly the residence of Governor William Blount.

In the spring she visited friends in Georgia and Alabama. In May she was at the Battle House in Mobile. There she received the stunning news that her idol, General Stonewall Jackson, was dead. With a heavy heart and a strip of mourning ribbon tied about her left arm, she traveled to Charleston. Beauregard, now in charge of harbor defenses, gave her a dinner and personally accompanied her on an inspection tour of the gunboats.

The *Rockingham Register* of Harrisonburg, Virginia tells us Belle, "the great confederate heroine," was visiting Harrisonburg at the American Hotel on June 5, 1863.

At Woodstock she met an old friend, Major Harry Gilmor, who was setting out on a scouting expedition. Belle pleaded with him to allow her to go along. Gilmor refused. Belle insisted. At last as a subterfuge, he told her she could go if she obtained a pass from General Jenkins.

As he tells the story in his memoirs, *Four Years in the Saddle,* he tried to sneak out of the hotel before Belle awakened. To his chagrin he found she had taken his saber and pistol and hid them in her room.

There was nothing to do but wait. About nine she came down in a tight-fitting gray riding habit and two pistols in patent leather holsters. With a sweet smile she gave Gilmor back his saber and pistol.

Gilmor and Belle rode to the General's tent, where he sat in the sun, smoking a large cigar. Belle made her request. Jenkins looked over her shoulder. Behind her back, Gilmor shook his head violently. The General stroked his beard, thought for awhile, then solemnly told Belle he couldn't grant her request.

Belle "who was furious," rode off.

As Gilmor relates:

> I did not care to be accompanied by a woman on so perilous an enterprise; for though she was a splendid and reckless rider, of unflinching courage, and her whole soul bound up in the Southern cause, yet she was a little—mark you, only a *little* headstrong and willful, and I thought it best, both for her sake and mine, that she should not go. . . .

It would have been an adventurous journey for Belle. Gilmor and his ten men made a sweeping scout of the Federal lines about Martinsburg and Winchester and gave Ewell an excellent intelligence report.

When the guns boomed, Belle and a disabled officer watched the battle of Winchester from a hillside. Once a cannon ball came too close and they both had to dive for cover. When the battle was over

85

she returned to Martinsburg and here was welcomed by her father. The swift incredible marches he had made under Jackson had taken their toll of Ben Boyd, and he was home on sick leave.

Word that Belle was back spread throughout the countryside. At Bel Air, Lucy Buck groaned when she heard the news. She wrote in her diary: " 'Tis said Belle Boyd is back in town tonight. What next?"

In May and June the Confederacy rolled confidently along on the crest of their victories. Once again the cry was to storm Washington. Confederate troops marched into Pennsylvania, the long gray columns singing "The Bonnie Blue Flag."

Then in July, there was Gettysburg. The gray waves receded southward again. Weary, shoeless men marched by the hour down the streets of Martinsburg in a sad retreat. With her father Belle watched them. Reason told her she must go. But she couldn't. Her mother had just given birth to a baby and was ill. Belle had to stay.

The Federals marched in and occupied the town. Belle discreetly kept out of sight. For a week she thought she was safe. Then, one day as she was sitting by the window holding her three-day-old sister a horseman clattered to a stop in front of the Boyd house.

It was Major Nathan Goff, of the Third West Virginia Mounted, calling on behalf of General B. F. Kelly. The General it seemed wanted to confirm reports that Belle Boyd was home again in Martinsburg.

Belle pointed out that she wasn't the only Rebel in town. Goff, later under Hayes, secretary of the Navy, admitted that was true, but added, "but none so dangerous as yourself."

On July 23 an order was issued for Belle's arrest. It seemed as if some sort of a cat and mouse game was being played with Belle. It is interesting to note that the regimental history of the 123 Ohio Volunteers identifies the officer who arrested her, and the soldier who guarded her house with orders to shoot her, "should she appear on the balcony."

In mid-August a second order for her arrest was issued. At eleven o'clock on a scorching day she was put aboard a train under heavy guard and delivered to Stanton's detectives in Washington. This time she was imprisoned in the Carroll Prison, adjacent to Old Capitol. There were three other women in the prison; the famous Miss Antonia Ford, a Miss Nannie T., and her aged mother.

There is a wonderfully romantic episode in Belle's stay at the Carroll Prison. As she relates it, she had turned from the window as dusk was falling over the city when something whizzed past her. Fright-

86

ened, she fell to the floor. Her first thought was that a shot had been fired at her. When she had recovered she turned up the gas.

On the floor was an arrow. Wrapped around the shaft was a note. It read:

> You have many warm friends. Through me you will be able to correspond with them. On Thursdays and Saturdays I will come into the square opposite the window. Lower your gas. Do not worry I am a good shot.
>
> Try to get an India rubber ball in which to put your messages. Then sew the sides together. Throw it through the window with as much force as you can.

The note was signed, "C.H."

As Belle claims, she carried on a steady correspondence with the mysterious correspondent who evidently had the skill of William Tell. A Confederate flag, newspapers, friends' letters were shot into her room. In a way she doesn't explain, she obtained an India rubber ball and bounced out a few dispatches herself.

In September Belle helped plan an escape plot. A Mr. K. of Virginia smuggled her a note asking her assistance. She said she would do all she could and gave him forty dollars.

That night she turned the gas low, and flung her rubber ball out of the window. It contained an appeal to "C.H." to help in the plot. An arrow wizzed back the answer. He would help. Set the night and the hour.

As the fall days passed plans were completed. The night of October 1 was selected. K. was to sneak up to the garret occupied by two of his friends. From there he would get on the roof. Outside in the square, "C.H." would create a disturbance, after Belle had summoned Wood to her room on some pretext.

The plan worked without a hitch. While Wood was listening to a complaint Belle had made up, there were loud cries of "murder . . . murder" out in the square. Wood ran from the room followed by the guards.

Meanwhile, on the other side of the old building, K. slid down a lightning rod.

The *Washington Star* confirms the escape, reporting that on the night of October 1, a Rebel mail courier escaped from Carroll Prison, "by getting to the roof of the building and sliding down the lightning rod."

Records of the War Department also admit three prisoners escaped from Carroll Prison that month.

In October another woman was admitted to the prison. Belle saw her in the corridor. For a long moment they stared at each other. Then a something clicked in Belle's memory. The new prisoner was "Annie Jones" who had reported her to the Federals in the spring of 1862, at Front Royal.

At eight o'clock on the morning of December 1, 1863, Belle was sent to City Point under the guard of Captain James B. Mix, former commander of Lincoln's bodyguard. An Associated Press report states they arrived at Fortress Monroe, headquarters of Benjamin Butler on the morning of the second. Butler saw Belle within the hour. It wasn't a happy interview. Belle refused to accept a chair and told Butler he was a man "of atrocious conduct and brutality." She reminded him that such conduct had been commented upon by the English Parliament.

Butler jumped to his feet and ordered her out of the room. Later that morning Belle was brought to the wharf under guard and put aboard the Federal exchange boat, *City of New York*. It got under way the next morning at seven.

Ten minutes later the ship went aground. After an hour's delay they set out again. They had proceeded less than a mile when a tugboat put out in pursuit.

Belle's heart sank. She had a premonition that Butler, still smarting under her tongue-lashing had revoked her release. But the skipper of the exchange boat was not bothering about any tugboat. He had been delayed an hour and wanted to be off. He ordered full steam ahead and soon lost the tug.

Belle's fears were not unfounded. Butler had seen the letters of introduction to her by the prisoners of Carroll Prison, extolling her "great service to the Confederacy." He ordered that she immediately be taken into custody and sent on to Fort Warren in Massachusetts Bay, pending further investigation.

As Belle says, he was "in a great rage" when the tug returned empty handed.

At six o'clock, on the evening of the fourth, the *City of New York* docked at City Point. The next morning Belle was put aboard the Confederate exchange ship. At eight that night they entered Richmond.

There was a week of gay welcome-home parties. But one night during the week of the twelfth Belle had a strange dream, in which her room was filled with a bright light. Then General Jackson and her father appeared. After they had stood by her for a long time, Jackson touched her father's arm, saying, "It is time for us to go."

As Belle relates, they vanished with Jackson whispering, "Poor child."

On the morning of the fourteenth she received a note from an army officer friend to please meet him as soon as she had dressed. When she saw him she knew instantly that he carried bad news. Her father had died in Washington on the sixth. To the last he kept telling her mother Belle was standing at his bedside.

On March 29 Belle left Richmond under orders from the Confederate secretary of state, to carry important dispatches to England. At Wilmington, North Carolina, she boarded the steamer, *Greyhound.* Official records of the Union and Confederate Navies describe her as "a three-masted propeller, near new, painted lead color with a red streak, flies the Confederate flag and is a fast sailer." The *Greyhound's* master was a "Captain Henry" a well-known blockade-runner. One of Belle's fellow passengers was Edward A. Pollard, editor of the *Richmond Examiner.*

In his book, *Observations in the North,* published in 1865, Pollard, like Belle, keeps "Captain Henry's" real identity a secret. Both Belle and Pollard disclosed the Greyhound's master—"a splendid fellow"— had been wounded serving under Jackson.

The Official Records identify "Captain Henry" as George H. Bier, formerly a lieutenant in the U.S. Navy. Pollard and Belle were correct when they said Bier—or Captain Henry, as we shall call him here—fought under Jackson. The records of Stonewall's staff show a Major George H. Bier (C.S. Navy), C.O., who was released on January 12, 1863.

At ten o'clock on the night of May 8 the *Greyhound* pulled anchor. All lights were extinguished. Steam was gotten up slowly. Forward and aft, lookouts, kneeling on the mound of cotton bales, kept a sharp watch for Federal gunboats.

The hiss of the bow waves was the only sound. As Belle recalled, "It was a night never to be forgotten—a night of almost breathless anxiety."

Dawn of the next day—March 9 and Belle's twentieth birthday— found the *Greyhound* slipping past the wreckage of the ironclad *Raleigh.* There wasn't a sail or mast in sight. It looked as if the *Greyhound* had successfully slipped through the net of Federal gunboats.

At noon the lookout cried, "Sail ho!" and a gunboat soon came into view. From her wake, she was moving fast. Soon the *Greyhound's* passengers could see the guns roll out and hear the gunnery officers barking their commands.

The slam of the first gun sounded faint across the water. There was a short puff of smoke and a ball shrieked across the bow of the *Greyhound*.

Seamen rolled the cotton bales overboard. Kegs containing $20,000 in gold followed. The ship's papers were burned and at last her colors were struck. A boat left the gunboat and a lieutenant from the U.S.S. *Connecticut* climbed aboard. After examining Captain Henry's papers he ordered him aboard the *Connecticut* to be questioned by Commander John J. Almy.

Captain Henry returned to his ship along with a young prizemaster, acting Ensign Samuel Hardinge, of Brooklyn, New York. Belle was struck by his shoulder-length hair and large bright eyes.

She relates:

> . . . His every movement was so much that of a refined gentleman, that my Southern proclivities, strong as they were, yielded for a moment to the impulses of my heart, and I said to myself, 'Oh, what a good fellow he must be!'

Once he had taken over the ship Hardinge asked to enter her cabin. Belle gave her permission.

"I beg of you to please consider yourself a passenger and not a prisoner," he told her.

The *Greyhound* followed the *Connecticut* all that day. On the second day a whaleboat was lowered and Hardinge learned that the *Greyhound* was to be towed to Fortress Monroe. Tow lines were secured and both vessels proceeded north at four knots.

It was beautiful that night. There was a full moon and the vast dome of the sky moved with diamond fire. Like pale ghosts the two ships knifed their way along a floor of rippling silver. On the *Greyhound's* deck Belle and Ensign Hardinge sat in silence, listening to the hiss of the water as it fled past the ship's sides.

Then, above them on the bridge, Captain Henry began singing a love song "in a low sweet voice." When the song was finished he went below.

As Sam later recalled, he fell in love with Belle the moment he saw her after climbing over the *Greyhound's* rail, not only by her feminine charm but also by the special appeal, that in this quiet, tawny-haired girl lurked a desperate woman.

In the wonderful romantic setting, the Yankee prizemaster began to woo the Rebel spy. He moved close, took her hand and whispered passages from Shakespeare and Byron.

What happened next is best told by Belle herself: "From poetry he passed on to plead an oft-told tale. . . ."

On the deserted bridge, bathed in the soft moonlight Sam asked Belle to become his wife. She knew in her heart she had loved him from the moment he had stepped aboard. Still—she was a Rebel and he was a Yankee.

She told him they must wait—their worlds were too far apart.

On the morning of May 12, the *Greyhound* and the *Connecticut* anchored off the Capes. Hardinge reported aboard the flagship, *Minnesota* and returned in two hours. He told Belle he was unable to find out what his orders would be.

Meanwhile Belle was heartsick. She was sure Butler, who undoubtedly had been informed of her capture, would order her to Fortress Monroe.

But no courier arrived from Monroe. Belle evidently forgot that the Navy seldom delivers their prisoners over to the Army.

Captain Guert Gansevoort, an old friend of Captain Henry, commanding the ironclad *Roanoke* came aboard and brought enough champagne for a gay party. He gave Henry a written parole and told Belle she could go ashore in New York only if Hardinge accompanied her.

A few days later orders were finally received for Hardinge to take the *Greyhound* to Boston, stopping first at the Brooklyn Navy Yard to refuel.

In New York a crowd greeted Belle but was disappointed when the Navy ordered a tug to take her, Hardinge, and Captain Henry to the foot of Canal Street.

At the home of a friend of the Boyd family, Belle hurriedly excused herself and went upstairs to her room. There she quickly undressed and removed a heavy belt—filled with gold and belonging to Captain Henry who planned to escape at the first opportunity.

After a day of shopping and visiting Niblo's Theater to see Brougham's romantic *Bel Domonio,* Hardinge brought Belle back to the *Greyhound.* That afternoon they sailed for Boston.

In Boston Captain Henry made his escape by simply walking off the ship while Hardinge was occupied in the bow with Belle who was engaging him in a discussion of the city's skyline. The Confederate skipper's disappearance was not discovered until later that day. Hardinge reported it at once.

For Belle this was a grave matter. Apparently she was not troubled by the conflict in her heart of love for Hardinge and her act which exposed him to execution for treason. But it must be remembered that she had warned him aboard the *Greyhound* that their worlds were still far apart. She was still a Confederate patriot, and he (although her dearest enemy) was a Union officer.

Deputy marshals combed the water front but Captain Henry was on his way to New York. There he would stay in a Canal Street boardinghouse, amply supplied by the gold Belle had smuggled ashore, before leaving for Canada.

The escape of Henry was a newspaper sensation. The *Boston Post,* on May 20, listed Belle Boyd and Mr. Pollard "author of a Southern Historian of the Rebellion," as passengers aboard the *Greyhound.*

The reporter described Belle "as very lady like."

The *Washington National Republican* reported that Henry had escaped from the *Greyhound* and noted "the famous Belle Boyd is a passenger on the vessel."

On the twenty-first the *Post* reporter secured a beat where he obtained an interview with Belle. He described her as "a tall, blonde woman, graceful in her manners and obviously a person of intelligence and quick understanding."

The reporter also interviewed some of the other passengers and officers. He wanted to know how Belle acted when the gunboat crossed the *Greyhound's* bow with a shot.

He was told: "Miss B. came up on deck, took a seat under a bale of cotton and sat quietly fanning herself and watching the explosion of the shells."

Belle was soon ordered ashore by Marshal Keyes who told her he was waiting orders to send her to Canada or back to Monroe. Hardinge, meanwhile rushed to Washington, to see several influential persons to obtain her release.

Then Belle herself wrote to Secretary of the Navy Welles. On May 25, the *Washington National Republican* published a portion of the letter from "the notorious female Rebel spy Belle Boyd." The article said Belle requested permission to join her mother in Canada.

Navy Department records say Sam left Washington for New York on the twenty-sixth, boasting that he would soon get Belle released.

He was in New York when Washington ordered Belle exiled to Canada. That same day Hardinge was ordered to report to the commandant of the Boston Navy Yard. At noon he was writing Belle he had been "charged with conspiring to help Captain Henry escape."

Admiral Stringham, commandant of the Boston Navy Yard, however, paroled Sam until sundown to allow him to say good-by to Belle at the station. There was only time for a kiss and to let Belle whisper to Sam she would wait forever. For her their worlds now had joined.

Hardinge went back to the Navy Yard. The Official Navy Records states he was arrested by order of the secretary of the Navy on June 8. On July 8, he was dismissed from the service "for your neglect of duty in permitting the captain of the prize steamer GREYHOUND to escape. . . ."

At Niagara, Belle joined Captain Henry—now using his real name of Bier—and his wife. Detectives still followed them. It was only when Belle sailed for London that she was able to shake them. One tried to make reservations but was too late. In London she reported to Hotze, the Confederacy's agent at the Court of St. James's, that the dispatches she had been carrying from Richmond had been destroyed before the *Greyhound* had been overtaken.

Hotze gave her a letter—one of the most important in her life. It was from Hardinge in Paris. She telegraphed she had reached London and Sam replied he was racing to see her.

Their courtship—surely one of the most romantic in our history—came to an end on August 25, 1864, when Belle and Sam Hardinge were married in St. James Church in Piccadilly. Long accounts of the wedding appeared in the *London Morning Post* and the *Le Moniteur Universal* of Paris.

Among her guests were Hotze, James Williams, former American minister to Turkey and Confederate minister at large; and James L. O'Sullivan, special agent of the Confederate government in London.

Just about the time of the wedding, Stanton heard rumors Belle had stolen across the Canadian border and was in Washington. He notified Provost Marshal Colonel T. Ingraham who alerted his men.

A few days later an informer reported to Ingraham that Belle Boyd was hiding at the home of a Peter McGuinnis, 321-4½ Street [island] Washington. Ingraham sent a patrol under Captain J. C. Putnam to search the house and grounds.

The house was surrounded and Putnam broke in the door. Mr. McGuinnis ran down the stairs demanding an explanation.

"We are informed Miss Belle Boyd is hiding in this house," Putnam said.

McGuinnis stared at him. "Miss Belle is in the kitchen," he said, "drinking a cup of tea. But what do—"

Putnam rushed into the kitchen, pistol in hand.

A frightened young woman jumped up, upsetting a cup of tea.

"Miss Boyd?" Putnam snapped.

"Yes—yes—I am Miss Boyd," the girl said fearfully.

"We have a warrant signed by Secretary Stanton for your arrest," Putnam told her.

The girl stared at him. "For what," she cried.

"For being one of Jeff Davis's spies," Putnam said.

Miss Boyd swooned. That should have been enough to tell Captain Putnam this wasn't the lady he was looking for.

Later that day Putnam filed a report with Provost Marshal Ingraham. ". . . we discovered from her papers that she was Belle Boyd, a lady of the same name as the famous spy but from Havre de Grace, Maryland."

6

There is evidence that love had turned Hardinge a traitor, and the South accepted him.

On September 2, 1864 writing from their honeymoon suite in the Brunswick Hotel in Piccadilly, Belle informed Jefferson Davis of her marriage. "Mr. Hardinge has given up all his property. His father, a Republican, has disinherited him for marrying a Rebel and joining the Rebel Cause," she wrote. She ended the letter telling Davis to "command me" if there was any way in which she could serve the South.

In November Hardinge sailed for home. Why, is not clear. Belle says it was to see her family. That explanation is not logical when records show Sam sailed direct to Boston not Richmond. Perhaps Jeff Davis did "command" her to test her husband by letting him deliver some secret Confederate dispatches. But why to Boston, the place of his last arrest? . . .

After a short visit in Boston Sam paid a flying visit to his parents in Brooklyn. Then he journeyed to Martinsburg via Baltimore. In a journal which he kept for Belle, Sam says he was "greeted affectionately by the Boyd family." Belle's mother, he said, was expected to return the next day.

At five o'clock the next day Sam left the Boyd house, not even waiting for Mrs. Boyd's return. Evidently he had been warned. At

Monacocy Station he was arrested as a spy and taken to Harpers Ferry. There he was questioned by General Stevenson who demanded that he turn over to them the Confederate documents he was carrying.

Hardinge's arrest created a sensation. The *Washington Star* described him as a handsome, dark-haired man who wore a beaver hat and carried a cane. The *Star* suspected that Belle was lurking somewhere in the vicinity "in which Hardinge was captured."

In December he was sent to Forrest Hall Prison, better known as "The Last Ditch," then Carroll Prison and Old Capitol where the Superintendent greeted him as an old friend. After a few months he was transferred to gloomy Fort Delaware, near Wilmington.

Then, in another moment of exquisite aptness, life again turned artist in Belle's story.

Even the most romantic of writers would hesitate to have Belle securing the release of her husband by threatening the President of the United States with disclosures of scandal in his government. . . .

Yet we find that Belle did threaten Lincoln with publishing "many atrocious circumstances" of his government unless he released Hardinge by late March; that ten days after the letter was written Stanton's chief of staff sent a "special" order releasing Hardinge and requested a personal acknowledgement that the order was complied with; that the commandant of the prison anxiously inquired of Hardinge if he planned to take the next boat to England; that Hardinge sailed for England under special order of safe conduct issued by the War Department!

Belle's letter to Lincoln, discovered when the Lincoln Papers were reopened, was written from the Brunswick Hotel, Piccadilly, and dated January 24, 1865. It reads:

> I have heard from good authority that if I suppress the book "Belle Boyd in Camp and Prison," by Belle Boyd, 1865, I have now ready for publication, you may be induced to consider the case of my husband, Samuel Wilde Hardinge, now a prisoner in Fort Delaware.
>
> I think it would be well for you and me to come to some definite understanding. My book was not originally intended to be more than a personal narrative, but since my husband's unjust arrest I had intended to make it political. I had introduced many atrocious circumstances respecting your government with which I am well acquainted and which would probably open the eyes of Europe to many things which the world on this side of the water little dreams

—if you will release my husband and set him free, so that he may join me in London the beginning of March, I will pledge my word that my book shall be suppressed—should my husband not be with me by the 25th of March, I shall at once place my book in the hands of a publisher.

Trusting an immediate reply,
I am sir, your obedient servant,
Belle Boyd Hardinge

It is inconceivable that Lincoln would yield to such a threat. None the less, and charge it if you will to a strange coincidence, on February 4, Stanton's chief of staff sent the following message to General Schoepf, commandant of Fort Delaware.

SPECIAL ORDERS NO. 62.
The Secretary of War directs the release of S. Wilde Hardinge, a prisoner at Fort Delaware. Acknowledge receipt and inform me when Mr. Hardinge leaves the Island. (Signed) James A. Hardie, Col. and Insp-Genl.

Schoepf himself delivered the order to Hardinge in his cell. Schoepf seemed anxious about Sam's plans.

"I presume that you will leave on the first steamer?" he asked. Sam said he would.

Schoepf seemed so eager to get Sam off his hands, he ordered him rowed at once to the mainland. He was left off on a wind-swept dock, ill and weak, wearing a threadbare coat, a crownless black hat, one boot and the other foot wrapped in rags.

The weather was bitter and there were no wagons on the road to Wilmington. It took him all day to walk the sixteen miles.

Under a special safe conduct issued by the War Department he sailed for London aboard the Cunard steamer, *Cuba,* which docked at Liverpool on February 19—nine days before the deadline Belle had set.

If Lincoln didn't order Hardinge's release, who did? There is little doubt that some top-level authority acted, and acted immediately. The order signed by Hardie emphasized that this was no casual order.

Hardie's position must also be considered. After Rappahannock he was selected by McClellan to arbitrate the dispute between Burnside and Franklin; McClellan also selected Hardie to prepare his celebrated War Department memorial; and it was Hardie who had carried the secret message transferring the field command from Hooker to Mead before Gettysburg.

Had Hardie acted on Stanton's orders? . . . Did Stanton, who had jailed Belle twice, by-pass Lincoln because he was afraid of the "atrocious circumstances" she threatened to expose? . . . And what were Belle's terrible secrets? . . .

The answers may never be known. Belle kept her bargain and "suppressed" her secrets in her book.

However, the recently discovered memoirs of Pryce Lewis, the Pinkerton spy, who had been sentenced to death with Timothy Webster in Richmond, gives a hint of one of the disclosures Belle may have had in mind.

In 1863 Lewis and Scully, another Pinkerton operative, were released through the efforts of Humphrey Marshall, a Confederate general and Richmond lawyer. As Lewis wrote in his memoirs, he had promised Marshall one hundred dollars in gold or one thousand dollars in Confederacy money, for helping them. Lewis attempted to send the money to Marshall but his messenger was intercepted by Butler at Fortress Monroe and the money was returned to the War Department.

Lewis then appealed to Pinkerton who said he would "see Stanton about it." According to Lewis, Belle was released and delivered the money to General Marshall. Her escort was the former commander of Lincoln's bodyguard who may have been on hand to make sure she was not molested by Butler.

If Stanton did order Hardinge's release, he may have had this in mind. Certainly it doesn't make a pretty picture; the Secretary of War, giving an enemy spy a hundred dollars in gold to smuggle past his own general, to pay a Confederate general. . . .

There is additional evidence that Belle's threats were not those of a boasting woman.

George Sala, one of England's outstanding journalists at the time, in his foreword to Belle's book, writes that Belle, "is in possession of a vast amount of information implicating certain high officials at Washington in public and private scandals, which she deems it imprudent at present to publish. The time is not yet."

Then there is the observation of Dennis Mahoney to be considered. This experienced, well-balanced newspaper editor says in his memoirs that the notes which were passed to Belle from the other Confederate officers in Old Capitol Prison, contained secret information, and the publication of those letters would have been interesting. But then he too points out, "that must come later."

Meanwhile, Hardinge, unaware of the strange intrigue surrounding his release from prison, rushed to Belle's side after the *Cuba* docked at Liverpool. But they were to be together for only a few short months. Sometime in July Sam died in London, and the story-book romance of the Rebel spy and her dearest enemy came to an end.

The stage, two husbands, a daughter and death in June, 1900, followed for Belle.

She rests today under a white cross in beautiful Kilbourn Cemetery, Wisconsin Dells, Wisconsin. Her epitaph reads:

BELLE BOYD
CONFEDERATE SPY
BORN IN VIRGINIA
DIED IN WISCONSIN.
ERECTED BY A COMRADE.

Belle would have been proud of the last line.

Scout of the Cumberland

IN HIS biography of Pauline Cushman, written in 1868, and in that typically florid style of the time ("Lo! This was the beast she was to serve!"), F. L. Sarmiento portrays her as a desperate woman of great beauty whose intrigue and daring made her the *femme fatale* of the Civil War.

Few will dispute Pauline's gypsylike beauty. But compared to the intrigue and daring of those two romantic Confederate agents, Rose O'Neale Greenhow and Belle Boyd, her service to the Union as a spy behind the Rebel lines in Tennessee, appears to be not of great importance.

Instead, we like Pauline as Charles J. Eastman, an old Arizona pioneer remembered her in Case Grande on a windy night in January, 1884.

I was drunk as a coot [he wrote] when I met her on the corner of Top and Bottom Streets. The Major—that's what we called her —stopped me and asked me if I had seen that 'long-legged husband' of hers, Jere Fryer. I replied I didn't keep track of other women's husbands. No sooner had I said this when she yanked out that damned forty-five of hers, cocked it and stuck it in my belly.

"I asked you a civil question," she said real mad like, "and I want an answer due to a lady."

It seems I got sober in a hurry with that damn gun in my belly and I swept off my hat and gave her a bow.

"No ma'am," I said, "I haven't seen your illustrious husband, Mr. Fryer."

"Now that's the way to answer a lady," she said, and to my great relief took that forty-five away from my grub sack.

Although she is more colorful, more flesh and blood as a frontierswoman than as the ludicrous heroine of Sarmiento's biography it would be an injustice to her memory to ignore her services to the Union under Rosecrans in Tennessee.

Pauline was born in New Orleans, June 10, 1833. Her father was a Spanish dry-goods merchant with a good business. Pauline's picture at twenty, lends truth to the legend that her mother was a French beauty. When she was about ten her father's business failed and he moved his family to Grand Rapids, Michigan, where he opened a frontier trading post.

She grew up among the Chippewas who traded at her father's post. They called her Laughing Breeze and a chief gave her a pony. The young bucks taught her to ride bareback and the Indian women showed her how to prepare a pelt and cook a puppy stew. By fifteen she was a dark-haired beauty who had every Indian brave, trader, and soldier at the post pursuing her. She could ride, shoot and guide the frailest of canoes through the rapids with the greatest of ease.

Her biographer relates a highly fanciful story of an Indian chief, "Leaping Thunder," who falls in love with Pauline. A dramatic scene in which the chief steals out into the night to tell Pauline of his great love follows. Then the chief is off to the wars to win her heart!

There is a grand battle in which the chief kills a rival chief and is brought back to the post bleeding but triumphant.

With his tattered Buffalo robe thrown over his shoulder he gives Pauline a long and fiery account of his deeds. He ends with a plea to her to return to his tepee. But Pauline refuses and tells him in a farewell speech she is "the breath of civilization—the Indian and the pale face cannot mingle!" His face stolid and expressionless, the chief turns away and returns to his people. Of course it is all nonsense and typical of the popular literature of the time.

After the incident with the chief, Pauline left Grand Rapids for New York. There she met Thomas Placide, manager of the New Orleans Varieties, "who was struck by her handsome face and figure." He offered her a part in his show and she accepted. She was then about eighteen.

She graduated to lead parts, sharing top billing with John McDonough, the matinee idol of his day, in *The Seven Sisters*. The big scene had thirty-four girls in tights, each representing a state, lined up on the stage in front of a painting showing several politicians aboard the *Constitution* breaking a club over a Negro's head.

Pauline played the role of North Carolina. When asked by "Uncle Sam" what she thought of the painting, she cried out, "I say the only respectable figure in the whole batch is the almighty nigger."

In another scene, again as North Carolina, she is asked her opinion of a slave auction. At this point Pauline walked to the center of the stage, threw out her hands and recited, "There are greater sins at the doors of this nation, than the fiddle and hoe on a cotton plantation."

She never failed to bring down the house. As the *Louisville Journal* reported: "She was warmly applauded in every scene."

In January, 1863, the troupe opened at Wood's Theater, Louisville, Tennessee, with Pauline playing the role of "a young man of fashion," who closed the last act by opening a bottle of champagne and toasting the Union.

One night two paroled Confederate officers approached her with an offer of three hundred dollars to drink a toast to the Confederacy in this scene, "just to see what effect it would have on the audience."

Pauline told the officers she would think over their proposition and to return the next day.

That night after the play she reported the incident to the provost marshal to whom she had been introduced backstage a few days before, and asked his advice.

"I advise you to drink the toast," he told her. "I request you in the name of your country for a deeper reason than you know."

Then he outlined a plan in which she would join his secret service in the role of a Rebel sympathizer.

Pauline accepted. That afternoon she sent word to the Rebel officers that she would give a toast to Jeff Davis that night.

Three hundred paroled Confederate officers and men crowded the aisles and the balcony of Wood's Theater. The air was electric with tension and more than one fist fight broke out before the lights were turned low and the curtain raised.

The South and the North tried to outdo each other in applauding Pauline. The play was interrupted many times. Men in blue cheered and stamped their boots until the building shook, when Pauline appeared. But the Rebels knew the secret and they answered with "Dixie" and the high-keening Rebel cry.

A tense quiet fell as the vital scene opened. Pauline was seated at a table. The cork popped and champagne foamed in her glass. Walking to the edge of the stage, she held the glass and cried, "Here's to Jeff Davis and the Southern Confederacy—may the South always retain its honor and its rights!"

The Confederates roared gleefully; the Federals shouted, hooted, and jeered. Hats, cushions, and bottles showered on the stage. Fist fights broke out. Men leaped over chairs, wrestled up and down the aisles; sabres flashed and a shot rang out.

The curtain came down and a provost patrol came upon the double. The theater was a shambles when the last customer was booted out.

The outraged owner gave Pauline her notice with a prediction she would be arrested before sunup. Pauline ignored him but told her leading man she couldn't help her outburst; in her heart she was loyal to the South and the Cause.

She met the provost marshal in secret that same night to be congratulated. He told her her next assignment was to pose as a boy and loiter on Market Street, where the Rebel spies were supposed to be hiding. After a week of this the provost decided she was more valuable as a woman and sent her among the cafés and saloons frequented by her Confederate admirers.

Here she was much more successful. For months she danced and sang in the smoky saloons, charmed secrets from the Rebel officers, and became the toast of Louisville.

One night a Nashville producer saw her dance and asked the manager of Wood's Theater about her. He told him, "She's a good-looking girl and an accomplished actress, but she talks secesh. If you can keep her out of the provost marshal's hands you'll have a good thing."

The producer was opening a new theater in Nashville, and offered Pauline a leading role. She told the provost in Louisville who wired William Truesdail, chief of the army of the Cumberland's police. Truesdail urged Pauline to accept, hinting of a great task he wanted her to perform. The next day she left for Nashville with a delegation of Confederate officers to see her off.

In Nashville, Truesdail may have had Pauline in mind when he was writing to General Rosecrans in January, 1863, that he had "someone in mind who could get to Bragg's headquarters for us."

The Official Records tell us Truesdail wielded enormous power over headquarters of the army of the Cumberland. He was a close friend of General Rosecrans and evidently answerable only to him. In May, 1863, Assistant Secretary of War Scott, in a letter to Stanton, charged that Truesdail had deliberately "inactivated" the army of the Cumberland until "he and his contractors grew rich." Stanton did nothing and another general who tried to tell Rosecrans about Truesdail's corruption was advised to mind his own business.

Despite his crooked activities, Truesdail was an excellent army police chief. His reports to Rosecrans were intelligent and informative.

He employed a number of spies, most of them young and attractive women. After one of his operatives had refused to return behind the Rebel lines, he sent a "Miss Falcon" who sent a report in a loaf of bread," that 5,000 Rebels are in Cumberland Gap with two companies of cavalry."

Truesdail sent for Pauline after she had appeared in a week's run of *The Rake* at Allan's New Theater. He asked her if she was prepared to accept "an undertaking of unusual and extreme danger."

She agreed, "for I love my country very dearly." Then Truesdail went to a large wall map and with a pointer sketched for her the present military situation.

After the bloody battle of Stone's River in the last, bitterly cold days of 1862, the battered Confederates under General Braxton Bragg fell back to Shelbyville, twenty-five miles south of Murfreesboro, and some twenty miles north of Tullahoma. Bragg's right was posted at Wartrace, with a strong corps occupying the passes at Liberty, Hoover, and Bellbuckle Gaps. His extreme right was protected by cavalry with headquarters at McMinnville, while his cavalry on the left, under Forrest, had headquarters at Columbia.

As Truesdail told her, the Rebel army was strongly entrenched behind heavy works which had been feverishly prepared since the battle at Stone's River.

His pointer moved to Tullahoma, "a small straggling village," but a highly important railroad junction and Bragg's main supply depot. The Duck River, a deep narrow river with only a few bridges and fords, covered its front, with a rocky range of hills immediately south. Like Shelbyville, it was strongly fortified.

Truesdail explained that General Rosecrans needed information regarding the Rebel strength at both Shelbyville and Tullahoma. Would she go behind the enemy lines and find out what she could? . . .

"It is a rough road lined more with hemp than corn," Pauline said.

"The whole fate of General Rosecrans campaign may depend on the information we receive," Truesdail replied.

Pauline hesitated. Then she said she would go.

Truesdail sketched his plan. Under Special Order Number 16, she was to be "evicted" from Nashville, along with several other female Southern sympathizers. She was to make her way south, ostensibly searching for her brother, a major on Bragg's staff.

"When you reach the commanding officer of a camp, ask him to

103

give you a kind letter to the next commanding officer, and so on until you reach the command in which your brother may be," Truesdail said.

He instructed her how to answer questions of suspicious Confederate officers. Never, he warned, was she to ask outright as to strength of forces, movements of units, artillery, or locations of ammunitions.

He praised her beauty and said she would "undoubtedly" attract many Rebel officers who would ask her to inspect camps or go riding. Pauline blushed prettily when Truesdail suggested she accept these offers, "seeming cautious as to the propriety of such excursions." Once in the camp she was to ask to visit the "brave lads" in the hospitals.

Truesdail instructed her "to inquire if they had enough drugs, the number of sick and so on."

The next day Pauline was escorted to the Federal lines in a carriage and sent on her way. At a designated rendezvous, three miles from Nashville, she met one of Truesdail's men who gave her a horse and some clothes.

In the late afternoon she met a smuggler who bought her horse for three hundred Confederate dollars and guided her across the Cumberland to Columbia.

Several officers who remembered her from New Orleans gave her a rousing welcome. Word of her arrival spread through the town and as Truesdail had predicted, "Rebel officers were soon waiting upon her to squire her on riding trips."

Two weeks later she was on her way to Shelbyville. There a handsome and solicitous Rebel artillery officer took her on a tour of the works "searching for her brother."

That night in the hotel room she disobeyed Truesdail's orders and made several "crude but effective sketches" of the Rebel works. Before she left Shelbyville she executed a wonderful coup by stealing some plans from the desk of an engineering officer, who had left the room to write her a note of introduction to General Braxton Bragg's aide-de-camp.

She hid the sketches and the plans in her boot.

Capture by guerillas on her way to Shelbyville, and escape to Tullahoma in the south, where she had "several stirring adventures," which her biographer thought were so unimportant he doesn't give any details, followed. Then back to Columbia where she met a Rebel quartermaster from Vicksburg, "and Venus conquered Mars."

She stayed in Columbia for several weeks, gathering information from the quartermaster and other Rebel officers and wondering how she could return to Nashville without arousing suspicion.

Then, as she relates, Providence answered her prayers and sent her to the owner of the Richmond Theater who offered to star her in a new production. When she told him her gowns were back in Nashville he urged her to go there, collect her trunks, and join him in Richmond.

The Rebel quartermaster was brokenhearted but gallant. He wrote her a love poem in farewell, promising to meet her in Richmond "at all costs."

On her way to Nashville she was picked up by a Rebel scout and taken to General John Hunt Morgan, the Rebel Raider, whom she calls "the tenderest of captors."

Morgan sent her to Franklin under guard but Pauline escaped in a wild storm. In the darkness she managed to pass through two Rebel picket lines. But eight miles from the outskirts of Nashville she was recaptured and returned to Morgan's headquarters. The Rebel Raider, now not so gallant, sent her to General Forrest's headquarters.

Forrest in turn sent her to Bragg's headquarters, "because your case is a grave one."

She was court-martialed at Shelbyville after the provost marshal discovered the sketches she had made and the drawings she had stolen from the Rebel engineer some weeks earlier. In June she was sentenced to death, although it seems implausible that Bragg would have allowed her to be hanged.

On June 25, in a steady downpour, Rosecrans launched a three-pronged drive on Shelbyville, Wartrace, and Tullahoma. In her cell, Pauline could hear the booming of the guns and the rattle of musketry. On the twenty-seventh, the Federal cavalry smashed the advancing Rebel army and drove it back in disorder to Shelbyville. In the afternoon Bragg abandoned the town.

Union sympathizers removed Pauline from her cell to the home of a physician as Federal troops marched in.

A report filed by Brigadier General J. A. Garfield, of the army of the Cumberland, in the War Records, National Archives, states:

> Miss Cushman was employed by William Truesdail, chief of the army police, to make a trip within enemy lines. She was captured upon her return within eight miles of Nashville by Rebel cavalry. She was taken to Bragg's headquarters suffering from severe exposure during her trip. She was taken sick and found today in this

condition by General Granger's command. General Granger ordered her removed to Nashville.

Pauline disagrees with this version. As she relates, it was her idea to leave Shelbyville because it made her "dream of gibbets; of horrid hangmen coiling great ropes around my poor neck; of prisons with a rebel guard pacing up and down ceaselessly before my door. . . ."

Then, as she remembered, General Granger called her his "wilful, naughty girl!" and let her go.

A few days after her return to Nashville, Pauline collapsed from nervous exhaustion.

When he was advised of her condition, Truesdail wired his headquarters from Tullahoma that she was to have "every possible care."

She was removed in a litter to the boardinghouse of Mrs. Clara Kidel on Church and High Streets, and put under Mrs. Kidel's care. Pauline lists General Rosecrans as one of her visitors. This may be true. There is evidence that Rosecrans did take a personal interest in her case. A letter in the Archives, dated November 8, 1863, orders a Captain Goodwin "upon instructions of General Rosecrans to pay Mrs. Clara Kidel $80 for the care and boarding of Miss Pauline Cushman, while in the employ of General Rosecrans, commander of the Department of the Cumberland."

Apparently Mrs. Kidel had some difficulty collecting her board bill. Another undated letter from the provost marshal's office, endorses the bill and asks that it be paid "on instructions of General Rosecrans." The letter disclosed Mrs. Kidel dismissed three boarders "in order to take care of Miss Cushman."

While she was sick in bed, General Rosecrans and Brigadier General Garfield, his chief of staff, made her an honorary "Major of Cavalry," with permission to "procure and wear all the necessary equipment befitting her rank."

The women of Nashville presented her with a "costly riding habit trimmed in military style," and Granger came to the sick room to pin the maple leafs on her shoulder straps.

From her bed, Pauline made a pretty speech in which she promised to "honor and maintain her title as long as life continues."

Granger gave her a salute and the wet-eyed ladies cheered. Tea was served and as the Nashville paper reported, "It was a stirring afternoon."

Pauline was fully recovered by August. In September she set out on a highly successful personal appearance tour of the country. The *New*

York Herald described her as the "gallant Scout of the Cumberland who did such noble work for the Union in Tennessee."

In San Francisco hundreds lined up to buy tickets hours before the box office opened. The drama critic of the *San Francisco Bulletin* wrote:

> She appeared before the audience in a Major's uniform and looked every inch a man. The part she played in the Stereoptican Grand Combination was to recall, as the placard said, 'her startling adventures.' Her narrative was interesting and had she relaxed it apart from the rest of the show it would have been outstanding.

For the next ten years Pauline toured the country, reciting her "narrative" in theaters from New York to frontier mining towns where enthusiastic audiences saluted her with volleys from their six-shooters.

When her story wore thin she formed her own stock company in 1871. The rough mining towns of Virginia City and Carson, Nevada, applauded her that year in *Little Nell, The Marchioness,* and *Nicholas Nickleby.*

Before the tour ended her stage manager hired a handsome young dark-haired actor. He attracted Pauline's attention and she inquired about him. His name was James Ward, the stage manager told her, from New York. Young Ward seemed to hypnotize Pauline. As she later said, she "sensed" something of a great actor in him. At every opportunity she praised his ability to the stage manager and theater owners, predicting that some day he would be one of America's great tragedians. Ward, who fulfilled all of her predictions, repaid her kindness in a strange way many years later.

In 1875, somewhere in the east, Pauline met and fell in love with Dr. Samuel Orr, an army surgeon. It was to be a brief romance. The physician accompanied Pauline to San Francisco where she starred in *The French Spy* at the Metropolitan. As usual she was well received by the critics.

Pauline and Dr. Orr stopped at the Grand Hotel in San Francisco, then the most famous on the west coast. There they "occupied different sleeping apartments but had in common a reception parlor." One afternoon she called for a bellboy and young Mike Rice answered.

Mike's unpublished memoirs, written when he was eighty, for the Arizona Pioneer's Historical Society, described that first meeting. He writes:

107

It was my fate—or fortune if you will—to be the bell hop who answered the call of Pauline Cushman and Dr. Orr.

In the parlor I found a number of people seated around a large center table, one of whom I recognized as John McCullough, the most famous tragedian of that or any other time in Thespian history, another was Tom Hitch, the famous silver tongued orator of the West.

As I stood waiting I was accosted by a woman of magnificent physique, with large, lustrous, slow black eyes, raven ringlets falling almost to her waist, with the profile of a Madonna and a voice as melodious as a lute.

And this is no overdraft either, at the time she was all this.

She asked me if she could have allotted to her a special servant to wait on her during her sojourn. I informed her that such a service could be arranged by calling the chief clerk. She scrutinized me closely and after a few questions as to my knowledge of the city, and especially the theaters, she went to the tube, called the chief clerk and asked to have me allotted to her as special attendant, and I entered the Major's service forthwith. . . .

This was Mike's first meeting with Pauline. His last was to be memorable. *The French Spy* closed after a month's successful run at the Metropolitan. One day Dr. Orr packed his bags and left for Camp Bowie, Arizona, where he died not long after.

Pauline gave up her apartment at the Grand Hotel, moving to less expensive quarters. She devoted most of her time to writing her "memoirs." She may have been dissatisfied with Sarmiento's ludicrous biography and planned to publish her own story.

Mike left Pauline, "grudgingly on her part," to join Lotta Crabtree's stock company then touring the west. Mike played several minor roles, but, as he relates, "the Mummer's life did not appeal to me and I returned to San Francisco."

On his return Mike learned Pauline had left the stage and was managing the La Honda, a fashionable resort hotel, just south of San Francisco. He found her there, "Monarch of all she surveyed."

Mike stayed on as a bellboy until Pauline's "regime terminated in a very abrupt manner."

As Mike relates it, one Sears, the owner of the La Honda, was infatuated with Pauline's dark beauty. But Pauline found him "repellent and firmly resisted all his advances." When his attentions became unbearable she resigned.

Sears, a man scorned, plotted his revenge. In the saloons, barber shop, and general store, he boasted of "scandalous things about his relations with her." The tales reached Pauline who promised Mike that Sears would regret his lies.

It was a bright spring day when she left. Mike carried their bags to the waiting stage. Pauline spent most of the morning circulating around the guests, saying good-by and hinting that something unusual was planned for her farewell.

The stage was scheduled to leave at nine. There were so many passengers some were forced to sit on the roof and cling to the baggage rail. Mike climbed to his seat behind the driver "where I was in a good position to see what I knew was about to take place." Nearly every guest in the hotel was on hand ready to see the "unusual" farewell.

Pauline appeared dressed in a handsome red-velvet gown. For a moment she stood on the porch looking over the whispering crowd, a strikingly beautiful woman with a flood of glossy black ringlets flowing down her back from beneath a plumed hat.

The door opened and Sears came out, slightly bewildered at the sight of so many guests. But soon he was "bowing and scraping" among them.

Pauline ignored him. With the bearing of a queen she walked up to the driver of the stage.

"Let me see your whip, driver," she asked in a low voice.

"Surely, ma'am," the driver said, and handed down his six horse-whip. Pauline coiled it carefully and walked back to where Sears was bowing to a lady guest. He was in a perfect position. Pauline stepped back and the whip cracked like a pistol shot. Sears leaped high in the air, holding his rear. The whip cracked again. Sears started to run but tripped. Pauline was on him like a raging tigress. From where he sat Mike could see the dust rise from Sears' breeches and jacket and the heavy whip rose and fell.

Cursing and howling, Sears got to his feet and ran up on the porch. Pauline chased after him. Just before he pulled open the screen door the black lash whizzed through the air, coiling about his neck and face like an infuriated python. Screaming with pain, Sears plunged through the door, without bothering to open it.

There wasn't a sound as Pauline carefully coiled the whip. As calmly as though she was going to tea, she walked up to the stage driver.

"Thank you, sir," she said. "It is a good whip."

The driver lifted his hat. "Thank ye, ma'am. All aboard!"

A gentleman opened the stage door. Another gentleman jumped up and offered Pauline his seat. She thanked him with a flashing smile. The whip snaked through the air—this time above the heads of the horses, and the stage lurched forward. The driver whooped and shouted and Mike clung to the seat. He told himself that the slanderer, Sears, had "received a genuine horsewhipping."

The incident made headlines in San Francisco with graphic eye-witness accounts. The *Chronicle* headline read: A TRADUCER TROUNCED.

Pauline stayed in San Francisco for several months, "leading a sedentary life." Later, in partnership with a man named Chandler, she moved to Santa Cruz, California, where they staked a large claim in the great redwood forest of the Santa Cruz Mountains.

They built an enormous log house which became well known as a hotel for fishermen and hunters. The partnership lasted a year. Pauline sold out her interest "for a liberal sum" and moved to Santa Cruz.

Another admirer, name unknown, began to pursue her. Pauline asked him not to annoy her. He refused. One day he insisted on joining her at dinner.

"Please leave me," Pauline said.

"No . . . no . . . I must see you . . . talk to you . . ." the admirer said.

"Please go . . ."

"No . . . No . . ."

Pauline jumped to her feet. As the man started to rise, she broke a vase over his head. Her soup followed. Then the sugar jar. Another vase and a dish.

As Mike relates, "She didn't use a horsewhip on this occasion, but she piled on the unfortunate's head all the delft on the dining room table."

The incident didn't make her popular in Santa Cruz. Her admirer was a well-liked business man. As Mike remembered: "It was generally conceded that Pauline's action was uncalled for and a great indignity had been heaped (sic) on a reputable citizen."

From Santa Cruz Pauline went to San Gabriel Mission where she opened a large inn. Within a year it had become the most popular hostel in that section of California.

One day Jere Fryer, dark and handsome, appeared in San Gabriel. Pauline saw him and fell in love. Her courtship was direct but successful. She told Fryer she was in love with him and wanted to marry him.

Fryer was startled but, after thinking it over, said yes. Although Pauline was at least fifteen years older than Fryer, she was still a beautiful woman. There was no gray in her jet-black ringlets. Her dark eyes still crackled with fire, her lips were soft, and her voice remained melodious as a lute. Or so Mike remembered.

In 1879, the first year of their marriage, they bought the hotel and livery stable in Casa Grande, Arizona, a frontier settlement of only five permanent residents.

The hotel was incredibly dirty. Pauline scrubbed it from top to bottom while Fryer cleaned the livery stable. In a week's time it was opened for business.

July 4, 1879, was a memorable day for the tiny community. A rider had come in the night before with the news that the railroad had reached Tucson and Casa Grande was to be the terminal.

It was a clear hot morning with just enough breeze to make it comfortable. After the Casa Grande's guests had their breakfast Jere Fryer toasted the day with a drink. By eight o'clock he was roaring drunk.

"I'm going to get the Dutchman over and give him a drink," he shouted to Pauline and lurched out of the hotel, followed by his friend, Louis Dupey, who waved an American flag.

In the street, Fryer blazed away with his colt at the sign of the Buckalew and Ochoa General store. Dupey joined him. The quiet morning shook with the crash of six-shooters.

A model of propriety, Pauline appeared on the steps of the hotel.

"Mr. Fryer," she shouted, "you come in this minute and stop that damn shooting."

"Whoopee," cried Fryer and the B. and O. sign splintered under a fresh barrage.

"Let's get the Dutchman," he shouted.

"A god damn good idea," Dupey answered.

"We'll make him drink a toast to the good old U.S.A.," Fryer said, plugging the sign.

"Let's go," his friend said, waving his flag.

They advanced up the street, guns blazing.

Pauline watched them for a minute, then laughed and went inside. After all, it was Independence Day.

About the time Fryer and his friend were shattering the B. and O. sign, a frightened young man carrying a carpet bag, stepped down from the freight train which had chugged to a stop at the depot across the street.

He gulped when he saw Fryer and Dupey stagger out into the street and fire away at the sign. He stood petrified as they marched up the street, both guns working.

As Perry Wildeman recalls in his unpublished memoirs: "I will never forget my first impression of the country and its inhabitants."

In a few minutes, as Wildeman relates, Fryer and Dupey came out of the B. and O. store with "the German fellow, who had charge of the store, and whose place I was to take, walking between them."

Whooping, waving their flags, and puncturing the doors and windows of Smith and Watzlavzick, another general store, Fryer and Dupey escorted the German, "who was quiet and of a retired disposition," to the Casa Grande Hotel.

Pauline broke out a bottle of Monongahela. The German storekeeper protested he didn't drink. Fryer roared that it would be an insult to refuse to drink with him. To emphasize how grave an insult it would be, he placed his six-shooter on the bar.

The B. and O. storekeeper saw the light. He agreed it would be an insult. He lifted his glass, and they "drank to that great American Bird" of freedom and several other patriotic institutions.

Meanwhile, back at the depot, young Wildeman anxiously asked the agent if it was customary for citizens of Casa Grande to be escorted up and down the street with flag waving and gunfire.

The agent assured him there was "no danger."

"Why," he said, "those two men who are celebrating the holiday are the leading citizens of this town, namely Jere Fryer and Louis Dupey."

He then explained that "as the population consisted of only five persons, it was incumbent upon them to see that our national anniversary was properly remembered."

The celebration lasted all day. Families from the outlying districts drove to town to hitch up at the hotel. By late afternoon the B. and O. storekeeper was dead drunk. He had toasted every president from Washington on and every state from Maine to California.

The boisterous hours passed. Pauline saw to it that the little German storekeeper, her husband, and several other guests were laid side by side in the cool livery stable to sleep it off. Then she took over the bar, knocking together the heads of two young ranchers who thought they were gun fighters, and throwing one mule skinner out into the street when he insisted on trying to shoot a glass from another skinner's head.

At the station young Wildeman "remained in the shade trying to keep out of sight," wondering gloomily "what future this rough and tough frontier town which I had chosen as my home held for me." As he remembered many years later, it had been a shattering experience.

By late afternoon the celebration subsided, "owing to the heat and the effect of the stimulating beverage." Wildeman said a shaky good-by to the agent and walked across the street to the hotel.

The adobe house was cool and now very quiet. As Wildeman entered Pauline came out of the bar to meet him. Wildeman thought her face was familiar. Within a few minutes she had put him at ease. She gave him the best accommodations and "put aside any fear I may have had."

Suddenly a gear tripped in his mind. Now he remembered where he had seen her.

But no, it couldn't be. . . .

"Are you Pauline Cushman?" he asked.

Pauline smiled and said she was.

For young Wildeman it was a happy ending to this terrible day. As a boy he had seen her on the stage of Barnum's Museum in New York, where she appeared in the uniform of a Major in the Union Army reciting her "narrative."

"I had always admired her as one of our nation's heroines," Wildeman recalled. "Now as a tenderfoot in this out of the world place, I adored her for the courtesy and motherly way in which she made me comfortable."

But, he added, "I shall never forget my first Fourth of July in Arizona."

The hotel prospered. As the *Arizona Daily Star* in Tucson reported that December:

> Mrs. Pauline Fryer is very attentive to her guests and her house is very popular. Everything is kept clean and bright and not only travelers but residents of Casa Grande appreciate her efforts to please.

About 1880 the Southern Pacific Railroad came through and Casa Grande was made the terminal. The town boomed and grew overnight. Gun fighters, outlaws, horse thieves, skinners, and freighters rubbed elbows with homesteaders, ranchers, and pioneers. Pauline helped to maintain peace and order with a forty-five which now hung from her hip.

Charles J. Eastman, who had that interesting encounter with her on Top and Bottom Streets in 1884, recalls in his memoirs: "The Major was known as a 'square shooter' and an excellent nurse in taking care of anyone injured by bullet wounds and a woman who wanted to see fair play."

Pauline was also the unofficial referee in gun duels. One day in 1885, while preparing supper, she heard shouts. Strapping her forty-five about her waist, she ran out into the street. At Top and Bottom Streets two men slowly moved toward each other. Other men ducked into doorways and behind wagons.

Pauline recognized one of the men as Price Johnson. The other, Robinson, a rancher, she knew only by sight. There had been bad blood between them for a long time and each had sworn to kill the other on sight.

Both had a following. Now Johnson's men were gathering behind him; Robinson's already had their guns out. Top and Bottom Streets looked like the O.K. Corral in Tombstone when Wyatt Earp, his brothers, and Doc Holliday went in to wipe out Curly Bill Brocius's gang.

But Pauline had always vowed there would be no Tombstone gun fights in Casa Grande. She took her forty-five from its holster and walked to the corner and stood directly in the path of the two men.

"Fair play," she cried. "Let them kill each other but you boys keep out of it."

The gun leaped in her hand. The slugs ricocheted from an adobe wall. The two groups of followers hesitated. At this moment Price went for his gun. His draw was lightning fast. But Robinson's gun barked simultaneously. Neither man was hit. It became a running fight. They shot at each other from doorways and from behind wagons. Their followers had vanished. There was only Pauline standing in the street alone while the gun fighter and the rancher fought their duel around her.

She stood there, unafraid, holding the six-shooter, as the afternoon breeze played with her long dark hair and white apron.

Eastman, who witnessed the thrilling scene, writes: "Bullets whistled past within fifteen or twenty feet from where she was standing. At no time did she flinch."

The duel ended when Price fell with a slug through his stomach. Pauline slid her forty-five back in its holster and returned to her

114

kitchen—but only after she had prepared the body of the gun fighter for burial and had said "a few last words."

As Eastman says:

> This was the kind of timber our dear old lady pioneer was made of; afraid of nothing, open and above board in every way, and always ready to help her fellow man out. No one ever went hungry or wanted a bed while the Major was alive.

Next to her love for "fair play" was her affection for animals. Even the cantankerous mules which hauled the supplies for Florence and Silver King won a warm spot in her heart. She would never tolerate a man beating a dog, horse, or mule. One freighter discovered this on a hot summer day.

He was husky, bearded and mean. His name was Blue and it was said he'd take the whiskers from a fly with his long black snake whip. He came into the Fryer's corral with a string of sore-shouldered mules and started to put them in the lead of a string of twenty animals. Pauline came to the corral gate and watched him silently for a moment.

"Those mules aren't in working condition, Blue," she said.

"They are as far as I can see," Blue growled.

"Well, you can't see very far," she snapped. "They shouldn't be worked."

Blue turned and glared at her. "These here are my mules and it's none of your damn business, anyhow," he said.

"Well, I'll make it my business," she said, coming closer.

The freighter stood his ground. He said again they were his mules and no woman was going to tell him how to run his team.

"You won't take these animals out of my corral in this condition," she said.

Blue looked at her and sneered.

"I'm going to take them out of this corral and what are you going to do about it?"

Pauline, her eyes blazing with fury, turned and walked back to the hotel. She brushed past some guests coming to the bar, went to the wall and took down her Winchester.

There was a box of shells in the desk. She loaded the rifle.

"Hey major, you going hunting?" one of the guests called.

"Yes," Pauline said, "for a skunk."

She marched to the corral and climbed the fence. In a clear voice

115

she called out, "If you try to drive those animals from this corral, Blue, I'll shoot you down."

Blue turned. Black eyes stared unblinkingly down the barrel at him. The clear voice commanded, "Unhitch those mules."

Men tiptoed from the hotel to find the best spots to see the show.

Blue, big and ugly, studied Pauline. In one hand he held his coiled whip. For a moment it looked as if he might snap it at the woman straddling the fence. He licked his lips.

"Unhitch those mules, Blue."

There was a breathless moment. Then the freighter broke. "A man can't run his own team," he grumbled as he unhitched the animals with the festering sores and replaced them with a fresh team.

Pauline sat on the fence, the rifle across her thighs, watching Blue. She didn't get down until the heavy wagon rumbled out of the corral and disappeared down Main Street in a cloud of dust.

As Mike Rice, who witnessed the scene, said: "This act on her part was generally approved by teamsters who were more humane than Blue, and it tended to take the starch out of a bully."

2

As the town grew the hotel prospered. The handsome Fryer welcomed the arrival of prosperity. It gave him more time to dazzle some of the newly arrived widows and young girls.

The tongues of the gossipers wagged furiously. Someone made it a point to inform Pauline that Jere was spending the evenings with a certain pretty blonde widow, instead of seeing about supplies for the livery stable and the hotel.

Pauline was furiously jealous. In the bar one night she confronted Fryer with the accusations. He vigorously and self-righteously denied them. Pauline forgave him and then proceeded to denounce the widow in no uncertain terms, listing her among the ladies of the world's oldest profession.

The gossips made sure that the widow heard—in detail—all that Pauline had said about her.

The blonde, not only pretty but well built and many years younger than Pauline, put on a sunbonnet and marched up Main Street to the Casa Grande Hotel. The word that there was going to be a showdown between her and Pauline spread through the community like a prairie fire.

Men and women rushed out of houses and stores. The loungers' bench in the shade of the depot was empty for the first time since the explosive Independence Day. Pauline was rounding up some mules in the corral and the audience fought for the widest cracks in the fence to see the show.

Mike Rice, Fryer himself, and several cronies had box seats. As Mike recalls: "It was a magnificent Donny Brook event—and the major's Waterloo."

The widow marched right into the corral. There were a few words. Then the blonde swung from the hip. Pauline was knocked off her feet. But she was back in a moment. A whistling right almost tore off the blonde's head, but her left blackened Pauline's eye.

It was a long and grueling fight, fought in frontier fashion, with both parties completely ignoring the honorable rules laid down by the Marquis of Queensbury.

The blonde beat and kicked Pauline from one end of the corral to the other. Both of her eyes were blackened and her lips and cheeks cut. She used Pauline's long black hair to her advantage. When she left she had a large handful.

The name of Pauline's conqueror is lost to posterity because Mike refused to name her. And wisely so. He writes: "I would give the name of this belligerent female but I understand she is still in the ring, and is said to still possess that vigorous punch."

Her defeat seemed to have taken something from Pauline. Her cocksureness and her self-confidence seemed gone. Fryer himself, as Mike relates, was "visibly affected at the finis" and tried to comfort his wife. But her fire and zest were gone. Perhaps in the quiet of the hot room, where she brooded for days afterward, she first noticed the gray in her hair, the wrinkles in her neck, and the once flawless skin that the relentless Arizona sun had made coarse and tough.

Fryer soon tired of her brooding and sullen ways and sought gentler pastures to be soothed and loved.

Sometime in the mid-eighties he was elected sheriff of Puma County and he and Pauline moved to Florence, the county seat. Florence held more beauties and Jere became bolder and brazener in his transgressions.

Frantic with grief and driven almost out of her mind by jealousy, Pauline planned an elaborate plot to save her marriage. It ended only in tragedy and sadness. But as tragedy will often do, it brought them together for a brief time, perhaps closer together than at any other time in their rough, married life.

One of the few people who knew her secret was Mike Rice. In the twilight of his life he wrote it as he had witnessed it.

He gives no date but it must have been 1882 when Pauline heard of an unwed woman in from Picket Post who was going to have a baby. Ordinarily the news would never have disturbed Pauline. Preachers on the frontier weren't too numerous and many a couple went through the marriage ceremony about the time the third child was ready to be born.

But that night the news stuck in her mind. Her marriage was crumbling . . . she could read the pity in the eyes of other women . . . Jere's affairs were the talk of the town . . . this woman . . . a baby . . .

A child could save their marriage!

She saw the woman the next day, and, as Mike relates, "conspired to get the baby and pass it off on Fryer as his own."

Then Pauline went to Fryer with shining eyes to tell him he was about to become a father. Jere was stunned, then deliriously happy. When Pauline begged him to allow her to go to San Francisco to a big maternity hospital he consented at once.

As Mike remembered: "She was gone for several months."

One day Fryer ran into the sheriff's office, waving a telegram.

"I'm a father," he shouted, dancing about the office. "I'm the father of a girl."

"Never was a man so elated as he at the glad tidings, and he celebrated the event, regardless of expense," Mike remembered.

A week later Pauline arrived with the precious bundle in her arms. Jere approached, hat in hand. She tenderly opened the blanket. He stared, a foolish smile on his face.

"I am the happiest man in Arizona," he whispered.

The child brought about a complete reconciliation. Fryer was home every night. The blondes and widows were forgotten. Both he and Pauline showed an almost "fanatical devotion" to the child.

The child was baptized and christened Emma Pauline. Tragedy struck a few months later. One night the little girl's body suddenly stiffened, then shook with spasms. When the doctor arrived he told them gravely that the little one had an incurable nervous disorder and could live for only a few years.

They were both stunned. When Pauline wept bitterly, Jere took her hand and for the rest of the night they clung to one another listening to the labored breathing of the infant that had become the only real thing in their rough lives.

A bitter six years passed. There was scarcely a night that Pauline or Jere did not walk the floors until dawn with the screaming little girl.

Mike, sharing Pauline's terrible secret, also shared her grief. As he tells it, he too carried the child up and down the room as the spasms shook her little body.

"Once," he writes, "her little limbs contracted and she actually bounced out of the cradle onto the floor."

As a last resort doctors suggested a change of climate. Pauline had relatives in Michigan and took the child there. On April 18, 1888, Jere and Mike were in the sheriff's office when a telegram arrived. Jere tore it open. His face hardened and he turned away.

"The baby is dead," he said bitterly.

In its account of the child's death the *Arizona Weekly Enterprise* said little Emma was stricken while on the train returning to Arizona. A stop was made at Gremont, Nebraska, but the child was completely paralyzed. Death came an hour later.

Her place of birth was given as San Francisco, California. Her age, six years, five months and three days.

The sad homecoming and the funeral followed. Pauline had aged considerably. Her face was drawn and her hair streaked with gray.

Then, like a horrible vulture preying on the dead, the dead child's mother appeared demanding her baby. The secret burst like a bombshell in the quiet community. Grief-stricken and shaken with shame, Pauline faced the man she loved, who demanded to know if this were true.

Had she denied it, Fryer would have undoubtedly believed her. But Pauline courageously admitted it was true. She told him that she loved him and that was why she had done it.

Had Fryer been a man of stronger character, such courage and devotion would have humbled him; but he only denounced her as a fraud. Pauline left soon after for San Francisco. Only Mike was at the station to see her off.

In San Francisco Pauline tried to make a comeback on the stage, but nobody was interested. Stage managers, in the back rows of dark theaters, only snickered when she recited her "narrative" in a harsh, cracked voice.

Nobody was interested in the Civil War any more, they told her. This was a new age of gas buggies and telephones. A few who remembered when the magic of her name filled their houses week after week were touched and promised her a spot "as soon as it was convenient." It was never convenient.

About 1890 Mike met Pauline for the last time. She was stopping at the Hotel Baldwin, "quartered in a magnificent suite of room."

Mike was surprised to discover she was again the old Pauline; once again she was the fiery woman who had been heroine of the army of the Cumberland and toast of a thousand audiences from New York to Deadwood.

She bounced to her feet and gave him a big hug. In the long visit old times were relived. Then, as he was leaving, Pauline "commanded" Mike to call again in the afternoon as "she had an important mission."

In his memoirs Mike underlines the word "command," adding: "And I mean that word. Even then a command from the Major brooked no denial."

He returned in the late afternoon. Pauline handed him an envelope.

"Take this to the box office of the Baldwin Theater and there wait for a reply," she told him.

The theater was just down the street. Mystified, Mike delivered the envelope to the box office.

"Oh, Mr. Ward," the ticket seller said, turning to a distinguished black-haired man who stood next to him, "this is addressed to you."

Ward ripped open the note. He read it rapidly, exclaiming, "Good God! Pauline Cushman!" Turning to the box office man he said, "Give me the best two in the house."

"But Mr. Ward—" the man began to protest.

"Dammit, give me the best two," Ward snapped.

The clerk gave him the tickets. Ward handed them to Mike, who was listening, open-mouthed.

"Tell Miss Cushman these are with my regards. I look forward to seeing her this evening," Ward said.

When Mike gave Pauline the tickets she threw them on the table as though she had never doubted for a moment that Ward would refuse her.

"You will escort me to the play tonight," she told Mike.

Mike declined, but she insisted "and as insistence with her was just that, I consented to appease her whim."

When Mike returned that evening he was horrified. A painted and roughened harridan greeted him. Her face was thick with powder and paint; her hair done up in a colonial style. She wore a flowing ancient and mildewed robe of black satin, topped off by a Gainsborough hat with two towering white plumes.

"Your arm, if you please," she said. Mike, wishing the earth would open and swallow him, weakly offered his arm.

All activity in the lobby stopped as they appeared. Men and women stared at the terrible apparition stalking toward the door, on the arm of the obviously embarrassed man in evening clothes. The startled doorman swung open the door. Pauline and Mike walked down the street. Passers-by gaped. Hansom cabs jerked to a stop. A policeman forgot to direct traffic.

In the theater they were ushered to a box on the level with the stage. Mike recalled: "It was the most conspicuous place in that big and fashionable theater overlooking the dress circle."

Pauline made him sit alongside her. Every lorgnette and opera glass was trained on the box. An usher spread the news "that Pauline Cushman, the spy of the rebellion was an occupant."

Mike sat there, sweating and wishing "there was some means to crawl out and enter myself into oblivion. Any old Arizona burro puncher would appreciate how I felt."

The show was a horror. Pauline's cracked voice commenting on the play and the actors could be heard all over the theater. She hailed Ward's appearance with a burst of applause and called out to him. Ward gallantly bowed and blew her a kiss.

Between acts she held court in the box. Reporters, actors, actresses, society matrons, fought to shake her hand. She whistled and hooted to friends in the audience, waving her fan furiously and talking continuously. As she grew more excited the sweat rolled down her face, crisscrossing the layers of powder and melting the rouge.

It was the worst night in Mike's life. As he remembered: "I was so badly shattered that I don't know to this day the name of the play."

After the play Ward waved away his followers and entered Pauline's box. He insisted that she join him and the cast for a supper at Taits, a fashionable restaurant. But Mike could stand no more. He weakly shook his head and went out.

The next day when he came to say good-by she upbraided him fiercely for his "lack of gallantry." She wept when she recalled how he had left her at the hands of "notoriety seekers," but she forgave him on his promise to attend another supper planned by Ward for that evening.

At the supper Mike heard Senator William M. Stewart of Nevada announce that he had introduced a bill demanding $10,000 from the government to pay Pauline for her services in the Civil War. The bill, he said, would be passed just before Congress would adjourn.

That night Pauline and Mike said a sad good-by. They both knew they would never see each other again.

Pauline never made her comeback. The royal suite at the Baldwin took all her savings, forcing her to move to Mrs. Taylor's Lodging House at 1118 Market Street.

Finally the woman who had thrilled a country with her deeds behind Rebel lines in Tennessee; who had known the cheers of the audiences at Barnum's in New York; the six-shooter salutes in the frontier theaters; who had stood unflinchingly between two killers as they shot it out on the streets of Casa Grande; horsewhipped a scandalmonger and made a tough mule skinner back down—went to work as a scrub woman.

She did it quietly and shamefully. Mrs. Taylor was sorry for the proud old woman who quite plainly had once been beautiful, but whose face was now haggard and worn, her untidy hair almost all gray, her shoes broken and her dress ragged.

Pauline lived at the lodginghouse for three years, scarcely leaving her back room except to go to work two or three times a week. All that was left were memories.

Rheumatism and arthritis racked her body. Night after night she lay alone, moaning with pain. The doctor prescribed morphine tablets but she told Mrs. Taylor she was afraid to take them "because she feared they might reach her heart."

At ten o'clock on December 7, 1893, Mrs. Taylor knocked softly on Pauline's door. She became alarmed when there was no answer. Another lodger forced in the door. They found Pauline dead.

The police were notified and the body was taken to the morgue. A coroner's inquest, according to the *San Francisco Call,* found she had died from an overdose of morphine, "taken without suicidal intent and to relieve pain."

No next of kin could be located and the coroner ordered the body buried in Potter's Field.

Mrs. Taylor, who had grown to like the quiet old lady, was horrified. She stormed down to the headquarters of the Grand Army of the Republic—the American Legion of its day—and told them about the old lady who lay alone in the morgue.

The *Call* and the *Chronicle* played the story on page one, retelling the story of Pauline's life. Contributions flowed in, "to prevent this indignity being offered to one whose love of country made her risk her life so much in its cause."

The whole city was aroused. Pauline was removed from the bare morgue and taken to the undertaking parlors of Craig and Cochran, on Mint Avenue. A "handsome, cloth-covered casket" was supplied.

The Woman's Relief Corps sent over a large American flag and an honor guard.

On Saturday morning, after a simple service at the Central Methodist Church, the funeral procession wound its way through the city. There were at least a hundred men in faded blue uniforms present, and the Women's Relief Corps.

In Oakdale Cemetery, in the Grand Army plot near the Cliff House, Pauline was laid to rest, with Federal rifles crashing in tribute.

The simple marker read:

PAULINE CUSHMAN, FEDERAL SPY AND SCOUT OF THE CUMBERLAND

The headline in the *Arizona Daily Citizen* might have pleased her more. It read: PAULINE CUSHMAN IS NOT FORGOTTEN.

Spinster of a Rebel Parish

THIS is the most dangerous woman in Richmond. Watch her tiny figure shuffle along the street: large poke bonnet, sweeping black dress, a market basket laden with fruit and books on one arm. She has a thin face and eyes like dark stars. Her lips form a thin line. There is something vital about her, as of a mind, constantly alert, active, nothing of a dreamer. Her personality is magnetic.

She is Miss Elizabeth Van Lew, age forty-seven, looking like the maiden aunt of Jo March but living as desperately as any woman in our history; visiting the Confederacy's prisons, administering to the sick, dying, lonely, and heartsick; planning mass prison escapes and hiding the fugitives in her secret room. Spies and couriers constantly come and go at her beautiful house. An angry mob will threaten to burn down her home but she will defy it. Hidden in her library is a horse who nibbles at the bindings of her classics. On a windy April night she will stand over an open coffin, calmly instructing her agents how to smuggle the corpse of the famous boy through the Rebel lines. She will raise an enormous American flag over burning Richmond, hours before the Union Army enters.

"For four years she was the sole representative of the power of the United States Government behind Rebel lines," wrote General George Henry Sharpe, then chief of the United States Army's Bureau of Military Intelligence.

"Ma'am, you have given me the most valuable intelligence I received from Richmond during the war," General Grant told her, as he sat drinking tea on the piazza of her mansion.

"There is no lady in the country whom I would rather meet than yourself," wrote General Benjamin Butler, whom the women of New Orleans called "The Beast."

"A damned witch," a man said thirty years after her death.

Her private physician remembered she had a "sharp and brilliant mind."

She was "God's angel," to a sergeant, to whom she had given some grapes when he was burning with fever on his straw pallet in Libby Prison.

Miss Van Lew's story is to be found in her five-hundred-page "diary" now in the Manuscript Room of the New York Public Library. It is not a diary in the sense that is a day-to-day account, nor does it flow chronologically. Rather it is a collection of impressions, graphic descriptions, philosophies, letters jotted down on ledger paper and stationery of the army of the Potomac, in hasty, almost illegible hen-scratches. She is always reticent and cautious.

It is obvious why she was careful not to incriminate herself. As she remembered after the war:

> If you spoke in your parlor or in your chamber to your next of heart, you whispered. You looked under the lounges and the beds. The threats, scowls, the frowns of an irritated community—who can write of them? I have had brave men shake their fists in my face and say terrible things. We had threats of being driven away, threats of fire and threats of death.
>
> "You dare to show sympathy for any of those prisoners," said a gentleman, shaking his finger in my face—"I would shoot them as I would blackbirds—and there is something on foot up against you *now!*"
>
> I would bring my writing to the bed each night—only to destroy it in the morning. Oh, God we had no friends . . .

Her diary describes the Van Lew family. Her father, a Hollander, was born in Jamaica, Long Island. He was an only son. His great-aunt, "Aunt Letitia Smith, nee Van Lew," was a heroine of the Revolution, carrying dispatches to Washington's army in New York after the evacuation of Long Island. She was finally imprisoned in an old church, used by the British, "where she witnessed fearful scenes of suffering." Family tradition ruled the eldest become a Latin professor. But Miss Van Lew's father scorned tradition; he wanted to become a merchant. His father was angry but finally agreed. His son left Jamaica, "on good terms with all," for Virginia. In Richmond he became a partner in a hardware business with Dr. John Adams, son of a Richard Adams of the House of Burgesses and the Virginia assembly.

The business failed. Young Van Lew's share of the debt was $10,000.

"My father always said that debt had to be honorably paid," Miss Van Lew writes, "and it was."

Van Lew returned alone to the hardware business. This time it prospered, "to become the first and distinct hardware business in Virginia."

On a trip to Philadelphia about 1820, he met and fell in love with Elizabeth Baker, the tiny, bright-eyed daughter of Hillary Baker, mayor of Philadelphia, who died in the yellow fever plague in 1798. The young merchant brought his bride to Richmond, and they were married in St. John's Church, made famous by Patrick Henry's ringing speech. Across the street was the beautiful Adams' home where their wedding reception was held.

Van Lew was well acquainted with the Adams' house on Church Hill, highest of Richmond's seven hills. Many times he had sat on the rear piazza with Dr. Adams and the children to watch the setting sun tinge the waters of the James a golden hue. He loved the terraced gardens and the roses Mrs. Adams sent down to his store.

The house had been built in 1799 by Dr. Adams, "in a choice spot." It was three-and-a-half stories, its stuccoed walls bleached with scotch limestone brought over as ballast in pre-Revolutionary ships. In the front was a high porch with four white pillars. Twin, semi-circular steps with decorated iron balustrades lead up on either side to the porch. The rear of the house was most attractive, looking down on the terraced gardens, gravel walks, summer houses, rustic iron seats, a moss-rimmed spring, and out to the waters of the James.

The rooms were large with an eighteen-foot hall running through the house. There was an enormous library where, of course, Lafayette accepted a glass of water from one of the Adams children in 1824.

After dinner one night, over their brandy and cigars, Van Lew asked Dr. Adams to sell him the house he had cherished for so long. But the scholarly doctor told him he would never sell as long as he lived.

On October 17, 1817, the Van Lew's first child, a girl, was born. She was christened Elizabeth. When she was seven, Dr. Adams died and his widow sold the house on Church Hill to Van Lew. Before she left, Mrs. Adams showed Van Lew the mansion's secret room.

It was on the top floor at the end of a hall. A small door opened into a large closet. Neatly fitted into the plaster was a door which in turn opened into the south portico. Under the broad roof was a room large enough to hide twenty to fifty men.

The yellowing diary tells of her childhood; of tutors and private schools, of music teachers, dancing instructors, and a gay young groom who taught her how to ride. When she grew older her father sent her to Philadelphia where she stayed with her mother's family and attended a private school.

The city of brotherly love would mold her conviction that no man, white or black, should be enslaved. While she was there her brother, John, was born.

Shortly after her return from Philadelphia, she persuaded her father to free their fifteen slaves. One, Mary Elizabeth Bowser, she sent to Philadelphia to be educated.

In Miss Van Lew's teens the great white house was a center of Richmond's social activities. Her diary tells of great balls, garden parties, of rides through the countryside in the family coach drawn by four white horses, all evenly matched; of vacations at White Sulphur Springs.

There were many distinguished guests. Bishop Moore, Justice Marshall, the Lees, Robinsons, Wickhams, Adams, Cabells, Carringtons; Fredericka Bremer, the Swedish novelist, recalled her visit to the Van Lews in her book, *Homes Of The New World;* Jenny Lind's magnificent voice filled the music room one soft April afternoon; Edgar Allan Poe solemnly read "The Raven" in the library. The windows rattled under the last of a spring thunder storm, and the wind moaned about the house as the melancholy voice read on for the shivering listeners.

The question of slavery occupied much of Miss Van Lew's time. The *Richmond Times* says that upon her return from Philadelphia, "where she absorbed Abolitionist principles and contracted a fevered hatred for slavery," she and novelist Fredericka Bremer paid many visits to the tobacco warehouses and colored jails, "weeping over the conditions of the inmates."

Miss Van Lew remained a spinster. In about 1855, her brother John had married. In 1860 her father—"a good man and a Whig"—died, leaving "a substantial fortune." John took over the management of the hardware business.

Miss Van Lew and her mother now lived alone attended by a number of devoted servants. There were no longer elaborate balls and dinners but Miss Van Lew and her mother gave an occasional tea for the ladies of Richmond.

Their quiet, cultured world tumbled down about them when John Brown led his fanatics against Harpers Ferry. It was then Miss Van Lew really began her war "diary."

"From that time [Brown's raid]," she wrote, "our people were in a palpable state of war." Virginia passed the Ordinance of Secession and Richmond went war mad. Upon her return from a trip to town, Miss Van Lew wrote:

> Such flag-making, such flag presenting—the drums, the fifes and the marching! For my life I would not have dared to play Yankee Doodle, Hail Columbia, or the Star Spangled Banner, our hallowed national anthems. Instead it was the blood-stained Marseillaise resounding through the streets.
>
> My country— Oh, my country! God help us these sorry days!

Then in 1861 Sumter fell and civil war was upon the land. Miss Van Lew now had reached the crossroads in her life; would she travel the easy road and side with old friends and neighbors against the North, or would she take the other path which stretched out before her, strewn with thorns of hate and bitterness, black with hopelessness and despair.

She never hesitated. With an amazing courage she openly declared that she and her mother were sympathetic to the Northern Abolitionists.

When she appeared in town, dressed in black and wearing a large sunbonnet, a servant at her heels, she was always the center of bitter arguments, "speaking dispassionately but making it clear to all of Richmond, whose side she had taken."

As she wrote after one such trip in town:

> "We have gone to war in the nick of time, and John Brown's raid was a God-send," say the women.
>
> The women all work, sewing and knitting, making clothes for the soldiers. "Kill as many Yankees as you can for me" is the favor they ask. Mr. Lincoln's head, or a piece of his ear or some precious relic, is coveted.
>
> Our favorite heroine is Charlotte Corday. For once the whole South has something to do. Hospitals were put under charge of the women and everything is on a war footing. The arrest of suspected loyalists goes on every day. . . .

Marching troops filled the street, and "Dixie" was heard everywhere. One day a delegation of women from Richmond called at the Van Lew mansion. The air was chilly as the ladies balanced their tea cups discussing new babies, flowers, and the weather.

128

The formalities over, one of the ladies said bluntly, "Miss Van Lew, we would like you to help us make shirts for our gallant soldiers."

Miss Van Lew, who was standing at a window, walked across the large room and took her mother's frail hand in hers.

For a moment the two women clung to each other. Then Miss Van Lew said quietly, "I am sorry but we cannot. Our sympathy is with the North in this unhappy war."

There was a moment of shocked silence. The ladies rose. A servant brought their wraps. Without a word they left. And in the silence of the room, Miss Van Lew surely heard the crackling flames of the bridges she had burned behind her.

Threats, revilement followed. Old friends turned their heads when she came to town to market. Street toughs hooted when the coach and four passed.

Beauregard's victory over McDowell at Bull Run, July, 1861, rang through the South like the clang of a giant bell. The Union troops had been completely shattered and sent reeling back into Washington. For a time it looked like Beauregard and Johnson would storm Washington itself.

Federal prisoners and wounded streamed into Richmond by the hundreds to soon fill to capacity the old ship's chandlers warehouse, called Libby Prison; Castle Thunder, and Belle Isle.

With a servant carrying a large market basket filled with fruit, Miss Van Lew haunted the official departments of the Confederate Government for permission to visit the Federal prisoners.

When she visited the tobacco warehouse on East Cary Street, Lieutenant Todd, President Lincoln's brother-in-law, told her, "You are the first and only lady to make such an application."

She was shunted from office to office. At last she was told Brigadier General J. H. Winder, provost marshal of Richmond, was the only one who could issue her a prison pass.

She made several discreet inquiries. She was told Secretary of Treasury Memminger, "a gentleman who loved flattery," could intercede for her with Winder.

Miss Van Lew paid a visit to the Treasury Department. Memminger was horrified and indignant when he heard her request. He told her that the prisons "were not fit for a lady to visit" and that she should be sewing for the Confederate troops and not visiting the captured Yankees.

She gave Memminger a soulful glance. "Mr. Memminger, I once heard you speak very beautifully on the subject of religion."

Memminger "relaxed" with a smile. "Ah," he said, "and you liked my discourse."

"Very much," Miss Van Lew answered. "You said that love was the fulfillment of the law, and if we wished our cause to succeed, we must begin with charity to the thankless and the unworthy."

Memminger straightened up with a self-conscious cough. "Yes, yes," he said, "now about this pass?"

A few minutes later she was on her way to Winder's office with a letter of introduction. The head of the secret police was conferring with his detectives when she entered but, "I was graciously received."

As Miss Van Lew wrote: "His beautiful white hair was waved in beautiful locks. After sitting a moment I said to him, 'your hair would adorn the Temple of Janus, it looks out of place here.'"

Miss Van Lew was granted her pass, permitting her "to visit the prisoners and to send them books, luxuries, delicacies, and what she may please."

For four years she visited Libby Prison, Castle Thunder, Castle Goodwin, and Belle Isle, administering to the Federal prisoners. Lieutenant Todd "was won by gingerbread and my buttermilk," but she never tells us how she won over "Anti-Christ" Caphart, the notorious jailer of Belle Isle.

In the Van Lew Collection there is mute evidence of the affection which the half-starved Union prisoners held for her. A small cardboard box holds pins and rings carved from bones and ivory. Some have tiny American flags painted on them in painstaking detail. There is a beautiful replica of a Bible carved from a solid block of kindling wood, with the appropriate lettering and inscription: "EVL —A Friend Indeed."

There are no records to tell us when Miss Van Lew became the North's secret agent in Richmond. It was probably shortly after First Bull Run. Either General Sharpe, or General Ben Butler sent an agent through the lines to give her the cipher on the two-inch scrap of green paper which she pasted in the back of her silver watch. The watch never left her.

The next step was a bold one. She summoned her ex-slave, Mary Elizabeth Bowser, from Philadelphia, "provided her with abundant references," and sent her to the Confederacy's White House, seeking work. Jefferson Davis hired her as a servant. It is more than legend that abstracts of military orders were often on their way North by one of Miss Van Lew's couriers, even before they reached Rebel commanders in the field.

A penciled note on a scrap of ledger paper, unsigned, and not in Miss Van Lew's handwriting, tells how she sent her dispatches through the lines:

> She had many ways of sending this information through the Rebel lines; sometimes she would send it by persons who were comparative strangers to her. In that case she wrote out her cipher in invisible ink, a liquid which looked like water and could be brought out by milk and heat.

Beside Mary Elizabeth Bowser, at Jeff Davis's elbow, Miss Van Lew's other sources of information were the Federal prisoners who established a method of counting horses, troops, and guns leaving the city. From the routes, Miss Van Lew was able to guess at their probable destination. Careless and boastful guards made their contributions. Some, like one, "Bull Head," could be stung by taunts to reveal troop movements or military moves.

In July, 1861, there were fifteen senior officers to be saved from the noose. They were held as hostages to be executed, should the North hang a similar number of the crew of the Confederate privateer, *Savannah*, captured in May by the United States brig, *Perry*.

The privateersmen had been taken to New York and placed in the Tombs, in cells set aside for felons. The North announced they would be tried as pirates. On July 6, President Jefferson Davis sent a vigorous protest to Lincoln under a flag of truce. Lincoln declined to see Davis's aide but the communication was forwarded through General Winfield Scott, who promised a reply. None was made.

After three sweltering weeks in jail, the manacled prisoners were paraded through the streets to City Hall Park and the United States Circuit Court, to plead innocent to Federal indictments charging them with piracy.

The case became an international cause *célèbre*. The British House of Lords severely criticized Lincoln's actions, with the Lord Chancellor giving the opinion that those who treated a privateersman "as a pirate would be guilty of murder."

In October the privateersman went on trial. The North's chief witness was a renegade crew member. After a stormy hearing, the jury retired. Twenty-three hours later they reported they were deadlocked. They were dismissed and the date for a retrial set.

In Philadelphia the captain and three members of the privateer,

Jefferson Davis, were tried in Federal Court and found guilty of piracy. They were all sentenced to the gallows.

All the South was enraged. In Richmond, Jefferson Davis announced that he would "demonstrate that the word retaliation in the Confederate vocabulary meant action." On November 9, he ordered General Winder to "choose by lots among the prisoners of war of highest rank," an equal number of prisoners who were to be thrown into "felon cells" and hanged, should the North carry out its threat.

On the tenth, in a dramatic scene in Winder's office in Richmond, the names of the hostages were placed in a can. In the presence of several captured Union officers and Congressman Ely of New York, who had gone out in a carriage to see the Battle of Bull Run, only to be captured in the debacle, the names were drawn. Six colonels, six lieutenant colonels and three captains were picked. They were all removed to cells in the city prison.

Among them was Lieutenant Colonel Paul Revere of the Twentieth Massachusetts.

When the Confederate Government made its announcement, Miss Van Lew hurried down to Winder's office to charm him into giving her a pass to see the hostages. With all that was positively known against her, the spinster of the Rebel parish got one as before.

During the anxious days she visited the prison, bringing the hostages food, smuggling out letters to their families, and giving Lieutenant Colonel Revere sums of money from her own purse.

The North was silent. The sands seemed to be running out. Winder's office prepared for the mass execution. With Miss Van Lew's help, Lieutenant Colonel Revere planned a desperate escape. But as the hour was about to strike, the North backed down. In New York the privateersmen were removed from the common prisons to military prisons "and accorded the status of prisoners of war."

Revere and his men were sent back to Belle Isle and Libby. He told Miss Van Lew he would never forget her kindness. He would die in the war but his account with her would be balanced.

The first year of the war passed. The gold shoulder knots of the cavaliers tarnished, their plumes drooped, their horses became leaner. In Richmond the guards no longer joked with Miss Van Lew. At the tobacco warehouse on Main Street, she overheard a guard say, "that he would rather know that he could only live for one week, than to live for six months on the food the prisoners got; that he could not imagine how they stood it."

A tobacco-chewing guard told her, "The German troops would just as soon shoot down these damn prisoners; just take them out and shoot them. . . ."

There is little doubt that both sides committed atrocities. In the North, guards at Old Capitol accepted bribes to allow Rebel prisoners to escape, only to shoot them in the back as they scaled the wooden walls; in Richmond, Miss Van Lew heard a snickering guard "boast how they had butchered some prisoners they were transporting to Richmond from points below."

In 1862, Miss Van Lew carried on a blazing feud with Owen B. Hill, acting assistant surgeon of Confederate prison hospitals. It began on a bitterly cold day in January. As usual, Miss Van Lew made her daily tour of the prisons. This day a servant carried jars of freshly made custard.

To her surprise the guards refused to admit her. However, she left the custard and returned home. At noon a captain returned the jars. There was a curt note from Dr. Hill. It read: "Nothing to eat shall go into the hospital except that furnished by the company of the post."

Miss Van Lew gently asked the captain, "Did you taste the custard, captain?"

The captain, who may have flushed under the gaze of the steady black eyes, replied, "Yes, ma'am."

"Was it good, captain?" she asked.

The captain nodded. "Yes, it was, ma'am," he said, "and would be beneficial to the prisoners, if I could give it to them—but I cannot."

Within the hour she was at the War Department in Richmond protesting Dr. Hill's order. Assistant Secretary of War Bledsoe told her Dr. Hill had no right to issue such an order. He promised to see Secretary of War Benjamin and have the order revoked.

"To prove the custard was innocent of all evil," she relates, "I left it at the War Office for the honorable gentleman, hoping that it might move them to humanity."

The next morning Miss Van Lew called on Bledsoe. He sent out a note saying Secretary of War Benjamin "refused to act on your application, which he has sent to General Winder's office."

Bledsoe ended his note: "The custard was very nice and thanks to you. I borrowed some cups from an eating place nearby and bought some crackers. So it was eaten in fine style. . . ."

She was at Winder's office the next day—with more custard. That afternoon the prisoners had their custard. How did she get the pass?

"Oh, I could flatter anything out of old Winder, so great was his love of flattery," Miss Van Lew told a niece many years later.

The gallant little lady did much more than just deliver custard to starving prisoners. As General Sharpe wrote in 1866: "Her whole library was strewn about the prisons." Some of the books left the prisons in her shopping bag. The guards never gave them anything but a casual glance. But in the candlelight in her room Miss Van Lew carefully studied each book, line by line and page by page. There were curious pin points above some letters. These she carefully wrote down. Hours later, eyes smarting from the strain, she was ready to send north a complete message.

Her favorite method of slipping dispatches past the guards was in the double bottom of an old French plate warmer.

One day Miss Van Lew heard a new guard say to another guard as she passed, "I think I'll have a look at that the next time she comes in."

On her next visit when she arrived at the gate, the guard demanded to examine the plate warmer.

"Certainly, sir," she said, slipping off the shawl she had wrapped about the bottom of the plate warmer, placed it into the guard's outstretched hands. He dropped it with a yell.

Her visits to the jail were not unnoticed. Among her papers is a yellowed newspaper clipping with the headline, RAPPED ON THE KNUCKLES. It reads:

> This is a warning to certain females of Southern residence (not perhaps birth) but of decidedly Northern proclivities. If such people do not wish to be exposed and dealt with as alien enemies to their country, they would do well to cut stick with their worthless carcass while they can do so with safety. . . .

In faded ink is written in the margin: "These ladies were my mother and myself. God knows it was little we could do."

Then McClellan sailed out of Washington and began his drive up the Peninsula. Intelligence trickled down from the North that his army was strong enough to smash the Confederates. Miss Van Lew and the few Northern sympathizers secretly planned to welcome him into the city. On Thursday a "charming chamber" was prepared for McClellan "with new matting and pretty curtains."

On Saturday June 21, a captain of the guards at Castle Thunder warned her, "You have been reported several times."

A few days later a shabbily dressed young man knocked on the front door of the Van Lew mansion. A servant ushered him into the library where Miss Van Lew was writing at a desk.

As she studied the young man a feeling of dread swept over her. She guessed correctly that he was one of Winder's detectives.

"May I inquire your business here, sir?" she asked.

"I wish to tell you something—something that will interest the government," he said vaguely.

"I know of nothing you can tell me that would be of interest to me," she replied.

"Perhaps you will let me board here," he asked.

"We have no room," she told him.

"Let me sleep in the library. . . ."

Miss Van Lew refused.

"Then I will sleep on the floor," he said. "I will sleep anywhere, it doesn't matter where. I wish the surroundings, yes, the surroundings —I must have them. . . ."

Miss Van Lew rang for tea, making countless excuses to the shabbily dressed young man, why he couldn't be her boarder. Finally she eased him out of the front door. Wearily she wrote that night: "We must be careful and circumspect—wise as serpents and harmless as doves, for truly the lions are seeking to devour us."

In Richmond, Winder's detectives plotted their next move to trap the lady in the great white house on Church Hill, with traitor's evidence.

A few days after the incident with Winder's detective, Miss Van Lew was awakened by the far-off rumbling of the guns. She sent a servant into Richmond with an order for her agents to gather.

In the afternoon she set out for the home of a Mr. Botts, where presumably the small group was meeting to greet McClellan. On the way Miss Van Lew had an excellent glimpse of war close at hand. That night she wrote a vivid report.

> The cannonading was heard more loudly as we approached. The excitement on the Mechanicsville Turnpike was more thrilling than I could conceive. Men riding and leading horses at full speed, the rattling of their gear, their canteens and arms, the rush of the poor beasts into and out of the pond at which they were watered; the dust, the cannons on the crop-roads and in the fields; the ambulances, the long line of infantry stretched by the side of the road, waiting their orders.

We enquired the news of the picket who stopped us. He told us that we were whipping the Federals, right, left and in the center and had taken many prisoners. The roar of the cannons grew louder. We were allowed to proceed as we were going only a short distance further. We found Mr. Botts and our friends listening to the roar of the artillery. The windows rattled and the flash of the bursting shells could be seen. The rapid succession of the guns were wonderful, the firing seemed to go around to the left. At nine o'clock it ceased. No ball could ever be exciting as our side this evening. I realized the bright rush of life; the hurry of death on the battlefield. . . .

It is a curious entry, hinting that perhaps love of the Union and hatred of slavery, were not the only motives which led Miss Van Lew to court danger and death. Under the bombazine was a fire-eater, a stormer of cannons, who loved the sound and fury of battle. It may be that the wounded, sick, and dying prisoners; the graveyards at midnight, the secret rooms, the prison escapes, the intrigue and spying were her symbolical battlefields, where in her heart she could experience "the bright rush of life."

Following McClellan's defeat, Miss Van Lew's position became more precarious. Threats were pinned to her front door. She was warned night riders would burn down her house. Winder's shabby young detective knocked again on her door. Again she gave him tea and made excuses as graciously as possible, why she could not take him in as a boarder. He stormed out, vowing to return.

As twilight fell she could see him through the curtains, "intently watching us" from behind the springhouse.

After the seven days of fighting, the carts rumbled into Richmond with the dying and the wounded. Miss Van Lew went down to the prison hospitals to beg her way past the guards. "The wagons, the carts, the private carriages, every vehicle that could be procured, was bringing in a sad load," she wrote. "The air was fetid with the presence of the wounded and the dead."

Day and night she nursed the sick and the dying. It was commonplace to see the little woman in black entering the prison early in the morning, and leaving as twilight fell over the city.

As the year came to a close, she was warned that Winder, under pressure of the ladies in Richmond, was about to cancel her prison pass, and perhaps place her under arrest.

When Miss Van Lew next visited the prisons the guards noticed that she had changed. Her dress was shabby and food-stained. The gray curls were no longer tied in a neat knot in the back of her head. When she passed through the gates the guards heard her singing softly to herself.

"Old Bet's gone crazy," they said. Soon they were calling her "Crazy Bet."

The townspeople took up the name. Children scampered after her in the street when she appeared, hooting and jeering, "Crazy Bet . . . look here Crazy Bet, you old witch . . ."

She only gave them a blank smile and continued to croon to herself. But in her diary she wrote: "They call me Crazy Bet but it helps me in my work."

2

During 1863, escapes were not infrequent from Libby Prison, Castle Thunder, or Castle Godwin. Sometimes they were almost unbelievably easy. Lieutenant Colonel F. F. Cavada in his *Libby Life* tells of a Union officer, formerly a tailor, who offered to make a new uniform for a Confederate major. The cloth was produced and the ex-tailor made not only one uniform, but two. The extra one he gave to a fellow officer. Dressed in the new uniforms they walked out of the prison, arm in arm. Several others, "attired like true Virginia gentlemen," wandered out through the surgeon's office. For weeks this trick worked, "only because of its confounded impudence."

But getting beyond the prison gates was only the first step to freedom. As Cavada says, "We all regarded the Confederacy as one huge military prison. To get through to our lines we had to have help from someone on the outside."

As the escapes increased Miss Van Lew became that "someone on the outside." By some mysterious underground, Union officers and men were delivered at night to the house on Church Hill to be hidden in the secret room.

One night in the winter of 1863, a child awoke in her room on the second floor of the Van Lew house. She was Miss Van Lew's niece, then about ten, paying her aunt a brief visit.

A sudden noise had awakened her. She sat up in bed, heart pounding. Outside her window trees creaked in the wind. Under each gust the house shuddered. There was a noise on the stairs. She slid out of bed, inching open her door. Her aunt, protecting the flame of a candle with one hand, was climbing the stairs to the attic.

The little girl tiptoed after her. She saw her aunt pause at the top of the stairs, then carefully lift out a panel in the wall. A man's thin, bearded face appeared like a weird jack-in-the-box. Miss Van Lew gave him a bag. The bearded face disappeared. After replacing the panel in the wall she climbed downstairs.

When the door of her aunt's room had closed her niece tiptoed up the stairs. In the moonlight the wall looked blank. She ran her hand along the plaster. Somehow the panel slid back. Terrified, she stared down at a man's bearded face. Before she could scream the man put his finger to his lips.

"If your aunt knew you were here, what a spanking you would get," he whispered. "Now put back the panel and go to sleep."

With trembling fingers the little girl pushed the secret door back into place. Just before it closed the man winked at her and roguishly put his finger to his lips.

Many years later, an old white-haired lady would remember that thrilling night and would again find the secret room, "for no one else knew where to find it."

In this strange melodrama of plots, escapes, prisoners, and secret rooms, appears a horse. If he had a name we don't know it. Nor do we know what he looked like. It is likely he was one of the four white horses that pulled the Van Lew family coach.

Lee had been forced to disband six cavalry units for lack of horses and the searchers for horseflesh were everywhere. It wasn't unusual for cavalry units to stop a merchant's wagon in the streets of Richmond and confiscate his horse. The *Whig* reported that one Williams, a baker, protested strongly to the government that a cavalry officer had taken his horse and left his wagon in the road.

On Church Hill there was only one horse left and Miss Van Lew was determined to keep him. For months she played a sort of cat and mouse game with the searchers. They tried to surprise her but she was always one step ahead of them. When the first cloud of dust betrayed the riders, the horse was hidden in the orchard or smoke-house, "sniffing the smokehouse air," in the shrubs, in the woods—anywhere. The searchers kept coming; the horse kept moving from place to place.

At last there was only one place left in which to hide the horse. The house. When the next riders were sighted, this incredibly inventive woman actually brought the horse up the front steps into the house, down the great hall to the library where the servants had covered the floor with straw!

She may be imagined, tired but triumphant, as she wrote that night:

He accepted at once his position and behaved as though he thoroughly understood matters, never stamping loud enough to be heard, nor neighing.

The library would serve as a stable many more times before Richmond fell. But the Van Lew's horse never became a Confederate mount.

3

The year turned. The high tide of the Confederacy was ebbing fast. The armies of Lee and Bragg faced an encircling movement from Sherman, from Butler on the James, from Meade on the Rapidan. In the other theaters of war, Beauregard was still at Charleston, and Kirby Smith at Shreveport. Shields and Geary occupied the Shenandoah; Banks was ready for his Red River expedition; Burnside at Knoxville. The South was defeated and some of their leaders knew it.

"We are rattling down hill," Colonel Ould, the Confederate exchange agent told Mrs. Chestnut at a dinner on the twenty-fifth of January.

Richmond's population had increased three times. Miss Van Lew scarcely knew the strangers on the streets; the rouged whores, fastidiously dressed gamblers; the beggars, thugs, thieves—all the scum that wars and armies attract.

It was bitterly cold that winter. In Libby, prisoners danced together in the light "of the near-sighted tallop-dips" to keep warm. Food was scarce. The Confederate commissary was low. In Libby, several hundred prisoners lived for a week on "stale corn-cake and cold hydrant water."

In January smallpox broke out in Libby and at Danville. Only a few died at Libby but as Lieutenant Colonel Cavada relates, the disease made "frightful havoc" at Danville with "hundreds carted to the graveyards." There was a mild epidemic at Belle Isle. Doctors examining the sick discovered a woman, "—a young girl of eighteen—" who had been a prisoner for a month. The gallant Confederates immediately discharged her and allowed the prisoners to collect a fund "to buy her garments suitable to her sex."

In the North, Stanton was saying that the South was starving Federal prisoners. In Richmond, General John Hunt Morgan, the Rebel raider, visited Libby and praised the jailers for their treatment of the prisoners.

The question of the prisoners was rapidly becoming a major issue with both sides. Miss Van Lew was to be vitally concerned with it as the bitterly cold days slipped by.

In the last week of January she learned momentous news. All Federal prisoners were to be removed from Richmond to the dread Andersonville Prison, the living ghosts of which haunted Northern homes for thirty years after.

How she learned the news she does not say. Nor does General Butler, commanding the army of the James, who received her dispatch. Mary Elizabeth Bowser, Miss Van Lew's spy in Jefferson Davis's household may have heard the news while serving dinner. Miss Van Lew indicates in her dispatch to Butler that the prisoners themselves told her.

She confirmed the information with two other spies. One she identifies only as "Quaker"; the other a "Mr. Palmer." Evidently they were both known to Butler.

On the night of January 30, with one of her couriers waiting to slip off through the darkness to the Northern lines, Miss Van Lew wrote the dispatch which was to have such fateful consequences.

The dispatch, written in cipher and addressed to Brigadier General Ben Butler at Fortress Monroe, reads:

It is intended to remove to Georgia very soon, all the Federal prisoners; butchers and bakers to go at once. They are already notified and selected. Quaker knows this to be true. They are building batteries on Danville Road. This from Quaker. Beware of new and rash councils. This I send to you by direction of all your friends. No attempt should be made with less than 30,000 cavalry, from 10,000 to 15,000 infantry to support them, amounting to all 40,000 or 45,000 troops. Do not underrate their strength or desperation. Forces probably could be called in from five to ten days; 25,000 mostly artillery, Stokes and Kemper's brigades go to North Carolina. Pickett's is in or around Petersburg. Three regiments of cavalry disbanded by Lee for want of horses. Morgan is appealing for 1,000 choice men for a raid.

The letter was signed, "Mr. Babcock," her code name.

Her messenger reached the Northern lines on the afternoon of

February 4. He was taken immediately to Butler. After he had given Butler "a private token" he was cross-examined by the General.

It would appear from his answers that the courier was one of Miss Van Lew's group and not a frightened farm hand. It doesn't require any exuberant fancy to imagine the scene in the dreary room of the old fortress: Butler with his bald head and bulging eyes looking like a huge toad, rumbling his questions at the weary courier whom he calls "boy," while his aide scribbles down the questions and answers.

This is the way the examination went. It is no fictionalized surmise.

Butler: Well, my boy, where did you get this dispatch?

Boy: Miss Van Lew gave it to me. I stayed with Miss Van Lew for a week before I went away. Miss Lizzie said she wanted to send you a letter and I said I would take it. Miss Lizzie said you would take care of me. I left there Saturday night. Miss Lizzie told me what to tell you.

Butler: What did she tell you to say? You need have no fear here.

Boy: She told me to tell you the situation of the army. Mr. Palmer got all the information he could for you. Lee has got about 25,000 men; there are about 15,000 men at Petersburg. The city battalion and two companies—Maryland companies—are at Richmond and about 1,800 or 2,000 at Chaffin's and Dewey's Bluff. Mr. Palmer said two brigades have gone to North Carolina about a week before I left. He found, though, just before I left that one stopped at Petersburg. The two brigades that went were Stokes and Kemper's. He thought that what (sic) available force could be got into Richmond in four or five days was 25,000 to 30,000 men. He says to say to you Richmond could be taken easier now than at any other time of the war. He thought it would take about 10,000 cavalry and 30,000 infantry.

Butler: Miss Van Lew says something in her letter about Quaker.

Boy: There is a man who goes by the name of Quaker. This is not his name but he does not wish anyone to know his real name. He does not wish to be known by any other name.

Butler: What of the prisoners?

Boy: They are sending the prisoners off to Georgia. Mr. Palmer said that he understood Lee was there in Richmond in secret session; but he said that was not reliable. Lee has about 25,000 available men. Miss Van Lew said not to undervalue

141

Lee's men. Quaker said his plan to take Richmond would be to make a feint at Petersburg; let Meade engage Lee on the Rappahannock, send 200 or 300 men and land there at the White House on the other side of Richmond so as to attract attention; then have 10,000 cavalry to go up in the evening and rush into Richmond the next morning.

Butler: How did you get past the lines?

Boy: Mr. Holmes got a man to guide me. He paid him $2,000 in Confederate money. He brought me to the Chickahominy and left me there. He fooled me. I came across the river. I got a boat. I don't think there are any men on the Chickahominy, or only a few cavalry. There are none nearer than Lee's army. At Chaffin's farm there is about a regiment. He told me to tell you that Dewey's Bluff is their strongest point; he said you must come around Richmond on the other side. Morgan is applying for a thousand men. The papers say he is going to make a raid into Kentucky. I don't believe that, though, for the papers would say so.

Butler: Anything else, boy?

Boy: Miss Van Lew said to stop the women passing from Baltimore to Richmond. She said they do a great deal of harm. She also said there was a Mrs. Graves who carried mail through to Portsmouth. She hoped you would catch her.

Butler sent a copy of the dispatch marked "private and immediate" to Stanton. He identified Miss Van Lew "as a lady in Richmond with whom I am in correspondence." He wrote that on the following Sunday "I will make a dash with 6,000 men, all I have that can possibly be spared. If we fail it will at least be in an attempt to do our duty and rescue our friends."

There was no raid that Sunday by Butler. Stanton evidently saw the folly of moving up the Peninsula with six thousand men when McClellan couldn't do it with two hundred thousand. To storm Richmond and free the Federal prisoners would require a stronger striking force.

There was a week of mysterious coming and going. The army was wild with rumors. Then Lincoln summoned General Judson Kilpatrick. The observers surmised that a cavalry officer meant a raid. Prisoners were on everybody's tongue lately. It must be a raid to free prisoners.

It was a badly kept secret. The Confederacy was not without spies in Washington and Jefferson Davis undoubtedly was well informed of the Federal's plans. As Colonel Lyman of Meade's staff wrote his wife:

For some days General Humphreys [Meade's Chief of Staff] has been a mass of mystery with his mouth pursed up and doing much writing by himself all to the great amusement of the bystanders who had heard even in Washington that some expedition or raid was on the tapis—a secret expedition with us is got up like a picnic, with everyone babbling or yelling. Kilpatrick is sent for by the President. Oh! Ah! Everybody knows it at once; he is a cavalry officer—it must be a raid . . . everybody devotes his entire energies to pumping the President and Kill—Cavalry! The idea is to liberate the prisoners, catch all the Rebel M.C. that are lying around loose and make tracks to our lines. . . .

Later he wrote: "All Willards [hotel] chatters of it . . ."

On the twenty-seventh General Meade wrote his wife that he was "occupied" with an attempt to send a cavalry force into Richmond to free Federal prisoners. Two days later he wrote her to say, "My cavalry expedition for Richmond got off last night. I trust they will be successful; it will be the greatest feat of the war, if they succeed and will immortalize them all. Young Dahlgren with his one leg went along with them."

Briefly this was the plan, based on Miss Van Lew's intelligence: Kilpatrick with four thousand men was to move from the left on to Richmond; a diversion from the right toward Charlottesville was to be made by Custer with two thousand cavalry, supported by the whole Sixth Corps and part of the Third Corps; a picked force under "young Dahlgren" was to move between Lee and Kilpatrick and make for Belle Isle, south of Richmond in the James, liberate the prisoners, then join Kilpatrick near Richmond. Both forces would then come out through the Peninsula to join Butler's army of the James.

"Young Dahlgren," who was to play such an important part in the life of Miss Van Lew, was Colonel Ulric Dahlgren, son of Rear Admiral J. A. Dahlgren.

At Gettysburg his right leg had been irretrievably shattered. In October it was amputated. But after a convalescent leave he had

143

joined Meade's cavalry, the youngest colonel in the army. He had an artificial leg but still required a crutch. He was a tall, slim lad with a tawny goatee. He was twenty-one.

On the twenty-sixth, two days before the raid, he wrote a note to his father. It was to be "a grand raid," he said, and if successful "will be the grandest thing on record." But if it failed, he said, he was prepared to "go up," as they said in that war.

On the night of February 28-29, Dahlgren picked three hundred raiders inside the arm of Kilpatrick's four thousand men and crossed the Rapidan. They separated at Spottsylvania, hurrying toward the South Anna River which he crossed on the night of the twenty-ninth. Guided by a Negro they crossed the James River Canal on March 1. The guide searched for the ford to cross the James River but couldn't find it. Accounts differ as to whether Dahlgren hanged the Negro. The force hurried toward Richmond. The next day they were on Plank Road, five miles from the city. They turned northeast, stopping at the home of Secretary of War Seddon where Dahlgren had a goblet of blackberry wine. Then on to the Pamaunkey River with the Home Guards sniping at them as they crossed on a ferry. He turned south with the countryside aroused. Rebel cavalry was closing in and the avenue of escape was lost. A heavy rain added to their misery.

At one o'clock on the night of March second the weary column halted for a few minutes. Suddenly the woods on all sides blazed with musket fire. Five bullets toppled Dahlgren from his saddle. Thirty-one of his men followed. The rest of the force withdrew into a meadow nearby. The Rebel cavalry ringed the meadow and waited through the night. In the dreary, wet dawn, an officer approached with a flag, demanding their surrender. After a consultation with his men, a captain turned over his sword.

Dahlgren's body was found face down in the mud. His memorandum book was taken, the little finger of his right hand cut off and a ring stolen, along with his coat.

That same morning, unaware the Union raiding party had been destroyed, Miss Van Lew walked about the city trying to buy corn.

The miller told her they were only grinding "for those who bring them corn." At the city dock she found a peck of corn selling for five dollars in gold. Prices were spiraling upward everywhere in the city. Apples were seventy-five cents apiece and a tiny slab of tobacco cost fifty cents.

A twelve-year-old boy found Dahlgren's body a few hours after he had been killed. He searched the body and found a gold watch. Some soldiers were amused when the boy told him he had pulled off the dead man's wooden leg. They rode out to see if this was true. It was and they left with the artificial leg. As the *Richmond News* said: "His artificial leg was a beautiful one. Such things were rare and in great demand in the Confederacy, and some of the officers or soldiers took possession of it."

Also found were Dahlgren's special orders and instructions to his command. The body was then buried, as Miss Van Lew says, "in a slashy mud hole, at the fork of the road where he fell."

On the fifth, the Richmond newspapers, which heretofore had called the captured officers "good looking men," lashed themselves into a frenzy over the documents which supposedly had been found on Dahlgren's body.

The orders were to sack Richmond and assassinate Jefferson Davis. On the seventh, the *Whig* demanded death for the "bandits." The dispatch on the ninth, tenth, and eleventh, called Dahlgren "a miserable wretch no worse than the rest of the Yankee commanders in crime."

The *Richmond Examiner* thundered that the name of "Ulric the Hun shall be linked henceforth with eternal infamy."

The corpse was disinterred and sent to Richmond where it arrived at the York River railroad depot, Sunday afternoon, March 6. The *Whig* and the *Examiner* reported "large crowds" viewed the body, laid out in a plain pine coffin.

On the seventh, Major Turner, commandant of Libby Prison, ordered "Captain" Martin Meredith Lipscomb, who held the contract for burying all Federal prisoners who died in Richmond, to bury the body. But when Lipscomb arrived at the depot, he found that the body had been claimed a few hours before by Major John Wilder Atkinson, commanding the Nineteenth Artillery.

Atkinson was acting under orders from Jefferson Davis to secretly bury the body "in the cemetery of a thousand grassless graves," the section of Oakwood Cemetery where the Federal prisoners were buried.

Dahlgren's body was buried in strict secrecy. A two-mule "government wagon" brought the coffin to the cemetery. A horseman, who was undoubtedly Major Atkinson, rode ahead "to see if the road was clear."

The shallow grave was not dug parallel with the others, but at a right angle, a foot from a large stump, on the eastern boundary of the cemetery.

Despite the secrecy there was a witness to the eerie scene. As Miss

145

Van Lew relates, "a Negro hidden on a mound, providentially saw Colonel Dahlgren's burial." She is irritatingly vague at this point, refusing to explain how a Negro would "providentially" be on hand to watch a ghostly burial party.

The next day the Negro told Miss Van Lew. As she relates, she rode out to the cemetery the next day with the Negro and "marked" the grave with a small stick.

On the eleventh, General Butler, at Admiral Dahlgren's request, wrote from Fortress Monroe to Colonel Ould, Confederate Commissioner Of Exchange, requesting that the body of Dahlgren "be forwarded by a flag-of-truce boat." Butler added that he understood from the Richmond papers "some circumstances of indignity and outrage accompanied the death."

Butler enclosed five twenty-dollar gold pieces from Admiral Dahlgren to prepare the body for burial.

We next find Colonel Ould at Atkinson's tent, advising the artillery officer that he must see the grave at once because the body "is to be sent to Fortress Monroe for the next exchange."

Atkinson, under strict orders never to reveal Dahlgren's last resting place, refused. He told Ould the orders must come from President Davis himself.

Meanwhile one of the strangest dramas of the Civil War had begun. Miss Van Lew plays the leading role. She is supported by six men and two women: William C. Rowley, the Lohman brothers, Martin Meredith Lipscomb, Robert Orrick, and two German women. A frightened Negro supplies eerie humor.

Rowley and Orrick are farmers. Both Lohmans are former Richmond builders. Lipscomb is a civilian burial contractor. We know nothing of the slave. The two German women work for Orrick on his farm.

With the exception of Lipscomb they were all evidently Miss Van Lew's agents. Their motives were obvious. Lipscomb played his dangerous part only because of "humanity."

Unfortunately little is known about them. They are only names in brittle newspaper clippings found among her effects. She is guarded when she speaks of them in her diary. Years later they may have told the tale about a blazing fire with the wind moaning in the chimney— but even then only to a trusted few.

A quiet prologue to the melodrama opened when one of the Lohman brothers walked into Lipscomb's office in Richmond on the afternoon of the eighth or ninth.

There is no record of what he said or how he said it, but it can be imagined that Lipscomb sat up in his chair when Lohman told him the purpose of his visit. How the shiver of fear must have traveled down his spine when he heard Lohman say he wanted his help in digging up Dahlgren's body and smuggling it through the Rebel lines!

According to a brief account published in the *Richmond Dispatch* "by one of the principals" a few years after the end of the war, Lipscomb at first refused. But when Lohman kept insisting "with solemn and oft-repeated asseverations [sic] that what he was doing, he was doing for humanity's sake," Lipscomb agreed to help him.

There is a hint that Lipscomb was motivated not only by "humanity" but also by "pique." As another account published after the war says: "He [Lipscomb] was feeling some pique that the burial of the body had not been entrusted to him." But pique or not it was dangerous business.

The plot was not Lohman's but Miss Van Lew's. When she had learned of the secret burial of Dahlgren's body, she vowed to recover the corpse for his "bereaved father," evidently motivated by that deep, intangible drive which leads people to do something that is reckless but filled with glory.

Lipscomb set the night of the eleventh or the twelfth for the removal; the hour about ten o'clock. Lipscomb promised to have a Negro on hand to help them.

It is almost too trite to say that it was a wet, miserable night with a low ground mist blanketing the cemetery. The dripping trees and squish of the heavy wagon wheels were the only sounds when one of the Lohmans and Lipscomb and a terrified Negro pulled over to the side of the deserted road.

Years later, "one of the principals" remembered the lonely sound of their footsteps, the chattering of the Negro's teeth, a far-off howl of a farmer's dog, and the smell of the damp, wet earth.

The Negro, holding a lantern, stayed to one side of the big stump, mumbling prayers. Lohman found Miss Van Lew's marker and both men opened the grave among the ten thousand grassless graves of the youngest colonel in the Northern Army.

They dug hurriedly, their labored breathing and the sucking sound of the soggy earth as their shovels pulled free, loud in the silence. In the swirling mist they looked like disembodied spirits claiming a lost soul for their evil world of darkness.

They were about knee-deep when one of the shovels scraped on wood. Lohman knelt down and clawed at the mud.

147

"Here it is," he whispered.

"Dig . . . dig," Lipscomb said.

The shovels flew. The mound on the edge of the grave grew higher. When the rough pine coffin was cleared they lifted it out of the grave with ropes.

Lohman called for the lantern. The Negro, shaking like a man with the palsy, took a hesitant step forward and gave it to him. The pale light fell on the lid. In black stenciled letters was the name ULRIC DAHLGREN. Lohman carefully inserted his chisel under the lid. It creaked back with the sound of crunching dry bones. The face of the corpse stared up at them. Both men involuntarily shivered.

"Look at the leg," Lipscomb whispered.

Lohman gingerly ran his hand down under the military blanket. He found the right leg "wanting below the knee."

There was no doubt; it was Dahlgren's body.

The lid was hurriedly screwed back on. Lipscomb and Lohman carried the coffin to the wagon, the Negro lighting their way. It was slid in the back and covered with burlap sacks. Then they climbed up to the driver's seat. A whip snapped and the wagon splashed off through the dripping darkness.

The two white men would never forget how the Negro's teeth chattered or how their own knees trembled as the wagon jolted over the rutted road, the coffin bouncing dismally in the back.

Sometime later they arrived at the farmhouse of William C. Rowley, "who lived a short distance out in the country." When the wagon creaked into the front yard, Rowley, thin and bearded, came out with a lantern.

"Miss Van Lew is in the seedhouse," he said.

Lipscomb, Lohman, and the Negro carried the coffin into a small wooden house near the barn. Sitting on a box was Miss Van Lew. At her side was the other Lohman. She rose when they staggered in with the coffin, sliding it on a work bench. The chisel was again forced under the lid. It creaked back. Rowley held up his lantern. The four men and the tiny woman stared down at the corpse.

As Miss Van Lew relates with gruesome exactness:

The body, with the exception of the head, was in a perfect state of preservation, fair, pure and firm of flesh. Here and there was a spot of mildew. This was remarkable considering the length of time of the burial, unless as though it was becoming petrified, because the ground in which he had been buried was very damp.

148

The comeliness of the face was gone, but the features seemed regular with a look of firmness and energy stamped upon them. His dress was a shirt of the coarsest kind, not even fastened, pantaloons of dark blue cloth, a cotton sock was upon the left leg, the right was wanting below the knee. His left hand was carelessly thrown across his person, the left robbed of its middle finger, was resting on his left thigh. Around the body was wrapped a blue military blanket.

After Miss Van Lew had clipped a lock from the once handsome head, she ordered the two men to shave the corpse "so it would be hard to tell who he was."

After the ghastly barbering task had been completed, Lipscomb left, promising to return in the morning with a metal casket. The Lohmans escorted Miss Van Lew to Church Hill. Rowley sat through the night alone with the corpse. As Miss Van Lew writes: "It was a brave and honorable thing for Mr. Rowley to do."

In the morning Lipscomb returned to the farmhouse with a metal casket concealed in the rear of his wagon. But he told the Lohmans this was as far as he would travel along their dangerous road.

It was up to the Lohmans or Rowley to bring the dead man through the Confederate lines to Orrick's farm, ten miles from Richmond, where Miss Van Lew said the body was to be buried.

Rowley said he would do it alone. It is not clear why the Lohman brothers did not go along. Perhaps they were known Union sympathizers, and as such would arouse suspicion.

The body was removed from the rough pine coffin and placed in the metallic casket. As Miss Van Lew says there was no putty "to be found in all of Richmond," so the Lohmans made "a composition" to seal the lid.

It was at Lipscomb's suggestion that the coffin was covered with a thin layer of earth upon which were placed twelve peach trees, "packed as nursery men pack them."

After a brief handshake, Rowley drove to the highway, then west in the direction of the heavily guarded lines. The Lohman brothers said they would meet him a mile beyond the barriers—that is, if he wasn't already on his way to the city prison and the gallows.

As he drew near the pickets, Rowley broke out in a cold sweat, "realizing for the first time his peril." His hands trembled and he found it hard to breathe. Almost before he knew it he was pulling up in front of a tent at the side of the road. He dropped the reins "with an appearance of perfect indifference."

A lieutenant came out of the tent. He eyed the wagon. "Search this wagon," he said shortly and went back inside the tent.

A soldier came up. He stared at the peach trees, then at Rowley. "What's this?" he asked.

"Peach trees," Rowley answered, fighting to keep his voice calm.

"Whose trees are they?" asked the guard.

"They belong to a German in the country," Rowley replied.

The soldier started to walk to the back of the wagon when a cart creaked up to the barrier on the opposite side of the road.

Rowley waved his hand. "Go ahead and inspect him," he said, "I have plenty of time."

The soldier thanked him and walked across the road. He carefully inspected the other wagon, then returned to stare intently at Rowley.

"I know your face," he said after a long moment.

Rowley nodded. "We have met."

"Where?" the soldier demanded.

Rowley, who didn't know the man, took a wild chance and said, "At your mother's."

"Ah yes," the soldier said. He went around to the back of the wagon. "But whose peach trees are they?"

"The German's," Rowley repeated.

Another cart came up. The soldier inspected it, then waved it on. The lieutenant came to the doorway of his tent to bawl, "Dammit, guard, inspect that wagon!"

"Yes sir," the guard answered. The officer returned to his tent.

"It is late in the season to plant peach trees," the guard said deliberately.

"The German wants them," Rowley said.

They stared at each other. Then the guard said, "Yes, I know you from somewhere."

"We have met," Rowley said again.

Another cart came up. Again the soldier searched it and passed it on. Rowley, bathed in sweat, clasped his hands to keep them from trembling.

When the soldier returned he said, "I like peach trees."

"Yes, they are nice," Rowley said.

"But it is a mistake to plant them in April," the guard said.

"They are not mine—the German can do with them what he wishes," Rowley answered.

"That is true," the guard said. He stepped back a pace. "It would be a pity to tear them all up when you have packed them so nicely. . . ."

150

Rowley's heart sank. He forced back the inclination to leap from the wagon and run for his life.

"When I packed them," he said, "I didn't expect them to be disturbed. But as it is, I know a soldier's duty."

"Yes, we have our duty," the guard said.

Another cart came up. The same procedure followed. When the soldier returned the lieutenant poked his head out of the tent.

"God dammit," he bellowed, "search that wagon!"

"Yes sir," the guard sang out. The lieutenant disappeared back into the tent.

The soldier came close to the wagon to study the peach trees in silence. For Rowley a thousand years passed. Then in a low voice the soldier said, "I won't delay you any longer. I think it's alright, but at any rate your honest face is guarantee enough for me. Go on." He stepped back and waved his hand.

Rowley, bathed in sweat, picked up the reins and drove off. A mile beyond the pickets the Lohman brothers, "who had flanked the barrier," emerged from the bushes.

At the Yellow Tavern where Jeb Stuart had been killed, they left the highway, traveling west for ten miles to the home of Orrick, a German farmer. A grave was dug in the west pasture. "Two faithful German women, one with a shovel, the other a spade," filled it. Then Rowley planted a peach tree to mark the spot.

That afternoon they drove to Richmond. Again the Lohmans "flanked" the barrier. Rowley chatted jovially of peach trees to another guard who only glanced at the empty wagon. By nightfall Miss Van Lew had received the news. Colonel Dahlgren's body was safe. She wrote: "Every true Union heart who knew of this day's work, felt happier for having charge of this precious dust."

That night a messenger slipped out her back door, crossed the terraced gardens and the mossy brook to vanish into the darkness. A few days later the messenger arrived at Fortress Monroe to hand General Ben Butler a silver locket containing a lock of hair, the color of gingerbread. There was a note in cipher from Miss Van Lew, requesting him to notify Admiral Dahlgren that the body of his son was safe and would be turned over to him after "this unhappy war is over."

Shortly after he received the note from Miss Van Lew, General Butler wrote to Admiral Dahlgren:

The remains are not so far within my control as to be able to remove them from Richmond where every effort is being made by their [Confederate] detectives to find them but they are in the hands of devoted friends of the Union who have taken possession of them.

I hardly dare suggest to Ould [Colonel Ould, Confederate exchange commissioner] when he reports to me, as he will, that he cannot find them, and that I can put them into his possession because that will show a correspondence with Richmond and will alarm them, and will redouble their vigilance to detect their sources of information.

In Richmond the strange drama continued with a new cast of characters. A day or two after the body had been removed Colonel Ould returned to Major Atkinson's tent with "an autographed direction from Mr. Davis" to show him the place of burial. Atkinson and Ould rode out to Oakwood Cemetery. After the artillery officer had pointed out the grave, Ould thanked him and rode back to Richmond.

Late that afternoon Captain Sam McCubbin, chief of Winder's detectives, appeared at Major Turner's office in Libby Prison with orders to disinter Dahlgren's body. Turner sent McCubbin, riding a cart with a metallic casket, to Atkinson's tent. When McCubbin showed his orders from Davis and Ould, Atkinson, no doubt thoroughly disgusted with this macabre business, rode to the cemetery to again point out the grave.

While McCubbin and Atkinson leaned against the wagon, smoking, two gravediggers opened the grave.

They dug for some time, then announced that the grave was empty. McCubbin walked to the edge of the hole, looked in, and called back to Atkinson.

"What is the meaning of this, sir?" he asked.

Atkinson joined him at the edge of the grave. He too stared down into the empty muddy hole. As the *Richmond Dispatch's* account said: "When Captain McCubbin demanded an explanation, he could give none; all that he knew was that he had seen the body buried and that was all."

McCubbin had his own theory about what happened to the body. The *Dispatch* quotes him as "having a suspicion that certain citizens indignant over the orders found on Colonel Dahlgren's body, have found the grave, taken the body and chopped it into pieces."

It is not within the scope of this book to enter into a lengthy discussion of the authenticity of the Dahlgren documents. However, because it was on Miss Van Lew's intelligence that the raid was based, and because she herself labels the documents as forgery, we will briefly examine the evidence.

The documents consisted of an undated address to his troops on Third Division paper, signed U. *Dalhgren*. The special order was on the same stationery. The first reads:

> We hope to release prisoners from Belle Isle first, and having seen them started, we will cross the James and burn the bridges behind us, to destroy and burn the hateful city [and] do not allow the Rebel leader [Davis] and his traitorous crew to escape.

The second emphasizes the order to destroy the city and kill Davis and his cabinet. Both are on stationery of the Cavalry of the Third Division. Dahlgren's entire command, captured in that misty meadow, never heard of the "orders."

Braxton Bragg, when he saw the documents, immediately ordered the execution of the more than two hundred remaining troops. But Lee countermanded the order, commenting, "Assuming that the address and special orders of Colonel Dahlgren, correctly state his design, they were not executed. . . ."

Dahlgren was killed on the second, but the documents were not disclosed until the fifth, when the Richmond papers began its frenzied attacks on "Ulric the Hun." Then the President of the Confederacy takes time from his affairs of state to personally supervise a burial detail, which any noncommissioned officer could have supervised. The body is buried at eleven o'clock at night in a secret grave.

As for the documents: Dahlgren is made to misspell his own name and sign it U. *Dalhgren,* while every other letter in the Dahlgren Papers, Library of Congress, is signed Ulric *Dahlgren*. The handwriting is far from identical. The stationery of the documents appears authentic enough. It is certain that Dahlgren carried blank sheets of paper in his dispatch case. It must also be recalled that Colonel Dahlgren had been fighting a losing battle, hemmed in by the enemy at every turn. What leader of such a dangerous expedition, deep in hostile territory and with the game lost, would fail to destroy such incriminating evidence?*

---

* In his *Rebel Raider*, Swiggett, who had not seen the Van Lew Diary when his book was written, anticipated this point by asking what leaders had seen the documents. He informs me that he believes the papers were forged. However, he says Douglas Southal Freeman told him he believes them to be authentic Union documents.

153

Here are Miss Van Lew's conclusions written a few nights after Rowley and the Lohmans had reported to her that the body of Colonel Dahlgren had been brought through the lines:

Why were the documents, supposedly found on his body—that were seen only by a few people in high places, so studiously concealed?

The deduction is inevitable that the paper was prepared in Richmond to irritate and inflame the Southern people.

We have made capital out of exhibiting General Pope's coat; a Yankee skull, and certainly no one knowing us, would have suspected us of the false delicacy of withholding from public exhibition a paper—which if genuine—would wonderfully have endorsed our ends; unless we feared that the handwriting might be detected by Richmond experts and the fact made known to the world. . . .

The inescapable conclusion, as Miss Van Lew declares, is that the documents are forgery. Why?

In his excellent *Rebel Raider,* a study of the life of General John Hunt Morgan, Howard Swiggett believes the Northwest Conspiracy presents the reason. Davis already had sent several of Morgan's officers to Canada to direct the uprising of the secret movement of 490,000 members, which would crack Grant's western transportation service and the Union's western wall.

On the lakes, Colonel McDonnell of Morgan's command, and some officers from the Confederate Navy were plotting to steal steamers and trains, rob banks, and execute a wholesale prison escape of Confederate prisoners on Johnson's Island.

Details of the plots were brought out in the court-martial of John Yates Beall, a master in the Confederate Navy who was captured in Buffalo, April, 1864, attempting to derail an express train which was delivering two of Morgan's high-ranking officers to Johnson's Island Prison.

As the judge advocate declared in sentencing Beall to hang, "It was nothing but a plot hatched in Richmond to bring a reign of terror and to cause confusion among the loyal people of the Union living along the border."

With Mason and Slidell working feverishly on the alliance between the Confederacy and England and the Northwest Conspiracy moving to its climax, Davis realized that public opinion could not be outraged. The ill-fated raid of Colonel Dahlgren presented him an opportunity; the forged documents his alibi.

As the Beards point out in *The Rise of American Civilization* about the efforts of Jefferson Davis to win the support of the Confederacy's cause by the circulation of prepared ideas:

> Paying respect to the utility of religious emotions, a carefully selected Catholic priest was dispatched to the Continent—to work especially in Paris, Madrid, Vienna and Rome. As a stimulus to action, the Confederate Secretary of State, Judah P. Benjamin, an astute Jewish lawyer, informed this clerical diplomat that a recent raid had been made on Richmond for the purpose of committing it to flames, exposing its women to nameless horrors and putting to death the chief magistrate and principal officers of the government; and by way of elaboration, Benjamin added that the fury of the Federals spares neither age nor sex, nor do they even shrink from the shameful desecration of the edifice in which the people meet for the worship of God.

4

In the winter of 1864, Colonel Thomas E. Rose, of the Twenty-seventh Pennsylvania Volunteers and Colonel Abel Streight, the Union raider, finished their fifty-eight-foot tunnel under the foundation of Libby Prison. Battling sewer gas and a small army of water rats, they led 109 men and officers to freedom in one of the most thrilling escapes in our history.

Colonel Sharpe, in his résumé of Miss Van Lew's wartime activities wrote that he "understood and believes Streight and his party owed their escape to the Van Lews."

General Butler also credits her with planning the escape. But in her diary Miss Van Lew is strangely reticent. However, she gives an account of meeting Streight and Colonel McDonald a few hours after the escape.

The day "which I shall never forget" dawned clear and cold. Before noon she had a mysterious visitor who she describes only as a "Union friend." A servant ushered him into the library, the floor still covered with straw and ready for the next visit of the horse-hungry Confederate raiders.

What took place is a tantalizing mystery. Did Miss Van Lew and her friend climb the attic stairs to prepare the secret room as the alarm guns slammed and the church bells throughout the city pealed wildly? . . .

Sometime during the day she was taken by her "Union friend" in a carriage to a farmhouse near "Howard's Grove." They knocked. The door opened an inch, then wider to admit them, then quickly closed.

Miss Van Lew walked into the parlor. Two men in tattered blue pants and filthy shirts rose to their feet. One was short and black-haired, the other a blonde giant.

Colonel Streight, the blonde man, smiled and said, "Ah! Miss Van Lew."

He introduced the smaller man as Colonel McDonald. Miss Van Lew saw that they appeared "feeble" and insisted they be seated.

A "Mrs. Rice," who evidently owned the farmhouse, came in with some tea. As they sipped the tea, Streight and McDonald told her of the terrible day and nights they had spent digging the tunnel. When he had finished his part of the story, McDonald gave Miss Van Lew the chisel, "their digging tool, now worn to half its size" to examine.

When she reminded Streight that the South hated him particularly for leading a Negro regiment, he smiled and said wryly that "it was a lie but he would have no objection."

She tells us only that they discussed the war, and when Streight asked her why she thought they were fighting, she replied, "For Democracy but secretly I thought it was against slavery."

That's as much as Miss Van Lew tells. The only other paper in the Van Lew collection, in connection with the sensational escape, is a long thesis on the causes of the Civil War, which she says she wrote for Colonel Streight "after thinking over his question as to why we fight."

Did Colonels Streight and McDonald and some of the forty-nine men who safely reached the Union lines, read this thesis by candle-light in the secret room of the Van Lew house? . . .

John Reynolds of Boston, executor of her estate, to whose mother Miss Van Lew told her secrets, says they did. We have Colonel Sharpe's and General Butler's comments on Miss Van Lew's part in the mass escape.

All the Richmond newspapers credited her with planning the escape, hiding the fugitives in the secret room, then hiring guides to take them through the Rebel lines.

The *Times Dispatch* reconstructed the escapes as follows:

Following Miss Van Lew's instructions, the fugitives, led by Colonel Streight, scurried to a number of unfrequented spots about the closely guarded city, where her agents met them and placed them in temporary shelters, providing them with clothes—farmers, laborers, civilians and women. When their escape was discovered alarm guns were sounded and churchbells rung. Many were quickly recaptured but those who followed her [Miss Van Lew's] instructions, safely passed through the lines. . . .

But Miss Van Lew—
"I had a very pleasant visit," she writes. "I was driven home by a suspicious hack driver who took advantage of the situation to demand a round sum. . . ."

5

In the latter part of 1864, the number of dispatches containing military information arriving at Fortress Monroe from Miss Van Lew increased considerably. By 1865 she was almost in daily communication with Grant's headquarters, through what General Sharpe describes as "five relay stations."

So smoothly did her relay stations work, that scarcely a morning passed that flowers, fresh from the Van Lew gardens, did not appear on Grant's breakfast table.

To augment the information she received from her "Union friends," the mysterious spy called "Quaker," "Mr. Palmer," and the others. Miss Van Lew moved about the countryside at night or in the early morning, dressed in a farmwoman's buckskin breeches, a canvas coat, and a large poke bonnet. The troops marching out of Richmond never gave the old woman carrying the bag of farm products a second glance. Under the rim of the big bonnet, eyes black and bright, she carefully counted cannons and men.

When Grant took City Point she used as her courier an old Negro who worked on her farm, located below Richmond on the James River.

The Negro's "large brogans" carried her dispatches between the thick soles. At night the old Negro would walk from the farm across the Union lines to Grant's headquarters. Because of his "humble station in life," as the *Richmond Dispatch* called it, he was never questioned by the guards.

Couriers were continually going and coming from the house on Church Hill. Once Winder's detectives forced their way into the house to "search rooms, drawers and cupboards. But they found nothing."

In the secret room the Union couriers or spies, waiting to set out for the lines, could hear the tramp of boots, jingling of spurs, and the orders of the officers.

Miss Van Lew put on a good show. She followed the chagrined and empty-handed raiders down to Winder's office.

"Sir," she told him, "your ordering underling officers to search my home for evidence to convict me in league with the enemy, is beneath the conduct of an officer and a gentleman."

As the *Boston Sunday Herald* remarked, in telling the story, "General Winder turned livid, behind his mustache and said nothing but with mighty thinkings in his heart all the same."

It was about this time that Miss Van Lew's brother John, who lived with his family in Richmond, was finally drafted into the Confederate Army, although he, like his sister, was outspoken in his sympathy for the North and the Abolitionists.

He only wore the gray for a few months. At the first opportunity he slipped through the lines to Fortress Monroe where he gave General Butler "valuable information."

In mid-March it was common gossip that Richmond was to be evacuated. A. P. Hill heard it while spending a few days in the capital. He was outraged and declared that if this gossip was true he did not care to survive the fall of the city. His wish was granted. On the morning of April 1, his stricken aide stood in the hall of the Venable House listening to a sweet clear voice singing a love song. A few minutes later he was telling Mrs. Hill that her husband was dead.

The sands were running out. A veteran major in Curtis Lee's command wrote that he "could not see" how the troops could be held together without food.

Petersburg fell. The retreat to Richmond was a horrible ordeal. Men dropped from weariness on the side of the road. Artillery horses fell dead in their shafts from lack of grain. Soldiers who were fortunate to find a scrawny chicken or a pig, wasted no time in building a fire. The carcass was sliced in pieces with bayonets and the flesh eaten raw.

By daylight officers wept when they saw the gaping holes in their brigades. But there was no thought of surrendering. Said one colonel, "The idea of subjugation never dawned upon us."

On the night of April 2, part of Lee's army began moving through Richmond. The city was in an uproar. Mobs were everywhere, looting and burning in a drunken frenzy.

They came from everywhere—the whores, gamblers, drunkards, thieves, and thugs. The few policemen were helpless. Convalescent

158

soldiers who were to replace the provost marshal's men now were removing the Federal prisoners, assembled in Capitol Square. But the mob swept them aside.

Strict orders had been given that whisky stores were to be destroyed. Some barrels were stove in but many more were rolled out of the warehouses. Drunken men and women fought to dip in their cups or pans.

Ewell rode his staff through the mobs, desperately trying to restore order. But the mobs shouted him down. Drunken men staggered down the streets with torches. Burning lamps were flung across rooms in flimsy shacks of the red-light district. They burned, the flames leaping from one to another like blazing trees in a pine forest. A warehouse on the water front, set afire by the provost marshal's men, crimsoned the river. Troy was dying.

The fires burned all night. Dawn broke with a scorching breath. The fires had spread and the business section of the city was a roaring inferno.

From Church Hill Miss Van Lew watched Richmond burn. In the afternoon she rode down to the city accompanied by a servant. Cries of "Crazy Bet—Look there's Crazy Bet" greeted her. She ignored them. The servant cracked his whip. The horse, fat from hay and the book bindings in the library, lengthened his stride. They traveled only a few more blocks, then she ordered the servant to turn back.

She wrote:

> The city was burning. Our beautiful flour mills, the largest in the world and the prize of our city, were destroyed. Square after square of stores, dwelling homes, factories, warehouses, banks, hotels, bridges, all wrapped in fire—all filled the city with clouds of smoke as incense from the land for its deliverance. What a moment. Avenging wrath appeased in flames!

Miss Van Lew had returned to her house for an important reason; she had remembered an American flag she had smuggled through the lines months before. It was to be raised when Richmond fell. With trembling hands she took it from the hiding place. With a servant she climbed the attic stairs to the roof and ran up the flag. The breeze fanning the burning city caught the twenty- by nine-foot flag with its thirty-four stars, smoothing out the wrinkles and fold marks.

A Yankee flag now flew over Richmond, heart of the Confederacy. In the city the people gasped. Crowds gathered to peer through the smoke. There were jeers, shouts, and drunken threats. A mob moved through the city and up Church Hill, vowing to tear down the hated flag which rippled in the afternoon breeze.

How many were in the mob we do not know but we know it flowed into the graveled lane, over the terraced gardens to stop at the edge of the front porch. It demanded in an angry voice to tear down that flag or—

Suddenly a little woman dressed in black appeared on the porch. Her dark eyes were blazing but there was no fear in her thin face. The shouts and jeers died away. In the tense silence Miss Van Lew stared over the sea of angry faces. Then in a shrill voice she cried, "Lower this flag or hurt one bit of my house and I will see that General Butler pays you back in kind . . . everyone of you!" She raised her hand. A finger picked out those she knew. "I know you . . . and you . . . and you . . ."

There was a dead silence. Then, like snow in the sun, they dissolved, flowing back over the lawn, back into the road, back to burning Richmond.

When he heard that the Confederacy was evacuating Richmond, General Grant summoned his aide, Colonel Parke, ordering him to hurry to Richmond "to see that Miss Van Lew is properly cared for."

Parke galloped to Richmond, entering with the first troops. A thick haze of smoke hung over the city; wood ash covered uniforms and horses. Negroes came dancing from their hiding places to be joined by secret Union sympathizers. Looters were arrested, snipers disposed of, and fires extinguished.

A soldier named Louis Grund raised the American flag over the courthouse—the second to fly over the city. On Church Hill the large flag still flapped in the breeze.

Parke galloped to the Van Lew house. The servants told him their mistress had gone down to the city when she heard the troops were approaching. Parke returned to the smoldering city to search for her. He described her numerous times but none of the guards remembered having seen her. Then one of Miss Van Lew's friends told Parke where she was.

The dusty, sweaty officer found her inside the Confederacy's War Department. She was knee-deep in scattered papers, documents, and ledgers. She explained that she had rushed to the high office of the Confederacy before someone burned the papers "because General Grant might find them valuable."

160

Unknown to her, Secretary of War Benjamin had already burned the Confederacy's secret service papers.

In the Van Lew Collection are some of the papers she found that day in the Confederacy's War Department. One is a sketch of a new Confederate Flag.

About this time General Butler at Fortress Monroe was writing Colonel James A. Hardie, aide to Secretary of War Stanton, recommending a pass to Richmond for John Van Lew.

> The sister of John Van Lew [he wrote] is my secret correspondent in Richmond and has furnished me with valuable information. Their family is most loyal.
>
> She [Miss Van Lew] is now the repository of the secret of the burial place of Colonel Ulric Dahlgren's body, whose remains were taken by the Unionists of Richmond from a dishonored grave and put in a place of safety known but to her.
>
> She is mentioned with commendation in some of my dispatches to the War Department.

John was granted the pass and hurried to Richmond. There is nothing to tell us when he reached the city, nor how he was received. But surely it was a happy hour for Miss Van Lew when the servants came running with the news that John was coming up the road.

A few days later Lee surrendered at Appomattox. The Cause was lost. In the house of Church Hill, Miss Van Lew furled her flag, tied together all her papers and notes, putting them in a large black box. The poke bonnet, canvas jacket, and buckskin shirt were put away in the attic. The servants swept the straw from the library; the horse went back to a more prosaic existence in the stable.

Miss Van Lew reported to General Grant where Colonel Dahlgren's body was secretly buried. The body was disinterred and shipped to Philadelphia on a special train draped with mourning. There was an elaborate military funeral and at last the gallant young Colonel was laid to rest. Admiral Dahlgren offered Lipscomb, the Lohman brothers, and Rowley "a reward" but they all refused to accept it.

"I did it for humanity," Lipscomb told Miss Van Lew, "and I cannot see accepting money from this poor boy's father."

Months after the surrender, when Grant, accompanied by his wife, visited Richmond, he immediately called upon Miss Van Lew. In a letter to a "Mr. Carpenter," Mrs. Grant wrote that she had never heard of Miss Van Lew until they reached Richmond, "when General Grant said he must call upon Miss Van Lew, that she had rendered valuable service to the Union."

The bearded General, his lady, and Miss Van Lew sipped tea that afternoon on the rear piazza of her house. It would be delightful to know what they talked about. It is almost certain Miss Van Lew told him how she had recovered Colonel Dahlgren's body and smuggled it through the lines. Mrs. Grant must have felt like an interloper as she listened to her husband and this tiny woman talk of dark plots, grave-yards at night, couriers and ciphered dispatches.

Grant never forgot Miss Van Lew. When he became President in 1869, his first official act, fifteen days after his inauguration, was to appoint her postmaster of Richmond, at the yearly salary of $4,000.

His selection was a popular one. The Seventy-ninth Regiment of Highlanders, Fourth Brigade, First Division, New York, from their annual reunion at their regimental armory in New York City, sent Grant a huge elaborately engraved "resolution" approving his appoint-ment of Miss Van Lew. Grant thoughtfully sent it to Richmond. Miss Van Lew carefully folded it away among her private papers. It was her proudest possession.

Necessity now brought her in contact with her former friends. But to the people in Richmond she did not exist. Eyes stared through her; her nods of welcome were ignored.

In 1870 her mother died. The large house became intolerably lonely. At her request her widower brother, John, and his two daughters came to live with her. The children's laughter brightened the gloomy house and Miss Van Lew was happy again.

When Grant was re-elected, he appointed Miss Van Lew despite the advice of his political advisers. Even when he was no longer presi-dent he tried to help her. In 1877 he recommended her to President Hayes, enclosing a letter from W. C. Wickham, formerly a Confederate general but after the war an executive of the Chesapeake & Ohio Rail-road. Wickham had written a letter praising her work. On the back of the letter Grant scrawled:

Miss Van Lew was appointed by me as Postmaster of Richmond, Va., soon after my entrance (sic) from a knowledge of entire loyalty during the Rebellion and her service to the Cause. She has filled the office since then with capacity and fidelity, and is very deserving of continued confidence of a Republican administration . . .

162

Rose O'Neil Greenhow, from the frontispiece of her book. *Courtesy New York Public Library.*

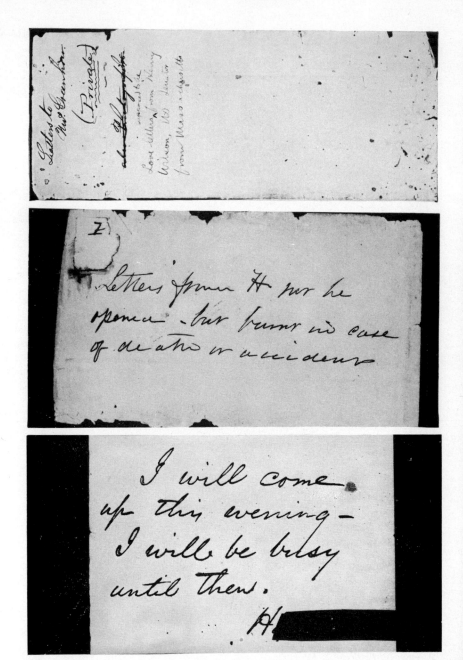

Three documents from the National Archives taken from Mrs. Greenhow's papers: a) The envelope in which the letters from H. are located;
b) Mrs. Greenhow's instructions on the packet of letters; and c) one of
the letters from H. His name was cut out, presumably by Mrs. Greenhow.
Courtesy the National Archives.

Mrs. Greenhow and her daughter in the courtyard of Old Capitol Prison in the fall of 1862. The photograph is by Brady. *Courtesy the Library of Congress.*

Belle Boyd. *Courtesy Harriet H. Shoen.*

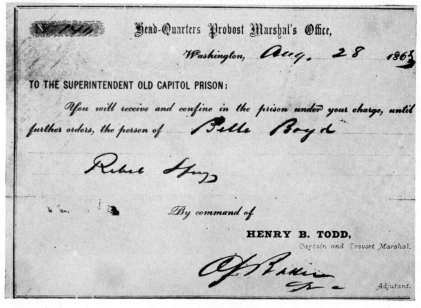

One of the documents regarding Belle Boyd's imprisonment in Old Capitol Prison. *Courtesy the National Archives.*

The Major, Pauline Cushman. *Courtesy the National Archives.*

Miss Van Lew, seated at the left of the portico of her mansion. It was over the portico that the secret room was located. *Courtesy the Valentine Museum.*

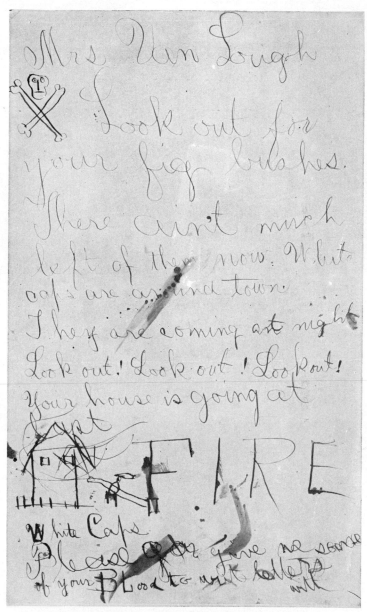

A warning left at the Van Lew house during the war. *Courtesy New York Public Library.*

Miss Van Lew entertaining members of her family in the garden of her Richmond home. *Courtesy New York Public Library.*

William Rawley, who drove Colonel Dahlgren's body through the Confederate lines. *Courtesy New York Public Library.*

Calamity Jane at Gilt Edge, Montana, having a beer with some of her contemporaries. *From the Collection of L. H. Jorud, Helena, Montana. Courtesy Montana Historical Society.*

Younger's Bend, Belle Starr's home, photographed in 1888. *Courtesy Oklahoma Historical Society.*

Belle Starr in 1889. *Courtesy Oklahoma Historical Society.*

Pearl Hart, the last stage robber in American history. *Courtesy Arizona Pioneers' Historical Society.*

Cattle Annie and Little
Breeches. *Courtesy Fa-
mous N. H. Rose Collec-
tion of Old Time Photo-
graphs.*

Poker Alice, taken in 1930,
just before her death at the
age of seventy-seven. *Courtesy Fred M. Mazzulla.*

Cattle Kate, who was hung with her lover, Jim Averill, by cattlemen in
Sweetwater Valley, Wyoming. *Courtesy Fred M. Mazzulla.*

Fort McKinney W. T.
May 3rd. 1890

Judge Andrews.
Laramie City Wyo.

Dear Sir:

You will no doubt be surprised to hear of my having shot Chailey Johnson. But I was compelled to do so or be shot myself; according to his own words which were not only spoken to me, but to others and the people at large. I sincerely regret that such things had to happen - but I avoided it by keeping out of his way since March 20. until yesterday when he met me where I could not get out of his way in safety. you know the character of this man.

I want to know when you will be here and if you can assist

me by counsel. I would like to see you here. and if you had been here this awful affair would not have happened as you know I intimated to you that I wanted to put him under bonds to keep the peace and leave me alone.

Please let me hear from you soon as possible and your advice be of assistance to me I believe

Respectfully Yours

James Averell

A letter from Jim Averill to Judge Andrews, explaining how he happened to shoot "Chailey" Johnson. *Courtesy Fred M. Mazzulla.*

Little Jo Monoghan, before and after. *Courtesy State Historical Society of Colorado.*

China Polly and Johnny Bemis, outside their cabin, in Idaho's wild Salmon River Country. *Courtesy Sister M. Alfreda, St. Gertrude's Monastery, Cottonwood, Idaho.*

China Polly with her two horses, in the twenties. *Courtesy Sister M. Alfreda, St. Gertrude's Monastery, Cottonwood, Idaho.*

Hayes, however, refused to accept the recommendation and re-appointed someone else. She still had powerful friends left in Washington who saw that she received a position as a government clerk.

In the eighties, tragedy struck her. Her brother John died suddenly, followed a short time later by his eldest daughter.

Stunned by grief, she clung to her remaining niece, a gay, laughing, blonde child, whom the servants worshipped as "young Miss Lizzie." As her mother had done, Miss Van Lew hired tutors and sent her niece to the best schools. But there was no longer a Van Lew fortune, and to meet her bills she sold her beautiful collection of antique silver plate, "piece by piece to keep the wolf from her door."

There were always old Union veterans dropping in to see her. Louis Grund, who raised the second flag over Richmond, paid her a visit in the late eighties to talk of the old days. She carefully preserved his calling card in a small envelope, where it was found after her death.

Little girls were always welcome to come into the Van Lew gardens. But there was an "embargo" on boys. Miss Van Lew probably never forgot the imps who ran after her in the streets of Richmond, hooting "Crazy Bet" and pelting her carriage with mud balls.

As the *Richmond Times Dispatch* said, "Only once was this embargo lifted, and that was for the son of the vestryman of St. John's."

She terrified most of Richmond's children. To them this tiny old lady with the mass of jumbled gray curls that bobbed about her head as she walked; whose snapping eyes glittered like black buttons under the rim of her old-fashioned bonnet; whose long black dress swept the street, was a witch as real as the one who stuffed Hansel and Gretel into the oven or gave Snow White the poisoned apple.

One middle-aged woman remembered a visit she had paid to the Van Lew house as a child.

"I was so terrified Miss Van Lew was going to lock me in her secret room, that I was ready to cry. But she was very kind and gave me an apple and some of her beautiful roses. . . ."

Mrs. Littlejohn Fitzgerald recalled for the editors of *Houses of Old Richmond,* that beautiful book about beautiful homes, how, as a little girl, she had been taken to see Miss Van Lew by her father.

As they stood on the porch waiting for the door to open she tried to pull away, crying, "I don't want to see a Yankee."

To her amazement the door swung open, and an old lady in black was saying, "Good afternoon—and I am not a Yankee!"

Years passed. The wheel made a full turn. "Young Miss Lizzie" never married. As her aunt had done she chose to remain a spinster, voluntarily cloistered in the big house behind the boxwood hedges, the terraced gardens, and the beautiful magnolias.

During Cleveland's administration Miss Van Lew was either fired or forced to resign, possibly because of her letter writing. She was a regular contributor to the Boston and Washington papers. Some of her letters were two columns long. Many times the *Boston Herald* printed them in full. They were politically astute but sometimes unfavorable to the administration.

Miss Van Lew tried to see President Cleveland many times but was always refused an audience. At last in desperation she wrote to his secretary:

> The only purpose of my visit to see the President. I was never permitted an interview hence my repeated visits. I thought I had won a right in times of peril, to courtesy and recognition there. The war which marched many loyalists north impoverished my family. Only the most resolute needs from the great depression of my property caused me to ask for the Richmond Post Office job, and with my record I believe if the question was left to the nation, it would be decided in my favor. . . .

In Washington the *Star* sadly commented: "A nomination having been made for the Richmond Post Office, Miss Van Lew will come no more. It seems as if another landmark is gone."

That same afternoon the managing editor of the *Star* received a tart note from the "landmark" informing him she was not "'gone" and that she intended to stay in Washington for some time.

But Miss Van Lew was not without friends in the North. The Grand Army of the Republic heard of her plight and registered indignant protests. Men who had worn the blue, from privates to generals, let the White House know their feeling in the matter of Miss Van Lew.

Despite the protests Miss Van Lew was not reappointed. She returned to Richmond "with only a few dollars in my purse." More of the silver plate and Chippendale went to dealers.

Her last years were spent in terrible loneliness. Old friends died away. To the people of Richmond she still did not exist. For Miss Van Lew there was never an Appomattox.

Dr. William H. Parker, who became the Van Lew's family physician, remembered her last years.

"When your friends are gone, there is not much left in life," he said. "Miss Van Lew never had a friend here in Richmond after the war. People shunned her like a plague."

One old resident remembered that one day she came timidly to the gate as he passed to whisper, "I have no more friends—nobody loves me anymore. I am all alone. . . ."

When the precious heirlooms were all gone and with scarcely money left to buy food, Miss Van Lew turned to the family of Captain Paul Revere in Boston, whom she had helped when he had been held hostage in 1863. It was not a begging letter. She said simply that she was in need and perhaps the family of a man for whom she had done so much might help her.

Mrs. John Phillips Reynolds, sister of Colonel Revere, immediately sent her son, John, to Richmond. At his mother's orders he established a fund which brought her a small annuity.

May, 1889, was the blackest year in Miss Van Lew's life. After a long and lingering illness, her beloved niece died. Day and night Miss Van Lew stayed by "Young Lizzie's" bedside, refusing to eat or sleep, only begging the nurses, "Save her! Don't let her die! Please don't let her die! She is all I have!"

It was just dawn, the garden alive with the comings and goings of the birds, the air fresh with the dew when "Young Lizzie" died. For Miss Van Lew the world stopped that day.

"I guess her tired old heart just about broke in two," one of her old friends said.

During the next months Miss Van Lew never left the house. She refused to allow the servants to remove some Christmas decorations her niece had put up before her illness. In the soft summer twilight she would sit on the rear piazza, looking out over the terraced gardens to the burnished waters of the James.

During the year, she received two visitors, one a nun, the other a German tavern owner. The nun, representing the Order of Monte Maria, offered her twenty thousand dollars for the house to be used as a convent. Miss Van Lew served the nun tea and gently refused her offer.

It would be delightful to know what she said to the tavern owner after the man told her he wanted to buy the lovely old house to turn it into a "German beer garden."

Before the summer was out, she fell ill "with dropsical tendencies." Dr. Parker remembered her as "a little old lady with marvelously bright eyes. I can see them today. And much interested in politics.

She loved to open a bottle of champagne and chat with me but she studiously avoided any mention of the war. She was lonely but not neurotic, and she had a bright mind."

In September 1900, she was very weak but her mind was alert. She had great difficulty in breathing and spent most of her last days sitting up in a chair. She never complained but whispered an apology to a relative from Philadelphia after each spasm shook her swollen little body.

On the morning of the twenty-fifth she slipped into a coma. At eleven o'clock, her gallant heart fluttered, then stopped.

Late that afternoon, complying with her request, she was laid out on the rear piazza. The sun was going down when the undertaker wheeled out the coffin. The Negro servants who had been free years before the end of the war which had been fought to free them, watched through the night, with the relative, Mrs. Louisa Nicholls. It is not hard to imagine the eerie scene; the sounds of the night insects, the candles fluttering in the wind, and the weeping Negroes who stood just beyond the rim of candlelight, praying for "Miss Lizzie. . . ."

Two days later she was buried in the Van Lew plot in Shockhoe Cemetery. Ironically, because there was no room, her grave was dug —like Colonel Dahlgren's—perpendicular with the others.

As red October closed, her home was auctioned off. The doors were opened and the people of Richmond trooped in. The great gloomy halls resounded with their whispers. They peered into nooks and corners, as if expecting to see one of the ghosts which they had heard from childhood inhabited the gloomy old mansion. They handled the quaint old furniture, gazed with curiosity at the cracked canvases of family portraits, and with lifted skirts waded through the debris of three-quarters of a century.

All day, instead of the whisperings of stringed instruments, the shuffle of satin slippers, the ring of spurs over the polished floors, and the clink of crystal cups from the feast in the great banquet hall, there was only the droning cry of the auctioneer.

As a reporter for the *Boston Herald* wrote:

Not a person there but felt the subtle influence of historic suggestion—the unconscious hypnotism of that which breathes from every crack and cranny, such thrilling romance, grave dangers and dark mysteries. . . .

All of Miss Van Lew's personal property was left to distant relatives. Mr. Reynolds received her "diary" and private papers.

As he said then, "The diary is fascinating reading, but unfortunately Miss Van Lew, in her reticence refused to tell in detail much of her activities." It was also learned that immediately after the war the War Department, at Miss Van Lew's request, had returned all her original dispatches and messages. They were never found.

On November 22, 1900, the remainder of her personal property went under the auctioneer's hammer in Leonard's Auction Room on Bromfield Street, Boston. The sale netted only a thousand dollars. As the *Boston Herald* said in its headline: BOSTONIANS LACK SENTIMENT IF THIS SALE IS ANY INDICATION.

The flag she had raised above burning Richmond was sold for seventy-five dollars; five hundred classics—including *Commentaries of the Scriptures,* which her horse had nibbled on—went from twenty-five cents to three dollars.

"A small boy staggered off under the weight of three huge dictionaries, one French and two English, sold for three dollars . . ." wrote the reporter. "And a box of letters from Oliver Wendell Holmes, General Grant, President Garfield, President Hayes and Federal Generals, went for ten dollars. . . ."

Two cities always remembered her: Boston and Richmond. Boston with love, Richmond with bitterness.

In 1902 a huge slab of gray Massachusetts stone, two feet high and four feet long, weighing two thousand pounds was delivered to Shockhoe Cemetery as a marker for her grave. In the center was a bronze tablet. On it was the inscription:

ELIZABETH VAN LEW
1818   1900

She risked everything that is dear to man—friends, fortune, comfort, health, life itself, all for the one absorbing desire of her heart, that slavery be abolished and the Union be preserved.

THIS BOULDER

FROM THE CAPITOL HILL IN BOSTON, IS A TRIBUTE FROM HER MASSACHUSETTS FRIENDS.

Sometime after the turn of the century, the Virginia Club took over the old house, then the subject of so many tales and legends.

There were strange stories of a ghostly figure climbing the attic stairs, shielding a candle, and the clink of spurs on the steps going to the secret room.

An undated clipping of the *Richmond Journal* tells of a Negro "shaving ice" in the cellar who looked up "and saw Miss Van Lew staring out at him from the wall." With a shriek he bounded upstairs. Even after it was pointed out to him that the "ghost" was only streaks in the newly calcimined wall, the servant took his pay and left. As he said, "I gwine 'way from here. I done hear Miss Lizzie walkin' 'bout. I knowed all 'long she was here. No sir, I done with this house."

In 1911 the Van Lew house was condemned to make way for a proposed school. It seems incredible but no one raised a voice against tearing down what had been one of Virginia's most beautiful and historic homes. When the White House of the Confederacy and Jeff Davis's birthplace were similarly endangered, there had been indignant protests.

There was no one to oppose the ruling of the school board. The wreckers moved in and the lovely old house crumbled into a pile of brick and mortar and a cloud of dust.

Richmond, who never forgot nor forgave her daughter's treason, had her revenge.

Book Two: 1870-1900

You won't see the like of such women today. They could ride and shoot as good as any man. They asked no favors or gave any. When they went on a high lonesome, all you could do was hogtie them until they sobered up.

Then there was the other kind; the homesteading kind. They didn't kick up a fuss and get talked about but many of them killed a hostile when they had to in defense of their home. They were good, God-fearing women, who raised sons and daughters and helped civilize the frontier.

Personally I went for the Hell-raising kind. They were more interesting.

—From a letter to the author from a former outlaw, who recently died at the age of ninety-two.

Calamity Jane: White Devil
of the Yellowstone

THE story of Calamity Jane is best told before an open fireplace, with the logs burning briskly, the boughs of the big oak creaking in the wind, and some fine bourbon close at hand.

In such genial surroundings, the old tales bring her vividly back to life. In the dancing firelight it is easy to see her dressed in her famous buckskins and white sombrero, "cursing out" the other freighters in her deep, rasping voice, as the lumbering supply wagons join Crook's army, moving out of Fort Fetterman against the Sioux; or proudly riding into boisterous Deadwood in '76, at the side of Wild Bill Hickok; or backing out of the grocery store in Deadwood, a six-shooter in one hand and a package of food in the other, on her way to the smallpox victims whom everyone else had refused to help. . . .

We can see her cuddling a motherless child, "giving him the love that a lonely boy needs"; pistol whipping a bully and throwing him through a window; walking across a mountain "to bring old Jack some fruit"; wrecking a saloon and fighting four policemen; pleading with Buffalo Bill to help her return to the West, "away from these damn Eastern snobs," then coming back to her beloved Deadwood to die, a strange, tragic misfit, who had become a living symbol of America's wild West, and of adventurous women who since time immemorable have followed the advance of the frontiers.

In such surroundings we told Jane's story.

The firelight shone on the faces of old friends, the precious few cedar logs burned with a bright blue flame. The wind was up and across the hills where cannon balls had been made for Washington's army, a farmer's hound howled at the moon, thin and curved as a silvery sickle.

When the tales had been told there was a brief silence. A log broke, the sparks flew up.

Then someone in the shadows of the room said musingly, "I think her life was very tragic."

It was a woman's voice. Perhaps women best sense the tragedy in Calamity Jane's life.

2

For nearly half a century Calamity Jane has been ridiculed as a rough, tough, ignorant woman. She has been pictured as a moron, a female outlaw, a cheat, a gambler, and a prostitute.

Doane Robinson, historian of South Dakota, who knew Jane and made a study of her life, said, "She was woman low down, even in her class. Her fame was almost entirely outside the Hills. . . ."

The passing years, however, have tempered the harsh criticisms which were so much a part of her life; a life that surely can be called unconventional, uncouth, unwomanly, but in which meanness had no part.

Dr. W. A. Allen of Billings, Montana, who knew Jane in the roaring days of Gilt Edge, says, "She swore, she drank, she wore men's clothing. Today nothing would be thought of these peculiarities, for where can you find a woman who doesn't do much the same thing? Then because standards were different, poor Calamity attracted unsavory attention. Today she probably would be thought of as a 'modern.' She was just fifty years ahead of her time."

There is no doubt that Jane was tragically miscast by nature in sex. There is little doubt she should have been a man. She had a marvelous constitution which withstood for years her horrible debauches. She was completely at ease in the roughest saloons with the most desperate of men. They accepted her as one of their own kind.

She rode "the cars," always sitting in the men's smoker puffing away at a cigar. She was the only woman ever to be admitted into Russell's famous saloon in Deadwood.

She was completely devoid of a female figure. Her body was slim and hard. She was a superb rider and could handle a six-horse team and heavy freighter's wagon with ease.

An old cowhand, himself an expert shot, recalled several years ago that Jane once gave "the finest demonstration of firearms" he had ever witnessed.

She had an impressive list of blistering curses, using them automatically, senselessly, cheerfully, boisterously, as any bullwhacker. She loved to drink, not only to get drunk but because liquor brought her among "the boys," filling her heart with a rowdy sort of happiness.

To Jane, time never existed, except that the price of a drink had increased. Deadwood of 1899, with its sedate macadamized streets, schoolhouse, and churches, was still Deadwood of the seventies when she returned. She went on a howling drunk. The author, Estelline Bennett, lying in bed, heard her going home in the early hours, whooping and challenging the world to combat. But she was still Calamity Jane to Deadwood. Who could arrest a legend? . . .

It is difficult to obtain a reliable physical description of Jane. Her pictures show her to be more of a man than a woman.

The *Rocky Mountain News* of 1877 compares her to a "Brete Harte heroine," adding, "there is nothing to disguise her sex, except her small neat frilly gaithers and sweeping raven locks."

An old miner in Deadwood insisted she was "tall and stooped."

The *Casper Weekly Mail* said she had "coppery, reddish hair, eyes brown, large and keen."

Johnson, a miner, gave the best description of Jane in 1880: "She swears like a trooper, drinks like a sailor, and roughs it with the roughest."

There are numerous stories surrounding her early life. In her seven-page "autobiography" which she sold to the miners for fifty cents to twenty dollars, depending on her thirst and state of finances, Jane said she was born in Princeton, Missouri, in 1848.

This may or may not be true. The United States census of 1860 lists a Martha Jane Canarray of Marion Township, age sixteen, born in Illinois, and an unnamed sister, age seven. The Canarrays presumably lived on a farm because a seventeen-year-old "farmhand" is listed as living with the family.

Other legends have her born near Fort Laramie in 1860, orphaned in an Indian massacre and adopted by a passing preacher who buried her scalped parents.

The Lander, Wyoming, correspondent of the *Cheyenne Sun,* claimed that Jane was brought into Miner's Delight about 1867 with a Major Gallagher and his wife. He describes Jane as "a young stray with the spirit of original sin."

The whole town, he said was "put on its ear by her escapades."

The *New North-West* of Deer Lodge, a frontier newspaper, said in 1877, Jane's "real name" was Jane Coombs, who was born in 1847, the youngest of four children. Her father was the Reverend W. R. Coombs, pastor of the Burlington, Iowa's First Baptist Church.

And so on.

Thirty years ago old men in Princeton remembered that Jane was her mother's daughter. Charlotte Canarray, a handsome, spirited woman, was evidently anything but conventional. Gossip was always being whispered about her. She wore gaudier colors and printed dresses, eschewing the traditional printless cotton.

Her plump, well-rounded figure was eye catching, and few of the Mercer County males let her ride past without smacking their lips and mentally taking her to the barn.

Duncan Aikman, in his *Lady Wildcats,* has Jane's mother on a rampage shortly after the Civil War, riding out of Princeton on the Collins Church Road, carrying a spread of calico like a trooper's flag. She pulled up at the door of a fifteen-year-old neighbor who recently had given birth to a baby, father unknown.

Jane's mother stared down at the ragged young farm girl for a moment, then with a laugh she tossed the calico flag at the girl's feet.

"Take that and make a dress for your bastard," she said, then rode off in a splatter of mud and with a shouted oath.

The first Canarray farm of two hundred acres in the Collins Church district was bought by Jane's grandfather in May 1855. In October 1859, Jane's father, Robert, bought an additional one hundred and eighty acres for five hundred dollars. On the other side of Mercer County, Jane's uncle, Thornton Canarray, was fast becoming known as one of the largest landowners in Missouri.

Jane's father worked the farm with Grandfather Canarray. Princeton's old-timers told Aikman in 1927 that they remembered "Bob working in the field with the old man." Grandfather Canarray died in 1859.

In 1863, when Martha Jane was twelve, the family sold their farm and moved West, weary of Princeton after eight years. Sixty-four years later, an old neighbor who had helped them pack recalled how they creaked off into the morning, riding a prairie schooner, driven by two horses, with two cows tied to the back and a brace of yellow Missouri hound-dogs trotting alongside. She remembered how Jane, "wild as a lynx's kitten," waved good-by.

There is now a blank in Jane's life. According to her "autobiography" they journeyed to Montana, taking the Overland Route. If this is true they perhaps joined some wagon train moving out of Independence, through Cheyenne, Laramie, down the Green River Valley of Wyoming, and into Utah and Salt Lake City. Then north across the desert and mountains of northern Utah across southern Idaho and into Montana.

Jane said the journey, roughly about two thousand miles, took five months. Before it ended she was an experienced teamster, skilled in the art of cracking the thirty-foot bullwhackers.

The wild, incredibly beautiful country, claimed her. She would never fall out of love with it.

According to her story, Virginia City was their last stop. It was then a raw, brawling frontier city. Saloons were open day and night, with endless card games, roulette wheels whirling continuously, and pianos tinkling above the screeching laughter of the dance hall girls and the chattering of chinamen. Gamblers, desperadoes, and outlaws swaggered down the main street. Death was commonplace.

Jane's story has the family staying in Alder Gulch until 1866, when her father died. With her mother she traveled in the autumn of that year, to Blackfoot, another gulch. After a year of washing miners' clothes, Charlotte, no longer the buxom lass of Princeton, died.

It's anybody's guess what happened to Jane after her mother's death. An old man recalled fifty years later that he sold her eggs in Banock in 1866, where she was learning the rudiments of poker from the famous Madam Moustache.

In 1867 she was in Salt Lake City. Again there is a blank in her life. Legend has her married about this time. The *New North-West* of Deer Lodge, in an account of her life in 1877, claimed she married "a young man named Washburn, who entered the army." Other accounts say she married a Lieutenant Somers, bore him a son, then disappeared.

A newspaper clipping in the Montana Historical Society says she next appeared in Rawlins, Wyoming, "where she led an unholy career." Evidently it is about this time that Jane decided to abandon the society of women forever, and join the male sex. She went to Fort Steele in men's clothes and her hair cut short to learn to throw a diamond hitch. She was hired as a mule skinner, but at Hat Creek "she got drunk and her sex was detected."

Jane went from job to job and town to town. She lived with the railroad construction gangs, swinging a pick and laying ties. She drank amazing amounts of liquor, cursing with a horrible eloquence that awed the tough railroad workers and mule skinners. She was an expert with a bullwhacker.

It may well have been no idle boast when she said to Wirt New-com of Montana, who told the story years later, "I'll bet you twenty-five dollars I can pick a fly off that oxen's ear four times out of five."

She was now about seventeen. Stories about her flew from camp to camp. She was fast becoming a frontier celebrity.

By Jane's account she drifted to Cheyenne in 1869. It seems plausible. The gold fields were dull except in Nevada. Cheyenne was booming, and it had a night life. There she could push her way to the bars, throw down her money, and drink with "her boys." She was never happier. The good women of Cheyenne watched her walk down the streets in her men's clothes and sniffed. But before she left Jane had become part of the cow-town's folklore.

According to her story she took part in the campaign against the Arizona Apaches in 1870-71. It may or may not be true. It is quite possible she went along as a bullwhacker.

Some accounts next have her in a cattle-driving train for the famous Majors Russell and Waddell, between Kansas City and Denver. Per-haps she left Cheyenne with a military operation then switched over to the rowdy life of the cattle-driving train.

Abilene and Hayes City, those two rough cow towns, next saw her. According to Pat Tucker, of Livingston, Montana, she had returned—temporarily at least—to a feminine dress. Pat says her elegant cowgirl's costume won her the name of "Prairie Queen."

According to her account she joined the army at Fort Saunders, Wyoming, in 1872, taking part in an Indian campaign called the Muscle Shells War. She says she took part "in a charge" on a Nez Perce Village, riding stirrup to stirrup with a Captain Pat Egan.

The charge was repulsed—as Jane's accounts describe it—and Egan wounded. "A hundred howling painted braves" started for him. Jane whirled about, beat them off to rescue her captain, riding off in a shower of arrows. Then Jane has Egan gratefully telling her, "Jane, you're a wonderful little woman to have around in time of calamity. From now on your name's Calamity Jane."

The incident of course, is a complete fabrication. Egan, a colorful cavalryman, never mentioned it. There is no evidence he "charged" an Indian village in 1872, and in at least two books written by men who rode with him, there is no mention of that lurid episode.

However, it is about this time that Jane did receive her nickname. There are two other versions of how she did. One is that William Nye, the famous Western editor of the *Laramie Boomerang* gave it to her in the early seventies; the other is a distorted version of the

Egan incident with "Buckskin" Frank Leslie, Tombstone's gun fighter, replacing Egan in an Indian fight. The reader can select the version he likes best.

By whatever means she received her nickname, she was now known as Calamity Jane, and she made the most of it during the rest of her life. It had a special ring of its own. It caught on, was repeated and repeated. The crowds in the rough saloons loved its overtone of sudden death and disaster.

"Here's Calamity," they would shout, stepping aside to let her reach the bar.

"Damn right, it's Calamity," she would boast in her harsh voice. "Step up and name your whisky. . . ."

The crowds roared. Calamity Jane, of Princeton, Missouri, played her role to the hilt.

3

In the Spring of 1875, while in Cheyenne, Jane heard of Crook's expedition against the Sioux. She hired a buggy, arriving at Fort Laramie the next day with the horse ready to drop in its tracks. Calamity always claimed she scouted for Sioux warriors on the Rosebud, took part in the skirmishes, carried messages from Crook to Custer, and scouted for Custer, missing the famous "massacre" only because she had been stricken with pneumonia after swimming the Platte River "with important messages."

There is evidence she joined the expedition as a bullwhacker, not as a scout. It is inconceivable that she was anything else. She was dismissed because of a river-swimming episode, but not as Jane told it.

She had joined the other bullwhackers for a swim sans bathing suits, after a hot, dusty drive, only to be spotted by a horrified young officer who notified his commanding officer. Jane was immediately ordered "sent back to Fort Reno in female attire," as the *Cheyenne Sun* said.

General, then Colonel, Anson Mills, in his autobiography, *My Story,* gives an amusing account of her dismissal.

Shortly after it had been discovered that Jane was a female, Mills passed through the camp. Jane, who was arguing violently with the wagon master, jumped up. Pointing to Mills, she shouted, "There's Colonel Mills—he knows me."

Mills, as he relates, froze in his tracks. Jane, hands on hips, stared down at him, with a roguish grin. All about the camp teamsters howled with laughter. Mills, red-faced, hurried off, "astonished and chagrined, being married."

Mills vigorously denied "knowing Calamity Jane or her calling." However, he said, "Nobody believed me," especially his fellow officers who would nudge him at mess, inquiring in a stage whisper, "Who is Calamity Jane, Anson?"

Years later Mills was startled to discover Jane working in the home of a fellow officer. But Jane never gave a sign she knew him. She only winked.

In the seventies she worked for a time as a cook for the Belly-Up stage station. One day a lonely, half-starved cowhand from Texas appeared.

"You look hungry, kid," she said.

"I am," the cowpuncher said. Without another word, Calamity "staked" him to a meal.

Before he rode off the cowhand said, "Some day I'll pay you for that meal, Calamity."

She grinned. "What's your name, kid?"

"Teddy Blue," he answered.

"Well, Blue, I don't give a damn if you never pay me," Jane said with a laugh.

Teddy Blue, who was to become one of the most famous cow-punchers of Montana, would repay her many years later.

In 1876 Jane appeared in her beloved Deadwood. The "gulch" was at its peak, crowded with miners, ex-soldiers, gamblers, outlaws, pimps, whores, bullwhackers, and mule skinners. Many of them remembered Jane and gave her a boisterous welcome.

A short time after her arrival, Deadwood's famous "Preacher Smith," the Reverend Henry Westton Smith, walked out of Deadwood on a hot Sunday morning, bound for Crook City, to give his weekly sermon. Eight miles outside the city he was mysteriously killed by bushwhackers, whether by Indian or white is not known. His body was brought back in a hay wagon.

The wooden sidewalks were packed as the wagon creaked its way down the street. Men took off their hats; there was a deep silence. Jane was one of the spectators. She had a case of the jitters and a terrific hangover. In a burst of remorse she said loudly, "Too bad the Injuns killed the only man that came in the hills to tell us all how to live." She looked around her. Then after a pause, she added, "And dammit, how we do need tellin'!"

O. W. Coursey, in his *Beautiful Black Hills* repeats a tale about

178

Jane that he heard "from a retired army officer." Jane, it seemed, became indignant when a freighter kicked his mule. The freighter told her to mind her own business and flicked off her hat with his bull whip.

Jane whipped out her six-shooter and made the freighter retrieve it, then put it back on her head.

When the teamster later heard that Jane was a woman he came "hat in hand" to apologize to Jane. She accepted it graciously, complimenting him for being "a gentleman."

The high point in Jane's life took place in 1876, when Wild Bill Hickok rode into her life. Their relationship has been, and will continue to be, debated by Western historians.

Many claimed she and Hickok were married. A so-called "confession," written by Jane for her daughter, which suddenly appeared in June, 1941, also makes this claim. The "confession" will be discussed later.

In 1937, in a discussion of the relationship of Jane and Wild Bill, G. R. Hickok, mayor of Lakin, Kansas, and second cousin of the famous gun fighter, denied that Wild Bill "was a close friend of Calamity Jane."

But Ben Greenough, famous rancher and guide of Red Lodge, answered Hickok, "I am convinced they were great pals. Calamity told me herself that she was quite fond of Bill and saw him often."

Charles Carson, only living son of the famous Kit, joined the discussion, published in the *Helena Journal,* by pointing out "Bill was a man who paid little attention to women."

His sister-in-law, widow of Carson II, had the same opinion, along with Antone Avvarra, "a famous stagecoach driver."

Jane first appeared in the company of Wild Bill in the summer of 1876. She had most certainly known him before. One old-timer's memoirs has them meeting in Laramie, at least on two different occasions.

Hickok was the genuine article among bad men of the West. He was a cold, calculating fighting man. In his capacity as gambler and frontier marshal he had killed at least a dozen men. The actual count will never be known. He dressed the part of a Western figure: long brown hair, stallion-tail moustaches, and buckskins. He had been East in Ned Buntline's *The Scouts of the Prairie* and had recently married a circus proprietress. There is no way of knowing how Calamity Jane teamed up with Wild Bill and his troupe, but one day in mid-June in 1876, Deadwood was delighted to see Wild Bill,

Calamity Jane, "Colorado Charlie" Utter, his brother Steve, and "Bloody Dick" Seymour, riding down Main Street.

They all wore creamy white Stetsons, brand new fringed buckskins and shiny boots. Revolver butts gleamed and the silver decorations on their saddles and bridles flashed in the sun.

Deadwood, which always loved a good show, whooped in glee. The dirty miners, gamblers, pimps, and outlaws surrounded them on all sides. They shouted for Calamity and she threw back her head to screech a welcome. Wild Bill let a smile flicker across his face. This was mob psychology at its best. It was wonderful for business—his gambling and his wife's circus.

For Calamity, this was her greatest moment. The crowds bought her round after round of drinks. She rolled from saloon to saloon, shattering the bar mirrors and bottles with her polished forty-five.

In his tent Wild Bill shuffled the decks, combed his moustaches, and appeared at Carl Mann's saloon, open for business. He had shrewdly guessed right, that there were many who were impatiently waiting to sit down with him in a game. And who cared if they lost—they could always brag to their grandchildren that they had lost to Wild Bill Hickok, "Prince of the Pistoleers," the greatest killer the West had ever known!

As the *Deadwood Telegram* said in 1922: "Wild Bill sought to accumulate gold by manipulating the picture cards rather than by digging in the earth for it."

Calamity Jane shone in the reflected glory of Wild Bill all that summer. There is little doubt Bill accepted her fawning with quiet amusement. As the hero of the West he could have had the choicest female in Deadwood. There is evidence he was devoted to his wife, Agnes. In two letters to her, one in July and the other on the fatal afternoon of August 2, he said he "only lived" to love his wife.

At 4:10 P.M. on that August afternoon, Hickok was killed by Jack McCall who shot him in the back of the head. The bullet passed through the brain emerging from under the right cheekbone to shatter the left arm of Captain Massey, one of the three players in the well-known poker game.

Calamity claimed she cornered McCall in a butcher shop with a meat cleaver and later helped to hoist Jack sky-high. Of course, this is all nonsense. There was no lynching. A miners' court quickly freed McCall on his plea that Hickok had killed his brother in Kansas. However another court at Yankton, South Dakota found him guilty and he was hanged legally.

Calamity Jane wept long and loud for her hero. She knew the great days were gone. Now there was no hero to trail after, to affectionately slap on the shoulder and be given an amused smile in return.

Two years later she partially regained her lost glory during the dreadful smallpox plague which swept Deadwood.

The sick and dying were rushed to a pest house on the slope behind the town, and forgotten. Deadwood's only physician, Dr. Babcock, alone climbed the trail to the small shack to do what he could for his patients.

One day he climbed the slope to find Calamity Jane, hands on hips, watching him with a grin.

"My God, Jane, what are you doing here?" he asked.

"Well, Doc, somebody's got to take care of them. There's not even a damn bit of water for them."

Jane went inside the cabin with Babcock. When he left she said, "You just tell me what to do, Doc, and I'll do it."

That Jane really did this was confirmed by Dr. Babcock years later. Coursey, the Black Hills historian who interviewed Deadwood's pioneers, quotes several as saying they owe their life to Jane during the plague.

There is one persistent legend, told Coursey by a Colonel Brown, of Jane coming into Deadwood's grocery and calmly ordering a sack of groceries.

"That will be two ounces of dust," the proprietor said.

Jane drew her six-shooter. "Don't worry about your damn bill," she said, "I'll pay for it when the boys get better."

She backed out of the door, the parcels of food in one hand, the six-shooter in the other. Brown and the men in the store watched her climb the slope and disappear into the pest house. Other men told Coursey the same story. It's certainly characteristic of Calamity Jane, but as to its truth . . .

Before the pox was over Jane and Dr. Babcock had devised a scheme for her to get groceries. She would throw a list, written in pencil and wrapped with a stone, down the trail. It was to be picked up in the morning and in the evening replaced by a sack of groceries.

Before the plague was over, Jane asked Dr. Babcock to have "the boys" send up a water barrel. The barrel was delivered. The next day the line of wash appeared.

"Old Calam's washing their clothes," the admiring miners said and fired a volley to show their appreciation. Jane waved her hand to show that she understood.

One of Dr. Babcock's patients was a small boy named Robinson. He was Calamity's special charge. She was a rough but efficient nurse and apt to growl, "Here, you little bastard, drink this soup," or "Damn you, sit still while I wash your face."

The little Robinson boy recovered and will appear again in her life.

One day, when the plague was diminishing, Jane climbed down the slope and marched down Deadwood's muddy, stump-filled Main Street. She stopped near a saloon. Within a few minutes a crowd surrounded her. Someone brought a beer barrel and she climbed on top.

"Boys," she shouted, "there's a man back up there who has a wife and family back in the States. He has no dust. Untie your weasel skins and turn out enough dust to take him back where he belongs."

Jane held out her hat. "The dust came liberally."

Her role as heroic nurse ended; Jane returned to character. She reeled from saloon to saloon, nearly always ending up stupefied and sleeping it off behind a saloon or in a livery stable.

One day, walking down Deadwood's Main Street, she saw a small boy sitting on a doorstep. Jane, suffering from a terrible hangover, walked over to him.

"What's the matter, kid, you look lost?"

The little boy told her he was lonely "because he didn't have anybody to play with."

Jane flopped down beside him, pulling him up on her lap. Clearing her throat, she launched into a series of stories, probably about Indians, bullwhackers, Wild Bill Hickok, and dangerous men she had known. It was a strange sight to see the wild-eyed child sitting on the lap of this grotesque creature who was dressed in the buckskin Hickok had given her, now filthy from the debauches and barroom floors, her once white Stetson perched on the back of her head, telling stories in her harsh, rasping voice.

In 1926 that boy, Bud Hart, of Cooke City, recalled the incident for the *Cascade Pioneer*.

"I was then about eight," he said, "a motherless, lonely child. Father was a government engineer and had brought me to Deadwood during the rush. I was terribly lonely, and when this woman came by and asked me what was wrong I told her. I shall never forget her cuddling me and telling me those stories. Jane was a rough woman, but a kind one—at least to the little boy in Deadwood. . . ."

The tales of Jane in Deadwood are many. Tom Rivington of Gehring, Nebraska, recalled for the *Basin Star* in 1934, the evening when he walked into a saloon and saw Jane watching "the boys play their chips."

He pointed to a sombrero hanging on a peg in the rear of the saloon.

"Bet you twenty-five dollars, Jane, you can't hit that hat," he said.

Jane eyed the hat. "I'll take it," she said. The forty-five leaped in her hand. The players deserted their game to examine the hat. As Tom recalled, two shots had torn the hat's crown into bits. He paid the bet.

One of the most hilarious stories was told by Charles E. Chapin in 1943. The account is in the files of the Montana Historical Society.

Chapin, a well-known actor of his day, appeared in Deadwood, with the Lord Players about 1880. It was one of the first theatrical troupes to appear and Deadwood was excited. Mr. Chapin remembered the town "was one of the liveliest mining towns in the country."

The troupe opened with *East Lynne*. Jane swaggered down the main aisle of the Opera House, arm in arm with "Arkansas Tom," a notorious gun fighter. He was a short stocky man with long black hair and bristling moustache. They took a seat directly in front of "Seth Bullock, later a friend of Colonel Roosevelt."

The crowd whooped and shouted when Calamity sat down. Someone called for her to stand up and she did, a striking figure in a corduroy suit, long green gloves, and a pure white sombrero.

Mr. Chapin took a dim view of her. "She was not a very fascinating lady," he recalled.

Settled down in a seat just in back of the stage lights Jane took out a large piece of chewing tobacco and began "chewing as industriously as any miner present."

Jane was the model of decorum for the first act. But her mood changed when Lady Isobel eloped with Sir Francis. Jane grew indignant at such dastardly conduct.

Lady Isobel, strikingly beautiful in a long evening gown, walked majestically across the stage. Jane measured the distance. She pursed her lips and let go. A stream of tobacco juice flew through the air and across the pink dress.

Miners whooped with delight. The curtain slammed down. Mr. Lord, the manager and owner of the troupe, stamped out in a rage. But Jane was Deadwood's favorite daughter and for a moment "there was nearly a rough house." Lord, whose wife had been playing Lady Isobel "began to voice a protest over the indignity of what had happened to his wife."

But Calamity saved the day. She stood up, reached inside the pocket of her corduroy jacket "and threw some gold pieces across the stage to pay for the gown she had so ruthlessly desecrated."

The show went on—with Mrs. Lord in another dress. Jane remained quiet, "chewing her cud in respectable silence."

Tom left Jane two days after the show opened, to be shot down in a raid on a South Dakota town. Of Jane the old actor recalled, "She raised enough deviltry to have deserved a dozen hangings."

The *Deadwood Daily Champion* agreed with Mr. Chapin:

> As for her [Calamity Jane] she is a fraud and a dead give away. A hundred waiter girls or mop squeezers in this gulch are her superior in everything. She strikes out and lays around with a lot of bull whackers or road agents like an Indian squaw. . . .

Jane was taken in by the law of Deadwood only once, when a miner charged Jane with "rolling him for his money."

Jane was arraigned the next day. After the miner told his story, the judge turned to Calamity Jane.

"Did you steal this man's money, Calamity?" he asked.

Jane nodded vigorously. "Damn right I did, judge."

The astonished judge asked why. Jane said she had taken the man's money to "go to the hospital and pay the bill for Kitty Arnold who had been sick."

She turned to glare at the miner. "I had to take it, judge, before someone else took it. This damn fool was drunk under the table."

To Jane that was a monstrous crime. The judge agreed. He freed Jane and advised the miner to leave town. The miner took his advice and was gone before sunset.

Jane left Deadwood temporarily on September 24, 1878, departing on the Bismarck stage. She refused to say whom she was going to visit but the *Black Hills Daily Times* reporter made a shrewd guess. "Her destination is not known to this reporter," he wrote, "but probably she's going to see the boys in Blue. . . ."

In a few weeks Jane was back with a severe hangover and a bulging purse from her visit with "the boys in Blue."

In 1880 Jane finally left Deadwood. She next appeared at Pierre, working as a mule skinner. In 1932, Mrs. I. N. Walker of Great Falls, Montana, remembered her visit.

"In those days," Mrs. Walker said, "the children and so-called respectable people did not associate with Calamity Jane because of the life she led on the frontier. But the freighters, miners, and frontiersmen respected her and were always ready to help her when she was in trouble."

In Pierre, for some reason, Jane abandoned, at least temporarily, the men's clothing she always wore. Instead she wore "an old pink gown." She lived, Mrs. Walker said, "in an old shack by the water front where the poor people lived."

Mrs. Walker also reveals that Jane, besides being an expert mule skinner, was a skilled midwife.

According to Mrs. Walker, Jane was called in to take care of a woman expecting a baby. There were several other children in the house. Jane began to make preparations for the blessed event. The children soon got underfoot.

After almost falling over one small child as she was carrying a kettle of boiling water, Jane exploded. She viewed the children with a cold eye. Then, grabbing them one by one, she deposited them in different places about the room.

"Damn you little bastards," she boomed, "now you stay there."

They stayed.

Jane was still her generous, impulsive self, Mrs. Walker remembered. "Even when she was destitute, her services were rendered free if the people could not pay . . . she had a kind heart and was always thinking of others before herself. . . ."

Mrs. Walker remembers Jane as a slender woman about five foot eight, weighing approximately 140 pounds, "with a little gray in her hair." She was then "a woman of the world."

From Pierre, Jane drifted to Montana, where she claimed she bought a ranch. Two years later she opened an inn where "weary travelers could be afforded food and drink."

She was now part of the Western folklore. Dime novels called her "the White Devil of the Yellowstone." Magazines exploited her as solid frontier history. Horatio N. Maguire included her among the empire builders in his *The Coming of the Empire,* supposedly a serious study of the Western scene.

In 1885 she traveled to California to marry a man named Burke. A daughter was born about 1886 or 1887. Legend has Burke's family raising the child.

A few years later Jane turned up at Gilt Edge, Montana, her hair more gray, the lines of dissipation etched deeper in her face. Doctor W. A. Allen of Billings, bought her a riding outfit of which she "was beamingly proud." It was the physician who took her picture in the buckskins and boots, holding the Winchester with which she has appeared many times in books and magazines.

There was a small crowd watching Allen take the picture. A cowboy riding past pulled up. He studied Jane for a moment, then slid from his saddle. Walking up he held out a fifty cent piece.

"I think I owe you this, Jane," said Teddy Blue, the hungry cowhand Jane had fed many years before.

Jane studied him for a moment, then grinned. "I always said, Blue, I didn't give a damn whether you ever paid me for that meal. Come on, boys, let's drink it up. . . ."

Blue stood next to Jane at the bar. It was to Blue that she proclaimed her philosophy: "I want to be left alone to go to Hell in my own way. I want to be with you boys, that's the only life I know."

Blue also recalled a hilarious night in Gilt Edge, where a number of cowhands had stopped off after a long drive. They were dry, they told Jane, but couldn't enter a saloon. When Jane asked for the reason they explained that their herd boss was a religious fanatic who imposed his own morals on his men.

Jane thought for a moment, then said, "You boys be in the lobby of the hotel at eight."

At eight, the lobby was crowded with curious cowpunchers. Blue recalled how they wondered among themselves what Jane "had up her sleeve."

At eight the solemn-faced herd boss walked in. Jane let out a scream and ran up to him, clutching him in a bear hug.

"Darling," she cried. "How are you? Don't you remember how you and I set up the drinks in Miles City . . . and at Carson City when we stayed at the . . ."

The herd boss pulled free. "Madam, I don't know you," he began, but Jane threw her arms around him.

"Darling! Sweetheart! That night when you wanted me to . . ."

The boss fled, "leaving the boys to celebrate with all the hilarity of their pent-up youth."

Jane was the lioness of the hour.

Blue said that for all her generosity and childish improvidence, there were days when Jane was "real hungry." She would drift into a town, craving a drink and really hungry. First she would solicit a few coins then buy a tub and washboard. The rest of the day would be spent in touring the saloons and boardinghouses collecting dirty clothes.

When she had enough "for a toot" she would disappear, "leaving behind a tub and washboard not much worse for the wear."

Jane drifted about the West. The *Cascade Pioneer* in 1923 recalled she lived in a shack a few miles west of Billings, Montana, "sharing a rickety cabin with two horse thieves." Jane made a living chopping down pine trees and selling them for fence posts."

When Chief Joseph fought the Seventh Cavalry to a standstill and the wounded were brought back to Miles City, Jane "turned her back on the horse thieves" and hurried to help care for the wounded.

In 1883 the Rawlins, Wyoming, *Journal* reported that "Calamity Jane has just left accompanied by her best man who serves a hangman's knot." However, the account ended, "Calamity is not half as bad as the ghouls who abuse her."

In 1889 the *Casper Weekly Mail* reported the Sweetwater Valley quiet "except for the musical notes of Calamity Jane."

In 1890, Ben Arnold, the famous Indian fighter, found her in a small town in South Dakota at the end of the Milwaukee Railroad. She was then "old and haggard."

"Know Bill Bivens of Virginia City?" he asked her.

"I can go to his grave as straight as an Indian goes to dog soup," she snapped.

In the summer of that year she appeared at Deer Lodge, Montana. Twenty years ago "Count" Menard, first treasurer of Powell County and secretary of Montana's well-known Overland Tallyho Club, remembered her visit.

It was a warm day, Menard said, and he and the boys were lined up at the bar of the old Brewery saloon.

Suddenly Jane appeared with a tin "growler."

"Fill 'er up," she said.

Someone playfully flipped a lemon peel across the room. It struck Jane on the cheek. She whirled around. A pool table caught her eye. She scooped up the racked balls.

There was "a general exodus for the door but the portal proved too small for assemblage to get through," Menard says.

Jane always had an excellent eye for marksmanship. The pool balls whizzed through the air. One flew past the Count's ear. Another "banged Bud Brown on the skull and he went down and out."

Windows smashed, pool balls bounced off arms, shoulders and skulls. Two more customers went down. Finally the saloon was empty. The bartender cautiously peered from behind the bar.

"Fill 'er up," Jane said quietly. The can was soon filled to the brim.

Then Jane "returned to the small house behind the saloon where she was 'entertaining'."

Her fame spread. More and more tales were told about her. More paper-backed novels appeared with her "confessions." The legend makers were hard at work.

Jane was fast becoming a symbol of the lurid West; the fast-drawing, "say-that-with-a-smile-pardner" West. Jane was conscious of her mission and did her best to live up to it.

In 1934, writing for the jubilee edition of the *Miles City Daily Star*, W. H. (Wirt) Newcom, a well-known frontiersman and former cowpuncher recalled Jane in Miles City in 1894.

He had come into town looking for a job. There weren't many to be had but he managed to find sleeping quarters at Loveridge and Thurman's livery stable on Park Street.

Jane at the time, was living in a shack in the rear of the Gray Mule Saloon. Her husband, Burke, had joined her.

Newcom commented on Burke's good looks. Jane agreed, saying, "I never had a fellow with a hell of a lot of money, but I always got the good-lookers."

One night Jane went on a "toot" and was arrested. She was fined one hundred dollars but managed to slip out of jail. She went to Newcom who persuaded a cowhand to leave his poker game to drive her to the next town. Jane left, swearing to come back and "beat hell out of the police chief," and promised Newcom she would repay him some day.

Years later she would in an amusing way.

In 1899, Calamity was in Billings after a trip to Bozeman and Livingston. The town was alive with cowpunchers waiting to get cattle shipped up from Texas. At the time Billings was built largely about the Northern Pacific Depot. Cowhands coming in to town usually "hurrahed" the town in the best wild West tradition.

In May, 1899, Andrew Malum, formerly a member of the Troop F., Thirteenth Cavalry, and a rider for the Circle Diamond outfit, arrived in Billings to pick up a shipment of cattle. There had been shipping delays all month and with the town crowded with restless cowhands, "events began to happen with Calamity Jane in town."

In an interview in 1930 with the *Cut Bank Pioneer Press,* he recalled one such "event." He was with his ranch boss, Bob Dorset, whom Jane knew, and together they went to the Castle Dance Hall. It was a wild night. The small band played continuously and the whooping cowpunchers "stamped up a cloud of dust."

About midnight there was a stir at the door. Someone pushed through the crowd, six-shooters in both hands. It was Jane, "her eyes sparkling with mischievous intent."

The band stopped. There was a dead silence. Jane jumped up on a chair.

"Everybody leave the house except Bob Dorset and Andy [Malmum]."

There was a scramble for the exit. To make them move faster Jane fired. The glass behind the bar shattered. The bartender ducked. The dance hall emptied, leaving Malmum and Dorset in the middle of the floor "waiting for her next move."

Jane walked toward them, twirling her guns and shooting at the floor. Malmum, no novice with a six-shooter himself, remembered "It was the finest demonstration of gun handling I ever saw."

Jane walked across the floor to the bar followed by Malmum and Dorset. As Malmum said, "The bartender regained his composure and served us the particular liquid we called for. The expense was ours."

Jane was still an expert at cadging drinks.

The next night Jane borrowed a horse from a Circle Diamond cowpuncher and rode right into the dance hall, claiming the horse wanted to dance. Later, at the head of a band of whooping cowhands she rode up and down the street shooting out the street lights.

Rawlins, Cheyenne, Livingston claimed her for the greater part of the eighties. An old man remembers how she leaned out of a window above a saloon, "cursing out" a defaulting teamster. Old-timers in Livingston recall how she was thrown out of a brothel for making two "tenderfeet" dance as she shot about their toes. In Rawlins she stampeded a bull train. Casper, wild and woolly, would have none of her nonsense. She was roped and hog-tied and thrown into jail until she sobered up. One wonders if she ever met Cattle Kate, who was notorious at the time in Casper.

In 1896 she was sober enough to join the Palace Museum at Minneapolis. She toured Chicago, St. Louis, and Kansas City. Once again she was the flamboyant scout of the plains, polished six-shooters at her hip, new buckskins, moccasins, and a Winchester. She had her seven-page "autobiography" published and it sold by the thousands.

But Jane could never remain sober long. She was drunk most of the time and unable to make appearances. Reluctantly, because she had been an excellent attraction, the management fired her.

In 1899 she appeared again at Deadwood. Estelline Bennett, in her *Old Deadwood Days,* recalls the scene. Jane was now a sick woman, aged far beyond her years. Her straggling black hair was iron gray, her eyes bloodshot, her hands trembling from a recent "toot." She was wearing an old musty black dress, a weird hat, and "arctics" (overshoes). She explained later she had given her shoes to a woman on the train "who had to go a long way and might get her feet wet."

She shuffled slowly down Main Street, dragging her daughter, now seven, behind her. Deadwood, she soon realized, had changed. Once it had been a dirty little town in a gulch, the main street filled with boulders, mudholes, and tree stumps. The houses had been shacks or part logs and canvas. Where was the Big Horn Grocery, where she had stolen the groceries for her "patients"? . . . or the saloon where she had . . . ?

It was so hard to believe. The creek now ran red from the trailings of the great Homestead, the towering pines on the slopes were thinner, the muddy street was now macadamized; on Main Street there were now three-story buildings, a schoolhouse and beautiful homes on Forest Hill.

Curious townspeople watched the grotesque figure pass down the street, dragging the child behind her. Word soon spread that Jane was back. Calamity Jane, White Terror of the Yellowstone! They greeted her at the bank. Doc Babcock, Porter Warner, editor of the *Times,* Mike Russell, Buffalo Bill's friend, and all the others, older, white-haired and sentimental.

They stood in the sunshine remembering the "old days." When Jane told them she was trying to make some money to send her daughter to "the sisters to be educated," someone suggested a benefit be staged for Jane. It was greeted with approval.

The Old Opera House was selected. The place was jammed, the show was a financial success. The money was turned over to Jane, who became so exuberant she ordered the boys to join her at Pat's Place.

It is characteristic of Jane to forget her child and spend most of the "benefit money" across the bar. Luckily someone took it away before she could squander all of it.

Miss Bennett heard her come home that night, howling like a wolf and offering to battle any one of the good citizens of Deadwood, who lay in their beds listening with amused smiles.

The next day was a Sunday and the visiting editors of "The National Association" holding their convention in Deadwood found Jane "an object of curiosity."

That afternoon she left Deadwood and took a seat in the men's smoker. Word got around that Calamity Jane was aboard and soon the smoker was filled with admirers "and smoke so thick you could cut it with a knife." Jane sat back when someone produced a bottle and began spinning the tall tales of the "early days."

The reporter who wrote the story for the *Deadwood Times* observed, "She is not as robust as she was fifteen years ago but she still possesses her original traits and characteristics. . . ."

Deadwood never saw her alive again.

4

The sands were running out for Jane. Her magnificent constitution weakened. She no longer had the vitality to shake off the effects of her terrible debauches. She lay in her bed for days, wracked with rheumatism and delirium tremens.

In May 1900, the editor of the *Livingston Post* and Josephine Winifred Blake, the well-known novelist, found her in "a negro house of ill repute, sick and half dead from a long debauch."

Miss Blake asked Jane to accompany her to the East to recuperate. She said she had been promised that Jane would be hired by the Pan-American Exposition as a Western feature.

While Jane lay half in a coma, one of the Negro prostitutes whispered to the newspaperman and Miss Blake that this sick and half-delirious woman had faithfully carried a basket of fruit each day to an old pioneer friend in a hospital at Aldridge, ten miles away, "walking every day along precipitous trails," as the *Post* later said.

The editor urged Jane to accept the novelist's offer. Calamity reluctantly did so—only after Miss Blake had hired a man to "carry fruit to old Jack, my friend in the hospital."

Jane recovered and went to Buffalo where she was featured. Again she appeared in her "scout's" costume, "driving a six-horse team and wagon recklessly around the ring."

One day, Wirt Newcom, who had helped Calamity Jane escape the one-hundred-dollar fine in Miles City, stopped off at Buffalo to visit some relatives.

Inadvertently he said he knew Jane. His relatives would give him no peace until he agreed to introduce them to Jane. As he said in

1930, "Hell's Bells! This crowd never failed to go to church twice on Sunday and prayer meetings on Wednesday night. Here I was in a spot and not a balloon in sight."

Newcom brought his relatives to the fair. Jane appeared in a blaze of bugles, whooping and bellowing to her horses as they roared around and around the ring. The ladies were entranced. Here was a Brete Harte character in real life!

Backstage, Newcom waited apprehensively for Jane to appear. The ladies tittered excitedly among themselves. Jane burst out of her tent. She spotted Newcom.

"Slim!" she roared, "why you old——"

Newcom caught her just in time. He whispered an explanation. Jane put on her best manners, "polite as any of the party."

Alas, the "manners" vanished the next day. As he was passing through Chicago, Newcom read where Jane "went on a high lonesome, fighting two policemen who tried to arrest her."

She was held overnight on a disorderly conduct charge. Still the magic of the name held. She was released the next morning by an admiring justice of the peace. Jane gave the two police officers—one sporting a big black eye—passes for the show and copies of her "autobiography."

But Jane was unhappy. She yearned for Deadwood, Virginia City, and Rawlins, where, to coin a phrase, men were men. It is said that Buffalo Bill found her like this, weeping maudlin tears in her beer.

"For Gawd sakes," she whispered hoarsely, "get me out of this rig." She swept her hand about the tents. "Look at this outfit. It's got me thrown and tied. I want to go back, Bill. Give me the price of a free meal and a ticket to send me home."

It is said and is probably true that Cody sent Jane back West. He was a fine showman and knew the value of publicity. Buffalo Bill helps Calamity Jane, "Scout of the Plains," to go back to the West she loved! It was a natural!

For the next two years Jane wandered about the West, a grotesque creature, dressed in a ragged black dress, battered flowered hat, worn boots, a drunken grin framing two yellow teeth.

In the spring of 1902, the *Daily Yellowstone* reported her in Red Lodge, then Billings, Montana, where she "shot up a saloon." Over the protests of the saloon owner, who recognized a publicity break when he saw one, she was locked up to "sober up." Jane was indignant the next morning, cursing the police and swearing never to return to Billings.

Calamity Jane next appears on a street in Yellowstone in the warm dusk of a summer's evening in 1902. Louis Freeman, the noted American explorer, in his *Down the Yellowstone,* gives an account of his meeting with Jane.

As he was walking down the street he was hailed, "Short Pants, oh, Short Pants, can't you tell a lady where she lives?"

Freeman, wearing knickers, stared through the thickening blue light. He thought he saw a drunken cowpuncher holding on to a lamppost.

"Well, you show me where the lady is and I'll try," Freeman answered.

"She's me, Short Pants. Me—Calamity Jane," the hoarse voice protested.

Freeman came closer. Now he could make out the rough, coarse face, burned to the color of old leather by countless suns and winds of the plains. Two hazel eyes tried their best to focus on him. A foolish grin framed two yellow snags.

"Sure, I'll tell you where you live, Calam," Freeman said, "only you'll have to tell me first."

"Well, come on, Short Pants," Jane roared, "help a lady."

The explorer took Jane in tow and together they sailed down the main street. He managed to discover that Jane had arrived in town sometime that afternoon, hired a room, then went on a "toot." Now she had forgotten where the saloon was. However, she cried triumphantly, she knew the bartender's name was "Patsy" and there was an outside staircase leading to her room.

Freeman and Calamity made a tour of the town's hostelry-taverns. Calamity was always greeted with a shout, "Here's Old Calam," and someone would buy a round. Jane would then introduce "Short Pants," plant a foot on the rail, cock an eye at herself in the bar's mirror, speckled with fly dirt, and down a tall glass of beer—first blowing off the suds with powerful gust.

At each stop Calamity recited her troubles. There was always a murmur of sympathy.

When she wept someone would buy another drink. And so on. Soon volunteers joined Freeman and Calamity. They grew at each stop. Before the night was over there was a sizable crowd staggering behind Jane and Freeman, all alert for Patsy and the outside staircase.

At last the barroom was found. Calamity embraced Patsy who

bought a round on the house. Finally Jane was ready for bed. She fumbled in her pocket. Her eyes glazed, her face became blank.

"Short Pants." Freeman, fearing the worst, asked gently, "What's the matter, Jane?"

Calamity sniffed. "I lost my damn key," she cried, holding on to the bar. "I lost it, I tell you—my damn key."

Chivalry never flourished so strongly in the West as it did that night. The volunteers borrowed a ladder from the fire department. Jane, who had difficulty in finding the rungs, climbed to the second story. A window was opened, and, as Freeman said, "We helped her unprotesting anatomy through the window."

He remembered, "It was the proudest night on which I was able to look back."

In his boyhood, Freeman, as many other American youths, had spent a great deal of time with the lurid paper-backed thriller, *The White Devil of the Yellowstone*. Although the slobbering old wreck he had helped through the window was a far cry from the beautiful woman of his young dreams, she was *still* Calamity Jane. The name *still* had a ring to it. He couldn't wait to see her in the morning.

At about eight he knocked on her door. The hoarse voice commanded him to enter. Freeman found Calamity smoking a thick black cigar, about to prepare breakfast.

"Have a cigar, Short Pants," she growled.

Freeman declined with thanks.

Calamity, a true believer of the iron code of Western hospitality, ordered him to draw up a chair "and have some breakfast."

This sounded better than black cigars. Freeman had ham and eggs. All during the meal Calamity kept calling him "Short Pants," then shortened it merely to "Pants."

In the daylight she looked like a woman of about seventy, with bloodshot eyes and straggling gray hair. From her waist down she had a slender, cowboy's figure. Her hands were well formed but calloused and dirty.

After breakfast, Freeman, still the romanticist, asked to hear the "story of your life."

Calam nodded. "Sure thing, Short Pants. Rush down and fetch me a can of suds. I'll rattle off the whole layout for you. Meet me by those empty beer barrels."

An hour later Freeman was stretched out comfortably in the warm sunshine, alongside the beer barrels, while Calamity lovingly caressed the "can of suds" Freeman had brought her.

"Now, Pants," she rasped, "what do you want to know?"

Before Freeman could answer, she began. "I was born in Princeton, Missouri, in 1848 . . ."

She paused, looked thoughtful for a moment, then squinted down at Freeman.

"This must be my birthday, Pants. Drink to the Queen of the May!"

Wiping the foam from her lips Calamity began again. "I was born in Princeton, Missouri, 1848 . . ."

Her voice droned on monotonously. Her family emigrated from Missouri in 1865 . . . Overland Route to Montana . . . Mother died in 1866 at Blackfoot . . . scout with Custer . . . Captain Eagan whom he brought back to safety, how he whispered, 'I will call you Calamity Jane.' . . ."

Freeman, remembering *The White Devil of the Yellowstone,* was shocked. "But Calamity," he protested, "wasn't it Major Percy Darkleigh, and didn't you say, 'For life and love,' as you caught his reeling form? . . ."

Calamity exploded. The air turned blue with her curses.

As Freeman said, he "gathered" she didn't care too much for *The White Devil of the Yellowstone.*

Calamity took a long swallow. Then she began again, curiously at the beginning. "I was born in Princeton, Missouri . . ."

She went on, a scout for Custer, pony express rider . . . swimming the Platte with the "important dispatch." . . .

Freeman wondered where he had heard this story before. The tin bucket was emptied and refilled. Calamity went on. Tears appeared when Wild Bill's name was mentioned. A long swallow took care of that nostalgic moment.

The story was finally ended.

Freeman lay back, eyes closed against the sun. He smiled to himself. Now he knew where he had heard the story. It was Calamity's own seven-page "autobiography" which she had recited by heart.

That spring of 1903, the *Pioneer Times* reported her traveling "from town to town and camp to camp, visiting pioneers and others who knew her during the early days."

In July, 1903, Calamity Jane appeared at the Calloway Hotel in Terry, a short distance from Deadwood. She stood in the doorway, whispering, "I'm ailing—I guess I'm ready to cash in. . . ."

The owner of the hotel, who knew her of old, thought she had been on one of her famous debauches. He helped her to a room, ordered a maid to assist her to undress, then returned to his work. In the late afternoon the maid appeared, saying Jane was violently ill and had a high fever.

Doctors were called. When word came to Deadwood, some of the old people rode up to Terry to see her. It was four o'clock and the sun was setting, filling her small room with a garish light.

"What's the date?" she asked in a hoarse whisper.

August 2, 1903, she was told.

"It's the twenty-seventh anniversary of Bill's death," she said. She seemed to sink into a coma. Once she opened her eyes and whispered, "Bury me next to Bill."

At five her breathing became labored. Finally, with a shudder, she died.

The women of Deadwood washed and dressed her body in a neat dress. A local undertaker donated a plain pine coffin.

On Monday, August 4, Jane was buried with one of the largest funerals in Deadwood's history. Dr. C. B. Clark, a Methodist minister, preached, as one old man said later, "one of the finest orations I ever heard."

"He spoke with a fervor greater than I have ever heard him use before. He said nothing about Calamity's depredations but stressed the good in her life."

There was one last wonderful touch. The man who sealed her casket and lowered her into the grave in Mt. Moriah Cemetery, next to Wild Bill Hickok's, was C. H. Robinson, rector of the cemetery. He was the young boy whom Calamity Jane had nursed so carefully during the smallpox plague of '78!

6

Calamity Jane settled into Western history. Thousands of tourists began to travel annually to see her grave and Hickok's. Her depravity was lost in a sea of newspaper clippings which repeated the old lies of how she saved Captain Eagan's life, who called her "Calamity Jane"; was a scout for Custer, served under Crook on the border, and so on.

Then in June, 1941, the West rocked with the news that Calamity Jane's daughter had appeared with her mother's "diary and a so-called confession."

The *Billings Gazette* identified her as Mrs. Jane Hickok McCormick, a quiet, gray-haired lady who lived in a small hotel on North Broadway in Billings.

In her "confession" Jane said she was married twice, once to James Butler (Wild Bill) Hickok, and after his death to Charles Burke in 1891.

The confession is dated June 3, 1903, and was witnessed by the Reverend N. K. Sipes, James O'Neil, and R. R. Ryan. The so-called diary does not give a continuous account of her life. In reality it consists of a series of letters dated sometimes four years apart. They were all intended to be given to her daughter after her death.

The first entry is dated September 25, 1877, at Deadwood, Dakota Territory, with the notation: "Jim O'Neil, please give this album to my daughter, Janey Hickok, after my death. Jane Hickok."

Part of the letter reads:

My Dear: This isn't intended for a diary and it may even happen that this may never be sent to you. But I would like to think of you reading it someday, page by page, in the years to come after my death. I would like to hear you laugh when you look at these pictures of meself [sic]. I am alone in the shack and tired. I rode sixty miles yesterday to the post office and returned today. This is your birthday. You are four years old today. Jim [James O'Neil who allegedly adopted Calamity Jane's daughter] promised me he would always get a letter to me on your birthday each year. Was I glad to hear from him. He sent a tiny picture of you. You are the dead spit of meself at the same age. . . .

The next letter is dated three days later and boasts how the Sioux never "bother me because they think I am a crazy woman." Also enclosed was a picture "of your grandmother. She and your grandfather came across the plains in a covered wagon when I was a child."

The next entry dated October, 1880, has Jane driving a stagecoach. She said the Reverend Blue and Teddy Blue got her the job.

She wrote: "One day I have chickens to eat, and the next day feathers."

A description of Billings is included in the next letter dated May 10, 1893. Life, she wrote was "hectic" in Billings, "like Hell let out for noon."

In July, 1893, a letter described a howling hailstorm in which she was trapped while driving a stage. She also revealed that Buffalo Bill had asked her to join his show.

July 25, 1893, she writes she joined Cody's show. She also told of

197

buying 320 acres in "Canyon Creek" where she cooked for some out-laws. Her price was twenty cents a loaf of bread, fifty cents a pie, and cake a dollar.

In the same letter she advised her daughter to seek Ben Greenough, "if you want to find someone to speak a good word for me."

The diary then includes letters written while she was supposedly traveling with Buffalo Bill's show. Once she went to England with James O'Neil and saw her daughter who was not then aware that Calamity was her mother.

The next entry is dated July, 1898, in which she tells how she dis-liked "the snobs" she had met in Europe and in the East. The last entry is April, 1903, when she writes she is going blind. It concludes on this pathetic note: "What have I ever done except to make one blunder after the other? . . ."

Mrs. McCormick explained that she hadn't made her identity known before to avoid "embarrassing friends." Friends who knew her relation-ship to Calamity Jane, notified the radio commentator, Gabriel Heatter, who invited Mrs. McCormick to New York. Over a nationwide broad-cast, she disclosed she was Calamity Jane's daughter.

Mrs. McCormick died in Billings Hospital on February 22, 1951, at the age of seventy-seven, from a heart attack. According to her obituary notices in the *Livingston Post,* there were no survivors.

In a letter, a copy of which the author has, written in 1947, Mrs. McCormick gives the background of her relationship. She wrote:

> I was born at Benson's Landing, near where Livingston now stands. The year, 1873—and my parents were Wild Bill Hickok (James Butler Hickok) and Calamity Jane (Jane Canarray).
>
> Of course Calamity Jane had left Wild Bill early that year. She had been posing as his partner, the Jack of Diamond's, in Abilene, Kansas, and down on the border. She left him in Deadwood and hit the trail alone up the Yellowstone Valley.
>
> She was only nineteen when I was born. She had no care of any sort and almost died from lack of medical care.
>
> A man appeared near the cabin Jane had built and upon hearing a baby crying investigated and found a two-day-old baby and a very sick mother.
>
> This man was Captain James O'Neil,* British master of a

---

* The Liverpool office of the Cunard White Star Line, after a search of their records, has informed the author that there is no evidence that a Captain James O'Neil was ever employed by the line.

Cunard liner who was also investigating the death of his brother. A report came to him that his brother had been killed by Howling Wolf, a Sioux Chief.

He had located the place where his brother had been buried, and was ready to leave when he chanced on the cabin Calamity Jane had been hiding out in. He made arrangements for Jane to bring the baby girl to Omaha, the nearest point to a R. R. connection east. I was nearly a year old before the O'Neils adopted me and took me to England with them.

I was raised as an O'Neil and never knew who my real parents were until the death of my foster father, Captain O'Neil in 1912.

Twice in my life I saw Calamity Jane—once when I was about eight years old, and again when I was 18.

She was considered just a woman of the West and a friend of the O'Neils.

I have her diary written all those years after she adopted me to the O'Neils. It is a pathetic sort of a diary written in an old family album in form of letters to me. It was given to me upon O'Neil's death. . . .

Mrs. McCormick told the *Billings Gazette* which devoted two and a half columns to the story, that she saw Calamity once in Richmond when she was eight. Calamity had $10,000, "reportedly half her winnings in an all night poker game with officials when the Northern Pacific reached Billings."

The money was given to the O'Neils by Calamity for her daughter's education.

Mrs. McCormick returned to Montana in 1898, teaching penmanship" in Butte schools until 1902. She married, was divorced, then went East for several years. She was a volunteer nurse in France and married Edward McCormick, an aviator on November 11, 1918, in a deathbed ceremony in a rear-line hospital.

In 1922 she returned to Montana. For several years she worked as a cook on dude ranches in Montana, Washington, and Wyoming.

What of this alleged confession and diary? Of course, without an opinion of a handwriting expert it cannot be flatly labeled spurious.

To this author it seems highly improbable that Calamity Jane, during her riotous, drunken life, ever took time to write such letters or keep a "diary."

Again it is doubtful that she ever "married" Hickok, who certainly only viewed her as an amiable bar fly who lent some color to his entourage.

There is one error in the "diary." Jane supposedly wrote in July, 1893, that she had joined Cody's show and was going to tour Europe. Buffalo Bill didn't take his show abroad until two years later. A search of his programs in the circus collections in the New York Public Library fails to show any listing of Jane's name. It seems implausible that Cody would fail to capitalize on such a colorful attraction as Calamity Jane.

Yet for all its improbability, someone who knew a great deal about Calamity Jane must have written those letters. Teddy Blue, the Montana cowhand is mentioned, also the fact that she shared a cabin and cooked for horse thieves. This may have been the same winter recalled by an old-timer who said "she shared a cabin with thieves at a place called 'Horse Thief Cache,' a few miles west of Billings."

Putting aside all the arguments for and against the legitimacy of the so-called "confession and diary," this author fails to conjure up a picture of Calamity Jane, feebly picking up a pen in one of her dismal shacks, and in a befuddled alcoholic haze, writing a "Dear Janey" letter.

Belle Starr: A Woman Who
Has Seen Much of Life

FOR more than eighty years men have told the story of Belle Starr. She is described as a woman of dazzling beauty, loved by many men, a female Robin Hood who led a colorful band of outlaws during the last days of the old West.

They recall how she thundered into Fort Smith, dressed in a velvet gown, two six-shooters on her hip, a Winchester strapped to her saddle, riding "Venus," a mare black as a raven's wing. They remember that she was "educated" but swore like a mule skinner and could outride the best of the bronc riders and outswagger and outshoot most of the gun fighters who pushed their way along the wooden sidewalks of Fort Smith.

Above all they recall how she played the piano in the rough saloons, stilling the shrill laughter of the dance-hall girls, the bawdy jokes, and the clink of poker chips.

Perhaps because the legend makers of the old West always insisted that their outlaw heroines be "educated," Belle's piano playing stands out in most of the legends told about her. Homesteaders, squatters, nesters, ranchers, and outlaws swore she had a piano in the rough, one-room shack on the Canadian River which she called Younger's Bend.

"When I passed I heard Belle playing—it sure was beautiful," one old-timer says.

Nothing could convince him that Belle never had a piano in her shack. A close examination of Younger's Bend shows it would be almost impossible to squeeze a piano through the door of the one-room cabin in which slept Belle, her current husband, her daughter and son, and the outlaws—"jolly lads"—as Belle called them, who were always hiding out at Younger's Bend.

Strangely enough there is some truth to be found in the legends told about Belle. There is evidence she could play the piano. Richard Young

Auld, in his memoirs published in the Oklahoma Historical Society, Indian Pioneer History, recalled Belle Starr playing in the Ingram Hotel in Eufaula, Oklahoma. He says in part:

> My attention was attracted by her general appearance. She wore two large pistols in a belt buckled around her waist and her wearing apparel was not of the delicate feminine type generally worn by her sex, though everything appeared to fit with her type of character and was worn with perfect comfort and composure. On my way to my room I asked Mr. Ingram who she was and he told me it was Belle Starr.

As for being a "Bandit Queen," an indictment handed down in Fort Smith charged her with being "the leader of a band of notorious horse thieves. . . ."

Her theatricalism was mentioned many times in newspapers of the day, while men and women still living in Fort Smith recall her black mare "Venus," her velvet gown, her six-shooters, and her thundering entrances into town. As for her being "educated," strangely enough she did attend a private school in Carthage, Missouri, whose curriculum included music!

The only part of the legend told about Belle which does not stand up, is the one describing her as a dazzling beauty. Belle may have been a wholesome, fresh-cheeked country girl when Cole Younger, home from the wars, first seduced her. But at thirty she was a thin-lipped, hawk-nosed woman with coarse, weather-beaten skin, cold gray eyes, gray-streaked hair, and hands calloused and hard from gripping the reins of the wild horses she loved to break.

It was Richard Fox's hack writers who made Belle a Western Robin Hood. Until they filled the Police Gazette with columns of fictitious accounts of Belle's exploits, she was only a frontier character known for her theatrical activities in Dallas, Fort Smith, Arkansas, and "the Nations." Fox's hacks soon made her "Queen of the Bandits," "The Petticoat Terror," and so on.

Belle, to one writer, was "a woman as remarkable as Cleopatra, more amorous than Anthony's mistress, more relentless than Pharaoh's daughter, and braver than Joan of Arc." She was also pictured as a woman of "extraordinary musical and literary talents which were thrown away through the basis of her nomadic and lawless disposition."

To strengthen their title "Belle Starr, the Female Jesse James," Fox's writers had Belle robbing trains and stagecoaches. Belle, of course never committed a major robbery. She confined her thievery mostly to rustling, horse stealing, and "passing horses" as a frontier fence. She was arrested but never convicted of robbery.

The pink-sheeted *Gazette* passed from hand to hand in the old West. The tall tales were accepted and elaborated upon. Some historians accepted the legends and they became fact. Many times Belle Starr had been confused with Belle Boyd, that truly glamorous Confederate spy. Only a few years ago one Western writer solemnly declared that Rose of the Cimarron, who rode with Doolin gang of Oklahoma, was "the daughter of Belle Starr." This ridiculous error was repeated in another book. Perhaps it will be repeated again. It may be that some years from now Belle Starr will be pictured as Stonewall Jackson's courier, while Belle Boyd steals horses and cattle in the Oklahoma territory. . . .

2

It is generally accepted that Myra Belle Shirley was born on February 5, 1848 in a log cabin, somewhere along the Missouri frontier. We know nothing of her mother, Elizabeth. Her father, John, is said to have been a Southern "aristocrat" who came from Virginia, a state then popularly associated with fine cigars, excellent horses, beautiful women, and pure-blooded gentlemen.

It is traditional to call him "Judge" Shirley, although there is no record that he ever presided over a court. Like many of the frontiersmen, Shirley was consumed with wanderlust, the desire to see what was over the mountains.

It is believed that sometime before 1848, Shirley settled down in Washington County, Missouri, where his clan was so numerous they gave the name to the town of Shirley, still in existence. It was there that John Shirley married. It is possible that Belle was born in that town.

We next find Shirley, his wife Elizabeth, and their infant daughter, Belle, in Jasper County, Missouri. On June 30, 1848, Shirley's claim for 800 acres of land, ten miles northwest of Carthage, Missouri, was entered in the United States land office.

Their farmhouse was typical of the time; a three-room clapboard house with sheds and a barn in the rear, all enclosed by a zigzag rail fence. When Belle was two years old her father sold 160 acres for $700. The following June the family moved to Carthage, which then had a population of a hundred families. For three years, from 1855 to 1858, Shirley renewed the mortgage on his farm every six months. In the winter of '58 he had paid his debts and opened the Carthage Hotel. Evidently he had saved a fairly large sum. On the day he opened his hotel-tavern he bought two slaves to help with the work.

Now eight years old, Belle entered the Carthage Female Academy, a two-story brick building boasting of eight classrooms. Board and lodging was $10 a month. The curriculum included reading, writing, spelling, grammar, algebra, deportment, Greek, Latin, and Hebrew. Instructions in oil painting, piano, and organ were extra.

There is evidence that Belle also attended another school located in the town's Masonic Hall; tuition was from $1 to $1.50 a month.

In 1922, Mrs. James Brummett of Carthage, told the *Carthage Press* that Belle was her classmate in this school, conducted by a William Cravens. Mrs. Brummett gives us our only description of Belle as a child.

"She [Belle] was a bright, intelligent girl, but was of a fierce nature, and would fight anyone, boy or girl, that she quarreled with. Except for this fact, she seemed like a nice little girl." Belle was then about ten.

Shirley's tavern-inn business prospered. But the bitter war between Kansas and Missouri broke out. Civil War followed. Quantrill, "the bloodiest man in American history," swept across the border to burn and pillage Kansas. In retaliation Jim Lane led his "Red Legs" in plundering the farms of Missouri.

Belle's elder brother, Edward, joined Lane's bushwhackers and was killed at Sarcoxie, Missouri. Another brother, Prescott, ran away to Texas. Numerous writers have claimed the death of Belle's brother was her motive in becoming a female bandit. But the "revenge" motive appears in the life of almost every American outlaw; Jesse James was whipped by the Federals who tried to hang his father; Butch Cassidy was unjustly jailed for stealing a saddle; Bob Dalton, leader of the Daltons, was wrongly accused of cheating at cards, and so on.

Frank James, brother of Jesse, gives Belle a starring role in one border incident in which she helped to save her brother from the Federals. In his book, *Frank James: The Only True History of the Life of Frank James; Written by Himself,* he has Belle, then about sixteen, reconnoitering the Federal camp "to learn their movements." In some unexplained way she discovered the Federals' plan to attack her brother's camp.

James said Belle stayed in the neighborhood of the camp only to

be arrested the next day. The captain in charge of the camp ordered her held until the Federal troops rode out of camp "and had been gone a half hour."

The half hour passed and Belle was released. She ran to her pony "and was off like the wind, through fields and pastures, jumping fences, on and on." Of course she arrived before the raiders to warn her brother, who escaped. As Frank James said, "This famous ride gave Belle the name of a bronco rider."

Frank's book was published eleven years after his death. No ghost writer would have permitted such an illiterate, maudlin piece of trash to be published. There is little doubt that the book was written, as the title claimed, by James himself. He knew Belle quite well and the incident may have some truth to it.

Harman's *Hell On The Border* used Frank's incident but gave it much more embroidery. To make it more effective the incident is made to take place on Belle's sixteenth birthday. The cavalry major who captured her is pictured as releasing Belle, because "my men will have your brother under arrest before you can reach him."

Belle, sobbing "I'll beat them yet," vaults in the saddle, "a beautiful sight as she rode through the fields, her lithe figure clad in a tight-fitting jacket, erect as an arrow, her hair falling free and flung to the breeze. . . ."

The major, watching her fly down the road, is made to say, "Well, I'll be— She's a born guerrilla. If she doesn't reach Carthage ahead of my troopers, I'm a fool."

As in the Frank James version she roused her brother's camp in time for him to escape.

The continuous raids ruined Shirley's tavern business and he sold out. Early in 1863 he piled the family's meager possessions onto an ox-drawn Conestoga wagon, and with Belle on the front seat, rolled out of Carthage. He was, as they said in those days, G. T. T. (Gone To Texas.)

Shirley's youngest son, Preston, then about twenty-two, was living in McKinney County, north of Dallas. Shirley also had a brother who owned a farm near Scyene, ten miles east of Dallas. His goal was Scyene.

It must have been a long and torturous journey; through the Ozarks to Fort Smith, Arkansas, then to De Queene and westward to Dallas and southeast to Scyene. No matter how difficult was the journey, it was far more comfortable than being back in Carthage. On a quiet June afternoon Jennison's Jayhawkers rode into town like a band of howling Furies. When they left, the town was in ashes. Not a house remained. . . .

When Shirley's prairie schooner rode down the main street of Dallas, the town was booming. The population was more than 2,000 and growing daily. Saloons, gambling houses, and brothels were plentiful. Gun duels were commonplace. Belle eyed the town with interest. She would know it better before very long.

John Shirley, his wife, and Belle, moved in on Prescott, who was probably living in a "dugout"—simply a large hole dug in the ground, the dirt piled on all sides and covering the board roof. This type of dwelling was quite popular among the settlers. They were warm in winter and cool in summer. But they were much too small for more than two people.

Prescott soon found this out and made his father build his own dugout.

Burton Roscoe, who talked to old-time settlers for his biography of Belle, quotes them as saying the Shirleys were not liked by their neighbors. An eighty-year-old resident of Dallas recalls the Shirleys were hostile, unfriendly, and crude neighbors. He remembers how the farmers in the district rose up in arms when the Shirleys made a habit of draining the community well to fill their water barrels.

Others recall that Belle had a mule-skinner's tongue and a vicious temper. But most vivid in the memories of the old men and women was the furtive, close-mouthed nature of the Shirleys. To the loud, hearty, black-slapping Texans this was unthinkable. They would never understand the Doonelike clannishness of the Missourians.

A year after Appomattox, Cole Younger rode into Belle's life. Back in Missouri, Cole, his brothers, Jim, John, and Bob, and their neighbors, the James boys, had discovered there was no Appomattox for men who had ridden under Quantrill's black flag. There were lynchings and bushwhackings. Northern sympathizers who had suffered from Quantrill's raiders now struck back.

They had also found it hard to return to the peaceful ways of a farmer. Who could follow the plow after he had tasted the wild, thrilling moment when he had been one of the three hundred screaming horsemen who had thundered down on Centralia, reins between their teeth and Colts blazing?

The former guerrillas gathered at the Samuels' place. Riders pounded along the dark roads and back lanes. Then on St. Valentine's Day, 1866, Jesse James led his brother Frank and the Youngers into Liberty to hold up the Clay County Savings Association Bank—the first robbery of its kind in the nation's history. They rode up and down the street, guns blazing and shrieking their wild cries. A fourteen-year-old boy, bewildered by the firing, started to run. One of the ex-guerrillas took careful aim and fired. The boy dropped dead, a bullet through his brain.

The senseless killing infuriated the community. Posses scoured the countryside. But the bandits had vanished like fog in the sun.

Before the posses had reached the Samuels' place, Jesse and the Youngers had G. T. T. with $60,000, $15,000 of it in gold.

Cole was a handsome man who emerges as perhaps the most personable and likable of the gang. Jesse was a moody, cold-blooded killer; Frank a sanctimonious, Bible-quoting hypocrite. But big Cole was a complete extrovert. Women always wanted to love him. More than one female heart skipped a beat when, at Madelia, Minnesota, following his capture, he stood up in the wagon taking him to jail, to tip his hat and bow to some ladies on the sidewalk. Not even eleven bullets could make him forget that he was the Gay Desperado, first and always.

Belle never had a chance. While the gang drank her father's corn and played poker, Cole wooed Belle in the moonlight. Before the gang rode off she was pregnant.

When Belle told Cole he adopted the attitude of man eternal. He made promises and told her he would "love her always." Then with Frank and Jesse James he rode off to rob the Hughes and Mason Bank in Richmond, Ray County, just east of Clay where Jesse lived. After fighting off the angry townspeople they escaped with $4,000 in gold.

Cole returned to the comparative security of Texas, where he bought a small farm near Scyene, which soon became a hideout for outlaws and horse thieves.

The Youngers stayed in Texas off and on until about 1874. Bob Younger took a clerk's job in a general store, Jim served as a deputy sheriff in Dallas. Cole evidently did nothing but woo Belle.

The author has read a signed statement by E. G. Bower, district attorney of Dallas from 1874 to 1876, which tells of the activities of the James and Younger brothers in Texas.

Bower described Cole as "a young man of kindly nature, entire truthfulness and heroic gallantry." He added: "Cole, Bob and Jim Younger sang in the choir of the Baptist Church in Dallas, where they were on the side of law and order. The boys were often called in by the sheriff to assist in the arrest of desperate characters and they always responded."

The "boys," Bower also disclosed, were civic minded. "They not only sang in the choir," he said, "but they also assisted in taking the scholastic census of Dallas in 1870."

District Attorney Bower may have been slightly prejudiced in favor of the James and Younger brothers. As he stated, "I was a war comrade of Cole's."

It makes a wonderful picture: Cole, Jim, and Bob in the choir loft, sharing a choir book, and lifting their voices to the glory of heaven, each wearing a brace of six-shooters under their frock coats; or big Cole, tipping his hat and asking the housewives of Dallas their age, number of children, and salary of their husband—all of course for the purposes of good government.

There is a legend that Cole joined Jesse and the gang in a two-room shack they had built on Tar Creek, near Miamai in Otowa County, Oklahoma. The *Daily Oklahoman* said the cabin was a hideout for the gang after the "Galena raid in which Jesse was shot."

Shortly after the raid Belle is said to have appeared at the cabin in her search for Cole. She stayed to nurse Jesse and to bring back supplies for the gang from nearby Venita.

There is a strange romantic twist to the legend. One day when Jesse had recovered, a mysterious rider, dressed in a worn blue Confederate cavalryman's coat, pulled up before the cabin, calling loudly for Belle.

Belle came to the door and when she saw the rider "screamed and staggered back into the house."

One of the outlaws rushed out with a drawn gun and demanded the stranger "to tell his name."

"None of your damn business," the stranger said as he pulled his horse about. The outlaw fired, killing the mysterious rider. Belle, "with an outraged scream," fell on the outlaw and tried to pull her gun to kill him but was prevented by Cole who disarmed her.

When she quieted down, Cole asked, "Who is this man, Belle?"

Belle cursed him out and began packing her few belongings. Outside the shack the gang was burying the dead man. Before she rode off, Belle said to them, as she rode past the new grave, "You'll pay for this."

The identity of the man was never learned. Of course flowers appeared once a year on the grave, placed there by Belle. In 1918 a local newspaper reported finding a faded picture of Belle Starr and a young man in the shack.

There is little doubt that the cabin existed and some young outlaw was killed and buried there. His grave is now covered with a large pile of mine chat.

It is doubtful that Jesse James and the Youngers hid out there or that Belle paid them a visit. There is no record of Jesse taking part in a Galena bank robbery, which the newspaper writers or legend makers may have confused with the Gallatin robbery in December, 1869, when Jesse and his gang raided the Daviess County Savings Bank. Jesse, however, was not wounded in that robbery.

There is also this to consider. Why should Jesse have fled to Oklahoma when he was unusually safe in Clay County, protected by his spy system, sympathizers, kinfolk, corrupt or fearful officials?

Upon his return to Texas, Cole saw Belle and his daughter, christened Pearl Younger. There is nothing to tell us how Cole felt about fatherhood. But there is little doubt that he was quite relieved when Belle began to show a romantic interest in Jim Reed, bank and train robber who had G. T. T. with a sheriff's posse from Vernon County, Missouri, at his heels.

For Belle it was a renewal of an old romance. As one of Reed's brothers said in 1889, "Brother Jim and Myra Belle Shirley" were childhood sweethearts.

When Jim arrived in Texas he joined the notorious John Fischer outlaw band. "Judge" Shirley's farmhouse at Scyene was selected as a hideout. Jim asked Belle to join the gang, and Belle, bored with the farm drudgery, agreed. Fischer gave his blessing.

Her father was furious when she told him. To prevent her from leaving he locked her in the closet, then drove Fischer and his gang from his land.

Belle banged on the closet door all that afternoon but her father would not allow her mother to open it. One can easily visualize the future "Queen of the Outlaws," hoarse from shouting, sitting among the old shoes and hats, wondering how she could get out to join her outlaw sweetheart.

That evening in a bar in town, the disconsolate Reed began drinking heavily. Fischer and his gang joined him, promising each other to kill Shirley on the spot when they saw him. Then Jim brightened up. He rubbed his whiskers, admiring himself in the mirror behind the bar, as he announced to the gang he had an "idea."

They eyed him expectantly when Fischer asked cautiously if he was going to kill "the Judge." Jim shook his head.

"We'll rescue Belle tonight," he shouted, "and I'll marry her!"

The outlaws looked at each other. Then, as the novelty of the idea grew, they whooped and slapped each other on the back.

"What about a preacher?" asked Fischer.

That only stumped Jim for a moment. The gang whooped again

209

when he announced Fischer would be the "preacher" who would "marry" them.

From somewhere in town the gang obtained a ladder and rode out to the Shirley place. While the others stumbled in the shadows, drunkenly shushing each other, Reed climbed the ladder.

Belle, who had been released from the closet by her father when night had fallen, carefully raised the window. Before Jim was half-way up the ladder she was on her way down. The gang galloped off with Belle riding behind Reed. Before they reached the town, Fischer, in the center of a circle of his grinning outlaws, solemnly "married" Jim and Belle.

Jim and Belle returned to Missouri where they bought a small farm near Rich Hill. They had only a few months of "married" life when Jim rode off for Texas to avenge the killing of a younger brother. The hack writers in the nineties made much of this incident. In one version Jim is pictured as leaving Belle and her daughter under an oak tree, after she had promised to return to the same spot "twenty days from today at one o'clock. . . ."

Of course at the very hour Jim Reed returned, "reaching over her shoulder, and taking the baby from her arms, tossed it in the air, then kissed the baby and her. . . ."

Reed did return, in how many days we do not know. With him was a dark-skinned young man, whom he introduced as Sam Starr. Belle eyed the stranger with interest. He was a handsome man, straight as an arrow, with the unmistakable features of a pure-blooded Cherokee.

Jim was home only a few weeks when he was informed that law officers from Texas were inquiring about him. He said a hurried good-by to Starr, and packed Belle and baby Pearl into a wagon.

This time it was G. T. C. (Gone To California). The strangers had been Pinkerton operatives and Texas deputies. As Reed explained to Belle, he had been exceedingly busy in Texas, taking part in a few holdups and killing two men to avenge the murder of his brother.

The Reeds found old friends in California. Jesse James, his brother Frank, and the Youngers were enjoying the West Coast climate. Law officers later found the Missouri outlaws had stayed at the home of Jesse's uncle, Dr. Woodson James, who conducted a sanitarium at Paso Robles.

They stayed on the Pacific coast for about two years. During that time Belle presented Jim with a baby boy, whom they named Edward. Probably to support his growing family Jim turned his hand to outlawry. Once again they escaped the posse when a kindly neighbor informed Jim the man hunters were on their way.

Jim and Belle returned to Texas where they bought a small ranch near Scyene. Evidently "the Judge" had forgiven Jim for eloping with his daughter. Meanwhile the James-Younger gang was terrorizing the border states. After each strike they apparently vanished into thin air. It wasn't until years later that it was learned the gang hid at Frank's ranch, or the Shirley place in Scyene. In 1869 the Dallas authorities obtained a warrant for the arrest of Shirley on the grounds of harboring fugitive criminals but there is no record of the disposition of the case. "The Judge" probably had it squashed.

On one of the long rides into Texas to hide out, the Youngers were accompanied by John Younger, the youngest in the band. Then about sixteen, he had killed a man in Clay County. From the records it appears he shot the man "who had struck him on the head with a dead fish." Cole brought his brother to Texas "until it was safe for him to return."

Supplied with funds by Cole, John soon began to swagger about Dallas, boasting of his name and his brothers' fame. He took to wearing six-shooters and bragging of his marksmanship. One day in the winter of 1871, he persuaded a drunken old bar fly to let him shoot the pipe out of his mouth at ten paces. The old man, so drunk he could hardly stand, agreed for the price of a drink.

John aimed and fired. Pipe and part of the old man's nose disappeared. So did John. A warrant was sworn out for Younger and Deputy Sheriff Nichols of Dallas County went to the Shirley place, where John was staying, to serve the warrant.

The *Dallas Weekly Herald* of February 5, 1871, tells the story under the headline "Obituary." Nichols, at the head of the posse, was "shot down" by the young outlaw and died the next day.

Belle hid John, then sent him back to Missouri.

In 1873, Belle herself took to the outlaw trail. With Jim Reed and two other outlaws she tortured a wealthy old Creek Indian in his house on the North Canadian River, until he told them the hiding place of his $30,000 in gold. Belle took part in the robbery dressed as a man.

After the loot had been divided, Jim and Belle returned to Dallas. While Jim went on "the scout"—looking for places to rob—Belle first played her role as "Queen of the Outlaws." She dressed in a long, black velvet gown with a high collar, chiffon waists, glossy black leather boots, and a creamy white Stetson with an ostrich plume stuck in the band. Around her waist two six-shooters hung from a cartridge belt.

She made it a habit to gallop into town on a splendid black stallion, pulling up at the nearest saloon or gambling house. With the train of her long velvet dress draped over one arm, she would call loudly for whisky or plump herself down at the nearest faro table, announcing she was ready to play with the sky the limit.

As the months went by she played her bandit queen role to the hilt. The velvet dress was replaced by a fringed buckskin suit and beaded moccasins. The guns always hung from her belt.

She was never arrested, although on some occasions she rode through the town whooping and firing her guns. Windows crashed and signs were splintered. Men ducked behind wagons and into alleys. But no one ever tried to disarm or arrest her.

Doc Holliday, that cold-blooded, nerveless fighting machine, is said to have been in Texas at the time, earning his living as a gambler. One wonders what would have happened had Belle tried any of her theatrical stunts on him. . . .

In April, 1874, Reed, Jesse James, and Cole Younger held up the San Antonio-Austin stage. A few weeks later Jim was arrested in Dallas. However, he was released a short time later for lack of evidence. In August he was killed by a member of the gang who had been granted immunity by the United States marshal, on the promise to get the evidence on Reed and arrest him.

Belle continued to live with her daughter, Pearl, in Dallas. Her son was raised by his grandmother on the Shirley place in Scyene. Belle lavished all her attention on her daughter. Piano and dancing instructors were hired. When she was fourteen Pearl made her debut in a Dallas theater, but collapsed on the stage "from a brain hemorrhage."

Belle took up her old way again. The saloons and gambling houses saw much of her. But behind the theatrical pose was a bewildered and lonely woman. Harman, in his *Hell On The Border,* quotes one of her letters, which he said he had copied from the original, to Reed's kinfolk in Missouri. In it she tells of her father's death, and the decision to let her mother, who was leaving Texas, raise her son.

> I don't know if I shall ever see him again. [she wrote] He is a fine manly boy as you ever seen and is said to resemble Jimmie [Reed] very much; he is still motioned and I don't think there is a more intelligent boy living. . . .

She closed the letter saying she was "far from well and so nervous I can scarcely write."

Pearl stayed with her mother about two years in Dallas. Then Belle sent her to relatives in Missouri. With no children to burden her, Belle cut loose, "and again began to exhibit her roving disposition."

Once she was saved from a jail term for arson by a wealthy stockman who was attracted by her charms and paid her fine. As the story goes, she gave the panting stockman only promises. When his efforts to collect his "collateral"—probably a night or two with Belle—failed, the stockman's friends urged him to sue. But Texas chivalry dominated, and the stockman declined.

From 1875 to about 1880, Belle became the undisputed leader of a band of cattle and horse thieves who made their headquarters in "The Nations," the Indian-held sections of Oklahoma. Outlaws sought her out for advice, or for refuge. To Belle they were all "jolly lads." Some of them she accepted as lovers, but it was Cole Younger who had the choicest spot in her heart.

In 1876, the people of Northfield, Minnesota, blew the James-Younger gang apart with rifles, shotguns, pitchforks, and rocks. Cole was captured and sentenced with his brothers to life in the Stillwater Penitentiary. Belle was untiring in her efforts to get him paroled. Legend has dust-covered riders coming into the office of Cole's lawyers and dropping on their desk thick rolls of greenbacks "for Cole from a friend." The money is said to have been sent by Belle to aid the fight for Cole.

Belle also showed in another way she never forgot the big, handsome outlaw from Clay County. After she built her home on the Canadian River she called it "Younger's Bend." But Belle was never a lady who would weep and wait for her lover. Cole was behind bars; a stocky, mustached Indian, with the strange name of "Blue Duck" took his place.

One day in 1877, Belle and "Blue Duck" traveled to Dodge City to sell a herd of stolen cattle. She entrusted the money to Blue Duck and went off on a shopping spree. Blue Duck visited the nearest saloon and promptly lost the roll to gamblers.

When she heard his story Belle silently strapped on her guns and started out of the hotel.

"Where you going, Belle?" Blue Duck asked anxiously.

"To get back the money you lost, you damn fool," she replied.

Belle swaggered through the saloon and up the stairs to the gambling rooms. The tinkling piano stopped and the dancing girls stared. There wasn't a whisper when she kicked open the door and yanked out her guns. At her command the gamblers threw down their guns, butts first. Then she backed out of the room with $7,000, saying, "There's a little change due you, gentlemen. If you want it come down into the Territory and visit me some time."

It makes a grand scene even if the serious historians of the *Queen of the Cowtowns* forget to mention it.

In 1880 Belle married Sam Starr, the tall, slim Cherokee who first appeared in her life when he had accompanied Jim Reed back from his revenge trip to Texas. Sam was twenty-eight, Belle thirty-two. The honeymooners settled down on Sam's sixty-two acres on the north side of the Canadian River, near Briartown.

Belle was surrounded by the enormous numbers of the Starr clan, presided over by "Uncle Tom" Starr, an incredibly vicious old villain. In *Chronicles of Oklahoma* there is a story of how in 1843 he burned a whole family to death including a five-year-old boy who came running out of his burning house, only to be tossed back into the flames by "Uncle Tom."

From the memoirs of J. W. Weaver, reporter and editorial writer for the *Fort Smith Independent* (Arkansas), and *New York Herald* correspondent, we learn of a peculiar incident which happened a short time after Belle became Mrs. Starr. From time to time Belle gave Weaver biographical sketches which he promised would not be printed until after her death. Weaver was a seasoned newspaperman and we must respect his statement when he classifies as authentic the information Belle gave him.

One day a well-dressed stranger, mounted on a fine horse, rode up to Younger's Bend. He was of medium height with a light brown beard and a weather-beaten complexion. He had blinking blue eyes, cold as frozen seas. Belle seemed startled to see him. He was a "Mr. Williams, an old friend" from Texas she explained to Sam.

Mr. Williams was a quiet, inoffensive man, who didn't do much talking, smoking, or drinking. If Sam noticed the well oiled six-shooters in the holsters of the cartridge belt strapped about the stranger's waist, he never mentioned it. There were few men in the Territory who didn't carry guns.

The stranger from Texas stayed on for several weeks. Only once was Sam suspicious. That was when one of the Starrs came riding up to Younger's Bend. Mr. Williams was on his feet with the grace of a

214

cat. Before Sam knew it the Colt was out of the holster and in his hand. He stood by the window, his eyes blinking furiously.

Then Belle whispered something to him and the gun dropped back into the holster. When Sam mentioned the stranger's actions, Belle said simply he was "on the dodge" and was suspicious of strangers.

One day Sam returned to Younger's Bend to find "Mr. Williams" gone. As she told Weaver, her editor friend, "He was unknown to my husband and he never knew until long afterward that our home had been honored by Jesse James' presence. . . ."

3

One of the strangest sights in Belle Starr's time was the "tumble-weed wagon," a large caboose-type building set on huge iron-rimmed wheels, which roamed the plains like dogcatchers, seeking humans and not canines.

The tumbleweed wagon was Judge Parker's black maria on wheels. Named after the roving tumbling weed of the prairies, it traveled hundreds of miles, seeking robbers, desperadoes, whisky peddlers, horse thieves, cattle rustlers, killers, and Indians charged with minor crimes.

Its crew consisted of four men, a driver, cook, and two outriders, both marshals, who were armed to the teeth with six-shooters and Winchesters. The prisoners wore leg irons and at night helped to gather firewood, draw water, and wash the dishes. If they refused to work they went hungry.

When they went to bed for the night, each prisoner was shackled to a heavy chain which in turn was wound around a tree. If there were no trees a chain was locked about the wagon wheels.

The "tumbleweeds" were a familiar sight on the prairies. When the word spread like grass fire to the gullies and camps of the outlaw gangs, they scattered like wheat in the wind with the marshals in pursuit. Some outlaws never made the wagon. They were buried after being shot down on the run.

The prisoners also served as fire fighters. When a prairie fire broke out and the wagon was endangered, or a farmer had galloped up crying that his farm was in the path of the flames, the prisoners would be unshackled and given shovels or sacks to beat out the flames. Then they were herded back into the wagon to be leg-ironed to their seats.

Orrington Lucas of Wagoner, Oklahoma, told a WPA writer in 1937, how he and Heck Thomas, the famous marshal, and another deputy, William Brothers, were ordered out on a "swing" to corral some outlaws. He told how the tumbleweed wagon rolled into the Western towns, the people staring at it from the sidewalks. When it was hitched up they walked about town, "showing their badges and visiting with various people. Sometimes we would walk up to a man we suspicioned; if he tried to avoid us, then we knew we had a man worth investigating. Sometimes he would evidence a desire to get out of town. We would mount our horses and give chase, usually wounding the horse. Then we would pick him up and ask the questions we had in mind."

Once, Mr. Lucas said, crime was so rampant, three tumbleweeds were sent out, returning with twenty-two white and Indian prisoners. As he said, "Sometimes they would quarrel among themselves but usually they reserved their ill-will for us."

The last of Judge Parker's famous two hundred rangers, Elias Rector, of Fort Smith, now past ninety, has a vivid recollection of the day Belle was picked up with Sam Starr by the tumbleweed wagon on a horse-stealing charge, "a pastime that had a deep appeal for her."

Belle was taken into custody through a ruse. The deputies had no easy time holding her. As Rector recalled, "She fought like a wildcat, screaming, kicking, scratching, and fighting. Finally when we had a chance to search her, we found a forty-five strapped around her waist, under her skirt. She was then only half-dressed. You can draw your own conclusions as to what she wore when she was fully dressed."

Belle was put into the tumbleweed wagon which started out for Fort Smith and Judge Parker's court. Soon she had her revenge. When the driver or outriders weren't looking she tossed out blankets, pots, knives, forks, and food. When she was discovered trying to throw out the stove, the furious marshals had to retrace their tracks and recover the wagon's utensils and food. The marshals evened the score by making Belle sit on the floor of the wagon. After jouncing over the uneven prairies and along the rutted roads, Belle found it easier to stand than sit in court.

Mr. Lucas also had a hilarious story of how Belle avenged herself on the marshals. One day word came to her that a tumbleweed had been sighted. Belle knew she was safe; neither hse nor Sam had been stealing any horses lately.

To make sure the marshals were coming to Younger's Bend she climbed the crow's nest built in a tree on the bluff and scanned the prairie. There was a spot of dust on the horizon. As it grew larger she made out the riders and the boxlike wagon. As the thought came to

216

her a smile curved her thin lips. She hurriedly descended the ladder and ran to the kitchen of the shack, shouting to Sam to draw some water for they were having "guests." Sam was puzzled at first but when she explained his round swarthy face broke out into a grin. All the way to the spring he roared with laughter.

The marshals arrived and Belle invited them to dinner. The surprised officers accepted. Belle served up a boiling hot stew, bread, and coffee. The hungry officers filled their plates. When the last cup of coffee had been finished and the stew pot cleaned, Belle stood over them with a wide grin on her face.

"Well," she said, "everybody enjoy the meal?"

Her guests nodded. There were belches and murmured "thank ye, ma'am."

Belle chuckled. "Well, I guess you law officers would like to know what you had to eat?"

The officers looked blank, then uneasy. Had Belle deliberately poisoned them? . . .

"Well," Belle continued, "I just want you to know you ate a damn old rattlesnake I killed yesterday. Now you can go outside and puke it all up."

They all did, Mr. Lucas added.

Despite the marshals and Judge Parker's tumbleweed wagons, Younger's Bend continued to be the hideout for outlaws. They included bank and train robbers on the "dodge," horse thieves, cattle rustlers, killers, and whisky peddlers. They were all part of Belle's loosely connected gang, of which she was the undisputed "Queen."

In no way did her gang resemble Butch Cassidy's closely knit "Wild Bunch," the Dalton or Doolin gangs. The outlaws who served her stayed on for short periods, then moved on to the next hideout. The places were always filled by new arrivals. Belle held them by sex, fear, or her rough, personal magnetism. The criminals who stayed at Younger's Bend were undoubtedly intrigued by riding with a female outlaw who was also "educated." To some of her illiterate followers, Belle may have appeared as a genius because she could read the wanted posters to them.

For all her rough ways, Belle never allowed her riders to forget that she was "a lady." Once, as legend has it, she was riding to Fort Smith when her hat blew off.

Belle pulled up and looked at the outlaws. They stared back at her questioningly. In a rage she drew her Colt and aimed it at "Blue Duck."

"Get down there and pick up that hat, you ignorant bastard," she snarled. Blue Duck was out of his saddle in a flash to retrieve her hat. Belle accepted it with a dignified politeness, slid the gun back in her holster, put on the hat, then waved her hand. The gang carefully followed the woman in velvet and the white hat and flowing plume as reverently as the servants followed Maid Marian through the forests of Sherwood six hundred years before.

Belle was now as well known in Fort Smith as she had been in Dallas. She always made a theatrical entrance, galloping furiously down the main street on her magnificent black mare, scattering the pedestrians right and left to pull up at the nearest saloon.

The battered piano off to one side of the room would inevitably catch her eye. After buying a round for the "professor"—the regular piano player—Belle would sit down and play several maudlin numbers. Before she had finished there wasn't a dry eye in the house.

4

In the winter of 1883, Belle made her appearance as the first female ever tried for a major crime in the courtroom of the celebrated "Hanging Judge" Parker in the Federal Court of the Western District of Arkansas.

The indictment charged she was "the leader of a band of horse thieves." Belle put up the bail and a date was set for their trial. The arrest was a frontier sensation. The telegraph wires hummed with the story and stories appeared in some of the nation's largest newspapers. Belle was dubbed "The Petticoat of the Plains," "The Queen of the Bandits," and "The Lady Desperado." Fox's *Gazette* turned out reams of lurid and fanciful copy.

Belle and Sam went on trial in February, 1883. Spectators fought for choice seats in the jammed courtroom. As the *Fort Smith Era* said:

> The very idea of a woman being charged with an offense of this kind, and that she was the leader of a band of horse thieves, and wielding a power over them as their queen and guiding spirit, was sufficient to fill the courtroom. . . .

The *Era* reporter tells us that Belle was not only the guiding light of her outlaws, but also her lawyers. All during the four-day trial, she listened intently to the "mass of testimony" placed against her with a "devil-may-care expression on her face," scribbling furiously on a pad, and sending notes to her attorneys. As the *Era* reporter wrote: "It was a subject of remark that they paid strict attention to the contents."

Once the name of Jim Reed was mentioned in the testimony of a government witness and Belle appropriately wept. "Tears welled in her eyes and trickled down her cheeks, but they were quickly wiped away and her face resumed its wonted appearance."

On the afternoon of the fourth day the case went to the jury. The jurors deliberated for only an hour before returning with a verdict. Belle was guilty on both counts in the indictment, Sam on one. Judge Parker put off the date of sentencing until March 8.

On the morning of that day, Belle showed up in court, dressed in her finest velvet gown. For the occasion she had bought a new ostrich plume. When she walked to the bench at Judge Parker's summons, the spectators, standing on tiptoe in the rear of the packed room could follow her progress up the aisle from the gently waving plume.

Although she could have been sentenced to two years, Judge Parker, who had sent eighty-eight men to the gallows, was unexpectedly lenient. He gave her only six months on two counts and Sam a year on his one count. He gave them only a few hours to arrange their affairs before leaving for the Federal Prison in Detroit.

During these few hours Belle had only thoughts of her young daughter, Pearl. Just before she left for prison, the bandit queen wrote her:

Pandemonium, February, 1883

Baby Pearl,

My dear little one; it is useless to attempt to conceal my trouble from you, and though you are nothing but a child I have confidence that my darling will bear with fortitude what I write.

I shall be away from you a few months, baby, and have only this consolation to offer to you, that never again will I be placed in such humiliating circumstances, and in the future your little tender heart shall never more ache, or a blush called to your cheek, on your mother's account.

After reviewing the case against her, and explaining Judge Parker's sentence, Belle added:

Now, Pearl, there is a vast difference from that place [Detroit] and a penitentiary. You must bear that in mind and do not think

219

of your momma being shut up in a gloomy prison. It is said to be one of the finest institutions of its kind in the United States, surrounded by beautiful grounds and fountains and everything that is nice. There I can have my education renewed, and I stand sadly in need of it. Sam will have to attend school and that is the best thing ever happened for him. And now you must not be unhappy and brood over our absence. It will not take the time long to glide by, and when we come home and get you we will have a nice time.

We will get your horse and I will break him, and you can ride John while I am gentling Loco. We will have Eddie [her other child] with us, and will be gay and happy as the birds we claim at home. . . .

Belle gave the letter to a friend and it was delivered. While her daughter read the letter her mother and stepfather were on their way to the penitentiary.

Instead of "renewing" her education, Belle spent her time in prison weaving chair bottoms out of split cane, while Sam split rocks with a sledge hammer. Good behavior reduced their sentences by three months.

After leaving the federal penitentiary Belle and Sam returned to Younger's Bend. There is a gap in their lives until the fall of 1884, when Belle is said to have taken part in a wild West show in Fort Smith. Belle played the part of an outlaw holding up a stagecoach. One of the passengers was Judge Parker!

In the spring of 1885, a dashing young Missourian, John Middleton, a cousin of Jim Reed, appeared at Younger's Bend. Belle always preferred men younger than herself and Middleton caught her eye. Middleton was no novice in outlawry. He had a price on his head for cold-blooded murder and was wanted in Texas and parts of Arkansas for assault, arson, and train robbery.

Middleton stayed for Christmas and there was a round of wild parties. The whisky flowed freely and Middleton and Belle were seen whispering together. Sam watched them, his dark Indian's face inscrutable. A few days later he vanished.

Accounts vary as to why Sam disappeared. More prosaic reports had him "down with the measles" and recuperating at his father's place in the hills.

Belle and Middleton were left alone. Romance bloomed. When the Missourian proposed they leave Younger's Bend for more fertile fields, Belle eagerly agreed to go. Probably not to arouse the suspicions of any of Starr's relatives, Belle told Middleton he could accompany her as far as Keota, then traveling by different routes would meet somewhere in Logan County.

On a beautiful May day, Belle and Pearl drove off in a covered wagon. Middleton rode ahead on a sorrel mare stolen from one of Belle's neighbors, his forty-five hanging from the saddle horn. Belle carried her Winchester alongside her in the wagon. At Keota the lovers parted. Middleton struck off southwest, traveling by a dangerous and circuitous route to their rendezvous, probably to by-pass the larger towns where his picture could be seen on the wanted posters.

Belle arrived first at their rendezvous in Russellville. She waited for three days, fuming with rage and impatience. At last, cursing all mankind, she drove back to Younger's Bend, glibly telling Sam when he next appeared, that she had gone off to visit relatives.

Meanwhile a posse of Texas marshals and Indian police were on the trail of Middleton. They heard of the "elopement" and visited Belle. She drove them off with the best bagnio language at her command but they believed her when she said she hadn't seen Middleton since they had parted on the trail to Russellville.

While the posse searched the badlands, a Choctaw Indian found a dead horse on the banks of the Poteau River. He summoned the sheriff who found the badly decomposed body of a man, half submerged in the mud. The corpse was buried in nearby Pocola, after descriptions had been sent to the editor of the *Fort Smith Elevator,* in the hope that someone would identify the dead man.

One of the possemen hunting for Middleton saw the story in the *Elevator* and on a hunch had the body exhumed. It was established from the clothing and the forty-five caliber gun that the corpse was definitely Middleton.

The deputies rode back to Younger's Bend. When they told Belle Middleton was dead, she screamed and cursed them. When one of the deputies showed her the outlaw's gun found on the saddle horn of the dead horse, she seemed stunned. When they left, Belle hitched the covered wagon and with Pearl asleep in the back, set out for Pocola.

She hired a laborer to exhume the body so she could herself identify it. Satisfied it was Middleton's body Belle ordered a coffin and an "appropriate" marker for the grave.

Belle next appears in May, 1886, riding down the main street of Fort Smith, escorted by United States Marshal Hughes who had arrested her on a charge of horse stealing and robbery.

The frontier newspaper made much of the robbery charge, picturing

Belle dressed as a man, leading a four-man bandit gang who had robbed a Choctaw Indian family. The neighbor, whose horse had been stolen by the luckless Middleton, was the complainant in the horse thievery charge.

The arrest was unexpected. As Belle later told a reporter for the *Dallas News,* she was accustomed to the marshals "coming to the Bend with a crowd of twenty-five to forty men, crawling on their knees in the darkness." But Hughes just rode up in broad daylight and ordered Belle to ride in with him.

"Hughes is a brave man," Belle said, "and acted the gentleman in every particular, but I hardly believe he realized his danger."

Belle vigorously denied the charge, when arraigned before Judge Parker. She was released in bond and spent the rest of the day shopping. It is characteristic that she bought two beautiful forty-five caliber Colts for which she paid twenty-nine dollars.

In the afternoon she met the *Dallas News* reporter who persuaded her to submit to an interview. Belle talked for some time, sketching her early life in Missouri, her elopement and marriage to Reed, while "John Fischer, one of the most noted outlaws in the state of Texas was holding her horse." Belle revealed she had been wearing her best velvet gown that night.

From the story in the *News* we get an idea of Belle's position in Fort Smith. As the reporter wrote:

> Belle attracts considerable attention wherever she goes, being a dashing horsewoman and exceedingly graceful in the saddle. She dresses plainly and wears a broad-rimmed white man's hat, surmounted by a wide, black plush band, with feathers and ornaments, which is very becoming to her. She is of medium size, well formed, a dark brunette, with dark and intelligent black eyes. . . .

After the long interview, Belle summed up her philosophy. She said, "I am a friend to any brave and gallant outlaw, but have no use for that sneaking cowardly class of thieves who can be found in any locality, and who would betray a friend or a comrade for their own gain. There are three or four jolly, good fellows on the dodge now in my section, and when they come to my house they are welcome, for they are my friends and would lay their lives down in my defense at any time the occasion demanded it, and go their full length to serve me in any way. . . ."

Belle returned to Younger's Bend to learn that Sam had been shot by the Indian police after robbing the treasury of the Creek Nation. The police had held Sam overnight in a farmhouse but a mob of his followers had freed him. Now Sam was "on the dodge" somewhere in the hills.

Belle left Younger's Bend at a gallop as a posse of Indian trackers and federal marshals left Fort Smith. She located Sam at his father's house, heavily armed and ready to shoot it out.

Squatting before the crude fireplace in the miserable one-room shack, Belle persuaded Sam to surrender. With typical shrewdness she pointed out he had all to gain and nothing to lose. Once in the hands of the tribal council he would face horrible torture or be whipped to death publicly. In the white man's court he could go free on bond—perhaps permanently free—Belle promised. From her neighbors she knew the Indian police had no direct evidence linking Sam to the robbery.

Early the next morning the people of Fort Smith witnessed a strange spectacle. Coming up Main Street at an easy lope, was Belle, guns flapping at her side and ostrich plume rippling in the breeze, escorted by Sam Starr and United States Marshal Tyner Hughes, the only law officer to ever visit Younger's Bend at Belle's request.

Sam's case was the first called by clerk of Judge Parker's court. As Belle had promised he was allowed to go free after his relatives had posted bond. Sam wanted to ride back to Younger's Bend at once and celebrate. Belle told him they must wait until the late afternoon. Sam soon knew the reason for the delay in leaving.

That same day Belle was summoned to Judge Parker's court to face the robbery and horse stealing charges still lodged against her. She never took the stand in her own defense. Both charges were dismissed. The whooping pair rode out of town in a cloud of dust. Now there was something to celebrate.

Sam never went back to Fort Smith. At a Christmas celebration near Whitefield, on the south side of the Canadian River not far from Younger's Bend, he was killed by a dying Indian deputy, whom he had shot down after a drunken argument.

5

Belle wasn't a widow long. Jim July, whom the *Dallas News* described as a "tall, well formed Creek Indian, with long black hair falling down over his shoulders," came into her life. July, who changed his name to Starr to please Belle, may have been one of those "jolly" outlaws Belle had described to the *Dallas News* reporter months before. The young Indian buck had visited Younger's Bend, while "on the dodge" from horse stealing.

July was not an illiterate. He had been educated at Indian schools and could speak nearly all the Indian dialects. When he moved in with Belle he announced to all the neighbors and to their friends in Fort Smith that they were "married." It was close quarters at Younger's Bend. Also sharing the one-room cabin were Belle's daughter, Pearl, and son, Ed.

Pearl was her mother's daughter, Ed his father's son. Sometime in the spring of 1887, Belle sent her daughter to Soloam Springs, Arkansas, to have an illegitimate baby; in the summer she was sending money to her son in the federal penitentiary at Columbus, Ohio, where he had been sentenced for robbery. A few months later Belle herself was again arrested for stealing horses but the case was dismissed.

On a hot July day in 1889, Belle rode with her new husband part of the way to Fort Smith where he was to surrender to the United States marshal on a larceny charge. They stayed overnight in a farmhouse at San Bois, about fifteen miles from the Bend. Jim set off alone the next morning.

Sometime that afternoon, a Sunday, Pearl was surprised to see her mother's horse, still saddled, come galloping up the road. Frightened, she called her stepbrother and they began to search for their mother.

A short time later a neighbor appeared to inform them Belle had been found dead in the mud of the road, a mile from Younger's Bend. A bushwhacker had killed her with a charge of buckshot in the back. To make sure she was dead he bent over and fired a second shot from a Colt which tore through the left side of her face.

According to an interview a *Fort Smith Era* reporter had with Jim July, or Starr, shortly after the killing, Belle was still alive when Pearl knelt at her side and lifted her head. Jim insisted that Belle whispered some last words to Pearl but that is doubtful.

In Fort Smith, Jim heard of Belle's death.

As the *Fort Smith Elevator* said: "There was bad blood in his eyes when he heard the news, and without delay he saddled his horse, provided himself with a quart of whiskey, struck out on a run for home, saying somebody was going to suffer. . . ."

Belle was buried on a Wednesday morning. The women of the neighborhood had washed the corpse with turpentine and oil of cinnamon and dressed it in a black dress and frilled collar. Her coffin was of plain pine. All morning under a piercing sun, the measured strokes of a pick and the scrapings of the shovels wielded by the gravediggers in the front yard were heard in the quiet. Inside the one-room cabin, the Indian women sat on benches and chairs, their stolid faces expressionless.

Grim-faced men, some of Belle's "jolly" outlaw friends, and Sam Starr's relatives, stood about the front yard of the cabin, examining intently each horseman that appeared.

At noon the pallbearers, six-shooters dangling at their hips, came out of the house with the coffin. They set the coffin down beside the grave, and stepped back, their hands on their guns, their eyes hard.

A single file of whites and Indians filed past the open coffin. As each Cherokee passed they dropped a small piece of cornbread inside the coffin.

The lid was nailed down and the coffin lowered into the grave. At a signal from Pearl the gravediggers began to shovel the dirt into the hole. Suddenly, in the stillness, there was a loud cry, "Throw up your hands!"

The gun fighters and outlaws wheeled about, their hands going for their holsters.

To their amazement they saw Jim Starr standing in front of one, Watson and his wife, who lived a short distance from the Bend.

"You murdered my wife . . . you killed her," Starr shouted.

The circle about them widened. Men let their hands rest on the butts of their Colts. Watson stared back at Jim.

"You have the wrong man," he said calmly. "If you kill me you will have killed the wrong man. . . ."

Starr refused to listen. He said he wanted to bring Watson back to Fort Smith and stand trial. Watson agreed, first asking some of his friends to stay with him "because he was afraid he would be killed if he was left alone with the Starrs."

Jim bound Watson's hands and the next morning brought his prisoner into Fort Smith and signed a murder warrant against him. To the *Era* reporter he charged Watson killed Belle as a result of some ancient quarrel.

Watson vigorously denied the charge. The *Era* reporter who interviewed him found Watson to be "the very opposite of a man who would be supposed to commit such a crime."

Watson was soon discharged, because of insufficient evidence. There is no doubt he was not guilty. Even Ed, Belle's son refused to testify against him. And for good reason. Ed might have murdered his own mother. Harman, in his *Hell On The Border,* accepts Watson as the killer, but curiously tells how Ed threatened his mother's life after she had given him an unmerciful beating with a horse quirt. As he says:

> The beating greatly angered the boy, and he was not home for two weeks; it was said he had threatened his mother's life in return for his chastisement, and there was talk of his arrest and trial by the Indian police, but the matter was finally quieted and he was not arrested. . . .

A few months after her mother's death, Pearl hired a stonecutter to mount a stone monument over her mother's grave. On the top of the stone was carved an image of her favorite mare "Venus." Carved on the stone was this inscription:

BELLE STARR
BORN IN CARTHAGE, MISSOURI, FEBRUARY 5, 1848.

DIED FEBRUARY 3, 1889.

Shed not for her, the bitter tear,
Nor give the heart to vain regret,
'Tis but the casket that lies here,
The gem that fills it sparkles yet.

A more appropriate inscription had been supplied by Belle herself, in an interview a year before with the *Fort Smith Elevator* reporter. As she said, "I regard myself as a woman who has seen much of life."

Cattle Kate

HAD Jim Averill never discovered that the pen is mightier than the sword, the dark and terrible events which shook Wyoming in the years from 1889 to 1892, might never have taken place. Jim might have lived to become a crotchety cattle baron; a young boy might never have died from "Bright's Disease"; men riding the lonely roads would not have been shot from their horses by bushwhackers; Frank Buchanan, Jim's friend, would never have ended as a pile of sun-bleached bones; the "invasion" of Wyoming might never have taken place, and a president of the United States would not have been summoned from his bed in the early hours of the morning to save the invaders from a mass lynching.

That, of course, is all supposition. This we know: Had Jim never taken up his pen, buxom Ella Watson, "Cattle Kate" to the frontier, would never have strangled to death on the end of a rope in the cool July twilight, on the banks of the Sweetwater River, more than half a century ago.

The story of Kate and Jim Averill is more than a Western legend. It is still one of the touchiest subjects in certain parts of Wyoming. Only recently a friend of the writer spent a vacation near where Kate was hanged. When he mentioned he would like to see the gully where the lynching took place, "the subject was abruptly changed and my request ignored. Later I was privately requested not to mention her name again."

A young lady in Wyoming who gathered material on Kate, agrees in a letter that "the subject is still a very touchy one out here."

One man tersely replied to an inquiry, "I know nothing about her [Kate] except that she was hanged for rustling." Several other inquiries were ignored.

The names of Cattle Kate and her lover, Jim Averill, are to Wyoming what Sherman is to Georgia.

It is difficult to find anything on Jim and Kate. Long-dead frontier newspapers best tell their story. But before we begin the reader should

227

be warned. As the *Weekly Bonanza* said piously, "their story is an awful one. . . ."

2

Their story began sometime in 1888. In his general store, part saloon, in Sweetwater Valley, Jim Averill took up the pen for the first time. He carefully smoothed down the writing paper before him and began writing in the lamplight.

Jim could turn a phrase—evidently from the letters he wrote, smoothly and with ease. This particular evening he was writing to the editor—that great American pastime. The words flew. He was protesting to the editor of the *Casper Weekly Mail* against the land and cattle barons who ruled the Sweetwater Valley. They were "land-grabbers, speculators . . . land-mad men who are opposed to anything that would improve the country and make it anything but a cow-pasture for the Western speculators. . . ."

It went like this for almost a column. When he had finished and reread his prose, Jim was satisfied. The next day his foreman, Frank Buchanan, delivered his letter to the editor.

When the *Mail* went to press, Jim's letter was quoted in full. There is little doubt that Jim bought several copies. Who can resist the magic of seeing one's name in public print for the first time!

Averill was fascinated. The next week he sat down again and dashed off another letter. He pointed out that the cattle kings owned nearly all of the Valley, "four men alone claiming the Sweetwater seventy-five miles from its mouth."

His pen flew across the pages. Change the irrigation, he cried, and watch the orchards and the rolling farm lands spread across the entire state of Wyoming. . . .

As the weeks went on the name of Jim Averill was on everyone's lips. He always had been a semiofficial spokesman for the smaller ranchers and now he was being hailed as their leader. Men began to stop by and congratulate him on his letters. Jim began to dream, and in his dreams, of course, he was a prophet of old leading the ranchers, the homesteaders and the nestlers, against the mighty cattle barons to the promised land.

It is important to understand the situation in the Valley, at the time. Wyoming had not yet been admitted to statehood. Cattle, more than men, were important. There were two groups involved in the raising and selling of beef; the small ranchers who owned herds that ranged

228

from one hundred to three hundred head, and the land gentry, the cattle kings, who "owned" mile after mile of government land and herds running into the thousands.

None of the large cattle kingdoms bothered to obtain land claims. It was anybody's land. The usual practice was to get a small claim upon which a ranchhouse would be built, then use the government lands for grazing.

Strangely enough, the cattle kings were seldom the men who had wrestled the land from the Sioux and Cheyenne. In general they were playboys of the nineteenth century, heirs of English fortunes, who had been lured to the last frontier by the call of adventure, or the purple prose of Ned Buntline.

For example, the Scottish owned Swan Company controlled half a million acres and more than 100,000 head of cattle; the Powder River Land and Cattle Company, ruled by a British nobleman, consisted of 50,000 cattle and 100,000 acres.

An Austrian archduke ruled the Big Horn Basin and a grandson of Queen Victoria slept in a royal bed in the rambling ranchhouse on the Powder River.

Territorial legislatures elected the governor of the Territory and the supreme court justices. The ex-governor, in most cases, later became the president of the powerful Wyoming Stock Grazer's Association. The courts had already ruled it wasn't a crime to fence in government land but it was a crime to cut that fence!

In 1884 the famous Maverick Bill, which aroused Jim Averill and his followers in the Valley, was passed. Under this law all mavericks (unbranded cattle) on the ranges were declared to be the property of the Association. Simultaneously, all "rustler brands" were treated as maverick cattle. In other words, a rancher who owned cattle but could not belong to the wealthy Association was a "rustler" and it was within the power of the Association to confiscate his steers as stolen cattle!

The disastrous winters of 1887-88 almost swept the range clean of cattle. Price of beef in Eastern cities boomed. Embittered small ranchers seeing their own stock wiped out began to appropriate the already depleted herds of the cattle barons.

The courts did little to help. In Carbon County there was one conviction in 197 arrests. A man and his wife caught with stolen hides and beef were acquitted.

It was in this period that Averill rose as the spokesman for the smaller ranchers. A short time later Kate was to join him.

By the spring of 1888, Jim was the undisputed leader of the discontented small ranchers, homesteaders, and squatters in Sweetwater Valley. A grateful Democratic administration, impressed with his outspoken campaign against the plutocratic Republicans of the Valley, made him the postmaster. The small salary was unimportant but the prestige was invaluable. The general store and saloon were doing an excellent business; business in stolen cattle was booming.

Averill had also adopted direct actions. He had horrified the land barons when he made John Corbin prove a claim. He had taken some of Robert O'Connor's big holdings and had prevented the powerful A. J. Bothwell, lord of the Valley, from fencing off the rest of the lush government land.

To the cattle barons, Jim Averill had become a dangerous menace. Sometime in '88 Jim had a plan.

More than once the cowhands and rustlers who patronized his saloon had wished they could be joined in their levity by a female. There had been spirited discussions in the saloon, all of them about women. To the rough, tough cowpunchers, who never saw a woman for months at a time, the subject of women was one of endless interest.

Why shouldn't a lady of easy virtue settle in the Valley, Averill wondered? It was an intriguing subject. He thought about it for days. Finally he sat down and wrote a letter to a woman he and the frontier knew as Ella Watson. Ella, then living in Rawlins, was the glamor girl of the cow towns. For some unknown reason she had recently changed her name to Kate Maxwell. Jim had probably met her while "relaxing" from his vast political and business worries.

A few weeks later Ella, or Kate appeared. As the *Cheyenne Mail Leader* described her a few months later:

> She was one of the most unforgettable women on the range. She was of robust physique, a dark devil in the saddle, handy with a six shooter and a Winchester, and an expert with the branding iron and lariat. Where she came from no one knows, but all agree, she was a holy terror. She rode straddle, always had a vicious bronc for a mount, and seemed never to tire of dashing across the range. . . .

We know something of Kate's background from an interview her father gave to the editor of the *Rock Springs Miner*. Mr. Watson was described as "a well-to-do farmer from Lebanon, Smith County, Kansas." Kate was the eldest of ten children. At eighteen she had married a Kansas farmer but two years later she divorced him, as her father said, "because of his infidelity." She then worked as a domestic in the

230

home of the county's leading banker. A year later she left for "a respectable position" in Red Cloud, Nebraska. Denver was next, then Cheyenne and Rawlins. Sweetwater Valley was her next stop. She was then twenty-six.

Her father described Kate as "a fine girl, of handsome form, handsome and rugged, modest and unassuming, with not a particle of fastness in her action or her disposition." He also confirmed the Cheyenne editor's description of "robust physique." Kate, he said proudly, weighed "between one hundred and sixty to one hundred and eighty pounds!" *

When she arrived in the Valley, Jim outlined his plan to Kate. She agreed to it enthusiastically. With his help she located a homestead on the Sweetwater, one mile from Averill's ranch and saloon. In the old records of the government land office her claim is still listed, Number 2003.

Averill, always chivalrous, sent over some of his hands to build her a neat, one-story log cabin, with the door and window casing painted a light green. Kate soon gave it a woman's touch. A cowboy riding to Averill's saloon one day reported there were curtains and a geranium in the window.

She hired one hand, a fourteen-year-old boy, who took care of the two cows Jim sent over as a house-warming present.

The establishment was a huge success. The cowhands and rustlers could get drunk at Averill's, and after a short ride, could sample Miss Watson's charms. Kate let it be known that she would take cattle in trade, explaining that in this way she hoped to start a herd, "and perhaps settle down to a life of reform and respectability." †

Surely, no more hilarious scene can be imagined than the picture of the sex-hungry outlaw or cowboy herding their stolen cattle down the lonely trails to Kate's place, then waiting impatiently while she estimated their value in trade!

To the people of the Sweetwater, she was soon "Cattle Kate." To the land barons and the cattle kings her establishment was simply a "hog ranch" and, in the frontier spirit toward commercialized sex, they treated it with rough humor instead of agonizing anguish.

---

* Kate may have been responsible for that nursery rhyme of the 'nineties which went: "K is for dear little Katie who weighed most a hundred and eighty. . . ."

† Unlike the modern criminal, the outlaws of the old West had an extraordinary yearning for reformation and respectability. Male or female, they all seemed to want to appear moral and law abiding. As Frank James said after he surrendered, "I want to be like other men, you know—have a wife and family and go out in the yard for firewood and not expect a ball in the back." It was a yearning few saw fulfilled.

231

The cows flowed in and out of the small corral. Business was so good, Kate hired another girl from a Rawlins *maison de tolérance,* as the French put it.

With conditions as they were in the Valley, a large number of the cattle Kate "received in trade" were rustled mavericks from the herds of the cattle kings. But Kate never questioned the source of her customer's goods. At night Frank Buchanan, Averill's foreman, several of her rustler customers, and Kate's fourteen-year-old cowhand would stage a quiet roundup and fix Kate's brand on the cattle. The herd would be driven to a small ranch used by the rustlers as a relay point, and driven to the railhead the next day.

Averill's campaign against Bothwell, and the rest of the land barons intensified. The *Casper Weekly Mail* printed more of his strong letters in which he demanded that the irrigation laws be changed, and the land claims of the barons be examined.

In their exclusive clubs in Cheyenne the cattle kings, who had dismissed him earlier as a rabble rouser and nothing more, now began to look worried. Jim's following was increasing. Fences were being cut and the small ranchers and homesteaders were carrying Winchesters and six-shooters. In Rawlins and Casper, there was even talk of a "cattle war."

The winter of '88 struck the state with an unprecedented fury. The range was almost cleared of the large herds. Some of the baronies were wiped out, sending the English and Scottish heirs back home to write their memoirs.

For the stockmen it was a difficult struggle to survive. The small ranchers who saw their lands and homes going for taxes, openly rustled the mavericks in the spring, to stave off starvation. The ranchers didn't see it as rustling; the land barons had stolen all government lands, so why shouldn't they steal some of their cattle? To them it was merely economic justice.

Some of the cattle began to show up in Kate's corral. When they heard of Kate's charms, rustlers came down to the Valley from Hole In The Wall to plunder the herds and drive the stolen cows to Kate's establishment.

The little log cabin began to become known as the hangout for outlaws and desperadoes, who came from as far as Casper and Bessemer, to escape the United States marshals. The wild parties increased Jim's liquor business.

Before the winter of 1888 had passed, Kate's place was posted as out-of-bounds for their employees by the cattle kings.

In the spring of 1889 Jim was ready to expand his operations. The excessive snows had left an enormous amount of moisture in the earth and the pastures became thick and lush. The cattle men began to rebuild their herds.

Jim decided this was a time to conduct his own roundup. He led his men out on the range to round up the valuable mavericks. There was only one trouble with stealing unweaned calves: their mothers would follow them. Even a rustlers jury would find it hard to acquit a man captured while driving a herd of mavericks, followed by a herd of bawling cows. Jim quickly solved that problem. He ordered his men to shoot the cows.

Kate's corral was used to house the stolen cattle. The rustlers took care of driving them to the railhead.

For Jim it was an ideal situation. He was the thunderous voice of the oppressed; the pen of the people. What if he were caught? Any jury would have to be selected from a panel of his friends and followers in the Valley. . . .

There was also this to be considered. The cattle were driven to Kate's corral. Who could prove she didn't innocently accept them in trade and put on them her own brand? . . .

And if they were found in the corrals of the little ranches, who could prove the rancher had not bought them in good faith, from Cattle Kate, who in turn had bought them in a lawful transaction?

Jim was quite smug about his plans. They were foolproof.

During the spring nights he rode the ranges "until he ached," as the *Leader* said. After each foray the plains would be scattered with dead cows, killed under Averill's new plan.

As the profits rolled in, Kate became a lady of fashion. The rough buckskin dress was replaced by a blue-flowered print from Cheyenne. Button-up shoes, in which she squeezed her man-sized feet, replaced the tough, dusty boots she had always worn. Jim bought her a saddle horse and an expensive saddle. There was also a buggy with a fringe on top.

Jim took to smoking good cigars and to wearing a heavy gold watch chain across the front of his vest. He also went off on drinking bouts with dire results. Once when Kate had a "visitor" from a Rawlins bagnio, Jim got drunk and chased the girl out into the bitterly cold night to rip off her clothes and beat her black and blue. There was even some murmuring among his constituents when she was found, half frozen to death and tied to a wagon wheel.

In June an angry stockman rode down to Kate's "hog ranch." He

233

counted twenty bawling mavericks which he insisted belonged to him. Kate came out on the porch of her cabin and watched him with a smile.

"That's my cattle you have in your corral," the angry stockman told Kate. "Where did you get them?"

Kate eyed him boldly. "Bought 'em," she said.

The stockman demanded proof. Kate drew herself up, each one of her one hundred and sixty—or eighty pounds—quivering with anger.

"Who the hell are you to question a *Lady?*" she shouted. "Now get out of here!"

The stockman stood his ground. Kate stormed in her cabin and came out with a Winchester. The stockman left.

On July 13, the *Casper Weekly Mail* solemnly warned that the failure of the courts to convict cattle thieves "will result in the stockmen taking the law in their own hands. . . ."

In early July, Jim, or his associates, led his men to the Bothwell ranges and drove off twenty of his calves. Unfortunately for Jim, Bothwell had been out inspecting his herd only a few days before and had picked out these particular calves as the best of the lot.

When a cowhand came galloping to the ranch house with the news that scores of cows had been shot and were rotting on the range, Bothwell, in a towering rage, went out to see for himself. It was exactly as his employee had described it.

The "hog ranch," of course was the first suspect. On Saturday Bothwell sent one of his hands down to "spy" on the corral.

"By his stealthy visit, the cowhand reported back to Bothwell that Kate's corral held no less than fifty of his steers, all yearling, with a few fairly grown," the *Cheyenne Leader* reported.

The statement of the spy circulated about the countryside. Riders pounded along the dark roads, carrying Bothwell's instructions to his neighbors. It was now time to take the law in their own hands.

On Sunday, July 20, nearly twenty men, "made desperate by their losses," gathered at a rendezvous and headed for Cattle Kate's hog ranch.

A few hundred yards from the cabin they stopped, then approached "with caution because Averill had murdered two men, and the woman was always full of fight."

The *Cheyenne Leader's* reporter wrote that the stockmen, peering in through the windows, saw Jim and Kate "sitting before a crude fireplace, the room clouded with tobacco smoke, a whisky bottle and two glasses on the table, and firearms scattered about so they were easily within reach."

The *Leader's* account adds that the vigilantes broke the glass of the windows, poked in their rifles and ordered Jim and Kate to come out with their hands up. But Kate, "always full of fight," put up a terrific struggle. When they tried to tie her up, she bowled over the night riders like tenpins. Finally they had to rush her en masse and sit on her while the ropes were strung about her body.

Even then they couldn't stop her tongue. As she sat in the smoky room, "she exhausted a blasphemous vocabulary upon the visitors, who assayed to stop the flow of bile by gagging her."

However, the *Leader's* account does not jibe with the later testimony of witnesses.

The fourteen-year-old boy said the riders came up, led by Bothwell, as Kate was walking to her log house. She tried to run for the cabin and her Winchester but two of the men cut her off. Hands on hips she demanded to know, in her best bagnio vocabulary, what the visitors wanted.

Bothwell said tersely, "You're coming to Rawlins."

Kate looked about at the grim, sweaty faces, "I can't," she said.

Bothwell snapped, "Why?"

Kate hesitated. Then she brightened. "I'm not dressed," she said.

Bothwell waved his six-shooter. "Get in the wagon," he said coldly. Kate got in.

One of the men cut the wire fence of the corral and let out the bawling calves. He ordered the boy to help him and together they began driving them up the road. The wagon, with Kate in the driver's seat, and the riders flanking her on each side, followed.

They stopped at the Averill ranch, a mile east. Jim was just closing his ranch gate, preparing for a trip to Casper, probably to deliver one of his blistering letters to the editor.

Bothwell rode up. "We have a warrant for your arrest, Averill," he said.

Jim looked up at him. "Let's see your warrant," he demanded.

Bothwell and another man, "threw" their guns on him. "This is our warrant," Bothwell said. "Get in the wagon."

The wagon with Jim and Kate slowly lumbered up the rutted road. Kate alternately cursed and joked with the riders. When the hard-eyed men refused to answer her, she lapsed into a sullen silence. Jim remained cheerful, pulling on his cigar, and blowing the smoke from

235

under the rim of his sombrero, which he had tilted down to hide his eyes from the sun.

The wagon rolled along for four miles. At the mouth of a small rocky canyon, the party dismounted. Jim and Kate were ordered out of the wagon and marched up the canyon. The vigilantes could not have selected a worse place. The gully was strewn with boulders and soon the cursing men in their high-heeled Western boots were slipping and falling over the rocks. It was a hot day and after walking several hundred yards to the south bank of the Sweetwater, hardly any one of them was in a frame of mind to pass sober judgment.

They stopped under a split cottonwood, "conspicuous by its presence among the red cedar and pines."

As all the men agreed later on, they never meant to hang the pair, especially the woman, but "only wanted to frighten them into leaving the county."

Bothwell ordered Jim and Kate to stand on boulders. "You must leave this county, Averill, and take this woman with you," he warned. "You know why. If you don't we'll—" he groped for the right warning—"well, we'll drown you right in the Sweetwater."

Kate cackled with laughter. She pointed to the river. "There ain't enough water down there to give you hogbacks a bath!"

Bothwell looked at the river. Kate was right. The Sweetwater was at its lowest summer ebb.

Jim Buchanan, Averill's foreman, now appeared. As he testified later on, he took out his six-shooter and began moving up, dodging from rock to rock. Soon he was within sound of their voices. He could see Bothwell shaking his finger at Kate who was roaring back insults.

When he was within range, he aimed and fired. One of the riders went down with a flesh wound in his thigh. The possemen swung into action. They ran for their horses and unstrapped their Winchesters.

The gully became a battleground. Winchesters and six-shooters barked. Bullets ricocheted off the boulders, horses reared when the slugs splintered the shaft and a wheel of the wagon. Kate gave Buchanan moral support. She bellowed loudly for him to "shoot the bastards, every one of them."

Buchanan fired until all his shells were used up. Then when the stockmen began moving in on his hiding place, he made a run for it and escaped to where he had hidden his horse.

Back at the cottonwood tree, a rope hissed over the lowest branch. A noose was put about Averill's neck.

"Be a man and jump," Bothwell said.

Averill grinned. He still thought they were only trying to scare him. Hell, the wild West was done with fifty years ago!

When Bothwell asked him if he was going to leave the county, he shook his head.

Kate, meanwhile, was no longer flippant. It took two of them to tie the noose about her neck.

She began screaming, "No . . . no . . . if you have a mother . . . a sister . . . no . . . no. . . ."

Bothwell pushed Averill off his boulder. Another rancher helped Kate into eternity. Legend has her first demanding that her skirts be tied.

As a hanging it was a terrifying affair. The *Casper Mail* said: "A point overlooked by the amateur executioners was tying the limbs of their victims. The kicking and the writhing of these two people was something awful. . . ."

It took a long time for them to slowly strangle to death. Jim died first. Kate kicked and tore at the tightening noose. Her beaded moccasins flew through the air. Her face darkened, her eyes bulged from their sockets, and a bloody froth appeared on her lips. Her struggles grew weaker. At last she was still.

The lynchers watched the struggling of the pair in fascinated horror. When the bodies were still they rode away, "each man occupied with his own thoughts." At the rendezvous Bothwell ordered them to go home and "keep mum."

Buchanan, meanwhile, rode aimlessly about the countryside. He testified later before the coroner's jury, "I was lost," a strange excuse for a man who had ridden that part of the range for years. The explanation is probably he was terrified at what he had seen, and was wondering if perhaps he should save his own skin by skipping out of the country.

His loyalty to Averill conquered his fear. He rode to a ranch house a few miles from the Averill place and told what had happened.

The rancher was dumbfounded. The day of vigilante justice was long dead. He was so dubious that Buchanan had to tell the whole story again. The rancher, now believing, galloped to Casper, fifty miles away, to summon the sheriff. On the way he stopped off at several ranches to spread the news.

About ten o'clock Monday morning the sheriff and his posse of thirty, heavily-armed ranchers, guided by Buchanan, rode to the gully, to find, as the *Casper Mail* said, "the bodies swaying to and fro by the gentle breeze which wafted the sweet odor of the prairie flowers across the plains. . . ."

The stiffened bodies were cut down and taken to the Averill ranch. In the main room of the ranch house a coroner's jury was impaneled from the possemen. Buchanan, the fourteen-year-old boy, and another ranch hand employed by Averill, testified.

A verdict of hanging was returned and six of the seven men, including Bothwell, were charged with the killings and arrested. Bail of $5,000 was fixed. Each of the defendants was allowed to sign another's bail bond!

The *Casper Mail* was outraged. Its editor wondered editorially: "Is human life held at no value whatever?"

The double hanging shocked the state. The telegraph wires hummed with the news. Newspapers all over the West gave the story a prominent spot, commenting on it editorially.

The state was soon divided into two camps. On one side were the powerful cattle kings, on the other were the small ranchers and homesteaders. The barons said Averill was a thief and a rustler and deserved to die; the small ranchers and homesteaders said bitterly that Jim was an honest man, a leader of the oppressed, "who was murdered because he wouldn't let Bothwell fence in the entire Sweetwater. . . ."

Curiously, both sides seemed to agree about Kate. To the stockmen's newspapers, she was an "abandoned woman"; in the editorial pages of the newspapers supporting the smaller ranchers, she was "a lewd woman, who got her cattle the way any prostitute does. . . ."

On July 26, Bothwell and the other vigilantes were arraigned and held for the Carbon County Grand Jury.

Two days later the county coroner wrote a blistering letter to Governor Warren, in which he charged that the case would be killed because officials of the state "and the governor of Wyoming were interested parties."

Warren sent back a swift reply denying that the case would be squashed, and that he was "an interested party."

Governor Warren evidently was a very naive man. Although the lynching was now a story of national interest, he admitted in a letter to the coroner, "I have had no communication with the officials of Carbon County since the crime was committed."

Warren naturally would have been prejudiced in favor of the cattle kings who were waiting indictment for hanging Jim and Kate. President Arthur's last act was to appoint him as governor before he had left the White House in 1884. Cleveland was immediately deluged with petitions to keep Warren in office. As a concession to the powerful stock interests, he did. However, he was finally forced to remove him when it was learned that Warren had himself fenced in large tracts of public lands.

As the hot summer days dragged on, the names of Cattle Kate and Jim Averill were on everyone's tongue. A violent battle of the editorial pages took place. Then the grand jury returned indictments against Bothwell and his vigilantes. One day the Valley hummed with the news: Buchanan had disappeared!

On September 10, Kate's father, Thomas, came to Casper. A bewildered, work-worn man, nearly sixty, he denied she was "a loose woman." And as for her rustling activities, he told the editor of the *Rock Springs Miner:* "She never branded a hoof, nor threw a rope."

Four days later, a slim, hard-eyed man rode into the Valley wearing a pair of six-shooters. In Casper he asked only a few questions about the hangings, then galloped out of town.

In a few days he was back. With him was Buchanan, who heatedly denied he had been driven out of the county by the threats of the cattle kings, but had accepted a job as a "mule puncher for the Niobra outfit."

The grim, silent man was seen everywhere; at the gully where the hangings had taken place; at Averill's ranch and at Kate's log cabin. He was also seen sitting on his horse staring down at the twin graves, not far from the Averill ranch.

A shiver of fear went through the Valley. Stories were whispered about "the avenger." The *Cheyenne Leader* printed a story identifying the mysterious stranger and the *Casper Weekly Mail* picked it up.

He was Averill's brother, from Tacoma, Washington, who had come down "to avenge his brother's death.

A wonderful paragraph in the *Leader's* account of the arrival of Jim's brother, sets the imagination working:

> He rode in quickly, without making his business known and went to the Sweetwater region to make his own investigation . . . he was quietly efficient. Within a week he had rounded up five witnesses. . . .

Evidently few people in the Valley had any desire to question his ability to use a gun. They may have remembered what the *Cheyenne Sun* said: "He was a quiet type, who didn't make much noise, and they are always dangerous."

239

Averill's brother stayed for several weeks. He located his witnesses and brought them one by one to the sheriff's office. Then, feeling as most of the smaller ranchers in the Valley felt, that it was now an open-and-shut case against the cattle barons, he vanished. He was never seen again along the Sweetwater.

Months after the indictments had been voted by the grand jury the Valley rocked with the news. The fourteen-year-old boy, a vital witness in the case, had been found dead, strangely enough from "Bright's Disease."

Then Buchanan disappeared again. Asa Mercer in his *Banditti of the Plains* charged he was bushwhacked, which is probably true. As late as 1935, an old-timer revealed that a pile of bleached bones was found four years after the lynching in the brush near Casper. The skeleton was identified as that of Buchanan, "because of a peculiar scarf ornament" found under the skull.

With all the witnesses murdered or disappeared, the cattle kings went into court. When their case was called, the indictment was dismissed for lack of evidence.

The verdict swept through the state like a prairie fire. "If it's lynching they want, two can play the game," a newspaper supporting the smaller ranchers cried.

The Cheyenne stockmen's newspapers applauded the court's decision, hinting the lynchers might hang a few more rustlers "to teach them a lesson."

Along the Sweetwater, feeling ran high. Again there was talk of a "cattle war" and men rode the range armed with Winchesters and six-shooters.

The cattle country was a keg of dynamite. A spark was all that was needed to touch it off.

Gradually the bitterness died away, only to flare up periodically for the next few years. There were several mysterious murders. One small rancher, who had loudly defended Averill, was shot from ambush as he was returning home with Christmas toys for his children. Another homesteader was killed by an assassin who hid behind a boulder. To make sure the body would not be found too soon, the bushwhacker killed the horse.

The cattle barons did not go unharmed. One of them, said to have been the man who pushed Kate into eternity, was killed by an angry ranch hand. Bothwell had his hat lifted off by a Winchester bullet. A few others narrowly escaped death or were wounded.

Meanwhile Kate's cabin fell into ruin. The high-keening wind of the range tore to bits the curtains and killed the geranium. The roof fell in and the door swung eerily on its hinges. Jim Averill's ranch was abandoned. After a few years the markers from their graves vanished.

There is a last ironical touch to the story of Jim and Kate. In the fall of 1891, Bothwell contested homestead claims of Jim and Kate on grounds of delinquent taxes. Through an in-between he bought them both for fourteen dollars and ninety-three cents. Kate's cabin, once the scene of her wild revels, was removed to the Bothwell ranch where it was used as an icehouse!

Rose of the Cimarron

SHE is remembered only as Rose—"Rose of the Cimarron"—and nothing else. For more than half a century her real name, her background, where she came from, and what finally happened to her, has been a tantalizing frontier mystery.

Slim and graceful as a doe, she was Oklahoma's most desperate woman. There are legends of the death and rebirth of the hero and the heroine, yet in her case there is evidence, as we shall see, that she may be still alive, a grandmother of seventy-four, wife of "one of Oklahoma's prominent men" and "mother of beautiful children."

Seven men knew her secret. Each swore never to reveal it. Most of them are gone. Until only a few years ago the last surviving three refused to tell who she was.

As the *Southwest Magazine* declared in 1951:

> She is cloaked in mystery, an Oklahoma puzzle that probably will never be solved, now that the principal actors in the old Indian Territory drama have departed from the scene . . . the chances are that Rose of the Cimarron will remain forever an enigma.

We shall deal later with this frontier "enigma."

Rose was one of the four women in the life of Bill Doolin, one of America's last great outlaws. Three were desperate; one not so desperate. Besides Rose they are Edith, his wife, and two teen-age horse thieves and gun slingers, known to frontier history as "Cattle Annie" and "Little Breeches."

Edith followed Doolin because she loved him; the two young girls "because they wanted to become outlaws"; Rose, because she loved one of his riders.

The story of Edith Ellsworth, the minister's daughter who married Doolin, falls in the familiar pattern of women of every century, who have married men outside the law, only to live bleak and strenuous lives, enduring much, suffering much. Cattle Annie and Little Breeches played only comic roles in this Western drama. It is Rose's story which is most attractive. The part she played in the bloody Battle of Ingalls, Oklahoma, more than fifty years ago, is the stuff from which the songs and ballads of a people are written.

Strangely enough she is not as well known as Calamity Jane, Poker Alice, Belle Starr, Madam Mustache, and the other familiar frontier female characters. Legend and folklore have distorted them all out of focus. But Rose still remains lifelike. This may be because her story is more contemporary. There are men still living who remember her. Zoe Tilghman, widow of that great frontier marshal, Bill Tilghman, writes me she knew Rose "to speak to" and remembers her.

The story of Rose of the Cimarron is primarily a melodramatic love story played before the backdrop of our last frontier, the Oklahoma Territory, just before the century turned. Her story and the stories of Edith Ellsworth, and the comedy team of the frontier, "Cattle Annie" and "Little Breeches," are a part of the rise and fall of the Doolin Gang.

Doolin was the son of Mack Doolin, an Arkansas cotton farmer. He was about fifteen when he left home to wander about the West, working as a transient ranch hand. Men still remember him, a well-built, good-looking youth with dark hair, hazel eyes, and a handlebar moustache. In disposition he was more like Butch Cassidy, leader of the Wild Bunch, than like Jesse Woodson James. Despite the romanticists, Dingus James from Clay County, was a sullen, vicious killer. But Butch and Doolin were always the Gay Desperado. Both had an enormous attraction for women.

We know that Doolin worked on Oscar Halsell's famous H X Bar Ranch, on the Cimarron River, not far from the future site of Guthrie. He was then about twenty, expert with a six-shooter, well known as a wild bronc rider, and skilled in the use of the lariat. Another cowpuncher on the H X Bar was "Bitter Creek" George Newcomb, then about nineteen, whom the Oklahoma marshal, E. D. Nix, remembers as "a fine specimen of manhood." Doolin and Newcomb were both reckless, easy-going, devil-may-care cowhands, loving women, liquor, and poker. From the beginning they struck it off and became firm friends.

In 1889, the Territory was opened and the H X Bar was abandoned to the settlers. Hundreds of cowboys became jobless. Doolin said good-by to Bitter Creek and drifted south to join Bob Dalton, whom he had met in his wanderings. In June, 1891, he rode with the Daltons in a daring holdup of a train at Red Rock, a station on the Santa Fe, a few miles north of Perry, Oklahoma.

It was the beginning of the Dalton gang's reign of terror. Under Bob Dalton, former deputy United States marshal, and police chief of the Osage Nation, the gang rode from one end of the southwest to the other, robbing trains, banks, and stealing large numbers of horses. Federal marshals were helpless. The gang was tireless, riding hundreds of miles using relays of horses to escape into "The Nations" where the law of the white man could not reach.

In the spring of 1892, they committed one of the boldest robberies in frontier history, holding up two trains at the same time at Red Rock.

Encouraged by his first success Bob Dalton planned a twin-bill robbery of the two banks at Coffeyville, Kansas. But like the citizens of Northfield who blew the James-Younger gang apart, the people of Coffeyville put a violent end to the Daltons in October, 1892.

The details of that famous day are well known and need no retelling here. Doolin escaped because a short distance from Coffeyville his horse went lame.

He heard of the massacre while on his way to the farm the gang had selected as a hideout. With a price of five thousand dollars on his head, he rode day and night until he reached Old Rock Fort, an outlaw's hideout on Deer Creek, in Payne County, Oklahoma.

In November, 1892, Doolin reorganized the gang, bringing in as his first in command, Bill Dalton, who had not been a regular member of his brother's band. One of his first riders was "Bitter Creek" Newcomb.

The new gang's first robbery was successful. The vault of the First National Bank at Spearville, Ford County, Kansas, was cleaned of every dollar. More banks and train robberies followed.

By the summer of 1893, Doolin was leading one of the most vicious bands of outlaws in Western history. Besides "Bitter Creek," his riders were George Weightman, alias "Red Buck"; "Little Dick," a fearless savage gun fighter, who had been raised by a foreman of the H X Bar Ranch who had found him, a homeless orphan, wandering on the prairie; Jack Blake, the "Tulsa Jack" of Oklahoma's frontier, as fast with the cards as he was with his gun; Dan Clifton, "Dynamite Dick," train robber and cattle rustler; Charley Pierce, a Pawnee, Oklahoma, race-horse owner who outraged Doolin on many occasions by his extreme recklessness; "Arkansas Tom," a slim, swift-moving gun fighter from Missouri, and "Little Bill," last name unknown, a short, muscular

244

man whose hair, parted in the middle, gave him the appearance of a jolly, German bartender. Bill was the "educated" member of the gang. One of the frontier newspapers said he "knew all about business" and had "a wide banking experience." He had. He robbed quite a few before he joined Doolin's gang.

They came from all parts of the West. They knew Hell's Fringe, the Oklahoma badlands, as well as they knew the backs of their own hands. From their faded pictures they might have been cut from the same mold. They were mostly all lean and rangy men, and like most cowpunchers, almost without hips. They were hard eyed and all superb riders. They were fond of fine horses, liquor, and dance-hall girls. Most of them were friendly until crossed, then they shot to kill. Unlike Jesse Woodson James, not one of them ever whined, "We were forced into it." They were outlaws only because they wanted to be. They were the quick and the dead and they knew it.

They had two hideouts, the famous Creek Nation Cave, a few miles west of the present city of Oilton, and Old Rock Fort Ranch, a well-known outlaw's rendezvous. The town of Ingalls was their main headquarters.

Named after Senator John Ingalls, it was a typical frontier community. It had one wide, dusty thoroughfare, inevitably called Main Street; a two-story wooden hotel called the Pierce Hotel after its owner, Mary Pierce; two saloons, Trilby's "where the dance-hall girls separated the boys from part of their swag and the professional gamblers raked in the rest" and Murray's Saloon, where the gang did its serious drinking, poker playing, and planning. There was also a town pump at the end of Main Street, two physicians, a blacksmith shop, and a livery stable. The gang ruled the town through fear, money, and friendship. They treated the townspeople with respect, never molested the women, and spent all their money there.

It was shortly after Doolin had organized his gang that Bitter Creek Newcomb met and fell in love with Rose, whose secret has been kept so well these sixty years; a secret which one frontiersman said only a few years ago, "Wild horses could not drag from me."

It is only because the truth is as stirring as the legend that we now tell Rose's secret. Here, published for the first time, is the solution of that "tantalizing frontier mystery."

Rose of the Cimarron was Rose Dunn, a convent-bred, dark-haired beauty who lived on a farm a few miles east of Ingalls. We know nothing of her father. Of her mother we know only that she was a vigorous and handsome woman.

Rose's parents made the Run in 1889. They settled on a one hundred and sixty acre homestead on Council Creek. They were apparently better off, intellectually and financially, than their neighbors. There never seemed to be any question of real poverty or want.

One of her brothers, Bee, probably the oldest, made the Run on his own, settling down with his wife and two or three small children on a homestead a few miles east of Ingalls. Rose was a frequent visitor.

The Dunn farmhouse, east of Ingalls, was large and comfortable and built of milled lumber, instead of the usual pole and hay roof dwellings used by most of the settlers. There were also barns, pens, and hog houses.

Rose came from a family which boasted of handsome men and women. One, Rose's cousin, won what was probably the first beauty contest in the Territory. Her gypsylike beauty took all prizes at a frontier fair.

Like most of the Dunns, Rose was slim and dark. Her shoulder length hair was blue black, her skin, tanned golden, was flawless. She had a tinkling laugh and a gay smile.

Rose grew up in the farmhouse along with several brothers and cousins. When she was about thirteen, her father sent her to a convent in Wichita, Kansas, "to be educated." She returned, poised and well spoken. As Mrs. Zoe Tilghman recalls, "Her good looks and presence made her stand out among the country girls who had no chance for 'polish.'"

There is no question that the Dunns knew Doolin. At least two of Rose's brothers were indicted for cattle rustling, and the gossip in Ingalls had Rose's father getting the money to pay for the lumber to build his house "from his association with Doolin."

Despite her convent education, Rose was a daughter of the frontier. It is no fictional surmise to say she was a superb rider, an expert with a six-shooter and Winchester, and skilled in the use of the lariat.

There is no doubt that on more than one occasion she crossed the border of the Pawnee Country, three miles east of Ingalls, to help her brothers round up their rustled cattle for the drive to Guthrie "where they had an agreement with a butcher." She was then about seventeen.

As Mrs. Tilghman points out, Rose was "no glamor girl" in the modern sense. She never had an evening gown in her life and may never have owned silk stockings. Like most of the girls on the frontier, Rose helped her mother tend the chickens, the stock, and the garden. Because her family was better off financially she had more and better clothes than the other girls. Still they were homemade on a sewing machine, copied from the issue of *The Delineator*, tattered and thumb-marked from being passed among the town's ladies.

Her social life revolved about the church box suppers and the dances held near Pawnee. On Sunday afternoon Rose would meet "the young set" of Ingalls to gather around a reed organ and sing.

It is indeed a strange picture to visualize: The slim and beautiful young girl soon to ride with the most vicious band of outlaws in the West, adding her voice to the young chorus, singing "Rock of Ages."

How Rose met Newcomb is not clear. She may have met him through her brothers, or through Doolin, who always found refuge in the Dunn house when the posses were chasing him. There is stronger evidence, however, that they met at one of the neighborhood dances near Pawnee, which the gang always attended in their "store suits." Legend has Doolin doing the fiddling and calling the turns.

What scenes in the barn those wild nights! Doolin, the outlaw, a price on his head, fiddling furiously; Bitter Creek looking down at Rose who smiles back at him; Red Buck getting drunk and trying to shoot out the lamps; Tulsa Jack swinging the Widow May about; Charley Pierce "working" the local farmers and ranchers to place bets on the next day's race which he invariably won; and Arkansas Tom, a preacher's son, the butts of his six-shooters showing under his frock coat, stamping and whooping with one of the other outlaws because there were never enough women to go around.

Rose and Newcomb fell in love. Men like the three frontier marshals, Bill Tilghman, Heck Thomas, and Steve Burke, saw more in their affair than the usual sex relationship of the bandit and the pretty girl.

Rose left home to ride with the gang, holed up in Old Rock Fort. When she rode into camp with Newcomb there were no lifted eyebrows. Our frontier outlaws had a curious sense of morals. They could casually kill a defenseless cashier in a robbery, steal a thousand head of another man's cattle, or rob a bank—but women . . .

Mother was to be wept over as you took off your hat; sister was an angel; a sweetheart must be worshipped and protected. Even the rouged harridans of the dance halls in their gaudy spangles were respected. A girl could ride with a gang but she belonged to one man. It was this way with Rose of the Cimarron. She was the nurse, scout, spy, courier, and horse holder for the gang. But no one, not even the vicious Red Buck, tried to force their attentions on her.

As Mrs. Tilghman recalls, "She was treated with respect by all the outlaws, and there was never a word against her character; even in a gossipy place like Ingalls. . . ."

247

About this time another of the gang, we don't know which one, was smitten by romance. We know from a later court hearing, love came on a summer's night at one of the wild dances near Pawnee. The girls involved were Jennie Stevens, age sixteen, and Annie McDougal, age seventeen. According to one account in the *Guthrie Daily Leader,* an admiring young cowhand played cupid. The dance was in full swing when the girls entered. They noticed some new faces and asked the cowboy about the strangers.

The cowhand shook his head admiringly. "Know who they are, Annie?" he whispered. "Doolin and his boys."

He pointed out Doolin sawing away at the fiddle; Arkansas Tom, tall, slim, and handsome; Red Buck and the others. Annie caught one of the outlaw's eye. It was love at first sight. Jennie, after being introduced by Annie to another member of the gang, was similarly smitten.

It was a grand evening. Red Buck shooting at the lamps, was cheerfully knocked out by Newcomb, and Doolin sawed away until all hours. As usual Charley Pierce collected several bets the next day on his race horse.

Annie and Jennie were frequent visitors at the dances after this. The outlaws made a habit of stopping at their farmhouse. The code of the frontier ruled that every door be open to a stranger. "Soon they were eating with them and in the corral they shook out oats and fodder for their horses."

One night Annie stole the clothes of a hired hand and rode off with her outlaw lover, to join the gang riding out of Ingalls for the hideout. Somehow along the way "her horse got away from her" and she was thrown. Whether or not this disgusted her outlaw lover, we don't know, but the account gives an amusing tale of how Annie was abandoned by her outlaw sweetheart and forced to walk ten miles across the prairie to a neighbor's house to be driven home, "to be welcomed by the jeers and taunts of her family."

The next day was the most humiliating of all. The outlaw appeared, "and being disgusted with her, asked for the return of his tokens." Annie, "heartbroken," turned them over.

That night, still in man's clothes, she left home with Jennie. The pair stole some horses and rode into the badlands, seeking romance and high adventure. In the months which followed, they trailed the Doolin gang, delivering their messages, stealing horses, watching the roads, and acting as sort of a comedy-relief team for the gang, now ready for their next strike.

On the night of May 2, 1893, Doolin led his gang into Cimarron,

Kansas, where they robbed the Cimarron National Bank of several thousand dollars.

As Doolin led the gang out of the bank, townspeople hiding behind fences and trees, opened fire. The outlaw leader went down with a bullet in his leg. With Bitter Creek's help he mounted his horse. Six-shooters blazing, they thundered out of town.

The telegraph clicked out the news. Posses formed and chased the gang to the border. Chris Madsen at Fort Supply took up the chase with a detail of soldiers and a running gun battle followed. But Doolin led his men to safety and the gang scattered to await the next strike.

Doolin went on alone to a ranch in the Cheyenne and Arapaho country where Arkansas Tom was working. Tom took care of Doolin until the wound healed, then drove him to Ingalls in a buggy. This is according to Tom's own version.

For the rest of the summer Doolin and his gang made Ingalls their headquarters, gambling at Trilby's and drinking at Murray's. Charley Pierce raced his horse against the best horseflesh the local ranchers could produce and seldom lost. Doolin planned the next robbery and Bitter Creek wooed Rose.

Rose evidently lived with her mother and her doctor stepfather while the gang "rested" in Ingalls. When she wasn't seeing Bitter Creek, she would ride up wide Main Street to the Pierce Hotel and visit the daughter of Mrs. Pierce.

Doolin ruled his roost like a medieval robber baron. He played poker with his followers, raced his horse, joked, gambled, and drank, but never relaxed his discipline. One of the gang was always riding out of town to meet Cattle Annie or Little Breeches for news of the posse said to be gathering at Guthrie.

In late July a red-headed stranger appeared. He said his name was "Red" Lucas and he was just passing through. It developed he was an excellent poker player and the gang liked his good humor. He stayed until late August, then disappeared. No one thought much of his disappearance. Men on the frontier seldom stayed in one place for very long.

In Guthrie, Lucas, a federal deputy, reported to Marshal Nix. He sketched the layout of the town, rattled off the names of the gang there, and gave his advice as to the best way of surrounding the town and wiping out the gang for the last time.

Back in Ingalls, Rose was telling Bitter Creek she didn't like Lucas. She said she was uneasy and wanted to pull stakes for Texas. Newcomb laughed away her fears. While he went down to Murray's to play a hand, she went back to the hotel to talk to Mrs. Pierce, "who had known her since she was eight."

Sometime around August, a young deputy sheriff of Payne County appeared at Ingalls, to arrest a Texas outlaw named "Ragged Bill." It is not clear whether the sheriff had been sent in as reconnaissance by the marshals. It is doubtful whether an experienced man hunter like Nix would use such a senseless young man.

The young deputy walked into Murray's, boldly announcing that he was ready to take in Ragged Bill. As the Stillwater and Tulsa newspapers reconstructed the scene, a dead silence followed his announcement. The gang lined up by the bar, turned to stare at the deputy.

"What's that?" someone asked.

The deputy repeated his statement. The men at the bar moved between him and the door.

Though it sounds like a scene from a bad Western, Doolin, at that moment, walked in.

"What's this?" he asked.

"He says he going to take Bill in," he was told.

"On what charge?" Doolin asked.

"For hitting an old man over the head and taking his money," the deputy replied.

"How much was it?" asked Doolin.

The officer said, "Forty dollars."

Doolin looked incredulous. "Forty dollars!"

The deputy nodded. Doolin turned to the fugitive. "Is this true, Bill?"

Bill nodded. "I hit him over the head just to get the money to join you," he said proudly.

"Get him out of here," Doolin roared. "Anybody who hits an old man over the head for forty dollars can't water Doolin's horses."

With a whoop the gang fell on Ragged Bill. In a few minutes they had tied him to a horse. The deputy rode out of town sweating but triumphant, leading the horse ridden by a cursing "Ragged Bill."

Meanwhile the posses under Marshal Nix were gathering at Stillwater, ten miles west of Ingalls. About twelve marshals and deputies rolled out of town in a covered wagon, disguised as a ranch outfit. Just before dawn on September 1, 1893, they pitched camp outside of Ingalls.

After breakfast, the attack on the town was planned. Unnoticed by the marshals, a small boy, fishing pole over his shoulder, had come through the camp and stood to one side, "all ears."

One of the marshals finally noticed the boy, who, by this time, "had heard much of their plans." It was decided to keep the youngster for safekeeping. The boy wept, insisting that he be allowed to go home. A short time before they started out for Ingalls the marshals released him after extracting a childish promise "he would not tell."

The barefooted boy streaked for town. Rose saw him racing down the dusty street, the fishing pole still over his shoulder. With Mrs. Pierce she ran out.

"What's the matter, boy?" she called out.

"The marshals are coming, they're up at the creek," the boy cried over his shoulder.

Rose ran down the street to Trilby's where Bitter Creek and the rest of the gang were playing poker. What happened then is not clear. Evidently they questioned the terrified boy but only half believed his story. Doolin, however, ordered the horses saddled and stabled at the south end of the town, near Trilby's. Bitter Creek calmed Rose's alarm and she returned to the hotel with Mrs. Pierce.

The morning passed. Horses and mules of other customers drooped at the hitching at Trilby's, shivering off the flies and whisking their tails. In the hotel, Arkansas Tom, "who was feeling sick," tossed on his bed.

Across the hall Mrs. Pierce was talking to Rose in her room. One wonders what was the subject of their conversation; Bitter Creek, the weather, the law, the last robbery? . . .

Back at the creek the posse was ready to ride. The prairie schooners were packed, guns and rifles loaded. They divided into three groups of about ten men each to come into Ingalls from three different directions. One group would cover the barn, another the hotel, and the last, Murray's and Trilby's.

Curiously no one saw them approach. Evidently Doolin was so convinced of the impregnability of his stronghold that he never bothered to set up barriers at each end of Main Street, or to post his men at vantage points on housetops or behind the fences or corrals.

About eleven o'clock the man hunters began to spread out, the marshals and volunteers scurrying down the side streets, along alleys and over fences, their rifle barrels gleaming in the hot sun.

The town was quiet in the breathless heat. Doc Bragg's fourteen-year-old boy, Dick, came down the steps of his house on Main Street and started toward the town pump. An elderly man named Ranson appeared riding a mule. Another man named Cushman came out of the blacksmith's shop, talking to the smitty, who went back to his forge. The measured strokes of his hammer began to break the quiet.

From behind the building Marshal Steve Burke rode up beside the boy. The boy looked up. Then Burke leaned over to say something to him, perhaps to warn him to get out of the line of fire.

On the second floor of the hotel Arkansas Tom called for a glass of water and Rose brought it to him. They spoke for a few moments then she went back again "to sit" with Mrs. Pierce.

In Trilby's, Bitter Creek "became restless." In the middle of a hand he threw down his cards and got up.

"Where you going, kid?" Doolin asked.

"Down to the pump to have a look around," Newcomb said.

Doolin nodded and the game was resumed.

Newcomb took a horse from the hitching post, swung up, and rode down the street. Rifle and revolver sights followed him. As he came up to the hotel, he whistled. Rose appeared at the window.

He asked how Tom was and she said he was sleeping. He gave her a wave and moved on, his horse going at a walk.

Suddenly he drew up short. He saw Burke talking to the boy. The boy said something and Burke turned in his saddle. He and Newcomb drew at the same time. Bitter Creek's hat jumped from his head as though pulled by an invisible string. His bullet tore through Burke's coat.

All around the town the revolvers and rifle fire crashed out. Glass shattered and the air held a strange, humming noise. The Bragg's boy screamed and fell to the ground, wounded in the side. Bitter Creek swung his horse around and dashed to the saloon. In the confusion he was not hit.

The scene inside the saloon has been duplicated countless times in scores of Hollywood's horse operas. The gang had overturned the tables and pushed them to the windows and the swinging doors. In a moment the wooden walls of the building were literally "riddled," as the *Stillwater Gazette* said that same day.

An innocent customer who had come in a moment before for a morning pickup was wounded seriously. In Murray's, the owner and a customer were wounded by rifle fire. In the street the elderly mule rider toppled over, shot through the heart. The hotel man to whom he was talking tried to run but was caught by the cross fire. "Dell Simmons, a young man of Ingalls," mistaken by the gang for one of the marshals, was killed.

In the first minutes the fire was rapid and hot. Doolin ran from window to window, firing and encouraging his men. In the hotel, Arkansas Tom was on his feet, revolver in hand, waiting. When Speed, one of the marshals, ran across the street Tom fired, killing him instantly. Several possemen directed their fire at his window. Tom ducked. A water pitcher crashed down on his head, the window was splintered and he was cut by flying glass.

In her room Rose and Mrs. Pierce crouched on the floor.

In Trilby's, Doolin, realizing their ammunition was getting low, ordered the gang to make a run for the barns and their saddled horses.

They emerged from the saloon, guns blazing. One of the marshal's rifles barked. Bitter Creek spun about, staggered a few feet, and fell in a small alley next to the saloon. The rest of the gang kept moving down the street, hugging the sides of the buildings, firing as they ran.

The possemen firing at the hotel, were now forced to keep under cover. From his hotel room Tom had killed two more marshals who had tried to rush the building.

Rose now had an opportunity to peep out the window. What she saw chilled her heart. Sprawled out in the dust was Bitter Creek. He still had his six-shooter in his hand but the chambers were empty.

Rose ran to a room down the hall. A Winchester, holster, and bandoleer of shells lay in a corner. She buckled the holster about her slim waist and ran out with the rifle and shells.

Mrs. Pierce came out into the hall. "Rose—what are you doing?" she cried.

"Bitter Creek is wounded. I'm going to him," she replied.

"Good God, child, you'll be killed out there," Mrs. Pierce said.

The tempo of the firing stepped up. In his room Arkansas Tom's six-shooter barked. The two women could hear the sharp smacking noise of the possemen's bullets hitting the flimsy hotel.

Without a word Rose ran to a room in the rear of the hotel. She took the sheets from the bed, tore them into strips, and tied them together. One end of the "ladder," as the newspapers later called it, was tied to a bed post. First she lowered the Winchester, holster, revolvers, and shells to the ground. Then she swung over the window sill and slid to the ground.

She may have banked on the chivalry of the West. With the rifle and shells under one arm and the heavy six-shooters slapping against her thighs, she ran out into the street, directly in the line of fire! It takes no exuberant fancy to imagine how startled were the possemen crouching in the alleys and behind the fences.

It was a girl!

The firing stopped. Rose reached Bitter Creek, gave him his six-shooters, then knelt at his side, to coolly work the Winchester!

The firing resumed. Above the crackle of gunfire Doolin shouted his orders; hold off the marshals until Rose and Bitter Creek reached the barn.

Bitter Creek was bleeding badly and weak from loss of blood. Rose helped him stagger to his feet, then leaned him against the side of the building. She took his guns and strapped them about her. Then, half-dragging, half-carrying her sweetheart, she made her way down the street, hugging the sides of the buildings protected by the Winchester and revolver fire of Doolin and his men.

All of them reached the livery stable. There Bitter Creek collapsed. Dalton ran inside the stable and came out with Newcomb's horse. While Rose held it, Dalton helped Bitter Creek to mount. The young outlaw, white to the lips, gripped the saddle horn and weakly kicked the horse down a shallow draw behind the barn.

The marshals cautiously approached. Doolin, Dalton, Tulsa Jack, Little Bill, and Dynamite Dick began blazing away with their rifles and six-shooters. Rose crouched behind them. The inside of the barn was thick with gunpowder smoke. The coughing outlaws, handkerchiefs about their mouths, kept firing through the slits of the old stable.

Doolin finally gave the command to make a run for it out a rear door. Bullets kicked up the dust about them but they made their horses "and rode down a draw." The possemen started in pursuit. A running gun battle started. The marshal, Red Lucas, shot Doolin's horse, shattering its jaw. The animal, wild with pain, reared up, but the outlaw kept his seat and managed to steady the animal.

Lucas fired again, cracking the animal's front leg.

The horse went down with the horrible scream of a wounded animal. Doolin jumped clear. Bill Dalton swung about and Doolin vaulted up behind him. The possemen came up, with Marshal Shadley sending a bullet past Doolin's head. Doolin, using Bitter Creek's Winchester, fired in return.

"Missed him, Bill," Dalton said calmly.

"Not this time," Doolin replied. Almost without aiming, he fired three shots.

Shadley bent over, then fell off his horse. The courageous law officer got upon one knee, clutched his revolver with both hands, and tried to pull the trigger. The effort was too much. He was down for good.

At the end of the draw the outlaws were stopped by a wire fence. Before the fence lay the unconscious Bitter Creek. While Tulsa Jack snipped the wire fence, Dynamite Dick and Dalton helped Newcomb on his horse. Dalton also mounted the horse, holding Bitter Creek in front of him.

At the edge of some timber they halted and made a crude litter of poles thrust through the sleeves of their coats. With the litter swung between their horses the band moved to their cave in the hills.

Back at the livery stable, Jim Masterson, brother of Bat, was the first to reach Marshal Shadley's side. He knelt down and lifted the dying man who still clutched his gun.

"I'm going, Jim," he said.

Then, in bitter admiration for the man who had killed him, he said, "He fired so fast he didn't seem to aim."

He coughed and died.

Masterson and the rest of the posse sadly brought the body back to Dr. Pickering's house in town. The physician, whose house was filled with the seriously wounded bystanders and the bodies of the dead, examined the marshal.

"The wounds are so close together," he told a *Gazette* reporter, "I can cover them with the palm of one hand."

In town Arkansas Tom had been taken prisoner. He had been trapped in the attic and the possemen were ready to burn down the hotel when Mrs. Pierce pleaded with them to let her try to persuade Tom to surrender.

Mrs. Pierce climbed to the roof. She told Tom that if he didn't come down they were going to destroy her hotel. Tom, a reasonable gent, said he would never allow such a thing to happen, so he climbed down and surrendered. The fact that he was out of ammunition and had thrown away his empty six-shooter at one of the possemen, may have been another contributing factor to his surrender, besides chivalry.

Evidently Rose had either eluded the possemen or had given them a logical excuse for being near the scene of the shooting, because we next find her riding back to town. The hamlet looked like a town hit by Quantrill's raiders during the border wars.

The reporter who did "a hurriedly written account" for the *Stillwater Gazette* counted five dead horses and three mules. Three marshals were laid out in the blacksmith's shop, at least four townspeople were dead, including the son of Doctor Bragg and another boy named

Jerry Simmonds. Several more were wounded. Murray's saloon and Trilby's were a shambles. Mirrors, windows, and fixtures were shattered by the gunfire. The table by the door of Trilby's was split in several places by the rapid fire.

"The walls of the saloon were completely riddled by the heavy firing of the marshals," the *Gazette's* reporter wrote.

Back in Ingalls, Rose rode up to Mrs. Pierce's hotel. The building was pock-marked with bullet holes. There was scarcely a window pane left unshattered. All day possemen galloped in and out of the town, passing the hotel in clouds of dust, while Rose waited for news.

Twilight, then darkness fell over the countryside. The excited cries of the man hunters; the thud of horses hooves, and the rattling and creaking of wagons, stilled. Then down the quiet street came a rider. He hitched up at the Pierce Hotel and knocked on the door. When someone asked who it was he whispered, "Dalton."

Inside Dalton faced Rose and Mrs. Pierce. No one knows what they said but surely Rose eagerly inquired about Bitter Creek. Dalton told her briefly: Newcomb was badly wounded and still unconscious from loss of blood. He must have a doctor at once.

It was Rose who roused the doctor that night and with Dalton rode back through the darkness to the outlaw's cave, where Bitter Creek lay before a small fire, started to protect him from the chill of the night wind.

It was Rose who nursed Bitter Creek back to health. She rode for the medicines and the food, always watching the roads to inform Doolin of the directions the galloping possemen were taking.

Meanwhile the "Battle of Ingalls," as it was called, had electrified the whole Territory. Citizens demanded action. Federal Marshal Nix gave it to them immediately.

Oklahoma's Bill Tilghman, Chris Madsen, and Heck Thomas were ordered by the government to find the gang and wipe it out.

In and about Ingalls, ranchers and farmers made up a volunteer posse. Led by some of the marshals who had been in the battle, they set out to find the gang and annihilate it. They were on their way to Old Rock Fort when they met a young girl, "heavily armed" and dressed in a pair of dungarees and a man's shirt.

One of the marshals rode up to her. In reply to his question she said she was returning to her father's ranch after visiting a friend. She said she hadn't seen any large group of men riding by. The marshal thanked her and rode on. She pulled her horse to one side of the road and watched the posse ride by.

The girl was "Cattle Annie," probably returning from a whisky selling tour among the Osage. When the last rider disappeared she found Little Breeches and both flew to a rancher, known to be friendly to the gang. The rancher rode to another with the warning. The message flew from ranch to ranch in relays. That night Doolin received the warning.

He ordered the gang to scatter and await orders. Within an hour the outlaw rendezvous was deserted. Doolin and Rose helped Newcomb into the saddle and, supporting him between them, rode to the Outlaw's Cave, deep in the Creek Nation.

Somehow Rose was able to get medicine and bandages. She stayed with Bitter Creek for several weeks, nursing him back to health. Then, when he was able to ride, they rode down to "Jim Davis' squatter's house on the Cimarron" where they hid out.

Sometime after the battle, romance entered Doolin's life. It was to be a brief, tragic affair.

It is not clear how he met Edith Ellsworth, daughter of the minister of Lawton, but it may have been while he was a fugitive. It was not unusual for the Western outlaws to pose as cattle dealers while on the run. Butch Cassidy did it in New York City before going to South America, and Jesse James and the Youngers always adopted that role.

Doolin's picture shows him to be a good-looking man. Edith, then about twenty, was charmed by his manners. She thought it strange that he came and went so frequently, but Bill suavely explained he was away on business trips.

Early in 1894, Doolin and Edith were married in the parlor of her home, by her father. Whether or not she knew he was an outlaw we do not know.

It would be delightful to know if they had a honeymoon and where they went. Did Edith in their intimacy plead with him to hang up his guns? Did she experience the first fear which was to haunt her for so many weary months—the creak of a board that made Doolin go for his guns . . . the rustling of a tree outside . . . a stranger on the road who looked at him queerly? . . .

At the time of his marriage Doolin had a price of six thousand dollars on his head. There is little doubt that he, like Frank James, had the feeling, "You can't go outside to chop firewood, you think any minute a gun will fire to take your life. You are afraid for your loved ones and wonder when they will come and kill you. . . ."

Bitter Creek and Doolin met in May. Little Bill, "who knew all about business," had sent word that the bank in Southwest City,

257

Missouri, was ready to be picked. Doolin was first an outlaw, then a bridegroom. With Little Bill, Red Buck, and Bitter Creek, they rode to Southwest City.

As always Doolin went in to look things over. He found the bank, as Bill said, "easy." On May 20, in the afternoon, the outlaws rode into town. The robbery was swiftly executed. As they swung up on their horses, J. Seaborn, Oklahoma's former state auditor, ran out into the street.

Little Bill fired one shot, killing him instantly. Across the street a window was thrown up. A shotgun roared. A burst of buckshot hit Doolin in the forehead. Almost blinded by the blood, but still firing, he led them out of town with the posses not far behind. But Doolin had selected the best horses he could steal, and they soon outdistanced the possemen.

They rode day and night across the Cherokee Nation, into the Creek Nation, and finally to Old Rock Fort. The loot was split evenly and Doolin rode off to join his wife. It must have been a terrifying experience to this woman to see the man she loved so deeply, ride up to the small ranch which they had selected for a hideout, his clothes blood stained and a crude bandage about his forehead.

The gang was quiet for several months. During that time Cattle Annie and Little Breeches spread the news; Bill Dalton had been killed. He had been hiding out with his wife at a ranch thirty-five miles west of Ardmore when he was shot down by a marshal while attempting to escape.

Dalton's death may have shaken Doolin. They had ridden the outlaw trail for years and were good friends. He rode out to see Bitter Creek and Rose and they all talked about hanging up their guns.

Rose was continually at Bitter Creek to leave the country. The frontier was fast becoming civilized and Tilghman, Heck Thomas, and Chris Madsen were reported everywhere. Rose and Mrs. Doolin probably knew each other by now and one can imagine the two women lecturing the two tough gun fighters on "crime does not pay," and painting a rosy picture of a quiet ranch somewhere in the West where they could raise a few head of cattle and their children.

Bitter Creek and Doolin told their women they would quit the outlaw trail after they had made a few more strikes. Sometime later Newcomb and Little Bill kidnapped a Wells Fargo agent at Woodware and at gun point made him open the safe. They got six thousand dollars.

Under the rules laid down by Doolin the loot of any robbery had to be split with the other members of the gang. They rode to Old Rock

Fort Ranch, took their share, and vanished again until the next call from their chief. Bitter Creek and Little Bill received the lion's share. Legend has them traveling to Chicago with Rose to see the World's Fair. It may be true. When Bill was killed later, two elaborately decorated guns with a Chicago stamp were found in his holster.

In January, 1895, Tilghman, still doggedly trailing the gang, appeared at Old Rock Fort Ranch with an Indian tracker and a deputy, ready to arrest a ranch hand on cattle stealing charge and squeeze out of him where Doolin was hiding out. They came up to the ranch in the midst of a howling blizzard. Tilghman told his Indian tracker and deputy to wait outside while he looked things over.

Inside there was a roaring fire of blackjack logs and one rancher sitting in a dark corner. There were tiers of bunks around the room with canvas drops. Tilghman was talking to the rancher when he noticed a revolver poking from under one of the canvas drops.

"Well," he said casually, "I guess I'll be going. How does a man get out of here?"

"The same way he got in," was the rancher's sullen reply.

Tilghman walked out into the storm. The place is full of outlaws," he told his companions. "Drive off but don't act excited."

In a moment they were hidden by the storm. Back in the cabin the outlaws scrambled from their bunks. Red Buck was in a rage because Doolin had refused to let him kill Tilghman.

"Bill Tilghman is too good a man to shoot in the back," the outlaw chief said.

In May, 1895, Chris Madsen caught up with Tulsa Jack and killed him after a train robbery at Dover, Oklahoma. Charley Pierce, Red Buck, and Bitter Creek escaped.

It was after this robbery that Doolin told Bitter Creek he was hanging up his guns. The last ten years were taking their toll. He was wracked by rheumatism and in constant torment.

Bitter Creek told Rose of Doolin's decision. Rose begged him to do the same thing. He said he would. They would leave the country, perhaps for Argentina, where many Western outlaws were buying land and starting a new life. We like to think they sat together in the darkness, the blackjack logs crackling in the fireplace, making plans.

In the morning Red Buck arrived with the news. Doolin was calling the gang together for the last time. At the Rock Fort Ranch, Doolin said good-by. Rose was there and so were Cattle Annie and Little Breeches, now selling whisky with a man named Wilson—"a rounder from Pawnee," as the *Tulsa World* called him.

The same night Doolin and his wife left for Burden, Kansas. Edith drove the wagon and Doolin rode ahead. They could have been any farm couple going home.

There was no escape for Rose and Bitter Creek. Day by day the misery and futility grew thicker about them. They took to the prairies and the hills. Spring passed into summer. They were reported in their Pawnee Country, then the Comanche Territory. Sometimes they spent a night in a crossroads village; more often they found their beds in barns and sheds, listening to wolves running in the hills; by day they were up at dawn and in the saddle until twilight to escape the relentless man hunters from Guthrie.

They ate when they could. From the endless hours in the saddle they grew thin. Rose's tanned face was burned dark by the sun and the keening wind. With her long hair streaming behind her in the wind she could have been a slim Pawnee buck galloping across the prairies.

They stayed together all summer and deep into the fall. Despite the hardships, the love between this rough, two-gun outlaw and the convent-bred girl, established its value. It remained intact; it intensified and never faltered.

In the fall they were almost captured but escaped. Their horses were weary and thin from lack of fodder. The edge of winter was creeping across the land; the sun gave less heat, the wind of the prairies chilled them. The nights were bitterly cold.

Sometime in the winter of 1896, Bitter Creek told Rose she must leave him. The posses were closing in; there were no places left to hide.

The year of 1896 was probably one of the bitterest in Rose's life. In the midsummer her brother, Bee, was shot and killed in Pawnee by Frank Canton, a deputy marshal, with whom he had a feud. Then in the late summer her mother died. Rose returned home, while two of her brothers, now under indictment for rustling cattle, sneaked down out of the hills at night for a last glimpse of their mother's face.

Bitter Creek rode on alone. Rose either stayed at her stepfather's house in Ingalls or went to comfort her brother's widow at the Dunn place outside of town.

Out on the prairie, Newcomb met Charley Pierce and they rode together. The plot of the melodrama turned to the stark irony of Greek tragedy.

Mrs. Tilghman recalls that in 1896 her husband persuaded the local district attorney to dismiss the rustling charges against the Dunns, Rose's blood brothers.

The two brothers were then made deputy marshals "and henceforth their homes ceased to be hideouts for the Doolin gang." By enormous duplicity this was accomplished without Rose being aware. She waited for Bitter Creek to come for her.

On a winter's day in 1896, Bitter Creek and Charley Pierce again appeared. We know what that day brought to both of them. They had been riding day and night, with Tilghman and Heck Thomas hot on their trail. Saddle-weary, chilled to the bone, and hungry, Newcomb and Pierce made their way to what they thought was their last refuge on the frontier—the Dunn ranch.

Surely this was the place they would be welcomed, be given food and oats for their horses . . . the Dunns always looked out for Doolin . . . they were friends of the gang and rustlers themselves . . . and there was Rose.

By some means we do not know the brothers had arranged that day that she should not be at the ranch. Perhaps she was at her stepfather's home in Ingalls.

Bitter Creek and Pierce reached the ranch in the late afternoon. Tilghman and Thomas had been there an hour before to warn the Dunns that the outlaws were headed in their direction. They had agreed to summon the marshals, waiting nearby in the hills, when they appeared.

Newcomb and Pierce rode up to the ranch gate. From behind the gate two shotguns roared simultaneously. Bitter Creek and Charley Pierce were dead before their bodies slipped out of the saddle. One of the Dunns fired a second blast "to make sure." It tore through Bitter Creek's boot.

Hearing the shots Tilghman and Thomas came up on the gallop. On Tilghman's orders the Dunns took the bodies to Ingalls, where, ironically, Dr. Pickering, who had examined the marshal killed by the gang, counted twenty-eight slugs in Bitter Creek Newcomb's body.

It may well be that they had killed him, not so much in gratitude to Tilghman for getting the indictments dismissed as to protect their sister from Newcomb.

They must have realized it would only be a matter of time before she joined him again, and that as in Ingalls, she would stay with him to the end.

The frontier hummed with the news of Bitter Creek's death. Men liked the happy-go-lucky bandit and talked about him. Before the flowers had wilted on his prairie grave, Bitter Creek was a frontier legend.

Who told Rose of his death is not known. As one account said with wonderful simplicity, "She wept a great deal for him." But the chariots were coming for all of them. The curtain was coming down on the last outlaw drama of the old West. Tilghman located Doolin in Kansas, captured him singlehanded, and took him to Guthrie.

A large crowd was on hand to meet them. As Frank James had done years before when he surrendered, Doolin called out to those he knew "and was greeted warmly," the lion of the hour. Hundreds stood for hours outside the jail to catch a glimpse of him. As always, the courageous law officer who had served justice faithfully was ignored.

On September 5, 1895, Little Bill was shot and seriously wounded by Tilghman at a ranch twenty-five miles northeast of Pawhuska, in the Osage Nation. Red Buck, the tiger of the Doolin gang, died not long after in a blaze of gunfire.

Then the country was shocked to hear that Doolin was again on the loose. He had not only escaped from jail but had released all the other prisoners.

At the risk of spoiling a romantic version which one contemporary historian insists is true, Rose of the Cimarron was not waiting outside the jail with a horse.

What happened was this; Doolin walked only a short distance when he came upon a couple riding in a buggy. He forced the couple to get out, then after apologizing that he was "sick" he rode off. The young woman, still living in California, has given Mrs. Tilghman a detailed account of her experiences.

Doolin fled to friends in Arkansas and Rose supposedly was taken into custody. According to Marshal Nix's autobiography, he ordered his men to arrest her. As Nix wrote in his *Oklahombres:* "The danger she might be tempted to aid Doolin in some way, denied us of the further privilege of chivalry in the matter."

Marshal Nix's version, which many Western writers have passed on down through the years, is wrong. The arrest of Rose by Bill Tilghman never took place, and existed only in the imagination of Nix's ghost writer.

Marshal Tilghman is also quoted as telling Nix after Rose's arrest, "Marshal, I'm almost ashamed of arresting that girl. She doesn't belong in our jail. I believe everything Doolin and the others have said about her is true."

Rose is said to have been arraigned before Federal Judge Brierer on a charge of "aiding and abetting outlaws." After pleading guilty she was supposed to have been sentenced to serve four years in Farmington Federal Reformatory in Massachusetts, after Tilghman is pictured as having made an eloquent plea for her, pointing out that she was reared on the frontier, "and never had a chance to meet anyone else but those outlaws."

Another account has a "boomer blade with a homestead" jumping up in court asking Judge Brierer if he can marry her on the spot. Then with a banality that was almost beautiful, Rose bowed her head and wept. Judge Brierer wept. A court clerk turned away to hide a misty eye. Then loudly blowing his nose, of course with a polka dot handkerchief, the judge reluctantly sentenced Rose to a short term after she had agreed to marry the young blade.

On the way to jail, glowing as the first rose of the morning, she paused to kiss the man who had saved her from a life of evil.

Alas, the tellers of those tales, as Cicero said of Cataline, "more easily believed that which he desired."

Rose was never arrested by Marshal Tilghman. She was never arraigned on any federal indictment, nor was she ever served with a bench warrant, nor did she spend one hour in a county or a federal institution.

Furthermore, the traditional picture of Rose of the Cimarron, wearing a dark-striped dress, holding a Winchester rifle and a six-shooter, which has been used in scores of Western and frontier histories is *not* her! The young girl in the picture was an inmate of the federal jail at the time. The picture was first used by Marshal Tilghman in an attempt to shield Rose's identity.

Because there never was a charge lodged against Rose, Tilghman, until his death, was always careful never to disclose her name or tell where she had settled after her marriage.

In 1927, Fred Sutton the frontier author of *Hands Up!* claimed that Rose was still alive, "married to one of Oklahoma's prominent men and mother of beautiful children." Only a few years ago there was an article in an Oklahoma newspaper on her life. The writer disguised her name but from the facts evidently knew who she was. He also hinted she was still alive.

2

There is much legend and distortion surrounding the death of Doolin. Here again Mrs. Tilghman gives the facts.

During his search for Doolin, Heck Thomas had the assistance of two voluntary informers, Charles and Thomas Noble, both black-smiths and well diggers. Their shop was in Lawson. When Edith, Doolin's wife, returned to her father's parsonage to await the birth of her first child, Thomas told the Noble brothers to watch for Doolin's return.

One day Edith drove up to the blacksmith shop and asked that the team be shod. It was an unusual request. The country was not rocky and horses were seldom shod. The blacksmiths reasoned the shod team meant a journey. They sent word to Thomas who arrived just before Doolin, his wife and their infant son, started off in the brilliant moon-light to what they thought was finally security and happiness.

Doolin walked down the road, leading his horse, a Winchester cradled in his right arm. Behind him, Edith drove the wagon, her infant son on the seat beside her.

Suddenly Thomas stepped out in the road. "Throw up your hands, Doolin!" he shouted.

Before Thomas finished his order, Doolin swung up his rifle and fired. This time his aim was bad. The bullet whistled past Thomas' ear. The Marshal fired. A shotgun blast tore through Doolin's chest killing him instantly.

His wife, who had no tears left, knelt by his side and took his hand, whispering, "Bill . . . Bill . . . I knew it would end this way. . . . "

Then the body was put across a horse and Heck Thomas and his posse led the horse and wagon back to the Ellsworth house. In the rear of the wagon was a chicken and a plow, mute symbols of the life Doolin had scorned so often but had at last frantically tried to embrace.

There is a persistent legend that Doolin died of consumption and a charge had been fired into the corpse as a part of a deal made by the Reverend Ellsworth and the marshals to split the reward money.

As Mrs. Tilghman points out, the records of the coroner's inquest, the financial records of the Department of Justice, and the records of the firms which offered the rewards, show Doolin was killed by Thomas while resisting arrest. If the legend was true, all of the mar-shals, the coroner and his assistants, the government agencies, and the business firms, would have had to have been "fixed."

The Western melodrama ended on a humorous note. Cattle Annie and Little Breeches, still peddling whisky with Wilson, "the rounder from Pawnee," had become quite troublesome to the authorities. Marshal Nix finally ordered Tilghman and Steve Burke to arrest them.

The *Daily Oklahoman* tells the story under the headline: A COUPLE OF BOARDERS FOR THE FEDERAL INN.

Tilghman and Burke, armed with warrants, located the pair in a farmhouse near Pawnee. As the Marshals rode up to the gate, Little Breeches leaped out a rear window onto her horse and galloped across the prairie in a cloud of dust.

"I'll get her," Tilghman shouted to Burke, "you get the other one."

Tilghman started in pursuit of Little Breeches Medkiff. As he later said he was torn between chivalry and duty. He didn't want to shoot the girl, nor did he want to allow her to escape. Little Breeches solved his problem. In the best tradition of the Hollywood horse opera, she turned in her saddle and began firing at Tilghman. Some of the shots were uncomfortably close. Tilghman decided to end the chase at once. He unstrapped his Winchester and brought her horse down with one shot.

The seventeen-year-old desperate woman tried to leap clear but one leg was pinned under the dead animal. As Tilghman swung out of his saddle she was pawing for her six-shooter, inches from her fingertips. She lay there tearing at the grass and "screeching like a catamount." When Tilghman bent down to pick up the gun she threw a handful of dust into his face almost blinding him.

After removing the shells from her six-shooter he lifted the carcass of the horse to free her. Little Breeches was still full of fight. She swung a right and caught big Bill on the jaw. Then she raked his face with her long and dirty fingernails. Tilghman spun her around and quite calmly administered several smacks with his very hard and calloused hand to her bottom. She had quite an ample rear and the dungarees were stretched tight. When he finished she was quite docile.

With Little Breeches riding behind him, holding on to his belt, Tilghman rode back to the farmhouse.

Burke was having his own troubles. He knew Cattle Annie, who was older and tougher, had a Winchester and a revolver. Despite her age she could shoot. Burke crept up to the house. He was underneath a window when Annie looked out. Burke reached up and grabbed her. With a shriek of rage she fell out of the window on top of the Marshal. Like Tilghman, Burke had a wildcat on his hands. Annie kicked, clawed, and bit.

When Tilghman came up, Burke, one of the most fearless of the frontier marshals, was standing in the front yard, holding the girl in a bear hug. He was hatless, minus some hair, and his face looked as if he had been in a fight with an army of frenzied cats.

265

The girls were taken to Perry and turned over to the prison matron who "scrubbed them and dressed them in attractive clothes." Under the men's clothes, the dirt, and grime, were a pair of attractive, but badly frightened young girls. Tilghman and Burke pleaded for them and Judge Brierer sentenced them to short terms in Farmington.

Marshal Nix and a deputy accompanied the girls on the journey east to prison. The century was drawing to a close and female outlaws were a curiosity. The wires of the news services hummed with their story. When they arrived in Boston a large crowd was on hand to see "Oklahoma's girl bandits." For the two frontier girls the journey had been thrilling. They were deeply impressed with Boston and stunned by the crowd. Soon they were behind bars.

They were released after serving two years. Cattle Annie, older and wiser, married and settled down near Pawnee. Little Breeches remained in the East. She stayed in Boston for some months working as a domestic. Then she went on to New York City "to do settlement work." Two years later she died in Bellevue Hospital of consumption.

What of Rose of the Cimarron? This is what we know. In 1898 she married Charles Noble, the blacksmith of Lawton, who informed on Doolin, *the man who for so many years had received refuge from the law in her father's house!* *

* A copy of their marriage certificate in the author's possession lists Rose, as Rosa Dunn. She was then nineteen. They were married by S. T. Peague, Minister of The Gospel in Payne County, December 5, 1897.

The Two Loves of Harry Tracy

IT IS hard at times to realize that heroes and heroines who played their roles in the past, were flesh and blood; that a man of consummate evil looked like a storekeeper or a bank clerk.

So it is with some of our most vicious American outlaws. Too often they are only names in yellowed newspaper clippings which tell us briefly, "He is tall and thin as a gallows post, and has a mustache and brown eyes," or, "He is short and squat with thick sideburns, a dark complexion and is now wearing shoes."

We know a little more about the man who was perhaps the most evil of them all. He talked in a soft voice, tipped his hat to a passing woman, liked flowers and a good cigar to smoke in the evening when he sat on his porch.

Not a dangerous man from this description, yet he killed at least fifteen men—three with shots through the head and heart on a pitch black night—held off a three-state posse almost singlehandedly, terrorized the Northwest for years, broke out of several jails and penitentiaries, walked three hundred miles through territory so wild Indian trackers refused to enter it, fought off numerous posses, and was the object of what is probably the greatest man hunt in American history.

Before the man hunters reached him he had captured a train and a small steamer, forcing the United States Government to hunt him both on land and on the sea.

He was of average height with a square, weather-beaten face, deep-set granite-gray eyes, and curly, reddish-brown hair. He was quiet and had a confident air. Men instantly liked him; women were attracted to him. In his criminal career there appears one outstanding characteristic; every act he committed had to be daring and executed in the grand style. He seemed eager to have the odds stacked against him.

The taking of a human life was commonplace to him. His basic philosophy was, if you want something, take it with a gun.

"I kill only those who get in my way," he once said.

He loved only two women in his life, both as evil as he. One became his road-agent partner, dying under the guns of a posse. The second one was an attractive dance-hall girl, of a criminal family, who deserted him when the sands were running out.

His name is Harry Tracy. This is his brief, violent story, and that of the two desperate women in his life, Genie Carter and Mollie Merrill.

2

There is little known about Tracy's early life. Two rare biographies, both not too reliable, agree he was born about 1871, but differ as to his birthplace. One claims Dutchess County, New York, the other a small village in Missouri. The latter seems more logical.

His correct name is not known. He has been called Harry Gard, and Harry Ward. Stewart H. Holbrook wrote in 1932 that he had learned Tracy's real name was Henry Severn, "from a woman who went to school with him" and who had died only a year before.

However, whatever his real name was, he was Harry Tracy to Butch Cassidy, Harvey Logan, the Sundance Kid, the Tall Texan, and all the other desperadoes of the Hole In The Wall country, who feared him.

Tracy's mother died when he was young. His father, a livery stable owner, is described by Clarence E. Ray, one of Tracy's biographers, as "a Spartan father who perhaps meant well, but who could not see any good in his son."

A few doors from his father's stable was the home of a Mr. Carter, a railroad man. His daughter, Genie, an attractive, brown-haired girl, grew up with Tracy. He pulled her pigtails, chased her down the street with worms, and carried home her books. Before they reached their teens she was considered Tracy's girl.

When he was about sixteen Tracy ran away from home, following a post office robbery. Later he offered the usual outlaw's alibi; he had been "framed." He took one of his father's best horses and rode off with Genie. At a crossroads they were saying good-by when a sheriff and two deputies came up. Tracy shot the sheriff and fled. He told Genie he would send for her some day.

We next find him in Montana in 1895, riding with John Shortell's gang of horse and cattle thieves. As Ray says in his *Life of Harry Tracy,* one of the few biographies not in the dime paper-back class: "His fine physique, daring bravado, utter recklessness in the face of danger and ready wit made him soon a leader in the band. . . ."

Unlike many of the Western outlaws, Tracy seldom drank to excess, nor did he ride into small towns, guns blazing away at signs and windows purposelessly. After each robbery he was content to hide out in the small cabin and corral the gang had in the Shoshone Reservation. Some of the gang noticed he wrote letters to a girl named Genie Carter in Missouri.

In the fall of 1895, Tracy killed Shortell when the outlaw leader tried to shoot an Indian girl.

Tracy gallantly tried to rescue her, but one of the gang killed her. A running battle followed but it ended when Tracy killed another member of the gang. He next appears in Cripple Creek, under the name of Harry Ward. In 1893 a man who knew him said, "He was regarded as a man who might take a desperate chance but who would not go out of his way to seek a quarrel. Suckers being plenty he generally had money and his clothes were made in Denver."

It is in Cripple Creek that Genie reappears. Evidently Tracy had sent her money to join him.

Genie is described as being "tall and fair, dressed modestly, but in good taste. She carried herself with an air of distinction that must have come from her intuitive good taste rather than from training she had."

They stayed at the local boardinghouse as "Mr. and Mrs. Ward."

The local badman was one Luke Theron. One day Genie slapped his face for a remark he made as she passed. One of the loungers rushed to tell Tracy who was playing poker, that Theron had insulted his wife and was looking for him.

Tracy apologized to the rest of the players, cashed in his chips, and walked down the street.

There was a strange air of deadliness about him. Law officers and outlaws who knew him said a chill ran through them when they looked into his cold, gray eyes. Later his soft, "I'm Tracy," made many a so-called killer tremble in his boots.

He walked slowly down the wooden sidewalk. The street was deserted. Men watched from doorways and windows. There was a dead silence as he pushed his way into the swinging doors of the saloon.

Theron turned. Tracy saw he was drunk. "If you're sober enough to go to hell in the morning, I'll kill you," he said and walked out. Theron pawed for his gun but bystanders disarmed him.

In the morning Cripple Creek waited breathlessly. Tracy left his boardinghouse, walking "nonchalantly" down the street toward the saloon. A few doors away Theron stepped out of an alley, a six-shooter

269

in his hand. Tracy's hand leaped from his coat pocket. Two shots barked. Theron clutched at the corner of the building, staggered a few paces, and fell.

Tracy calmly put the gun back in its holster and walked to the sheriff's office to surrender. At a preliminary hearing, witnesses testified he fired in self-defense but Theron's friends demanded he be held for the action of the grand jury.

Genie was Tracy's only visitor. She appeared faithfully every morning and afternoon. Two weeks passed. One rainy afternoon Genie appeared at the jailhouse and was escorted by the sheriff to Tracy's cell. The sheriff courteously brought up a chair, as was his custom. Genie leaned against the bars and they spoke together in soft whispers.

The sheriff watched them for a while, then turned away. Tracy's cold voice halted him in his tracks, "Just be good, sheriff, and nothing will happen to you."

When the sheriff had turned Genie had slipped a six-shooter from her sleeve through the bars.

Tracy disarmed the sheriff and handcuffed and gagged him. He was locked in Tracy's cell. There were two horses in an alley near the jail with slickers tied to the saddles. The few people on the rainy street scarcely bothered to raise their eyes as the two riders in green raincoats passed.

Tracy was no novice at fooling posses. The two horses were sold the next day. They continued their journey by stagecoaches, wagons, and trains. As Ray declares in his biography: "It may be that Genie entered into the spirit that controlled him, for she appears to have taken part in certain desperate ventures he engaged in when they arrived in the Green River country. . . ."

On November 4th, a mule skinner on his way to the Yellow Lode Mine was swinging about a curve in the road when a horseman dashed out, ordering him to stand and deliver. A box containing several bags of dust valued at about $10,000 was thrown down. The gold was tied to the saddle of a spare horse by a second road agent, described as "a boyish-looking fellow." Then he lined up the passengers to relieve them of their money, watches, and rings.

During the holdup the shotgun messenger went for his gun. A bullet shattered his elbow.

"Another move like that and I won't wing you," was the calm warning of the man on the horse.

As he was being searched by the "boyish-looking" bandit, the driver said, "This is tough on an old-timer to be frisked by a kid."

The young outlaw chuckled, replying in a "piping voice," "That may be, pard, but ain't I doing a good job?"

"There ain't no kick on the job," the driver said, "but I'll frisk you the same way some day."

As he said later he didn't think it was that much of a joke but the two outlaws roared with laughter.

Under the guns of the man on the horse, the younger outlaw cut the mule traces, tied up the driver, wounded guard and messenger. They also took a side of bacon and a $1,200 mine payroll they found in a pouch hidden in the provision box.

The "youngish-looking" highwayman, of course, was Genie Carter, riding the outlaw trail for the first time with Tracy.

Evidently they separated after the robbery, with Denver selected as a rendezvous. Five days later Genie appeared "in clothing suggesting primitive methods of dressmaking, but they were soon replaced by more fashionable garments." Later she was seen on the street by a miner's wife who identified her as the woman the ladies of Cripple Creek knew as "Mrs. Ward." Genie, after going on a shopping spree, remained in seclusion at the hotel, to wait for Tracy.

Meanwhile Tracy showed up in Provo, Utah, clean shaven and well dressed. He stayed only one day, changing some large bills, evidently the proceeds of the robbery at the local bank. Lady Luck deserted him while he was walking back to the hotel. As he entered a saloon, Willis, the wounded shotgun messenger, who lived in Provo and had come home on sick leave, spotted him.

A sheriff and two deputies closed in on him. Tracy, taken completely unaware, tried to draw but Willis, only waiting for the chance, fired. The bullet grazed Tracy's scalp, knocking him out. He came to in the Provo jail, handcuffed and leg-ironed.

As the *Provo Journal* said, "He got short shift, at the hands of the Mormon judge and was sentenced to ten years."

He entered the Utah Penitentiary in the fall of 1896, Number 1313. In her hotel room in Denver, Genie waited and wondered.

Tracy was never more dangerous than when he was in prison. He taunted the guards, broke numerous prison rules, and constantly plotted escape. All through his criminal career it would be the same. It seems incredible that he survived the beatings and black holes of the prisons of the time.

He was in Utah Penitentiary only a week when he kicked a guard into unconsciousness. In turn he was pistol-whipped into a bloody pulp by other guards.

Thirty days later he emerged from the black hole, still snarling at the guards and predicting he would soon escape. He flew into a rage when a trusty hung his prison number on him. He floored the trusty and again was beaten by the guards. Thirty more days in solitary confinement was his punishment.

When he came out he was labelled "a dangerous man, and not an official of the institution but would have visited the most extreme punishment upon him with slight provocation."

Once he made an attempt to escape by trying to wrestle a gun from a guard but was clubbed to his knees before he could use it. Orders came from the warden's office, "Shoot him if he tries to escape again."

For over a year he terrorized Utah Penitentiary. A special guard was set over his cell and he was denied any exercise period.

Meanwhile, back in Denver, Genie had opened a small millinery shop. Every week as they had arranged she sent a letter to him in care of General Delivery. By the listing of the unclaimed letters every Friday in the Denver papers, she knew he had not appeared.

One day she met Rawlins, whom Tracy had befriended in Cripple Creek. After staking him to a meal and some clothes he agreed to go to Provo to find out what had happened to Tracy. He returned to Denver and gave Genie the bad news.

Genie wrote to the Utah Penitentiary but her letters were returned because he was a "refractory prisoner without mail privileges."

Finally she and Rawlins moved to Provo. A guard was bribed to deliver a message to Tracy.

One day a slip of paper was dropped at Tracy's feet. On it was written in pencil, "Behave yourself. I have a note for you."

Overnight Tracy changed. He became meek and humble, whining that "he was through with his tricks."

It took weeks for the warden to accept the reformation. He did and Tracy was sent back into the cell blocks. On his first night back he found a note hidden under his supper plate.

Dear: Did you think I would forget. I have hope. Do nothing rash. I have a friend who is close to you. Be ready to take your chance. Expect a visitor next Thursday. Destroy this.

Genie

Tracy never destroyed the note. It was found on him six years later when he was arrested in Portland, Oregon.

On the following Thursday a woman dressed in mourning appeared

272

as Tracy's visitor. She explained she was his sister, lately widowed and had only just discovered her brother was in prison.

The warden permitted her to see his most dangerous prisoner— under the eyes of four guards. Genie played her role superbly, weeping delicately into a black-rimmed white handkerchief and berating her "brother" for bringing such disgrace to the family. Tracy bowed his head appropriately.

Genie came to see him several times. One day an attorney obtained a writ of habeas corpus requiring Tracy's presence in court at Provo. The sheriff from Provo, who served the papers, said he understood the attorney had been hired by Tracy's "sister."

Tracy was removed under heavy guard in a wagon from the penitentiary to the depot. He was then handcuffed and leg-ironed and bound to the seat in a deserted daycoach, by a chain.

"I think that'll hold him, boys," the sheriff told the guards. One guard, John Yairs, stayed with the sheriff. The sheriff settled down with a good cigar in the seat opposite Tracy. The guard, Yairs, sat with Tracy.

Tracy never blinked when the young woman entered the coach accompanied by a young man in a gray suit. She sat near the sheriff.

"Is that man insane?" she whispered.

"No, ma'am," said the sheriff, "but I wouldn't be surprised if he was a bit mad."

"A prisoner?" she whispered breathlessly.

The sheriff nodded. "Yes, ma'am, and a tough one."

Genie shuddered and "shrank back." The train jerked out of the station and began rattling down to Provo. When the sheriff finished his cigar he started to spin tall tales for Genie. The lies grew as the miles flew under the wheels.

As the train entered a wild and unsettled section of the country Genie dropped her role as a dewy-eyed young lady. A six-shooter appeared in her hand and the young man beside her stood up, a revolver in his hand. They bound and handcuffed the sheriff and the guard and freed Tracy.

"I'll take the rear platform, you get in front where the brakeman is."

At Taraum Junction, Genie and the young man stepped off on the platform. They nonchalantly waved to the conductor who signalled to the engineer. The train puffed out of the station. After it passed the depot Tracy swung off the rear car. In a moment he was swallowed by the forest.

Tracy met Genie next at Carson City, Nevada, where she had

registered as a "Mrs. Warren." Rawlins, handsomely rewarded, had struck out for Montana.

In his biography of Tracy, Ray states Genie was weary of the outlaw's life and for a time "they lived on the border of respectability." Such a life was not for Tracy. They went to Portland and he began gambling, "and was seen in the company of men who ask no questions of other fellows and require no vouchers for morality."

A streak of bad luck at the gambling table wiped out his luck. Genie gave him an ultimatum: go straight or she would leave him. Tracy agreed to leave Portland and try ranching in Wyoming. They got as far as Spokane. There some former gambling partners of Tracy persuaded him there was money in the camps along the Kootenai River north of the American border.

At Boundary Creek he opened a saloon. By what means he managed to get Genie to go along, no one knows. But she appears in his saloon for a time. However, the raw life of the mining camp was too much for her. She packed up and returned to Spokane. Tracy followed her a few weeks later—at the request of the Canadian authorities who charged he was the leader of a band of pirates who had looted a large quantity of gold dust from a mining barge on Lake Kootenai.

They stayed only a month in Spokane. Genie evidently at last persuaded Tracy to abandon the outlaw trail. They set out for the southeast planning to buy a ranch. They next appear at Lewiston, Idaho, then on the Snake River. Those who later recalled them, told Ray "They might have been fleeing from some pursuit."

During their journey, Tracy may have learned of a bank or stagecoach which was just waiting for the right robber to come along.

On the Snake they bought a small ranch, equipped with a herd of horses. The four-room ranch house was located at the east end of a lonely valley, lying between steep hills. The rear of the house rested against a wall of rock. A large corral strangely resembling a stockade, was built to one side. A narrow footpath passed through a ravine to the Snake River.

A few months after Tracy's appearance in the valley there was a noticeable increase in horse stealing. When two well-known horse thieves, Mike Morgan and Sam Wallace, were seen at the ranch, a posse paid Tracy a call "to leave a warning."

Tracy said very little. He fixed his hard gray eyes on the sheriff and suggested the possemen leave his property. The sheriff didn't need any encouragement. He and his men left in a cloud of dust.

274

In September, 1896, several stolen horses were seen in Tracy's corral. A vigilante committee was formed to visit the valley. The house and corral were surrounded in the early morning of September 4. The leader of the vigilantes, James McEwen, called for Tracy to come out.

Wallace, the horse thief, appeared on the porch. "What do you want?" he asked.

"I want to look at those horses," McEwen said.

"Go ahead if you think you can jump the fence and get away again," Wallace shouted.

McEwen swung off his horse and started toward the corral. Wallace stepped back into the house, reappearing with a rifle. Aiming at McEwen, he shouted, "I warn you—get out of shooting distance in two minutes . . ."

McEwen walked back to his horse. As he later testified at a coroner's jury, he saw a girl and Tracy standing in the doorway behind Wallace. The girl was weeping and tugging at Tracy's sleeve, but he pushed her inside. The vigilantes then left.

Wallace later testified Genie pleaded all day with Tracy to leave the valley. Morgan and Wallace urged him to take the horses and make a run for it. But Tracy, he said, "was stubborn," swearing to kill any "farmer" who tried to run him out of the valley.

At dusk, however, Wallace said Tracy finally capitulated to his weeping wife. A wagon was loaded and Tracy and the two thieves started to round up the horses. Suddenly Genie called out, pointing up the valley.

From where he was sitting on the top of the corral fence, Tracy could see a band of horsemen entering the valley. He climbed down and walked to the house with Morgan and Wallace.

"It's too late now," he said, breaking open a box of cartridges.

The posse was again led by McEwen, who appears to have been a foolish but fearless man. While the other vigilantes dismounted a distance from the ranch house, he rode up to the corral, shouting for Tracy to surrender "to save trouble for somebody."

Tracy's answer was to shoot McEwen's horse from under him. In his peculiar way, Tracy let McEwen run back to the shelter of some rocks without firing a shot.

The possemen blazed away all day. Tracy, for some unknown reason, killed three horses rather than men. When darkness fell the possemen fell back up the valley to re-form their lines and start their cook fires.

With the possemen in temporary retirement Tracy ordered his men to run for it. Genie packed food in their saddlebags and they crept outside to their horses. Morgan was ordered to lead the horses down the ravine and wait.

While Tracy and his men were preparing to leave the ranch house, McEwen and several other vigilantes returned on foot. As Tracy and Genie came out of the house they opened fire.

Genie fell. Tracy opened fire, shooting down two men in the darkness. Then scooping up Genie in his arms he ran down the ravine.

With two men shot down McEwen and the rest had little heart for chasing the sharp-shooting outlaw in the darkness in the narrow ravine. Picking up their dead they rode back up the valley to their camp.

On the bank of the Snake, Tracy knelt with Genie in his arms.

"Are you hurt?" he whispered.

"Yes, badly," she said.

When he asked her if she could ride, lying in his arms, she shook her head and wept.

Wallace brought some water in a pan but Genie almost choked when she tried to swallow it. Minutes later she was dead. Tracy remained in the same position, as if afraid to move and disturb the dead girl.

After a few minutes Wallace said nervously, "You might as well come on, Tracy, there's nothing you can do now."

Tracy shook his head. "Leave me a horse. You two get out of here."

Wallace joined Morgan, the horse holder. They whispered together, then mounted. In a few minutes they were gone.

The gurgling of the swift-moving Snake and the impatient pawing of the remaining horse were the only sounds. Suddenly Tracy rose and walked back through the dark ravine, Genie in his arms. He passed the corral to enter the ranch house. He carefully placed the dead girl on the bed, then walked out. The darkness swallowed him. There was a clatter of hoofs and then silence.

3

There is a blank in Tracy's life from 1896 to 1898. Then he appears as a member of Butch Cassidy's Hole In The Wall riders. There was no outlaw in the Hole's lawless community who was feared as much as Tracy. Even Harvey Logan, the Kid Curry of the West, kept Tracy at a distance.

An old outlaw who rode with the Bunch in 1898, and who recently died at the age of ninety, in a small mountain town in Wyoming,

276

told the author, "All the boys were afraid of him. He was quiet like and never did much talking."

On March 1, 1898, "Swede" Johnson, a tow-haired gun fighter and fugitive from a murder charge in Thompson Springs, Utah, shot and killed Willy Sprang, a young boy who had playfully tipped a water dipper from his hand.

Johnson, Tracy, and another outlaw, Dave Lant, joined the Bunch together. Tracy, bound by a strange loyalty of the Western outlaws, led the two others out of the Hole and headed east for Colorado.

The murder of the boy roused the citizens in the valley. Valentine Hoy, one of the leaders of the law and order group, formed a tri-state posse, from Wyoming, Utah and Colorado, setting out in pursuit a few hours later.

The trio was surrounded in a canyon. Jack Bennett, a whisky peddler whom Tracy had hired to bring them supplies, was captured and hanged on the spot. Hoy, courageously leading his men, was killed by Tracy, whose marksmanship drove off the posse. Hoy's body was lowered down the cliff by ropes and the posse re-formed.

The outlaw trio led by Tracy slipped out of the canyon, heading for Butch Cassidy's stronghold at Powder Springs. As they moved through the mountains a late snowstorm began. The possemen, led by expert guides, found their campfire where a colt had been killed and chunks roasted and eaten. The hide had been cut into strips for crude moccasins.

They were trapped in a small gully late that afternoon. Rifles and six-shooters barked until twilight. A spokesman shouted for them to surrender but Tracy shot off his hat. Next time, he cried, he wouldn't miss.

The temperature fell. As evening drew near the wind rose, driving the snow before it. Then suddenly through the snow came Johnson, face and hands blue with the cold. Lant followed. Tracy held back for another hour. Only after he was assured there would be "a fair trial" did he come out.

At the Hoy ranch, with the wind howling about the house, twisting the stiffened body of the whisky peddler hanging from the corral gate, Tracy, Lant and Johnson were arraigned before J. S. Hoy, Valentine's brother, as acting justice of the peace. There was a dispute over jurisdiction. Wyoming finally got possession of Johnson. Lant and Tracy went to Utah.

The governors of the three states began brawling in print over the

277

custody of the three prisoners. There were hysterical demands for the state militia to come in and wipe out the Bunch. Then one of the Hoys proposed hunting the outlaws down "like animals" by expert man hunters, "who would stay on their trail until the scoundrels are run down."

At Powder Springs Butch Cassidy heard of Tracy's arrest and Hoy's proposal. He ordered his riders to saddle up. On March 14, the outlaws swooped down on all the Hoy cattle camps, burning them to the ground.

Tracy only stayed in the jail at Hahn's Peak for fourteen days. He not only slugged Sheriff Neiman but robbed him of ninety dollars. He and Lant locked Neiman in his own cell and started off for Steamboat Springs, Colorado.

Neiman was a shrewd law officer, however. He reasoned Tracy would head for the Springs. Six miles out he ordered the stagecoach driver to stop. Two men jumped in.

"Good morning, Tracy," Neiman said, holding the shotgun, "breakfast is waiting for you back at the jail."

"Who the hell thought anybody in Hahn's Point would be up this early," Tracy said disgustedly.

After their capture, Tracy and Lant were removed to the Aspen, Colorado, jail.

It only took Tracy two weeks to break out again. He whittled a wooden gun, covered it with tin foil and subdued the guard. Thirty-seven years later John Dillinger would follow his example.

Tracy left Lant, moving north to Portland. It was there he met the second desperate woman in his life.

4

The stocky man in the blue suit ordered a drink and leaned against the bar. His face was weather-beaten and he wore a thick brown mustache. Off to one side card players were arguing loudly. Suddenly the battered piano tinkled off into silence. The man at the bar turned to watch.

A lumberman jumped up, drawing a knife from his belt. He started for a gambler who was rising to his feet. Tracy stared at them, then leaped forward. He swung hard at the lumberjack, who crashed over a chair and lay still.

The piano started tinkling again and a woman laughed drunkenly. The gambler, white faced, fixed his cuffs.

278

"Damn fool might have cut me," he said nervously. "Have a drink. My name's Dave Merrill."

Tracy smiled. "Thanks. I'm Tracy."

Merrill looked puzzled, almost as if he recognized Tracy. Then he brightened. He turned to the large mirror in the rear of the bar and looked again at Tracy. Both men turned to the mirror. They were alike enough to be twins.

Tracy went home with Merrill that night. There he met Mollie, Merrill's sister, a pretty, painted dance-hall girl, and her mother, "Mother" Merrill, a notorious fence for stolen goods.

Mollie completely captivated Tracy. He showered her with flowers and jewels. Mother Merrill approved. In a family of criminals what could be more beneficial than a son-in-law who was an expert killer and outlaw?

Mollie and Tracy were married legally in the Portland City Hall. Tracy hired a small white cottage with a garden near the Willamette River. To the neighbors they were a happily married young couple. An engineer who lived next door later told Portland detectives that Tracy once said to him, "There is nothing too good for my wife. I love her deeply. . . ."

To prove his love Tracy took in his brother-in-law as a partner in crime. Together they formed a small gang, robbing post offices and banks in Portland. The Brink's robbers of 1950 might be chagrined to learn they used false faces as disguises.

The money flowed in and the Tracys and Merrills lived high. Tracy spent money freely. Soon they were traveling about Portland in a buggy. Tracy grew a thick, reddish-brown mustache and looked the part of a prosperous young business man. Mollie told the neighbors he had been quite successful in real estate. She might have added: also in banking and jewelry.

Merrill basked in the reflected glory of Tracy. He began to brag in the saloons. The inevitable happened. Detective Weiner of the Portland Police heard the news from an informer. He picked up some stolen jewelry Merrill had pawned, then sprung the trap.

Merrill was taken into custody and given the alternative of helping them arrest Tracy, who, Weiner had been told by sheriffs of Utah and Colorado, was deadly with a gun, or going to jail for robbery.

"Mother" Merrill and Mollie came to the police station. They urged Merrill to play informer. At last he consented.

When Tracy walked to a rendezvous with Merrill the police were at his heels. At First and Market Streets they closed in. Tracy went for his gun. The bullet whizzed past Weiner's ear. Weiner fired but missed.

Tracy ran down the street toward the depot through a volley of shots. The Southern and Pacific was just chugging out. He leaped, gun in hand. Terrified passengers scrambled for cover.

Tracy looked at the engineer. "Jump," he snapped. The engineer leaped from the cab.

Tracy grabbed the throttle. The locomotive picked up speed. Then suddenly the big wheels ground to a stop. The conductor had pulled the emergency. Behind the train came the police, on horses, in buggies, and in wagons. Tracy turned to give them battle. Weiner fired. The bullet grazed Tracy's scalp, knocking him out.

Tracy and his brother-in-law, Merrill, were both found guilty. Tracy received thirty years in Oregon State Penitentiary, Merrill five. Mollie said good-by at the city jail, weeping appropriately and promising to wait forever.

From the moment he donned the striped suit, Tracy was planning his escape. In 1902 he was ready. Mollie's visits had fallen off but she pleaded that "Mother" Merrill's illness was too serious for her to leave the house.

In March of 1902 Tracy bribed a small-time thief to deliver a message to Mollie, outlining his plan to escape. She was to buy guns, ammunition, and a rope ladder. Then they were to be delivered to a mysterious intermediary inside the prison, possibly a trusty, who would hide them in the foundry shop in a box marked with chalk.

The thief promised to see Mollie. He found her in the dance hall instead of at her mother's bedside. When she read the note she laughed. She told the thief to tell Tracy she had no intention of helping him; she "was through with him."

The thief made another attempt to see Mollie but "Mother" Merrill threw him out of the house. Afraid to fail Tracy, the thief then stole a horse and buggy and sold them outside of Portland. With the proceeds he bought two thirty-thirty caliber Winchesters, ammunition, and a rope ladder. He returned to the prison, contacted Tracy's intermediary and gave him the guns, ammunition, and ladder—also a note describing Mollie's refusal to help him. Tracy was furious.

A few days later, on the morning of June 9, 1902, Tracy and Merrill scaled the walls of the Oregon Penitentiary, killing three guards and seriously wounding another.

From the evidence Tracy and Merrill may have been trying to reach Portland the next day. Just before dawn they entered the outskirts of the town of Salem, robbed two men of their clothes and horses, and headed for Portland. Bloodhounds from the Washington State Penitentiary picked up their trail.

Two law officers, riding ahead of the posse in a buggy were waylaid by Tracy and Merrill and robbed of their buggy.

A few hours later they drove down the main street of Gervais, with Tracy tipping his hat to the ladies on their way to market. On June 11, Tracy and Merrill evidently abandoned their effort to reach Portland. They entered the forest near Gervais where they were surrounded by a fifty-man posse.

"Every man who owns a gun," as the *New York World* correspondent wrote, was ordered to join the posse. But sometime during the night Tracy and Merrill squirmed past the campfires and guards, robbed two deputies of their weapons, and disappeared.

On June 13, the governor of Oregon ordered two hundred and fifty militiamen of Company F to join the posse.

A colonel of the militia boasted to the *World's* correspondent, "Tracy is so hemmed in, he'll be caught within a few hours."

The announcement was premature. In the morning it was discovered Tracy and Merrill had slipped through the cordon.

Once again their trail twisted toward Portland. Was it because Tracy was determined to reach his little cottage and kill the honey-haired girl who had betrayed him?

They only reached the outskirts of the city. After forcing a farmer's wife to cook them breakfast they stole two horses, galloping to the Columbia River. They discovered a boatman painting his boat. At gun point he rowed them across. In Washington they dined at another farmhouse, then bound and gagged their host. The bloodhounds were baying in the distance when Tracy decided to make a stand. The two desperadoes held off a posse of nearly a hundred men, with Tracy wounding two.

On the evening of the twenty-ninth, they shot their way past a road block near Chehalis, Washington. The next day they were seen on the Northern Pacific Railroad tracks at Tenino, about forty miles from Tacoma. That was the last time Merrill was seen alive.

Tracy next appeared alone. On the morning of July 2, he walked into the headquarters of a fishing company. He forced eight men to line up against the wall at gun point, then selected two to fix him breakfast.

"I'm Tracy," he said in a matter of fact tone, and sat down at the table. He was dressed in a rumpled, stained, blue suit, battered black homburg hat and a tieless white shirt. His face was worn and un-shaven. He carried two revolvers and a Winchester.

After he had finished breakfast he ordered the cooks to feed the other men. Then he herded all of them aboard a small steamer. At his command the skipper of the boat, a Captain Clark, was summoned.

"Get in," he ordered the Captain. "We're all going for a ride."

"Where to?" Captain Clark asked.

"Seattle," Tracy grinned.

As the ship pulled away from the dock he took a seat in the corner of the cabin, the rifle across his knee, the revolvers stuck in his belt.

By this time the alarm had been sent out. Steamers and tugs loaded with possemen began prowling Puget Sound. In the villages and towns along the sound heavily armed men stationed themselves along the water front, sweeping the misty water with high-powered glasses.

Meanwhile this incredible trip along a well-traveled waterway con-tinued. Tracy had a strange dominance over those he met. He was outnumbered at least eight to one, on a ship he had captured single-handed. The crew were all tough Washington lakemen, yet they all seemed awed. Tracy's shrewd psychology helped too. Several times he tested his marksmanship, shooting at small bits of driftwood. He never missed. ·

The war against Tracy had now become a naval one. Two steamers, the revenue cutters, *Scott* and *Grant,* were ordered by Coast Guard Headquarters in Washington to join the hunt. A large sea-going tug, crowded with sheriffs and deputies, joined the cutters late that after-noon.

Once Tracy pointed to the dim outline of Fort McNeil in the distance.

"Pull up near there, Captain," he ordered.

"What for?" the Captain asked.

"I want to shoot some guards from the walls," Tracy replied.

This was no idle bravado on Tracy's part. He really meant it. It took all the efforts of Captain Clark and the crew to persuade Tracy not to.

"Well, forget it," he said. "I don't want to see any of you men hurt."

One of the crew managed to gather enough courage to ask Tracy, "What happened to Merrill, Tracy?"

Tracy stared at the seaman. After a moment he said, "I killed him."

He looked out across the water. "I killed him because he betrayed me. He had no nerve and he was a traitor. I read in a newspaper how he gave me away before I stole that locomotive. In a situation like

282

this you must have someone you can trust." He paused, then went on. "We fought a duel in the woods. The play was to take ten paces, turn and fire."

He lifted his rifle and picked off a piece of driftwood. "I fired at eight. I knew he was planning to turn and kill me at nine."

About three o'clock that afternoon, nearly eight hours after he had captured the steamer, Tracy ordered Captain Clark to pull ashore three miles north of Seattle. He trussed up the captain and the crew but left the arms of one man free "because he had a sore wrist."

"Where are you going now, Tracy?" Clark asked.

"I'm going in to clean out a saloon," Tracy said. He waved, then disappeared into the brush.

Night fell. The sea search was abandoned. The cutters and tug, the *New York World* said, had covered one hundred and twenty-five miles without catching a glimpse of the steamer.

Tracy moved toward the north end of Lake Washington. Near Pontiac, in a pouring rain, he was cornered by a posse but he escaped, killing two men. Then like a wraith, he vanished in the fog.

Outside of Seattle he asked a farm woman to cook him some breakfast. He agreed not to tie her up if she didn't notify the police until the next morning. When a butcher's boy knocked on the kitchen door, the woman told the boy by signs that Tracy was inside.

At ten o'clock a posse surrounded the house. Tracy came down the walk with a Swedish farmhand whom he had captured earlier and was now using as a pack horse. As he climbed to the driver's seat of a wagon, a law officer ordered him to surrender.

Tracy turned, firing at the sound of the voice. The man dropped, a bullet through his head. Like a cat, Tracy leaped from the wagon. His rifle barked twice. Two men, standing in the pitch blackness, fell dead.

As the *New York World* correspondent said, "The bodies of the three dead men bear eloquent witness to the marksmanship of Tracy . . . ."

The state was now in alarm. Rewards mounted and the governor ordered more troops into the field. The bloodhounds bayed, the farm wives kept their doors bolted, and men rode to town at night with loaded shotguns.

Tracy was next seen at south Seattle, the Swedish hired man stumbling behind him, loaded down with a pack.

Then he cut around the end of Lake Washington at Renton. There he encountered a young woman and a boy picking berries.

Tracy swept off his battered hat, "apologizing for his appearance." He insisted upon escorting her home. There he entertained four other women, while he ate, telling them tales of the hunt, assuring them again, "I have never harmed a woman or a child."

When a posse appeared, he laughingly identified a man with a pad as "a reporter. They're the ones I'm afraid of." He chuckled when he saw a cameraman set up his equipment, wondering whether he should "capture a posseman and steal his pants so I will look decent."

The hours ticked by. The posse, not too eager to come to grips with this sharp-shooting outlaw, drew closer. Tracy finally left, thanking the ladies for a wonderful meal.

He had tied the Swedish farm hand outside in the woods. When the possemen found him, there was a great deal of confusion. Tracy calmly walked through their lines, telling one man he was a reporter, and warning him to be "on the alert, Tracy is in there."

In a moment the darkening woods had swallowed him.

For weeks the game of human hounds and hares continued. Tracy next appeared in Kings County and the bloodhounds picked up his trail. But he threw them off by walking along small streams. He was spotted in eastern Washington and it was believed that he was attempting to reach the outlaw high command post of Hole In The Wall Valley in Wyoming. Unknown to Tracy, the Wild Bunch had been scattered and the lost leader, Butch Cassidy, was leading two of his riders—one a beautiful woman—to South America, to introduce the American technique of outlawry there.

In mid-July in eastern Washington Tracy called a sheriff from a country store which he held up for food. After the usual "I'm Tracy" introduction, he told the law officer, "I just wanted you to know I'm still around." The sheriff sputtered and Tracy said soothingly, "Oh, don't get mad. After all, at least you talked with the man you're after. Good-by."

But in eastern Washington there were more telephone wires and Tracy's route could be traced more easily. The man hunters now gathered more swiftly. Tracy was hard pressed. He appeared at a logging camp and virtually captured it. Then, while eating, this incredible man entertained the rough and tough loggers with leisurely stories of the man hunt.

A few days later he came upon a deer hunter. When the hunter was slow in dropping his rifle Tracy fired a shot which grazed his cheek. The hunter told the *New York World* correspondent, the outlaw warned him: "I'm Tracy. I don't want to hurt anybody but those who get in my way—but when I say put up your hands—put them up."

The hunter hastily complied. Tracy pointed to the cooking pot over the fire. "That smells good, let's eat."

After the meal Tracy looked up at the sky. "I guess it's going to rain," he said. Then, "Well, good night, and thanks for the food."

East of Spokane he was spotted by a posse and wounded. He disappeared in a thick swamp and threw off the bloodhounds. How long this man of iron stayed there is not known, but it must have been a horrible ordeal; the shotgun wound glowing like a red coal, the swarms of mosquitoes, and the continual plodding through the slippery paths and scummy water.

He was seen again by a woman walking along a road. Although he was lean as a hungry wolf he still maintained his courtly manners, telling the woman "he had buckshot in his back which bothered him."

In the first week of August, Tracy reached the Eddy brothers' ranch near Creston, Washington, approximately 297 miles from Spokane. He had been free but hunted for fifty-nine days. In his flight he had covered more than 400 miles across the roughest country in the Northwest. He stayed at the Eddy ranch a week helping the brothers pitch their hay.

A party of five Creston citizens, all heavily armed, picked up his trail and arrived at the ranch on the afternoon of August 9.

The bandit saw them. "Who are those men?" he asked Eddy. Without waiting for a reply he disappeared into the barn where his rifle was.

The posse was approaching when Tracy ran out of the barn and down the valley. He selected a rock and made a stand. He fired several shots but none were effective. The possemen—at a safe distance—exchanged shots. One smashed Tracy's leg which stuck out from behind the rock.

Why Tracy, the superb marksman, missed so often, is explained by Lieutenant V. Hurley (Retired) of Concrete, Washington, in a letter to the author.

Commander Hurley recalls one of the possemen explaining that they had come over the hill just as the sun was setting. As he writes:

They would never have got him that day had it not been for the sun in Tracy's eyes. They came over the little hill as the sun was directly in back of them, and he couldn't see to shoot. He

285

would undoubtedly have got away except for that, as they were all afraid to get within shooting distance of him under normal circumstances. That, combined with the lucky shot which hit Tracy's leg as it protruded from behind the rock, did the business.

Behind the rock Tracy tried to stop the flow of blood with his belt. He kept winding it tighter as the red stream drained away his strength.

As the light purpled he stumbled from behind the rock into a wheat field. The possemen moved in. When night fell, a strange hush like an invisible mist hung over the valley.

In the field, Tracy gripped his rifle and waited. Maybe he knew that the sands had run out, that there was no longer any point in running away, that for him the only refuge—the only rest—was in death.

He put the muzzle into his mouth and pulled the trigger.

Outside the field the man hunters heard the shot.

All night they sat there in the tense blackness. Then in the morning at a command they sprayed the wheat, the gunfire rolling across the valley. Satisfied, the waves of men moved across the field.

They soon found Tracy, the side of his head blown away. His leg was so swollen that the thick belt could not be seen.

The most famous man hunt in America's history was ended.

Pearl Hart: The Last Lady Road Agent

BY 1899 the citizens of Arizona were quite sure their state was as safe for any visiting tenderfoot as St. Louis, San Francisco, or Chicago. Of course the deserts, the Gila monsters, and the cactus plants were still present, but they were fast becoming props for the romantically-minded tourist.

There were many signs that the days of the wild frontier were over. Buckskin Leslie, the killer of Tombstone, had exchanged the striped pants of the Yuma Territorial Penitentiary for a wedding suit, announcing to all he was ready to "settle down." In place of fearless editorials denouncing the killers who once swaggered past its doors, the *Tombstone Epitaph* was worrying about the "wretched work" of the Washington baseball club, some of whose members had been seen drunk "in a well known saloon" with the players of the Boston club before their game.

Patent medicines were having a big sale. One old prospector was heard to say he would rather have Mrs. Winslow's Soothing Syrup, or Dr. Pierce's Favorite Prescription for his rheumatism, than a drink of whisky.

Out in the ranch country the fence wars were almost forgotten. Most of the boom towns were falling into ruins, the weather-beaten signs creaking in the wind as an occasional old codger led his mule down the lonely and deserted streets.

The Mexican lottery was still running, but gambling was conducted sedately. The last male refuge, the saloon, was slowly but surely being invaded by insidious concoctions from the East called the Manhattan cocktail, Bronx, and Tom Collins. It was no longer considered the best of manners to enter a saloon, put your foot on the bar rail, announce to all it was your night to howl, and demand a slug of redeye.

Instead of the Earps, Doc Holliday and the Battle of the O.K. Corral, Tombstone, *The Epitaph* sadly said, had only "a tenderfoot from New Jersey named Markley who killed his horse and broke his own leg while playing cowboy." But all agreed that the old days were really gone when the CanCan announced it would start selling buttermilk.

In short, Arizona was heading for the Chamber of Commerce, Rotary Club luncheons every Tuesday, golf links, and checkered knickers.

Then Arizona had one last glimpse of posses and road agents. To make it all the more impressive one of the outlaws was a young girl scarcely out of boarding school.

Her name was Pearl Hart, plain, and slightly plump from Lindsay, Ontario. The girl's boarding school was straight out of the paper-back novels of the time. At seventeen, Pearl was seduced at the school by one Hart, "a personable young man who possessed considerable charm." They carried on their affair for several months, then eloped.

For some time they drifted about Ontario living in boardinghouses and cheap hotels, while Hart practiced his profession of small-time gambler and racing tout. When the cards and bangtails went against him he tended bar.

Pearl soon discovered the life of a gambler's wife was either feast or famine. When Hart cheated some bleary-eyed drunk of his money there was turkey and champagne; but when he was forced to rely on his skill with cards or his handicapping prowess, the menu consisted mostly of beans.

When more cans of beans were opened than turkeys sliced, Pearl became disgusted and went home to mother. Hart followed her. His charm still held. Pearl returned to "their nomadic life."

In 1893 Hart took Pearl to the World's Columbian Exposition in Chicago. He found himself ignored by the big-time gamblers and confidence men. The best he could do was to take a job as a barker in a side show.

While Hart did his best to lure customers into his tent to see Jo-jo the Dog-Faced Boy, or the dancing girls direct from the Sultan's Harem, Pearl explored the rest of the midway. She was attracted at once to the Wild West Show, which was complete with old Indian fighters, allegedly bad men, range riders, sharpshooters, and drunken Indians. Pearl attended every performance. Soon she was known to some of the cowhands and so-called bad men—as some cruel gossips said—compromisingly.

Hart could never measure up to the glamorous men she met at the fair, and after it closed Pearl sent him packing. She went on to Trinidad, Colorado. Again vicious scandalmongers whispered her ticket was paid by a cowhand who seemed fascinated by her not unattractive figure.

In Trinidad, Pearl gave birth to a baby boy, father unknown. For a year, as the *Arizona Star* said: "She wrestled with the world in a catch as catch can style making a living for herself and her baby son."

When she left Trinidad, Pearl was no longer the Ontario girl who worshipped the tall, silent men of the West as they shattered the clay pipes with forty-fives.

After sending her son to her mother in Ontario, she drifted about the Western towns working as a cook, domestic, and hotel maid. Now she could drink "with a stone head" and was an expert in controlling the pawings of the drunken prospectors who bought her drinks.

One day in 1895 she ran into Hart on the main street of Phoenix. Hart was still the charmer. He at once steered Pearl to the nearest saloon to pledge his love and weep on her shoulder. His luck was bad, he said, intolerably so since she had left. He must have her back, at any costs. Pearl demurred. Then Hart, in an uncontrollable burst of affection said that he would get a job!

The last was too much for Pearl. She consented to come back to him. Even Hart looked good after the life of a frontier camp follower.

For three years Pearl and Hart lived happily after a fashion in Phoenix. He worked as a bartender and hotel manager. A second child was born, a girl, whom they named Pearl.

But Hart was not the type to be tamed by domesticity. One night after three years of earning a legitimate living, he slapped Pearl into unconsciousness during a bitter fight and walked out to join the army. Many times Pearl was heard to say that she hoped Hart would walk into the path of a Spanish bullet.

Pearl kept working, as a mining camp cook. When the war was over and Hart came back, evidently expecting a hero's welcome, Pearl bought him a bottle of whisky and sent him off. He never appeared again.

The mine closed, ending her job. She sent little Pearl to her mother in Ontario and in the spring of 1899 found another job as a cook at the Mammoth Mining Camp.

There she met Joe Boot, a happy-go-lucky miner with flowing black mustachios. They struck up a friendship, "platonic," as one newspaper chivalrously described it.

One day Joe told Pearl he was leaving for Globe several miles away where he had a promise of another job. Pearl said she was tired of

289

cooking for a lot of "mule-eared miners" and asked to go along. Joe was overjoyed. To make sure she would be comfortable he hired a wagon and two "Mormon boys" as drivers.

It rained several days before they left their camp. The roads were helpless quagmires, the wagon sinking to the hubs of the wheels. Only three miles were made. They camped that night reaching Globe the next afternoon. Joe found his job waiting and Pearl was hired as a cook in a miner's boardinghouse. All was serene. Wedding bells were ready to tinkle. But Pearl, "after one disastrous voyage on the sea of matrimony," as one newspaper later called it, was cautious. She put Joe off, insisting they must wait. Joe twirled his mustachios. The day would just have to wait until his beloved was ready.

Disaster struck in the late summer. Pearl received a letter from her brother in Ohio where her family had moved, saying her mother was seriously ill. Could she send some money at once?

Pearl sent her meager savings. When another scrawled demand came Joe also sent what he could. A short time later there was another request. Medicine and doctors were very high-priced, could they send something more?

There is evidence Pearl was genuinely fond of her mother. As one account said: "She was frantic with worry over her mother and begged Joe to help her."

Joe proposed they make some money freighting miner's goods out of Mammoth. Pearl agreed. With the last of Joe's finances they bought a wagon. But the business soon failed.

They next staked out a claim near the closed-down works at Mammoth. The small vein was soon worked out. Over the campfire Pearl spoke frantically of her mother. She *must* get some money to send home.

Joe, no mental giant, said, "Let's hold up the stage, honey?"

Pearl was shocked. "The stage?" she echoed.

Joe explained. The stage, one of the last in the Territory, ran between Globe and Florence, a distance of sixty-five miles. There were always three or four passengers, usually drummers with well-lined pockets. As Joe explained, the days of the shotgun messengers were gone. It would be an easy job to "throw" their six-shooters on the driver.

Pearl at first indignantly refused to have anything to do with the idea. But as Joe ambled on describing the hundreds of dollars they would bring with them to New Mexico, she grew more interested. At last she agreed. Over the campfire they made their plans

They set out before dawn. Pearl had cut her hair short, tucking the ends under a wide white sombrero. She was wearing a man's gray flannel shirt, levis, and boots. In her belt was tucked a well-oiled forty-four caliber Colt. Joe had a forty-five.

They rode along the Globe Highway to a sharp bend in the road where they knew the stagecoach driver would brake his horses.

At about two o'clock they heard the stage rattling down the road, trace chains jingling and the driver's whip exploding like Chinese firecrackers over the heads of the two-horse team.

As the driver later said, "We were lumbering along with nothing of unusual interest to disturb the monotony."

At the curve he braked his horses. Suddenly there in the highway, were Pearl and Joe, "with revolvers cocked and aim steady."

"Stop and elevate," Joe shouted.

"Raise 'em," Pearl added.

The driver pulled up his horses "with a tug that set them back on their haunches." Inside the three passengers, who had been dozing, flew across the inside of the coach, landing in a heap. When Pearl yanked open the door, a face stared up at her through a tangle of legs and arms.

"What happened?" the man asked.

"Get out and line up," Pearl shouted. She waved her revolver. "Get out! Quick."

The three passengers, "a short fat man, a dude with his hair parted in the middle, and a pig-tailed Chinaman," tumbled out.

"Shell out," Pearl snarled.

The short fat man was trembling so badly he could scarcely take the bills from his pocket. In true road-agent fashion Pearl dumped them into a sack. The fat man was good for $390; the dude "assayed" thirty-six dollars for the sack, the Chinaman, five.

Pearl decided to play the role of Robin Hood to the hilt. She swaggered up and down before the three men, giving them the traditional cold eye and twisted lip. Then with a flourish she peeled three single dollar bills from the fat man's roll and gave one to each man.

"For grub and lodging," she said. Waving her revolver she cried, "Now climb aboard and don't look back for ten minutes. . . ."

The fat man missed his step and fell on his face; the dude and Chinaman fell on top of him. Pearl swung the door shut. She let out a screech and fired a shot. The driver's whip snaked over the restless team, exploding in their ears. The coach lurched forward, then flew down the road.

Joe and Pearl watched it disappear in a cloud of dust. They trotted leisurely down the road, roaring with laughter at the memory of the trembling little fat man.

2

The stagecoach driver broke all records to Florence. The coach bounced high in the air over ruts and stones but the driver never gave the passengers a thought. All he could think of was the robbery. To be held up by road agents in 1899!

Inside the coach the three passengers flew about like dice in a caster's cup.

The driver began to shout out his story as soon as he entered Florence. Idlers and storekeepers poured out of buildings. Someone summoned Sheriff Truman who came on the run. When he heard the story he only scratched his head, sniffing the air to see if the driver had had a drop too much.

Road agents! It was unthinkable. They belonged to the age of Curley Bill and Pummer of Idaho!

Then the battered passengers told their story; the short fat man embroidering his version to compensate for the loss of his three hundred and ninety dollars. The Chinaman chattered away in pidgin English but no one paid any attention to him.

The dude didn't say much. He still seemed stunned. Finally Truman brought the passengers and driver to his office. After some questioning he was able to determine that the robbers were Joe Boot and Pearl Hart, "who the driver recognized despite the fact that she looked like a young man."

The sheriff gathered a posse. The whole town turned out to see them thunder down Main Street. When they were gone the townspeople gathered in groups on the streets, chattering like magpies. Oldtimers who had lived during the stirring days of Tombstone, Casa Grande and the other wild frontier settlements, recalled those days and were given a respectful audience.

The alarm was sent out and the news service wires hummed with the story. The *Yuma Sun* called Pearl "the daring lady bandit" and Joe Boot, "a miner well known in Florence."

By nightfall all Arizona knew about the stagecoach robbery. Curiously when anyone told the story, it was with a particular sense of pride, as if some wonderful feat had been accomplished. Who said the old days were gone? Wyoming had her Johnson County cattle wars and Cattle Kate but who has a real, honest-to-goodness lady road agent?

Meanwhile Pearl and Joe were demonstrating they were rank amateurs in the art of road agentry. Instead of adopting the tactics of Butch Cassidy's Wild Bunch, or Jesse James's middle border bandit gang, Pearl and Joe began to trot about the countryside!

In a country twice as populated as it had been in the roaring seventies, they had committed a daylight robbery of a stagecoach without bothering to make any plans for their escape.

The outlaws of old would have had relays of horse holders hidden in gullies or canyons, clear across the state. By nightfall they would have been miles from the scene of the robbery, heading for a pre-planned rendezvous. But Pearl and Joe ignored all tradition. They trotted down the highway, still laughing over the way the little fat man had fallen on his face.

In the shades, the ghost of Jesse James surely shook with disgust.

Instead of heading northeast toward the New Mexico border Pearl and Joe decided to stay around Cane Springs Canyon. It was a wild place populated by mountain lions and a few old trappers. They supposed a posse would have a difficult time finding them in this place. Joe, who remembered something he had read in a penny dreadful, proposed they crisscross their tracks and confuse the man hunters. Pearl agreed, so they plunged into the wilderness, doubling back and forth on the narrow trails.

For the rest of the day they rode through the wilderness that was even less known to them than to the local inhabitants. It was inevitable that they lost their way. They kept on until they found a trail again. By twilight they reached a highway. It was a shocking discovery. They were back on the Globe Highway, less than a mile from the scene of the robbery!

There was nothing else to do. They galloped down the highway for about six miles past Riverside, crossing a creek to make camp in a thicket. The horses hobbled. Pearl and Joe rolled up in their blankets and slept.

The next day they started out for the railroad, ignoring the obvious fact they could easily be spotted by waiting posses, especially Pearl, "the young man," in her dungarees and white sombrero.

On the highway near Mammoth they plunged into the woods when they heard wagons approaching. When a group of riders passed, identified by Pearl as a posse, Joe suggested remaining in the brush for the rest of the day. Pearl said it was a good idea.

About ten o'clock that night, Joe told Pearl he was dying for a smoke. Over her protests he walked to his own cabin in the Mammoth camp returning with his pipe and can of tobacco!

The next morning they hid their horses and climbed the side of sandstone hill. Near the peak were several caves, where Joe proposed they hide out for the rest of the day. He entered the largest, crawling out in a hurry.

"There's a couple of eyes back there, bright as lamps," he told Pearl.

"Well, shoot them," Pearl said impatiently, forgetting that the sound of gunfire might attract passing possemen.

Joe crawled back into the cave. He fired one shot at the gleaming eyes. A furious growling and thrashing about followed. Frantically he fired five more shots then crawled out choking and gasping for breath from the gunpowder fumes.

They waited for some time, then crawled into the cave. Joe struck a match to find he had killed a wild hog. The acrid smoke deep in the cave had no way of escaping. As Pearl said later, she didn't know which was worse that day, Joe's snores, the dead hog, or the gunpowder smoke.

When darkness fell they slid down the slope to their horses. They passed Mammoth, crossed the Gila River at a shallow ford, and camped for the night at the end of a field near a schoolhouse. They stole some feed for their horses, then fell asleep on a pile of straw, "forgetting their troubles."

In the morning they set out again for the railroad. Their jaded horses gave up after ten miles of hard riding. Pearl proposed they turn their horses into a nearby pasture and steal two others. Joe, horrified at the thought of being called a horse thief, indignantly rejected her idea.

They pressed on after an hour's rest. At the edge of a field they came on a ten-foot ditch filled with water. Pearl a good rider forced her mount to jump. Joe, not to be outdone, put the spurs to his horse, which collapsed in mid-air.

Joe plunged in the water and went down twice before Pearl rescued him. For the next hour she was pumping muddy ditch water from the lungs of her outlaw lover. When Joe regained consciousness they built a fire. Joe, a bruise on one side of his head, sat Indian fashion before the blaze, occasionally hiccuping up some more water while Pearl prepared a supper of more bacon and beans.

But all heaven was against them. She had the food in the pan when a torrential thundershower fell. The fire sizzled, then went out. The

294

pan filled with water. Huddled under Joe's jacket they ate a miserably cold meal of beans and bacon.

Weary and soaked to the skin they fell asleep under a clump of trees.

Meanwhile the posse under Sheriff Truman had been following close on their heels, missing them several times by a hair's breadth. But now the jig was up. A Mexican who had seen them shivering over their cold fire notified the sheriff's office.

The posse quietly surrounded the field. Truman waved his men on. The ring of man hunters closed about the sleeping pair. Foot by foot the posses advanced, every minute expecting to hear the sharp crack of a rifle and the sound of a bullet screaming overhead. But there was only the dripping of the trees and the occasional twittering of a bird. After all the precautions Truman was dumbfounded to find the desperadoes sleeping peacefully. The sheriff carefully slid the pistols out of the holsters.

"Wake up, Pearl," he said prodding her with a rifle. "You're under arrest!"

Pearl jumped to her feet, groggy with sleep but pawing for her guns. She was furious to find herself surrounded by a circle of grinning possemen. Someone kicked Joe awake. He stumbled to his feet, rumpling the stubble on his chin and smoothing out his mustachios.

"Well," he said philosophically, "we almost made it."

Pearl was determined to play to the bitter end her role of a desperate woman. After blistering the ears of the deputies with a string of bagnio curse words, she turned to Joe, cursing him out for being "a damn coward."

"If you hadn't taken my guns," she boasted, "you would never have caught us alive."

The *Arizona Star* pointed out cautiously this may not have been an idle boast: "She is a wild-cat of a woman and had she not been relieved of her guns a bloody forray might have resulted."

The posse cooked breakfast while a courier was sent to spread the news. Hot coffee made Pearl more agreeable and she told her story to the admiring possemen. Then, with Pearl sharing Truman's horse and Joe behind another deputy, the posse rode to Benson, twenty miles away. There they took an afternoon westbound train to Pauline Cushman's town of Casa Grande. What a wonderful scene it would have been had Pauline been there to greet them. Surely the beautiful and fiery woman who cowed tough mule skinners and gun fighters would have provided Pearl with clothes and a good meal, along with a blistering lecture on why crime doesn't pay.

They stayed the night at Casa Grande, leaving at dawn for Florence. With a crowd at the depot to welcome her, Pearl forgot that Joe was "a damn coward." She put on a wonderful show, telling the reporters in the best Western tradition that she wouldn't be able to "stand it" were it not for Joe's presence. They "held hands" and Joe happily twirled his mustachios.

Sheriff Truman, however, was not swayed by love's sweet song. Being a practical man he immediately separated Pearl and Joe. In the Florence jail, Pearl held court for her countless admirers.

"Would you do it again, Pearl?" someone asked.

Pearl nodded. "Damn right, podner," she said, "if the circumstances were the same."

No one noticed that Pearl, the Ontario country girl, was now beginning to talk like one of Zane Gray's characters.

To a nation at peace and with its whole attention centered on itself, Pearl loomed high on the egocentric national horizon. She represented the romance of yesterday, a visitor from that wonderful world, which Lucy Lockwood Hazard described as, "A world made of dramatic incongruities, a world where anything might happen. . . ."

Overnight Pearl became a celebrity. She gave the audiences what they demanded. She provided love and a dying mother as her motives. She adopted the spurious and exaggerated sportsmanship of the outlaws of old, insisting Joe was not to blame. In the best Western tradition she worried about her horse, begging her captors to take care of it.

With Calamity Jane drinking herself to death in small Western towns, Belle Starr a dim memory, and Cattle Kate forgotten except by the citizens of Casper County, Wyoming, Pearl Hart "was exalted into a sort of arch-type of contemporary wild Western womanhood."

In the weeks which followed her capture, Pearl suddenly became a violent suffragette. She called upon the women of Arizona to fight against the laws made by the male sex.

This is the message the lady road agent, held without bail in a county prison, sent to the prosecuting attorney, "I shall not consent to be tried under a law which my sex had no voice in making."

Strangely enough the women of the County listened to Pearl's broadsides delivered to the reporters who visited her cell. The dinner table became their battleground. More than one husband hid himself in the evening paper as his wife demanded to know why she couldn't vote. Didn't women have as much right as any man?

The powerful *Arizona Star* took editorial cognizance of the question.

There is much to her [Pearl's] declaration. Why should a woman be indicted, put on trial, convicted and sentenced under a law she or her sex had no part in making . . . that laws should be enacted by the consent of the governed is a fundamental principle of our government.

The debate fizzled out. Peace again hovered over the dinner tables of Arizona. On June 30, Pearl undoubtedly in an attempt to revive the public's fading interest in her, tried to commit "suicide." It was a laughable attempt. She waited until a deputy appeared outside her cell, then with a melodramatic cry that life was too much to bear, or words to that effect, she threw a handful of powder into her mouth.

The sheriff tried to revive Pearl who lay on the floor of her cell, moaning as if in great pain. A doctor was summoned. He quickly examined Pearl, then told her to stop shamming. Pearl opened her eyes and indignantly demanded to know what he meant. When the doctor cheerfully told her no one could poison themselves with talcum powder, Pearl admitted the game was up. A few hours later she was posing in the jail yard for "the camera fiends" and looking as desperate as was possible.

But the suicide act was too much for the sheriff. He announced in the afternoon papers he was sending her to Tucson. As the Florence correspondent for the *Phoenix Republican* said, "For this trip, skirts and a hat were provided for Miss Hart. She proved not as good looking a girl as she had been as a boy."

Pearl was sullen because she had to leave Joe Boot. There was a last lingering kiss and the Arizona lady road agent set out for Tucson. Upon her arrival she was mollified to find a large crowd on hand to see her. That afternoon she was placed in a large room of the courthouse, directly over the county records room. Adjacent to the room was a smaller room, which had a spiral staircase to the towerhouse, and a door leading to the second floor landing of the building. A plaster and lath partition separated both rooms.

One of her fellow prisoners was a sandy-haired man named Ed Hogan, who was serving a thirty-day sentence for being drunk and disorderly. As a trusty he brought Pearl her meals. As he told the other prisoners, he found her very attractive.

Soon Pearl and Ed were exchanging sly smiles, notes under the plates of food, and soulful glances.

Two days before he was to be released Ed asked Pearl to escape with him. She refused to have anything to do with it. Ed insisted he would never leave without her. That night he disappeared. A routine alarm was sent out by the sheriff who congratulated himself on getting rid of a troublesome town drunk.

That night Pearl heard a tapping on the plaster partition. She placed her head against the wall. Ed, who had been hiding all day in the tower of the courthouse, said he was going to break through. Pearl insisted she didn't want anything to do with the prison break. Evidently she now realized the slim chance of escape, and the hardships an outlaw had to endure while "on the dodge."

Hogan was persistent. After he described how they could flee in the night and form an outlaw band with Pearl as its queen, Pearl's romantic heart was touched. She agreed to escape.

While she caught the plaster in a bed sheet, Ed dug a hole in the wall with a chisel. Soon the hole was big enough—or so Ed thought. Pearl pushed a table next to the wall and squeezed through the hole. She was caught halfway. Her ample rear was unable to make it. Ed tugged. Pearl huffed and puffed her way through the hole, inch by inch. Finally, with one last good tug, Pearl came through the hole in a shower of dust and plaster to flatten Ed.

After they got back their breath they tiptoed down the stairs, "making a bee line for the border," as the *Arizona Citizen* said.

Before she escaped Pearl wrote a long note to the sheriff. What was in it we do not know. The *Arizona Bulletin* described it as, "an epistle characteristic of her stamp." It would be wonderful to know what it contained.

Her escape caused a sensation. The townspeople filed into the courthouse to examine the hole, described by the *Star* as "a very small aperture, and it is evident that Pearl must have had considerable help in getting through. . . ."

Another bombshell was exploded by the *Yuma Sun*. Hogan was not Hogan at all! Their page one story disclosed: "Hogan is none other than Ed Sherwood, the notorious bicycle thief of Phoenix who will be remembered as the man who stole nothing less than half a dozen wheels. . . ."

The famous bicycle thief, the *Sun* said, had previously been an inmate of the Phoenix City Jail chain gang, "but escaped, chain, ball and all. . . ."

298

Reports that she had been seen escaping on a westbound train flew through the town by the afternoon, but they were unfounded. By nightfall rumors had her captured on the road leading to Florence, then on a train, then on a horse, buggy, and on foot. The sheriff scotched all the reports, announcing grimly, "She shall not escape us."

Pearl's escape added to her popularity. This is the land where men are men and women are women, the romanticists chuckled. Who said the old days were gone?

The *Star* said editorially this "popular sentiment was only because of the chivalry which so largely prevails on the frontier. There is no place where woman is held in such high esteem, and her protection is certain in this region of the United States. . . ."

3

Pearl and Hogan were recaptured in October by Sheriff Scarsborough of Deming, New Mexico, in an outlaw's hangout, "where she was starting a gang of which she was to be the bandit Queen," as the *Star* said. Pearl had taken the plans of Hogan, or Sherwood, the bicycle thief, quite seriously.

It was brought out that the Arizona man hunters hadn't been too anxious to find Pearl. Evidently they knew a tartar when they saw one. The Tucson sheriff was quoted as saying he had known "all the while" where Pearl had been hiding but had held off rounding up a posse to capture her until she had been joined by Hogan.

The *Lordsburg Liberal* scoffed: "This is a good enough story for the sheriff to square himself with the voters but it does not go."

When Pearl was captured she was again dressed as "a young boy," in a flannel shirt and sombrero, and overalls held up by a cheap pair of laborer's suspenders.

New Mexico, like Arizona, was thrilled to discover they had a real lady road agent in their midst. When the news spread that Pearl was being brought to Deming, there was a large crowd at the depot. Now the seasoned performer, she remained aloof and arrogant.

The night before her departure for Tucson, two elderly ladies with a small child appeared at the city jail.

"We would like to see Miss Hart," one asked primly.

"What for, ma'am?" the amazed Scarsborough asked.

"Well, we would like our little niece to see the famous bandit of Arizona," one said sweetly.

299

The law officer looked down at a child of about ten, dressed in a neat white dress and straw bonnet.

"I want Pearl Hart to sign my card," piped the child holding up a blank white card.

The startled sheriff said, "But ladies, this woman is the most foul person I have ever heard."

The two "nice appearing ladies" refused to be denied. "Oh, we are sure Miss Hart will noι insult us," they chorused.

"I want Pearl Hart to sign my card," the child piped up again.

The law officer threw up his hands, escorting the two women and the child into the jail.

"Luckily for the child and not those two women," the sheriff said later, "Pearl behaved decently and signed the child's card. She didn't make a bad break."

At the depot, waiting for the train to take her to Tucson, Pearl retold the story of the Globe stage robbery for her admirers. Then she told how she and Hogan—or Sherwood—had been chained together to the floor of a wooden shack after their capture.

Suddenly she stopped, looked about at the grinning faces, then chuckled. "Gawd," she said, "that's worse than being married!"

A few days later she was lodged in the Pima County Jail to await trial.

There were a few cynics, especially veteran newspaper editors, who had openly scoffed at Pearl's tale of a dying mother. But on November 26, 1899, the *Arizona Star,* under the headline, GRIEF OF A MOTHER, published the letter the sheriff had received the day before from Pearl's brother-in-law who was acting as spokesman for her family. It read:

To the Sheriff:

I see by the papers that you have Miss Pearl Hart in custody for some misdemeanor [sic]. Now, I am her brother-in-law and as such, am interested in her welfare. It has been a long time since we have heard from her, and we did not know what had become of her. The paper stated she wanted to go back to her mother. I assure you her mother would be very glad to have her at home.

I have seen her sit for hours and cry when we have spoken of Pearl, wondering what has become of her. Since unfortunately she has become an opium fiend,* we all have the more sympathy for her.

* There is no evidence of this.

300

She is the only one in the family to have become addicted to such a habit.

Now I would beg of you to be as easy with her as you can, for we have not dared to let her mother know anything of her, and much less that she is a prisoner [sic], as she is troubled with heart disease, and the news might affect her seriously. I enclose an envelope with my address on it for return. You will do me the kindness and tell me all the particulars in her case. . . .

As the *Yuma Sun* said editorially: "Had this letter been received much earlier it would have aroused much sympathy. The family is no doubt poor, and this makes the pity for the mother of the woman outlaw all the more keen. . . ."

On June 15, Pearl and Joe were arraigned in Florence. The *Yuma Sun's* correspondent gives a wonderful description of the scene. The courtroom was crowded and "camera fiends are taking all kinds of pictures, making her look as desperate as possible. Miss Hart is good natured about it all and seems to enjoy the situation. She says that if Joe Boot were not near she could not be so content."

In the detention cells the *Sun's* reporter said love again had bloomed between Joe and Pearl.

"Boot stretches his hand through the bars for the girl to caress and they seem happy."

The next day, Pearl went to trial in Judge Doan's courtroom. The people's case was brief. Pearl was identified by the stage's passengers and driver. Her attorney rested her case, evidently without her taking the stand. The halo of romance about her cropped head was still untarnished. After ten minutes the jury returned with a verdict of acquittal!

The furious judge "roasted" the jurymen, dismissing them from further panels. The court then directed the prosecutor to rearraign Pearl on a charge of stealing a revolver from the driver. The case was swiftly prepared and presented. The trial took less than an hour.

Under the stern eyes of the judge the jury retired. Thirty seconds later they were back with a verdict of guilty. Judge Doan immediately sentenced her to five years in the Territorial Prison at Yuma "to cure her of the habit of robbing stage coaches." Joe Boot was found guilty in a separate trial; he was sentenced to thirty years for highway robbery, the same charge on which Pearl had been found not guilty!

As he was led away he may have reflected on the sheriff's remark:

301

"It always pays to be the star actor, Joe. The dupe (sic) does the hard work and is seldom mentioned in the magazines."

On November 25, the *Coconio Sun* sent its reporter down to Maricopa to see Pearl pass through on her way to Yuma. The train stopped for a few minutes just after dawn. As the *Sun's* reporter wrote after talking to Pearl: "She had a big cigar in her mouth, rivalling the efforts of the locomotive to charge the atmosphere with smoke."

On November 26 at two o'clock, Pearl arrived at Yuma, as the *Arizona Daily Star* put it, "to be a guest for the next five years."

Pearl was a bigger nuisance behind bars than on the highway holding up stagecoaches. Yuma Penitentiary had been built exclusively for male prisoners. The warden was forced to isolate Pearl in a separate part of the jail. He had another headache. She was such a curiosity that he had to put a watch on the guards to prevent them from continually leaving their posts to call on "the lady road agent."

There was also the additional trouble of visiting newspapermen, tourists, and the "camera fiends" who always begged the warden to let her pose in the jail yard with a six-shooter or Winchester.

In May, Pearl was visited by a sister, Mrs. Frizzell of Silver City, New Mexico. The *Yuma Sun* identified her as an "actress" who has written a play about Pearl's adventures, called *Arizona Bandit*. Mrs. Frizzell held a dramatic press conference upon her arrival, announcing that Pearl would play the leading role, "when she is released."

Meanwhile in jail, Pearl ostensibly adopted religion. She became a vigorous lecturer—behind bars—on why crime doesn't pay, issuing grave warnings to mothers to watch their daughters. Her strategy paid off. She had spent less than a year and a half of her five-year term when the chivalrous citizens of Arizona began campaigning for her release. Most of the prison personnel were strong supporters of the movement, whether on the grounds that Pearl was a nuisance or because of chivalry, is not known.

Finally on December 19, 1902, Pearl was released along with another female desperado, Rosa Duran, who had arrived at Yuma after Pearl. Conditional pardons were issued by Governor A. O. Brodie, "on the grounds of the lack of accommodations for women prisoners."

Rosa demanded a complete new going-home wardrobe; Pearl asked only for a pair of long white gloves as her gift from the state.

The pair were released on a Monday. Pearl left that same night for Kansas City to join her sister, the playwright, and begin rehearsals as the leading lady of *Arizona Bandit*.

The *Yuma Sun's* reporter took a dim view of Pearl's acting ability.

302

As he wrote after seeing Pearl off: "Owing to a certain condition in the pardon which prohibits her being in the Territory until the expiration of her sentence, we are spared the pain of her playing Arizona for at least some time. Doubtless she will, however, play it with a vengeance though when she gets around to it."

Pearl was next heard from in May, 1904, when the *Arizona Star's* Kansas City correspondent reported that she had been arrested "for complicity with thieves."

Pearl, then going under the name of Mrs. L. P. Keele, at first refused to admit her identity but after the police chief ordered her picture sent to the Yuma Territorial Prison in Arizona, she broke down and confessed she was "the famous lady bandit."

From the meager evidence Pearl had disgraced the profession of outlawry. The Kansas City police chief said she had admitted buying some canned goods and a small sack of sugar, "from a youth who she said, had represented himself as selling flood goods."

While in the Kansas City police station, Pearl, now about thirty-two years old, reminisced to the admiring reporters and policemen about the stage robbery which had catapulted her to a brief and lurid fame. She became so enthusiastic about that great event, she wrote a poem about it. The *Yuma Sun* published it, commenting, "Pearl evidently desires to be known as a poet as well as a stage robber, and by such means perpetuate the history of her mis-deeds." For what it is worth here are some excerpts of Pearl's long poetical work.

The sun was shining brightly
On a pleasant afternoon,
My partner speaking lightly said the stage would be here soon,
We saw it coming around the bend and called to them to halt
Then to their pockets we did attend,
If they got hurt, twas their own fault.

CHORUS

While the birds were sweetly singing and the men stood up in line,
And the silver softly ringing as it touched this palm of mine,
There we took away their money but gave them enough to eat,
And the men they looked so funny as they vaulted in their seats.
Then up the road we galloped quickly, then through the canyon we
    did pass,
Over the mountains we went swiftly trying to find our horses grass,
Pass the station we boldly went and down the river side,

303

And our horses being spent of course we had to hide.
Now for the five long days we travel, in the day time we would rest,
Now we would throw ourselves on the gravel and to sleep we try our
  best.
Around us now our stamping horses looking for some hay or grain,
On the road the posse tramping looking for us all in vain,
One more day they would not get us, but my horse got sour and thin,
And my partner was a mean cuss and Bill Truman roped us in,
Thirty years my partner got, and I was given five,
He seemed contented with his lot and I am still alive.

After giving the reporters a copy of her poem Pearl disappeared.
There is no disposition of the case against her in Kansas City.

On a summer's day in 1924, a gray-haired woman appeared at the
Pima County courthouse, with the odd request that she be permitted
to "look the place over."

An attendant asked, "You will have to tell me why, ma'am."

The woman hesitated, then replied, "Well, I lived here many years
ago and I wanted to see if the place was still the same."

The curious attendant showed her about. The woman kept nodding
and smiling to herself as if recalling some far-off event connected with
the rooms, the stairway, and the old tower.

"Well it hasn't changed much," she said.

The curious attendant asked her name. "Pearl Hart," she said and
walked out.

Pearl may still be alive. In answer to an inquiry from the author, the
former warden of the Yuma Territorial Prison writes:

> Although I do not know of her present whereabouts, it is my
> understanding she is still alive. For a good many years she conducted
> a cigar store in Kansas City, and may be in that vicinity now.

A newspaper friend of the author's searched police records, newspaper reference room clippings, and interviewed several old-time residents but could not locate her in Kansas City. It is believed she moved
farther West ten years ago.

Women Not So Desperate

"LITTLE JO" MONOGHAN

In the spring of 1868, a slim young man of about twenty-one rode down the muddy main street of Ruby City, Idaho. The street was little more than a rough path, pockmarked with mudholes and littered with boulders and stumps.

The young man rode gracefully, carefully guiding his horse through the crowds that moved up and down the road on horseback, in wagons and on foot. There were rough miners with picks over their shoulders, cowpunchers, neatly dressed gamblers, and hard-eyed men with six-shooters on their hips.

The young rider pulled up at Gallagher's saloon. Several loungers watched him curiously.

"Is this Ruby City?" he asked "in a boyish voice."

They chuckled. This *was* a tenderfoot. "Sure is, sonny," one man said.

"Thank you, sir," the young rider said.

He swung out of the saddle and tied his horse to the hitching post. Then he went inside a rough two-story shack, with "Hotel" painted in black letters over the door.

The loungers watched him. He was a little man, no more than five feet tall in high-heeled Western boots. In a community ruled by the six-shooter he didn't wear a gun. The loungers closely examined the horse. It was a slim, brown mare, well groomed and showing evidence of a long journey. They wondered who he was.

When the young man came back to lead his horse to the livery stable, one of the men asked, "What's your name, sonny?"

The young rider said simply, "Jo Monoghan, sir," and smiled.

The lounger said he'd be damned; it was the first time anyone had called him "sir."

Like everyone else in Ruby City, Jo Monoghan tried prospecting for gold. He bought a pick and shovel and staked a claim. The digging seemed too much for him. The loungers at first laughed at him, but after a few days their contempt turned into a rough admiration for "the little fellow's guts."

His hands were raw with blisters but he wouldn't let anyone help him.

And he still called everyone "sir."

One night as he was coming past the saloon someone called to him. When he didn't turn someone said, "Hey Jo!" Then, "Little Jo!"

He was always "Little Jo" to the tough miners of Ruby City after that night.

A month after he arrived Little Jo abandoned his claim for a job as a sheep herder. He told the loungers in front of Gallagher's it was more to his liking.

"Hell, that's no job for a man, Little Jo," they said. "It's too damn lonely!"

"I like to be alone," Jo said simply.

For three years Little Jo herded sheep. His carefully groomed brown mare, and a sheep dog that never left him soon became a familiar sight on the ranges in the vicinity of Ruby City.

One day in about 1871, Jo came upon a chuck wagon camp. It was probably only because of his size and completely inoffensive nature that he wasn't ridden out of camp as a hated sheep herder.

One of the hands was breaking a wild bronc and Jo stopped to watch. "Want to try him?" someone asked.

"I wouldn't mind, sir," Jo said.

The cowpuncher winked. This was almost too good. A god-damned sheep herder busting a wild bronc. Word spread around the camp. Even cookie left his fire to come and see the sights.

Of course Jo rode him and rode him well. The foreman was impressed. The next week Jo was busting wild broncs.

In 1904 a man wrote in the *Boise City Capitol News:*

> No horse was too wild or savage that he could not be brought to saddle and butt under Little Jo's hands. To this day the countryside about Silver City and Ruby City tell of his remarkable ability in this line. Many a campfire is brightened by the stories of the little horseman and his prowess in subduing untamed steeds of the range. . . .

Jo stayed a year with his outfit. But he became restless. With his savings he bought a small herd and joined a larger outfit driving to a railhead. The large expanse of the range seemed to make him happy.

He still wasn't very talkative and about the campfires said little. But he liked to sing and the cowhands were always after him to sing in his choir-boy's voice.

Jo soon found he had to learn how to defend himself with a gun. He bought a six-shooter in Ruby City and faithfully practiced shooting "at targets." The loungers solemnly warned him not to shoot himself in the foot and he as solemnly promised not to. But later when he returned from a cattle drive with some more cattle they were impressed when "he hit a can thrown in the air four out of five times, and was quick on the drop." He said only that "some fellows from Texas" were kind enough to show him a few tricks.

Jo was liked by all the miners and cowpunchers and gamblers who lived in Ruby City but he had only one friend, an elderly mine superintendent. The barrooms and dance halls saw nothing of him. When he had returned from a drive, Jo would inevitably be found sitting with the mine superintendent on his porch.

Faithfully he gave the superintendent small sums of money to hold for him.

No man ever saw him take a drink. He never smoked or swore. His hands were always clean and his mare studiously groomed. He lived this way for almost fifteen years. In Ruby City he was a mystery and men liked to create legends about him. One had him a train robber hiding away from the law; another said he was a preacher who had killed his brother in the arms of his wife and had come East "to forget."

Tragedy came to Jo one day in about 1880. The faithful mine superintendent fled with his savings. The town was in an uproar when the secret leaked out and posses were sent out to head him off. It would be a delightful twist in Jo's story to have the superintendent captured by a posse of which Jo was a member, but the truth is the thief made good his escape.

After this blow Jo obtained a job at the Ruby City livery stable. A few years later he moved to Rockville, a few miles west of Ruby City, where he staked out a homestead claim. He built a small sawmill which was successful. With his profits from the sawmill he bought several cows. All his profits from the mill were poured into his ranch. He built a small log cabin which was kept spotlessly clean. There were curtains and a few china dishes. Visiting cowpunchers were startled one day to find him feeding several hens. He began buying horses and within a few years had half a hundred head.

At the turn of the century a man who knew him told a reporter for the *Rocky Mountain News:* "He was a familiar sight along the banks of Succor Creek with his band of buckskin horses all branded with the familiar J.M."

Jo made one concession in five years. He hired an old chinaman as a cook.

The country was growing fast. Jo was an established member of Rockville's community. Each election he faithfully voted and several times sat on juries.

However, Jo still lived the life of a recluse. When his Chinese cook died he appeared to shut himself up more than ever, "never visiting any of his neighbors, nor was he visited by them in return."

He had only one friend, a neighboring rancher, Fred Palmer. Whenever Palmer rode past the Monoghan place he made it a habit to whoop out a welcome. The slight, little man, now growing gray and stooped, would turn and wave if he was feeding his chickens. If he was inside the log cabin, Palmer later recalled, he never failed to open the door and shout a welcome.

One day in March, 1903, after a raging blizzard, Palmer noticed there was no smoke coming out of the Monoghan chimney. He broke a trail to the cabin and discovered the stock hadn't been fed.

He banged on the door, then forced it open when he heard someone coughing. He found Little Jo barely conscious in his bunk.

Palmer wrapped the slight figure in blankets and rode to the nearest ranch, owned by a Barney Malloy, on upper Succor Creek. Little Jo never regained consciousness. He died after a few hours, probably from pneumonia.

Palmer and Malloy and a few other ranchers brought the body to Rockville for burial. It was laid out in the local funeral parlor and the ranchers went to the local saloon, where they spun tales about Jo's ability as a bronc rider.

A short time later the door of the saloon swung open. The undertaker, white to the lips, staggered in. He lurched up to the bar.

"Give me a drink," he demanded.

He gulped it down. Palmer and Malloy stared at him. When they asked what was wrong the undertaker asked for another drink, then told them.

Little Jo Monoghan was a woman!

2

The rest of the story as we know it from the faded clippings of the *Boise City Capitol News* and the *Rocky Mountain News,* is that the ranchers went back to the ranch house and in the best romantic tradition discovered a small, black suitcase.

When they broke it open they learned Jo's secret. Her name was Josephine Monoghan, daughter of a well-to-do family of Buffalo, New York, that was in "exclusive society."

Her story was straight out of the paper-backed romances of the day. She had met a dashing playboy "of dissolute habits," who seduced her on their first rendezvous. She ran away to New York City where a baby boy was born in 1866. She obtained a job as a waitress in a Broadway restaurant and placed their child in a boardinghouse. The financial strain was too much and she gave her son to her younger sister and left New York.

The *Rocky Mountain News* account of her life said she donned male attire rather than travel across the country "as a woman alone."

Several letters, which the *Rocky Mountain News* produced, were found in the suitcase. All were from her sister in New York and addressed to "Jo Monoghan, Rockville, Idaho."

The first one is dated September 11, 1868, and addressed to "Dear Sister."

I have lain awake nights picturing you in your wild wanderings and with your boy pressed tightly in my arms I have prayed to a merciful God to keep you safe and unharmed.

When I think of all my comforts and luxuries and then of my Josephine sleeping by night on a blanket and traveling by day with that crowd of rough men and uncouth women you described in your letter I feel I cannot bear it.

I am glad you have decided to stay in one place although the camp sounds so awful. Still, I know where to find you.

Laddie [her son] is sitting on the floor beside me. He had a slight cold last week but is quite well now. I hardly know how to live without him. I also am well and still longing for your return. It takes so long for a letter to reach me that I hope you will not delay in answering this one.

Your last letter was such a comfort. Goodby now and with lots of love from Laddie and Helen.

Another letter, dated many years later, spoke of Laddie's graduation from Columbia Law School in New York City and his subsequent admission as an attorney to the New York State Bar.

From another letter it appeared the boy had been told his mother was dead.

There was also a faded daguerreotype of an attractive young woman in an evening gown. It was a picture taken when "Jo"—the sheep herder, the wild bronc rider, the lonely rancher of Jordan Valley—had made her society debut.

JOHNNY BEMIS AND CHINA POLLY

It was a summer's night in 1871. The saloon in the mining camp of Warren, Idaho, was strangely quiet. There was none of the usual shouting, singing, or the shrill laughter of the dance-hall girls.

The saloon was packed to the swinging doors. Two men sat at a table, an island in the crowded room. One was rather tall and thin with a weather-beaten, good-natured face. He was about twenty-one. Across from him was a pig-tailed Chinese of about fifty, dressed in a long black gown.

His skin, yellow as parchment, was stretched tight over the fine bones of his inscrutable face. Long yellow fingers spread out the cards.

Two pair.

Johnny Bemis grinned. He spread out his four aces, sweeping in the bag of dust in the middle of the table. It joined several others. The crowd sighed gently. The Chinaman's face was emotionless.

"I have nothing more to lose," he said.

Johnny eyed him. "Stake the girl."

The Chinaman's eyes dropped to the bags of gold, then lifted to study the weather-beaten face.

"You will put up the gold?"

Bemis nodded. "This and more." He stood up. The crowd opened. He walked to the bar, followed by the owner of the saloon. They knelt before a large iron safe. The saloon owner spun the dial and pulled open the heavy door. He silently handed Johnny three small bags of gold dust, each initialed in black ink: J.B.

Johnny walked back to the table. He plumped down the bags, pushing them and others to the center of the table.

The crowd stirred. This was more like it. The game had been going all day. Johnny had won, then lost, then won, cleaning the Chinaman out of every last ounce. Now they were going to play for the girl— the Chinaman's "slave girl," whom all Warren called "China Polly."

A hush fell over the crowded saloon. A man who witnessed the scene recalled twenty years later: "A pin could be heard to hit the floor had it fallen, and the intake of the breath of two men in the tense silence sounded like the exhaust from a steam engine. . . ."

Every eye was focused on the Chinaman. He stared at Johnny. After a long moment he said, "Bring in the girl."

A young Chinaman standing behind him vanished in the crowd. While the crowd waited impatiently the Chinaman stared into space. Johnny winked at a dance-hall girl.

Within a few minutes the young Chinaman was back, leading a beautiful Chinese girl, dressed in a sheathlike yellow dress, slit to the knees on both sides. Her skin was olive, her eyes only slightly almond shaped.

The miners, gamblers, outlaws, thieves, and all the rest of the scum attracted to a mining camp after a big strike, leaned forward. This moment would be remembered for years. . . .

The Chinaman chattered softly to Polly. She glanced briefly at Bemis, then bowed her head submissively.

The elderly Chinaman nodded to Johnny.

"One hand, winner takes all," Bemis said.

The Chinaman nodded.

Johnny shuffled his cards expertly. He slapped them down.

"Cut."

The Chinaman cut the deck. Bemis expertly dealt the cards. The Chinaman stood pat. Johnny took two. Silently he pushed the bags of gold dust to the center of the table.

The Chinaman laid down his cards. There was a gasp from the crowd. Three aces.

Johnny smiled. He spread out his hand. Five clubs, beats three aces.

The Chinaman's face remained expressionless. He said something to Polly. She raised her head and stared at Bemis with frightened eyes. He grinned, racked in the bags of dust and stood up. The crowd broke. He walked over to the girl, still smiling. Together they walked down the human aisle to the swinging doors—a cocky young man in checkered shirt, corduroy pants stuck into mud-splattered boots, whose arms were loaded with bags of gold—and a slender, young Cantonese slave girl, dressed in yellow, who followed him with mincing steps.

In a moment they were gone. The crowd relaxed with a collective sigh. It broke up and swirled about the saloon. Poker players picked up where they had left off when Johnny Bemis had started to win; dance-hall girls leaned on the bar, reliving in shrill voices the scene

311

they had just witnessed; the bartender began dishing out the "suds," glasses clinked, and the battered piano tinkled as someone sang in a drunken voice.

The elderly Chinaman walked out of the saloon, accompanied by the younger man. No one paid them any attention.

And in the light of the oil lamp in his log cabin outside of Warren where he had his placer claim, Johnny Bemis stared at the frightened Chinese girl named Polly, wondering, as he once said, "what the hell to do with her."

2

Incredibly romantic as it may seem, the story of Johnny Bemis is true. The Chinaman who had wagered and lost Polly was a tong leader from San Francisco, and the leader of the hundred or more Chinese who were working in the placer claims in and around Warren.

Polly was born in 1852. In 1871, at eighteen, she was smuggled into San Francisco to be shipped to the tong leader in Warren, who evidently had purchased her sight unseen.

According to the Idaho Historical Society, she was smuggled ashore and "passed from tong to tong, finally reaching the rich Chinese gambler."

There is another wonderful, romantic twist to their story, confirmed in letters to the author, from several residents of Warren and Grangeville, Idaho, who knew Johnny and Polly.

For months after the game in which he had won her, Polly faithfully followed the Yankee wherever he went. She cooked his meals and washed his clothes. Johnny was kind but whimsical. When her name came up he laughingly called her "my chink slave girl."

Several months after the game that was already becoming a legend, Johnny went back to Warren to try his skill. There was a new gambler dealing faro and Johnny spent the day "bucking the tiger." He won steadily. There were hard words and Johnny went for his gun. The gambler was faster, shooting him in the chest.

His friends placed him on a table and tried to stop the flow of blood while someone rode for a doctor.

Johnny lost a tremendous amount of blood; there didn't seem to be much more his friends could do. The odds were against him for pulling through.

It was Polly—who had sat behind Johnny all day while he gambled

—who took command of the situation. In pidgin English she ordered Johnny strapped to a horse. Then she took the reins and led the horse to the placer claim and their cabin.

It was Polly who nursed Johnny back to health. During the long weeks when he knew it was touch and go, he saw the beautiful young Chinese girl in a different light. Johnny fell in love with Polly. On his first trip into Warren he married her.

When the diggings around Warren petered out, Johnny and Polly disappeared in the backwoods.

The late Robert G. Bailey, author of *River of No Return* and Nez Percé County historian for the Idaho State Historical Society, found Polly and Johnny in 1901 in the wild Salmon River Country.

With Joe Randall, a noted Idaho guide, Bailey was on a prospecting trip through Central Idaho. After traveling along the Salmon River they came to the mouth of Cripple Creek. An "amiable" old ferryman hailed them. With his help, Bailey and Randall carried their gear aboard the flat boat and crossed the creek's mouth. Several trips were made and when Bailey asked the old man what he "owed" him, the ferryman grinned and said "nothing."

As Bailey recalled twenty years later, "Nothing I could do would induce him to accept pay for his services."

The ferryman, who said his name was Johnny Bemis, invited Bailey and his guide to stay for the night. Bailey was startled to find Bemis's wife was a tiny, smiling Chinese woman, who still retained traces of having been an oriental beauty.

After supper Bemis and the guide, Randall, regaled Bailey "with tales more lurid than is usually found in fiction."

The next day Randall told Bailey the story of how Johnny had won Polly. Intrigued with the story, the historian made several visits to the picturesque couple. From his interviews, Bailey pieced together the story of the life and adventures of Johnny Bemis and how he had arrived in Idaho.

Bemis was a Connecticut farm boy who ran away to sea in his early teens, sailing before the mast, as cabin boy, sailor, and mate. In San Francisco he heard the stories of the Idaho gold rush "and went there to seek his fortune."

He made his way to Lewiston, Idaho, then Warren. It was a rough camp with the usual frontier saloons, brothels, and gambling houses.

Johnny, "no better or worse" than the average adventurous miner, "took his pleasures as did his friends."

But women and liquor were not Johnny's passions. Gambling was.

313

His old friends told Bailey, "He was willing to wage everything he owned when the fever of the game was upon him."

Then came the game in which he won Polly. The shooting, his love for Polly, and their marriage followed.

After they had left Warren, Johnny and Polly traveled through the wild Salmon River Country, finally settling at the mouth of Cripple Creek, "where Johnny rocked some gold."

Polly started a vegetable garden, selling her produce to miners in nearby camps. With their savings they bought a small herd.

In 1920 Johnny died. A resident of Grangeville writes the author: "Friends brought Polly into Grangeville to live, but the noise and confusion frightened her."

Polly returned to the Bemis ranch and her beloved garden. She was now a tiny, smiling old lady with a host of stirring memories, who had no need for the outside world.

For years Polly lived alone with an aging sheep dog. Her two neighbors, Charles Shep and Pete Kleinkenheimer kept a careful watch over her. They gave her a radio, but, as an Associated Press story about her pointed out: "Alone in the Idaho hills she thought the radio was full of howling spirits."

When she became feeble Polly called in Kleinkenheimer and Shep.

"You have been good neighbors," she told them, holding out a document. It was a deed giving them the Bemis land. The only condition she attached was "that they take care of her for the rest of her few years."

Her neighbors agreed. A telephone line was strung from their ranches across Cripple Creek to Polly's house. Every morning and evening, Pete and Charlie called to say hello.

One morning in August, 1933, one of the ranchers called Polly.

When she didn't answer both men hurried to her ranch house. They found her critically ill.

According to an Associated Press dispatch, date lined Grangeville, Idaho, the nearest town, the ranchers "brought her on horseback over dangerous mountain trails" to the Grangeville Hospital.

Polly lingered three months. On the morning of November 6, "Her spirit passed to the great Beyond, there to give an accounting to her Maker of deeds well done."

POKER ALICE

The story of Poker Alice belongs to the romanticists. They need not search for melodramatic props and trappings. They are all here in real life; the gentle, refined educated English girl; her life in the raw frontier town and the tragedy which forced her to turn to gambling to make a living; the miners and the gamblers in top hats who test her skill across the green-blaized tables; the crowds in the hushed saloons who had come to see the slim young girl break the coldest, toughest gamblers in the West. . . .

The love affair in her life strangely resembles that of Annie Oakley in the musical *Annie Get Your Gun.* Annie married her rival sharpshooter; Alice married her rival gambler.

In her lifetime Alice estimated a half a million dollars slipped through her fingers, "but very little stuck." She lived a gay boisterous life, facing death at seventy-seven with a gambler's philosophical shrug.

When doctors told her the odds were against her surviving a dangerous operation, she said, "Go ahead. I've bucked worse odds."

2

Alice Ivers was born in Sudbury, England, February 17, 1851, the only daughter of a schoolmaster. She was educated in an exclusive girl's school and with her family emigrated to America. Her family settled in Virginia, then moved north to Colorado at the opening of the silver boom.

Alice was a slight woman, with a cloud of fair hair, and the flawless coloring of English gentlewomen. She had pale-blue eyes which turned cold as steel when they evaluated a man across the table in the smoky saloons of the West.

She was nineteen when she married Frank Duffield, a mining engineer. After their honeymoon they settled down in Lake City, Colorado. In 1870 the raw mining town consisted of a few log cabins and tents overshadowed by towering peaks.

Gold and silver were plentiful. Gamblers, in their checkered vests and top hats, were among the town's first arrivals. They set up shop in the rough saloons. The faro and poker games never stopped. From dawn to dusk fortunes were won and lost on the turn of a card.

Exactly how Alice was attracted to gambling no one knows. She first experimented with cards perhaps to escape the boredom. Soon she discovered she possessed a strange gambler's intuition. In the evenings she began to join her husband in the saloons where the games were often centers of attraction for the whole community.

Alice closely studied faro and poker. The gamblers, described by Professor Briggs in his *Frontiers of The Northwest,* as "usually the

315

best educated men in the community," came to know her. They answered her questions politely and described the finer points of the games.

Alice noticed their inscrutability as they played.

Behind the closed doors of her cabin she taught herself to sit woodenfaced as she played imaginary poker games with bags of gold dust as the stakes.

One night she asked her husband if she might sit in on a game. Amused he consented. A gambler stood up, tipped his hat, and Alice sat down. For most of the evening Alice played faro—and won.

The next several nights it was the same. Word spread through the camp and crowds gathered to watch the well-dressed young woman break the bank, with twenty-five dollars the limit.

Then suddenly her husband was killed in a mine accident. After the first rush of grief, she found herself in the wild mining town without friends, and as they say, without any visible means of support. She was educated enough to teach school but there was no school.

However, there were cards and gambling tables. After she buried her husband, Alice Duffield began gambling for a living. When she discovered she had to protect herself, she took to wearing a thirty-eight or a forty-five. As she remembered years later, her father had been an expert shot "and had taught me to shoot well."

She was to use her gun twice in her life.

The first week that Alice worked at the gambling tables her employer discovered she had one unbelievably queer custom. Alice said she would never deal a card on Sunday.

The saloon owner begged her to play, pointing out that on Sunday the miners would come into town with their "dust."

Alice was adamant. "I will never in my life deal a card on Sunday," she said—and she didn't.

Alice left Lake City to drift about the mining camps. Leadville, Central City, and Georgetown saw her, a refined, well-dressed young woman with a gay smile and the whisper of a British accent. But once behind a gambling table she was wooden-faced, "playing for keeps." She never smiled and spoke in monosyllables. She won and lost without the slightest expression.

When she was a white-haired old lady, she described her philosophy for Dr. Nolie Numey, the well-known physician-historian of Colorado. "We were all gamblers in those days; some staked theirs in mines, some in goods, some in cattle, some with a pan at a stream. I took mine at a table with a deck of cards. . . ."

316

Evidently Alice was without nerves. In Silver City, New Mexico, she once entered a gambling hall and placed a bet at a faro table. She won. She played another bet and won again. Her winning streak continued. She went from ten, to the twenty-five dollar limit. A crowd gathered. Other tables were deserted.

Alice carefully scanned the cards painted on the faro board, then covered one with her chips. The sweating dealer drew the top card from the metal faro bank frame, exposing the card. Nine out of ten times it was Alice's card.

Other players joined her at the board, laying their bets. But they soon lost their nerve to "buck the tiger," as it was called. Only Alice remained. At last the dealer threw up his hands in desperation.

"Bank's closed," he shouted, stepping aside.

He didn't notice the cold contempt in Alice's eyes. She walked around and took his chair.

"Gentlemen, the game is open," she said, "and the sky's the limit."

Word was passed along to the other gambling houses. Other gamblers left their tables to match wits and skill with Alice. All night they trouped down to the saloon to sit across from her. The crowd pressed close, watching the blonde woman slip the cards from the metal box, and rake in the chips.

Before dawn pushed its way into the grimy room, she had won several thousand dollars.

In the afternoon Alice left on the stage, bound for New York.

She recalled years later that her visit consisted mostly of shows, suppers, and fine clothes. Evidently no one asked her if she had been tempted to try her luck at some of Manhattan's luxurious gambling houses. It's a superb scene to imagine: the blonde woman with the emotionless face who broke the tough gamblers of the West, sitting sedately in some plush New York gambling salon, sipping at champagne while she coolly relieves the city slickers of their wealth—

As Alice said, the New York visit lasted "only as long as the money did." Again the frontier towns claimed her. In her absence a few more lady gamblers had made their appearances. Perhaps the most famous of them was Madam Moustache, a French woman of mysterious background who received her nickname from the dark hairs on her upper lip.

There were only a few. Alice summed up the reason. "Women have too many nerves."

As Professor Briggs points out, the gambler in Alice's time was essentially honest, and believed in a fair deal. If a game in camp was

317

rumored to be crooked, other gamblers closed their banks until the crooked game was broken up.

As a miner once observed, "If I were broke I'd rather ask a gambler for a lift than anyone else."

There were of course exceptions. Alice once met up with one, a crooked faro dealer. After losing steadily she began to study the dealer. Soon she realized he was cheating. When he clumsily slid a card from the bottom of the deck, she drew her forty-five.

"If you had done that cleverly," she said softly, "I wouldn't kick. I could admire a clever crook, I'll admit that, but I have no use for a clumsy crook like yourself. Now give me back the money I lost."

Without an argument the gambler carefully counted out the money.

In 1889 Alice became restless. She was now working the "graveyard shift," from midnight to about 8 A.M., for twenty-five dollars a week. But the same faces, the same hours were beginning to bore her. Then the Cherokee Strip opened. Alice hitched her team to a wagon and drove to Oklahoma "to see what was happening." She stayed two years, dealing faro and stud poker in gambling houses throughout the length of America's last frontier. Jim Masterson, Bat's brother, Heck Thomas, Bill Tilghman, the last great frontier marshals, all knew her and respected her.

About 1892, tired of Oklahoma, she left for Arizona. When Creede, Colorado was born and named after the man who discovered the fabulous vein of silver, Alice traveled across the mountains from Del Norte to be among the first arrivals.

There were few cabins. It was every man for himself. Alice scaled, cut down her logs, notched them, and with the help of a neighbor built her own log cabin.

It was the old West all over again. Bob Ford, who shot Jesse James in the back, arrived and opened a saloon and gambling house. Alice worked in his place as a faro dealer for a time. When Bachelor City, a few miles distant, was built overnight she traveled up there.

Gold and silver flowed like water. The stakes in the games were incredible. It was commonplace for the pot to hold thirty thousand dollars.

From Bachelor City, Alice went to Deadwood, Calamity Jane's beloved town. It was there she smoked her first cigar, that later became her trade-mark.

Legend has the miners of Deadwood protesting when Alice was hired as a dealer. They said they didn't like to lose to a woman. When the owner told this to Alice, she put on a corduroy coat and campaign hat and stuck a thick black cigar in her mouth.

At seventy-seven she said, "Other women smoke cigarettes. I happen to like mine thick and black and still do."

In Deadwood romance entered her life. The dealer at the next table was a good-looking man, named W. G. Tubbs. He was an expert gambler and a sharp rivalry developed between him and Alice. Each fought for their customers.

One night above the click of chips and drone of voices a chair crashed backward. A drunken miner reeled to his feet, drawing a knife. He advanced toward Tubbs, shouting, "You cheated me, damn you. . . ."

He was at the gambler's throat when a forty-five slug shattered his arm.

Tubbs turned to find Alice holding a smoking revolver. True love may have been born at that moment.

Shortly after Tubbs proposed. Alice, like Annie Oakley in the play, married her rival.

They both agreed to throw away their cards. Tubbs found a homestead forty-eight miles west of Sturgis and they settled down, to chickens and a garden patch.

Three years—as Alice once said, "the three happiest of my life"—passed. In the winter of 1910 Tubbs fell ill of pneumonia. There was a howling blizzard and during the storm he died in a wild delirium, with Alice holding him in her arms.

Then this indomitable woman carefully wrapped the body of her husband in a blanket, dragged him to a small room, closed off from the rest of the house. In the sub-zero temperatures the corpse was soon frozen.

While the wind shrieked across the land threatening to uproot the tiny homestead, Alice read the Book of Psalms in the lamplight, pausing only to keep the fire going.

After a few days the storm blew itself out. Alice broke a path through the drifts to the barn to hitch up a team. Then she dragged the frozen corpse of her husband to the back of the wagon.

She made the forty-eight mile trip to Sturgis under the most horrible conditions of bitter cold and almost insurmountable drifts. On the way she stopped at a small grocery store to pawn her engagement ring for twenty-five dollars.

She arrived in Sturgis, frozen and hungry. There was no undertaker.

However, she found a preacher and some men who promised to dig a grave for twenty-five dollars. The ground was so frozen logs had to be burned for hours before it yielded to the shovels and pickaxes.

While the preacher said the last words, and the gravediggers shivered in the sub-zero cold, Alice bent down and threw in a frozen clod. Dry-eyed she drove off through the snow.

Back in Sturgis, she went to the owner of the gambling saloon where she had worked with Tubbs.

"I want to deal," she said—"but only until I have earned twenty-five dollars."

The owner agreed. At noon she called that the bank was open. She dealt rapidly and skillfully. When the owner told her she had earned twenty-five dollars, she tossed down her cards, collected her money, and went out.

The ring Tubbs had given her was back on her finger before she reached their homestead that night.

Several bitterly lonely months followed. When the loneliness became unbearable she returned to the gambling tables.

After working as a dealer, she opened her own gambling bagnio where a man could find cupid after cards.

On Sunday it was never opened. Stories are still told of how Alice gave her girls Sunday-school lessons in the closed parlor of her house, while the good people of Deadwood walked past her doors to answer the clanging summons of the church bells.

It's a strange scene: the lady gambler, delivering her sermon on the Good Life in her refined, slightly English accent, to the bored whores who probably all had terrific hangovers. . . .

3

Alice married once again. But it was only a marriage of convenience. In a manuscript owned by Fred Mazulla, the well-known Denver attorney and collector of Western Americana, a friend of Poker Alice's describes her marriage to George Huckert of Sturgis. She writes:

> Poker Alice owned a place quite a few miles from the city of Sturgis where she was raising sheep. She hired Huckert to live on the ranch and raise sheep for her. He came to town every few months for supplies and she would give him what money he would ask for. In the meantime he fell in love with her and asked her time and time again to marry him, but she always said no, she

didn't want to marry again. This went on several years. One day Poker got to thinking she had not paid Mr. Huckert his regular wages for some time, so she sat down and figured what she owed him.

She said, "You know, I owed him about $1,008.00 and all I had was about fifty dollars on hand, so I got to figuring it would be cheaper to marry him than pay him off."

Poker married Huckert, who died a few years later. After his death she continued to use the name of Tubbs.

Poker Alice's place had become highly popular with the soldiers from Fort Meade, two miles from Sturgis. One night a drunken group tried to force their way in and Alice shot through the door, killing a cavalryman from "K" Troop, Fourth Company.

Alice was arrested and taken to the Deadwood jail.

"Have you a Bible here?" she asked the sheriff.

"No, Alice, we haven't," the law officer said.

"Well, would you mind if I sent home for mine?" she asked.

The sheriff said no and dispatched one of his deputies. Alice spent most of her time in jail reading her Bible and smoking the big black cigars she loved so much.

A jury found her not guilty and she was freed. But the reformers in town insisted Alice be arrested again, "for running a disorderly house."

She was found guilty and convicted. But the people of Sturgis petitioned the governor who pardoned the now white-haired old lady.

Alice now closed her "establishment," settling down in a small clapboard house. Chickens and a small vegetable garden occupied most of her time. She was a familiar sight; a slight, little, blue-eyed lady with her white hair twisted into an old-fashioned bun, wearing an army shirt and a black woolen skirt.

When Deadwood became conscious of its stirring history and organized the famous "Days of '76," Alice played her own role. As the crowds cheered she sat on a float behind a faro table, dressed in her familiar khaki shirt, chewing away at a big black cigar.

In the winter of 1930 doctors informed her she must undergo a serious operation. The chances of her survival at seventy-eight were slim. Alice's face, lined by the years, showed no emotion as she listened to the doctors.

She shrugged and told them to go ahead.

This time Alice lost.

321

Bibliography

Adams, Henry, *The Education of Henry Adams*. New York: Houghton Mifflin Company, 1918.

Aikman, Duncan, *Calamity Jane and the Lady Wildcats*. New York: Henry Holt & Company, Inc., 1927.

Aler, F. V., *History of Martinsburg*. Hagerstown, Md.: Mail Publishing Company, 1889.

Andrews, Matthew Page, *The Women of the South in War Times*. Baltimore, Md.: Norman Remington Company, 1920.

Annual Report of the American Historical Association. Washington, D.C.: Government Printing Office, 1889 (Vol. II), 1904 (Vol. II), 1905 (Vol. I), 1908 (Vol. I).

Ashby, Thomas A., *The Valley Campaigns*. New York: The Neale Publishing Company, 1914.

Auchampaugh, Phillip, "James Buchanan, the Squire in the White House." *Pennsylvania Magazine of History and Biography*. Vol. 58, 1934.

Avary, M. L., editor, *A Virginia Girl in the Civil War*. New York: D. Appleton Company, 1903.

Bailey, Robert, *River of No Return*. Privately printed, Lewiston, Idaho, 1935.

Baker, L. C., *History of the United States Secret Service*. Philadelphia: 1867.

Bancroft, Frederick, "The Life of William H. Stewart." *Political Science Quarterly*, September, 1891.

Basso, Hamilton, *Beauregard the Great Creole*. New York: Charles Scribner's Sons, 1933.

Bates, Samuel P. and Singerley, B., *History of the Pennsylvania Volunteers, 1861-65*. Harrisburg, Pa.: 1869-71.

Battles and Leaders of the Civil War, Vol. I. New York: The Century Company, 1888.

Beatty, John, *Memoirs of a Volunteer*. New York: W. W. Norton & Company, Inc., 1946.

Bennett, Estelline, *Old Deadwood Days*. New York: J. H. Sears & Company, Inc., 1928.

Beymer, William G., *On Hazardous Service*. New York: Harper and Brothers, 1912.

323

Bowers, Claude, *The Tragic Era.* New York: The Literary Guild of America, 1929.

Boyd, Belle, *In Camp and Prison.* New York: Blelock & Company, 1865 and 1867.

Briggs, H. E., *Frontiers of the Northwest.* New York: Appleton-Century Company, Inc., 1940.

Brininstool, E. A., *Fighting Red Cloud's Warriors.* Columbus, Ohio: The Hunter-Trader-Trapper Company, 1926.

Brooks, Noah, *Washington in Lincoln's Time.* New York: F. Defau & Company, 1888.

Brown, J. and Willard, A. M., *The Black Hill Trails.* Rapid City, S.D.: Rapid City Journal Company, 1924.

Buchanan, James, *Mr. Buchanan's Administration on the Eve of Rebellion.* New York: D. Appleton Company, 1866.

Buck, Lucy, *Diary of Lucy Buck.* Privately printed, 1940.

Butler, Benjamin Franklin, *Butler's Book.* Boston: H. M. Thayer & Company, 1892.

Calahan, E. W., editor, *List of Officers of the Navy of the United States, 1775-1900.* New York: L. R. Hamersly Company, 1900.

Calamity Jane, By Herself.

Case, R. J., *The Black Hills and Their Incredible Characters.* Indianapolis: Bobbs-Merrill Company, 1949.

Catton, Bruce, *Mr. Lincoln's Army.* Garden City, L.I.: Doubleday & Company, Inc., 1951.

Chambers, Robert, *Secret Service Operator 13.* New York: D. Appleton Company, 1934.

Chambers, Robert, *Special Messenger.* New York: D. Appleton Company, 1909.

Chestnut, Mary Boykin, *Diary From Dixie.* New York: D. Appleton Company, 1906.

Chester, Giraud, *Embattled Maiden.* New York: G. P. Putnam's Sons, 1951.

Cist, Henry M., *The Army of the Cumberland.* New York: Charles Scribner's Sons, 1882.

Coit, Margaret L., *John C. Calhoun.* Boston: Houghton Mifflin Company, 1950.

Connelley, William Elsey, *Quantrill and the Border Wars.* Cedar Rapids, Iowa: The Torch Press, 1910.

Connelley, William Elsey, *Wild Bill and His Era.* Elmira, N.Y.: Press of the Pioneers, Inc., 1933.

Coursey, O. W., *Beautiful Black Hills.* Mitchell, S.D.: Educator Supply Company, 1926.

Crawford, E. F., *Rekindling Camp Fires.* Bismark, N.D.: Capitol Book Company, 1926.

Croy, Homer, *Hang Them High.* New York: Duell, Sloan & Pearce, Inc., 1952.

Cunningham, Eugene, *Triggernometry*. Elmira, N.Y.: Press of the Pioneers, Inc., 1934.

Curtis, George Ticknon, *Life of James Buchanan*. New York: Harper and Brothers, 1883.

Dahlgren, J. V., *Memoirs of Colonel Dahlgren*. Philadelphia: J. B. Lippincott Company, 1872.

Davis, Jefferson, *The Rise and the Fall of the Confederate Government*. New York: D. Appleton Company, 1881.

Davis, Clyde Brion, *The Arkansas*. New York: Farrar & Rinehart, Inc., 1940.

Dee, D., *Low Down on Calamity Jane*. Rapid City, N.D.: 1932.

De Long, T. C., *Four Years in Rebel Capitols*. Mobile, Ala.: Gossip Printing Company, 1890.

Dictionary of American Biography, Allen Johnson and Dumas Malone, editors. New York: Charles Scribner's Sons, 1931.

Donald, Jay, *The Life and Adventures of the James Brothers*. 1882.

Doster, William E., *Lincoln and Episodes of the Civil War*. New York: G. P. Putnam's Sons, 1915.

Douglas, Henry Kyd, *I Rode With Stonewall*. Chapel Hill, N.C.: University of North Carolina Press, 1940.

Edmonds, Emma S., *Nurse and Spy*. Philadelphia: W. S. Williams & Company, 1865.

Freeman, Louis R., *Down the Yellowstone*. New York: Dodd, Mead & Company, Inc., 1922.

Foreman, Grant, *Advancing the Frontier*. Norman, Okla.: University of Oklahoma Press, 1933.

Gard, Wayne, *Frontier Justice*. Norman, Okla.: University of Oklahoma Press, 1949.

Genealogy of the Cutts Family in America. Albany, N. Y.: Joel Munsells Sons, 1892.

Gilmor, Harry, *Four Years in the Saddle*. New York: Harper and Brothers, 1866.

Greeley, Horace, *The American Conflict*. Hartford, Conn.: Case & Company, 2 vols., 1869.

Greenhow, Rose O'Neil, *My Imprisonment and the First Year of Abolition Rule at Washington*. London: R. Bentley, 1863.

Harman, S. W., *Hell on the Border*. Fort Smith, Ark.: Phoenix Publishing Company, 1898.

Harrel, Melvin, "The Outlaw Was A Lady." *Norfolk Sparks and Flashes,*

Harrington, Fred Harvey, *Hanging Judge*. Caldwell, Idaho: Caxton Printers, Ltd., 1951.

Harrison, Mrs. Burton, *Recollections Grave and Gay*. New York: 1911.

Headley, John W., *Confederate Operations in Canada*. New York: Neale Publishing Company, 1906.

Heitmann, Francis B., *Historical Register and Dictionary of the U.S. Army, 1789-1903*. Washington, D.C.: Government Printing Office, 1903.

Henderson, G. F. R., *Stonewall Jackson and the Civil War*. London and New York: Longmans, Green & Company, Inc., 2 Vols., 1936.

Hergesheimer, Joseph, *Swords and Roses*. New York: Alfred A. Knopf, Inc., 1929.

History of the Eleventh Pennsylvania Cavalry. Philadelphia: Franklin Printing Company, 1902.

History of the Fifth New York Cavalry. Albany, N.Y.: S. R. Gray, 1865.

History of the Fifth West Virginia Cavalry. New Brighton, Pa.: 1890.

Horan, James D., *Desperate Men*. New York: G. P. Putnam's Sons, 1949.

Hueston, E., *Calamity Jane of Deadwood Gulch*. Indianapolis: Bobbs-Merrill Company, 1937.

Kelly, Charles, *Outlaw Trail*. Privately printed, Salt Lake City, Utah, 1938.

Keyes, E. D., *Fifty Years Observation of Men and Events*. New York: Charles Scribner's Sons, 1884.

Leech, Margaret, *Reveille in Washington*. New York: Harper and Brothers, 1941.

Leovell, John, *Memoirs of John Yates Beall: His Life, Trial, Correspondence, and Diary*. Montreal: J. Leovell, 1865.

Little, James A., *Jacob Hamblin*. Salt Lake City, Utah: Juvenile Instructor Company, 1881.

Lossing, Benjamin J., *Pictorial History of the Civil War*. Hartford, Conn.: T. Belknap, 3 vols., 1868.

Maguire, H. N., *The Coming Empire*.

Mahoney, Dennis A., *The Prisoner of State*. New York: G. W. Carleton & Company, 1863.

Markens, Isaac, *President Lincoln and the Case of John Yates Beall*. Privately printed, New York, 1911.

Marshall, John A., *American Bastille*. Philadelphia: T. W. Hartley, 1872.

Matts, Merrill, "Fort Laramie, Guardian of the Oregon Trail." *Annals of Wyoming*, January, 1945.

McClintock, J. S., *Pioneer Days in the Black Hills*. Privately printed, Deadwood, S.D., 1939.

McGillycuddy, J. E., *McGillycuddy, Agent*. Stanford, Calif.: Stanford University Press, 1941.

McPherren, I., *Imprints on Pioneer Trails*. Boston: Christopher Publishing House, 1950.

Meade, George, editor, *The Life and Letters of George Meade*. Amber, Pa.: G. G. Meade, 1924.

Mercer, A. S., *Banditti of the Plains*. Privately printed. Cheyenne, Wyo., 1894.

Miller, F. T., *Photographic History of the Civil War*. New York: The Review of the Reviews Company, 10 vols., 1912.

Mokler, Alfred J., *History of Natrona County*. Chicago: R. R. Donnelley & Sons, 1923.
Moore, Frank, editor, *The Rebellion Record*. New York: D. Van Nostrand Company, Inc., 12 vols., 1861-65.
Moore, Frank, *Women of the War*. Hartford, Conn.: S. S. Scranton & Company, 1867.
Monoghan, James, *The Great Rascal*. Boston: Little, Brown & Company, 1952.
Mootz, H. Edwin, *Blazing Frontier*. Dallas, Tex.: Tradey Publishing Company, 1936.
Mumey, Nolie, *Poker Alice, the History of a Woman Gambler in the West*. Denver, Colo.: Art-Craft Press, 1951.
Nelson, B., *Land of the Dacotahs*. Minneapolis: University of Minneapolis Press, 1946.
Nix, Evet Dumas, *Oklahombres*. Chicago: Edew Publishing House, 1929.
Oklahoma: A Guide to the Sooner State. Norman, Okla.: U.S. W.P.A., 1945.
Paris, Comte De, *History of the Civil War in America*. Philadelphia: Porter and Coates, 4 vols., 1875-88.
Phillips, P. G., "Life and Adventures of Calamity Jane." *The Frontier and Midland*. Vol. 16, 1935-36.
Pinkerton, Allan, *The Spy of the Rebellion*. New York: G. W. Carlton & Company, 1883.
Pittenger, W., *Secret Service*. Philadelphia: J. B. Lippincott Company, 1882.
Pollard, Edward A., *Observations in the North*. Richmond, Va.: E. W. Ayres, 1865.
Raine, William McLeod, "The Hunt for Harry Tracy." *Wide World Magazine*, 1903.
Raine, William McLeod, *Guns of the Frontier*. Boston: Houghton Mifflin Company, 1940.
Ray, Clarence E., *Harry Tracy*. Chicago: J. Regan Publishing Company, 19—?
Richardson, Albert Deane, *The Secret Service*. Hartford, Conn.: American Publishing Company, 1866.
Robson, John S., *How a One-Legged Rebel Lives*. Durham, N.C.: Education Company, 1898.
Rogers, Cameron, *Gallant Ladies*. New York: Harcourt, Brace & Company, Inc., 1928.
Ropes, John Codman, "General McClellan." *Military Historical Society of Massachusetts Papers*, Vol. 10, 1895.
Rascoe, Burton, *Belle Starr*. New York: Random House, Inc., 1941.
Sala, George Augustus, *My Diary in America in the Midst of War*. London: Tinsley Brothers, 2 vols., 1865.
Sandburg, Carl, *Abraham Lincoln—The War Years*. New York: Harcourt, Brace & Company, 1939.

Sarmiento, F. L., *Pauline Cushman, Union Spy and Scout.* New York: John E. Potter & Company, 1865.

Scharf, John T., *History of the Confederate States Navy.* New York: Rogers & Sherwood, 1887.

Schmidt-Paulie, E. V., *We Indians.* London: Butterworth & Company Ltd., 1931.

Scott, General Winfield, *American Whig Review,* September, 1850.

Scott, Mary Wingfield, *Houses of Old Richmond.* Richmond, Va.: Valentine Museum, 1941.

Sigaud, Louis A., "Mrs. Greenhow and the Rebel Spy Ring." *Maryland Historical Magazine.* September, 1946.

Sigaud, Louis A., "When Belle Boyd Wrote Lincoln." *Lincoln Herald Quarterly.* Harrogate, Tenn.: Lincoln Memorial University, 1948.

Sigaud, Louis A., *Belle Boyd, Confederate Spy.* Richmond, Va.: Dietz Press, Inc., 1945.

Simkins, F. B. and Tatton, J. W., *The Women of the Confederacy.* Richmond, Va.: Garrett & Massie, Inc., 1936.

Stevens, W. O., *The Shenandoah and Its Byways.* New York: Dodd, Mead & Company, Inc., 1941.

Sutton, Fred, *Hands Up.* Indianapolis: Bobbs-Merrill Company, 1927.

Swiggett, Howard, *The Rebel Raider.* Indianapolis: Bobbs-Merrill Company, 1934.

Swiggett, Howard, editor, *A Rebel War Clerk's Diary.* New York: Barnes & Noble, Inc., 1935.

Tate, Allen, *Stonewall Jackson.* New York: Minton, Balch & Company, 1928.

Taylor, General Richard, *Destruction and Reconstruction.* New York: D. Appleton Company, 1897.

The Old Capitol, By a Lady. 1867.

The Westerners Brand Book. Chicago: Westerners, 1944 and 1945-6.

Tilgman, Zoe A., *Outlaw Days, A True History of Early Oklahoma Characters.* Harlow Publishing Company, 1926.

Trial of John Y. Beall As A Spy and Guerrilla. Military Commission. New York: D. Appleton Company, 1865.

Underwood, John L., *The Women of the Confederacy.* New York: Neale Publishing Company, 1906.

Walters, Lorenzo D., "Tombstones Yesterdays." *Progressive Arizona.* April, 1927.

War Department Official Records of the Union and Confederate Armies. Washington, D.C.: Government Printing Office, 1880-1901.

War Department Official Records of the Union and Confederate Navies. Washington, D.C.: Government Printing Office, 1894-1919.

Waterman, A. N., *Washington at the Time of the First Bull Run.* Washington, D.C.: Military Order of the Loyal Legion of the United States.

West, Ray B., editor, *Rocky Mountain Cities*. New York: W. W. Norton & Company, Inc., 1949.

Wharton, A. F., *Trial of the Crew and Officers of the Privateer Savannah on Charges of Piracy*. New York: Baker & Goodwin, 1862.

Willis, Carrie Hunter and Walker, Etta Belle, *Legends of the Skyline Drive and of the Great Valley of Virginia*. Richmond, Va.: The Dietz Press, 1937.

Williamson, James J., *Prison Life in Old Capitol*. West Orange, N.J.: 1911.

Young, H., *Hard Knocks*. Chicago: Laird & Lee, Inc., 1915.

MANUSCRIPTS

Abraham Lincoln Papers. Library of Congress.

Archives of Pinkertons National Detective Agency.

Autobiography and Letters of Captain Collins in the Civil War. Owned by the author.

Buchanan Papers. Library of Congress.

Captured Confederate Correspondence. Records of the War Department and of the State Department, National Archives.

Dahlgren Papers. Library of Congress.

Fishback Manuscript. Arizona Pioneers' Historical Society.

Jefferson Davis Collection. Library of Congress.

Memoirs and Letters of Dolly Madison. Columbus Historical Society Record.

Memoirs of a Friend of Poker Alice. Owned by Fred Mazulla, Denver, Colorado.

Memoirs of Charles J. Eastman. Arizona Pioneers' Historical Society.

Memoirs of Mike M. Rice. Arizona Pioneers' Historical Society.

Memoirs of Perry Wildman. Arizona Pioneers' Historical Society.

Memoirs of Pryce Lewis. Owned by Harriet Shoen, Ph.D., New York City, New York.

Memoirs of Richard Young Auld. Oklahoma Historical Society.

Miscellaneous Papers on Miss Van Lew. Library of William and Mary College.

Personal Miscellany. Library of Congress.

Records of the hearings of state prisoners before the Dix-Pierrepont Commission. National Archives.

Southern Historical Society Papers. Richmond, Virginia.

Van Lew Papers. Manuscript Room, New York Public Library.

Van Lew Scrapbook. Virginia Historical Society.

NEWSPAPERS

American Union	*Arizona Daily Citizen*
Arizona Bulletin	*Arizona Daily Star*

Arizona Enterprise
Arizona Republican
Arizona Star
Arizona Weekly Enterprise

Basin Star
Billings Gazette
Boise Capitol News
Boston Post
Boston Sunday Herald
Buffalo Echo

Carthage Press
Casper Weekly Mail
Cherokee Advocate
Cheyenne Daily Leader
Cheyenne Sun

Daily Boomerang
Daily Oklahoman
Daily Oklahoma State Capitol
Daily Yellowstone
Dallas Herald
Dallas News

Fort Smith Elevator
Fort Smith Era
Fort Smith Independent

Great Falls Tribune
Greensboro Daily News
Guthrie Daily Leader

Knoxville Daily Register

Laramie Weekly
Leslie's Illustrated Newspapers
Livingston Post
London Morning Post

National Intelligencer
New Brighton Daily News

New Orleans True Delta
New York Evening Post
New York Herald
New York Herald Tribune
New York Mercury
New York Times
New York World
Norman Transcript

Oklahoma Eagle
Oregonian
Oregon Journal

Paris Moniteur Universel
Philadelphia Inquirer
Philadelphia North American

Richmond Dispatch
Richmond Evening Journal
Richmond News
Richmond Times-Dispatch
Rockingham Register
Rocky Mountain News

Salt Lake City Herald
San Francisco Bulletin
Southwest Magazine
Stillwater Daily Press
Stillwater Gazette

Tulsa World
Tucson Citizen

Washington National Republican
Washington Star
Watonga Republican
Weekly Yuma Sun
Wilmington Daily Journal
Wyoming Bulletin
Wyoming State Journal

Yuma Sun

Index

C

Calamity Jane, legends of, 172; family of, 174; westward journey of, 175; takes part in an Indian battle and wins nickname, 176; joins Crook expedition, 177; appears in Deadwood, 178; joins Hickok, 179; death of Hickok, 181; legends of Deadwood, 182; returns to Deadwood, 190; is hired by Pan American Exposition, 191; meets Louis Freeman, 193; death of, 196; diary of, 197
Calhoun, John, approves of Dr. Greenhow, 7; death of, 10
Canarray, Martha Jane, see Calamity Jane
Carter, Genie, early years, 268; joins Tracy, 269; holds up a stagecoach, 271; bribes guard, 272; aids Tracy in prison escape, 273; death of, 274.
Cattle Annie, joins Doolin gang, 248; warns gang, 257; capture of, 265
Cattle barons, history of, 229
Cattle Kate, legends of, 227; description of, 230; opens brothel, 231; capture of, 235; death of, 236; father of, 238
China Polly, won by Johnny Bemis, 310; history of, 312; marries Johnny Bemis, 313; death of, 314
Collie, Alexander, writes to Mrs. Greenhow, 49
Condor, blockade runner, 52
Cushman, Pauline, birth of, 100; becomes spy, 102; goes to Nashville, 104; court-martial of, 105; tour of, 106; meets Mike Rice, 107; horsewhips a scoundrel, 108; marriage of, 111; opens hotel, 112; settles gun duel, 113; threatens freighter, 115; adopts child, 118; death of

child, 120; meets Mike Rice, 120; death of, 121
Cutts, James Madison, 6
Cutts, Mrs. James Madison, visits Mrs. Greenhow, 36

D

Dalton, Bill, 244, takes jail in Battle of Ingalls, 254; death of, 258
Dahlgren, Colonel Ulric, 143; raids Richmond, 144; death of, 144; removal of body of, 149
Davis, Jefferson, writes General López, 19; receives letter from Mrs. Greenhow, 45
De Long, T. C., describes Belle Boyd, 56
Dix, John A., examines Mrs. Greenhow, 43
Donellan, Dept. of Interior clerk, delivers note to Greenhow, 4; arrives in Washington, 14
Doolin gang, 244
Doolin, Bill, legends of, 242; history of, 243; joins Dalton gang, 243; takes part in train robbery, 244; forms gang, 244; raids Cimarron, 248; takes part in Battle of Ingalls, 254; kills deputy, 254; returns to Ingalls, 256; marriage of, 257; raids Southwest City bank and rejoins wife, 258; leaves for Kansas, 260; arrest and escape of, 262; death of, 263
Doolin, Edith, 242
Doster, General W. E., remembers Mrs. Greenhow, 5; talks of gossip about her, 11; visits Belle Boyd, 81
Douglas, Henry Kyde, 71
Douglas, Mrs. Stephen A., 11; visits Mrs. Greenhow in prison, 36
Duffield, Alice, see Poker Alice
Dunn, Rose, see Rose of the Cimarron

332

333